THE
AGNOSTIC
READER

THE
AGNOSTIC
READER

Edited by S. T. JOSHI

Prometheus Books
59 John Glenn Drive
Amherst, New York 14228–2119

Published 2007 by Prometheus Books

Inquiries should be addressed to
Prometheus Books
59 John Glenn Drive
Amherst, New York 14228–2119
VOICE: 716–691–0133, ext. 210
FAX: 716–691–0137
WWW.PROMETHEUSBOOKS.COM

11 10 09 08 07   5 4 3 2 1

Library of Congress Cataloging-in-Publication Data

The agnostic reader / edited by S. T. Joshi. — 1st American pbk. ed.
    p. cm.
Includes bibliographical references.
ISBN 978–1–59102–533–7
1. Agnosticism. I. Joshi, S. T., 1958–

BL2747.2.A33 2007
211'.7—dc22

2007022202

Printed in the United States of America on acid-free paper

A NOTE ON
THIS EDITION

This volume presents a variety of texts exemplifying different phases of agnostic thought. I have arranged them in six sections, in which the selections appear chronologically. For each piece, I have supplied a headnote providing biographical information on the author and some suggestions as to the selection's content and significance. I have added explanatory notes, enclosed in brackets, to many selections; the author's original notes are printed without brackets. I have inserted citations to the Bible directly into the text. I have not seen the need to preserve all notes in the original texts. At the end of the volume is a brief list of supplementary reading on the issues raised in this book.

I have done the bulk of my research at the Cornell University Library and the New York Public Library. I am grateful to the staff members of these institutions for their kind assistance. I am also grateful to the staff of Prometheus Books, in particular to freelance copy editor Heather Ammermuller, for the care and attention expended in preparing this book for publication.

CONTENTS

Introduction   11

I. SOME OVERVIEWS

1. Agnosticism and Christianity (1889)
   Thomas Henry Huxley   23

2. Agnosticism (1889)
   Edgar Fawcett   51

3. Why I Am an Agnostic (1929)
   Clarence Darrow   70

4. What Is an Agnostic? (1953)
   Bertrand Russell   79

II. THE CRITICAL STUDY OF RELIGION

5. The Life of Jesus Critically Examined (1835)
   David Friedrich Strauss   95

6. Primitive Culture (1871)
   Edward Burnett Tylor   115

7. About the Holy Bible (1894)
   Robert G. Ingersoll   134

8. Christianity and Morals (1939)
   Edward Westermarck   143

III. AGNOSTICISM AND SCIENCE

9. History of the Conflict between Religion and Science (1874)
   John William Draper   169

10. The Pre-Darwinite and Post-Darwinite World (1877)
    Moncure Daniel Conway   194

11. Science and Religion (1941)
    Albert Einstein   212

12. In the Beginning . . . (1981)
    Isaac Asimov   219

IV. THE DEFICIENCIES OF RELIGION

13. The Christian System (1851)
    Arthur Schopenhauer   233

14. The Ethics of Religion (1877)
    W. K. Clifford   242

15. Christianity and Civilization (1914)
    Charles T. Gorham   256

V. CHRISTIANITY IN DECLINE

16. Rationalism in Europe (1865)
   W. E. H. Lecky   273

17. Are We Christians? (1873)
   Leslie Stephen   283

18. The Twilight of Christianity (1929)
   Harry Elmer Barnes   309

19. God in the Modern World (1929)
   Walter Lippmann   330

VI. THE AGNOSTIC WAY OF LIFE

20. Secularism the True Philosophy of Life (1879)
   G. W. Foote   347

21. On Happiness (1927)
   H. L. Mencken   362

22. The Ethics of Humanism (1949)
   Corliss Lamont   368

Further Reading   385

INTRODUCTION

T he term "agnosticism" was coined by British scientist and
philosopher Thomas Henry Huxley in a lecture delivered in
1869. The word and its derivative, "agnostic," are neo-Greek coinages;
the closest analogue in classical Greek is *agnostos*, which occurs in
the *Odyssey* and means "unknown"; of greater relevance, Plato uses
the term in some of his dialogues to mean "unknowable." In the
broadest sense, agnosticism is an assertion regarding the possibility of
human knowledge; as Huxley himself states in "Agnosticism and
Christianity" (1889), the term denotes that "it is wrong for a man to
say that he is certain of the objective truth of any proposition unless he
can produce evidence which logically justifies that certainty."
Expressed in this manner, agnosticism is not so much a philosophy as
a theory of knowledge. Right from its origin, however, agnosticism
was applied, both by its proponents and by its enemies, to the specific
proposition of whether a god exists and such related matters (some of
them pertaining specifically to Christian doctrine) as the existence or
immortality of the soul, the existence of an afterlife, the divinity of
Jesus Christ, and the inerrancy of the Bible. Bertrand Russell defined
an agnostic as one who "thinks that it is impossible to know the truth

in matters such as God and a future life with which the Christian religion and other religions are concerned."

Agnosticism must be distinguished both from skepticism and from atheism. In a sense, agnosticism might be considered a subset of skepticism, which maintains that "sure knowledge of how things really are may be sought, but cannot be found."[1] Expressed in this manner, however, it can be seen that skepticism is much more agnostic than agnosticism itself, for the latter does not deny that reasonably certain knowledge on many scientific and other questions can be ascertained. Atheism—which skeptics would refer to as one of the "dogmatic" philosophies they repudiate—conversely declares that, if there is not an absolute certainty as to the nonexistence of God (few atheists are so philosophically naive as to believe that one can prove a negative), the evidence against God's existence is so overwhelming that the probabilities are all against it. As H. P. Lovecraft declared in 1932:

> All I say is that I think it is *damned unlikely* that anything like a central cosmic will, a spirit world, or an eternal survival of personality exist. They are the most preposterous and unjustified of all the guesses which can be made about the universe, and I am not enough of a hair-splitter to pretend that I don't regard them as arrant and negligible moonshine. In theory I am an *agnostic*, but pending the appearance of radical evidence I must be classed, practically and provisionally, as an *atheist*.[2]

From this perspective, agnostics have sometimes been criticized by atheists as being tentative fence-sitters, as if they maintained (implausibly, in the atheist's eyes) that there is a roughly equal probability of the truth of theism and of atheism and that therefore it is unwise to come down definitively on either side. This is, however, an inaccurate characterization of agnosticism. Huxley, Russell, and others are fully aware that the probabilities are, at the current state of knowledge, substantially on the side of atheism, but they would declare it a philosophical error to declare themselves atheists even "practically and provisionally."

It was no accident that Huxley's coinage of the term occurred when it did, for a remarkable confluence of events in Western intellectual history during this period all but necessitated it. Although skepticism in regard to religion, and even outright atheism, can be traced to classical antiquity, the definitive formation of agnosticism as a viable philosophical theory could not have occurred prior to the mid–nineteenth century. The roots of agnosticism can be traced at least to the Renaissance, when the revival of classical literature and philosophy brought to the fore the works of Plato, Aristotle, and, more significantly, Epicurus and the Stoics, all of whom put forward rich, complex philosophies untainted by Christian dogma. At the same time, the discovery of pre-Christian science in the work of Aristotle, Archimedes, and others—preserved and transmitted by the Arab philosophers of the Middle Ages—resurrected such inherently non-Christian, and even anti-Christian, notions as the heliocentric theory and the roundness of the earth. As John William Draper noted in his landmark treatise, *History of the Conflict Between Religion and Science* (1874), the findings of Copernicus, Kepler, Galileo, and other Renaissance scientists were furiously opposed by the church, which rightly recognized that dethroning the earth from its presumed position of centrality in the universe implied that a god would be highly unlikely to have bestowed his special favor upon the inhabitants of what was now seen to be an insignificant inkblot in a tiny corner of the cosmos.

Science proved to be, whether wittingly or unwittingly, destructive to religious dogma in other ways. The nascent field of anthropology was putting forth radical theories in regard to the natural growth of religious feeling. The eighteenth-century philosopher David Hume had made tentative forays in this direction in such texts as *The Natural History of Religion* (1757), but his work was unsupported by rigorous fieldwork. The same could by no means be said for the pioneering study *Primitive Culture* (1871) by Edward Burnett Tylor, who maintained, with an immense array of wide-ranging evidence, that primitive peoples came by their religious views as a natural and even inevitable result of their facing a universe whose operations they did not understand, and who therefore attributed the workings of nature to gods roughly like themselves but infinitely more powerful. Such views were popularized in a number of treatises, notably John Fiske's *Myths and Myth-Makers* (1872), and were later definitively expanded in such works as Sir James George Frazer's *The Golden Bough* (1890–1915).

That agnosticism as a coherent philosophy emerged a decade after the publication of Charles Darwin's *On the Origin of Species* (1859) is similarly no accident. As Moncure D. Conway established in the essay "The Pre-Darwinite and Post-Darwinite World" (1877), the theory of evolution was the final component of a purely secular world-view, although Darwin himself—who maintained, toward the end of his life, that "I for one must be content to remain an Agnostic"[3]—was in considerable doubt about the matter. A generation earlier, Charles Lyell had established, in *Principles of Geology* (1830), the immense age of the earth, far greater than the six thousand years put forth by orthodox Christian belief. Darwin, for his part, trumped the final Christian argument for theism, the argument from design: prior to Darwin, the origin of life on earth, and specifically the seemingly won-drous adaptation of human life to its manifold functions in society and civilization, had been inexplicable save by recourse to an all-powerful and benevolent deity. With the theory of natural selection, that con-ception fell to the ground.

But these scientific advances could not have had such widespread philosophical import and influence if other work, from a very different direction, had not played its part. For the better part of two millennia after the establishment of Christianity, the Bible had been regarded, not merely by "fundamentalists" but by virtually all Christians, as a work divinely inspired by God; after all, it said so itself ("All scripture is given by inspiration of God" [2 Timothy 3:16]). (There is, of course, a circular logic behind all this: God exists because the Bible says so; the Bible is true because it is inspired by God.) Work regarding the exact interpretation of the Bible, or of given biblical passages (gener-ally referred to as "lower" criticism), had been conducted since the Bible itself was established as a concrete entity; but investigation of the actual origin of biblical texts—what came to be referred to as "higher" criticism—was a product of the early to mid–nineteenth century. A cadre of German scholars systematically ascertained that the Bible was a heterogeneous text written by many hands over the course of centuries, even millennia, and a product of the social and political tendencies of the Jewish and early Christian society out of which it emerged. Without saying so, the higher critics suggested—in some cases unwittingly—that the divine inspiration of the Bible could not be upheld and that it was a mundane document that had its own history just like any other sacred or secular text from antiquity. One pioneer of this movement was David Friedrich Strauss, whose *Das Leben Jesu* (1835; The Life of Jesus) first interpreted Jesus' life in terms of myth theory and dispensed with the "miracles" attributed to Jesus and other figures as obvious fabrications of several generations, and in some cases several centuries, after Jesus' death. It is not surprising that the atheist George Eliot translated this revolutionary work into English, where it went through many editions.

This "perfect storm" of scientific discovery and philosophical advance—in the fields of physics, astronomy, biology, geology, anthropology, philology, and even the relatively new discipline of psychology, which was discovering that religious belief was, for many, a psychological bulwark against the miseries of their own lives and against the feeling of loneliness in the universe—resulted in a tremendous outburst of agnostic thought in the later nineteenth century, especially in England. Huxley was the spearhead, but many others soon joined him. Leslie Stephen, W. K. Clifford, and others spoke of religion, and specifically Christianity, in increasingly disparaging terms, challenging both the truth of Christian doctrine and its purported benefits to morality and civilization. Secularist and freethought societies sprang up and attracted wide notice and an enthusiastic membership. It is remarkable that, so early as 1877, a leading British magazine, the *Nineteenth Century*, could hold a symposium called "The Influence upon Morality of a Decline in Religious Belief."[4] Four years earlier, Leslie Stephen had published an essay with the provocative title "Are

We Christians?" the presumed answer being in the negative. Stephen did not state that he, or even a majority of professed Christians, were in reality atheists; instead, he asserted that the convergence of scientific discovery and moral and philosophical progress had caused many avowed Christians to be deliberately or unwittingly agnostic about certain dogmas that, in prior ages, had commanded universal assent: that Jesus Christ was a divine figure come to save humanity from sin, that hell existed and was populated by the sinful, that all those who did not believe in Christian doctrine were damned, and so on. A number of these dogmas had become acute embarrassments to the church, or at any rate to many of its liberal members. Rather than repudiate them explicitly, many Christians chose simply to ignore them and pretend that they did not represent contemporary Christian belief, even though they were all emphatically found in the Bible. This fudging on critical points of dogma has continued to the present day among mainline Christian churches. Yet it can be argued that even professed fundamentalists do not adhere rigidly to the principle of biblical inerrancy, even though they think they do. Few fundamentalists avow—at least publicly—such doctrines, unequivocally asserted in the Bible as proceeding directly from God, as the sun's revolution around the earth (Joshua 10:12–13), the death penalty for homosexuals (Leviticus 20:13) and violators of the Sabbath (Numbers 15:35), the condoning of slavery (Ephesians 6:5), the ownership of wives by their husbands (Exodus 20:17), and so on.[5]

The result of all this ferment in the nineteenth century was the conclusion, among intellectuals, that not only were Christianity's claims to truth false or, at best, unlikely in the face of scientific advance, but its role in the formation of the best features of Western civilization was doubtful This latter sentiment had been growing since at least the eighteenth century, when revulsion at the church's dogmatism and bigotry, its persecution of "witches" and heretics, the vicious wars conducted in its name, and other factors had led Voltaire and others to declare organized Christianity an "infamy" that must be crushed. That proved to be an impossibility in a literal sense, but political reform could, at any rate, remove religion from the province of law and government: it was this development that Irish historian W. E. H. Lecky studied closely and voluminously in *History of the Rise and Influence of the Spirit of Rationalism in Europe* (1865). Lecky is correct when, in noting the expulsion of religion from government, he wrote: "No human pen can write its epitaph, for no imagination can adequately realise its glories." The extent to which the Christian church controlled virtually every facet of public, and many features of private, life from the fourth to the nineteenth centuries in Europe and America can scarcely be comprehended by those of us who have lived outside its shadow; Lecky himself can only hint at it in his observation of the inexorable decline of the Holy Roman Empire to a tiny principality called the Vatican, locked within the state of Italy, its influence now restricted solely to a moral suasion that increasingly fails to affect even its professed adherents.

In the United States—although its founders had initiated the startlingly radical procedure of separating church and state in the First Amendment to the Constitution (a principle that no European country, save atheistic France of the post-Revolutionary period, would duplicate for many decades)—religious opinion even among the intelligentsia remained considerably more conservative. Christianity was the bedrock of education, artistic endeavor, and many features of public policy, and few were bold enough to challenge its supremacy openly. That changed somewhat in the later nineteenth century, with the emergence of Robert G. Ingersoll as the most popular public lecturer in the nation. Ingersoll, "the Great Agnostic," could not by any stretch of the imagination be called a profound thinker; his great virtue rested in the sheer courage of his onslaught against what he considered the most objectionable facets of Christian dogma and his unflinching exposure of the fallacies, contradictions, and moral turpitude of that dogma. He achieved his effects largely through a series of rhetorical flourishes that must have been thrilling to his hearers, and is conveyed in lesser degree even in cold print. Toward the end of the nineteenth century, Ingersoll passed his rhetorical torch to Clarence Darrow, who used all his skills as a trial lawyer to flay the Christian Church at every opportunity.

During the twentieth century, both science and agnosticism under-
went significant changes. For its part, science was forced to renounce
the somewhat cocksure certainties that had propelled nineteenth-century thought in physics, astronomy, and chemistry and to adopt a mod-
icum of uncertainty: in effect, with the advent of Einstein, Planck, and
Heisenberg, science became more agnostic. Although science could
no longer claim unequivocal truth but only strong probabilities (a
stance that allowed some mystics and religionists to resurrect outworn
dogmas that were no less fallacious than they had been before),
philosophers and other public thinkers came to believe that the new-
found indeterminacies of science only enhanced the credibility of
agnosticism as a viable philosophical creed. And thinkers like Harry
Elmer Barnes were still speaking of "the twilight of Christianity" and
attempting to devise moral, political, and cultural stances suitable for
a post-Christian age. Perhaps the most acute commentator on this subject was Walter Lippmann, whose *A Preface to Morals* (1929) remains
a textbook for coming to terms with the inevitable uncertainties of life
when religion has lost its authority and science cannot provide definitive answers in the realm of personal conduct.

One of the greatest advances that agnosticism made in the course
of the twentieth century was its advocacy of an agnostic way of life.
Religionists had long been able to accuse agnosticism of being merely
a negative creed, symbolized by the very first letter of the word—what
Greek grammarians called the "alpha-privative," indicating a negation.
If agnosticism merely meant "not knowing," how could it provide a
coherent guide to moral and social action? As early as 1889, Edgar
Fawcett had professed that agnostics were just as devoted to charitable
work as the major religions; and, given that religion had had many centuries' head start in such work, it could not be expected that secular
charity could rival religious charity in the near future. But the great
majority of agnostic thinkers emphasized secular advocacy of a variety
of social causes, while at the same time criticizing the Church for its
acquiescence in the root causes of social, political, and economic injustice. As Corliss Lamont wrote in *The Philosophy of Humanism* (1949),

Pope Pius XI's recommendation in 1931, at the height of the Depression, that the poor endure their suffering with "resignation" is an "excellent example of the typical religious defeatism that Humanism decries." Lamont also strongly criticizes Christianity's long-standing opposition to the liberalization of sexual practices, a product of what can only be regarded as hatred and fear of this most intimate and uncontrollable of human acts. The conservatism that the great majority of religions have exhibited in the wake of a pressing need for reform has itself alienated many who might otherwise have remained adherents in spite of the overwhelming scientific evidence against theism.

Religion's final argument—that the majority of human beings are simply unable to live in a state of uncertainty regarding the most significant issues facing us (Is there a God? Will there be a life after death? Is there a heaven and a hell?)—is a matter difficult to resolve without a wide survey of both believers and unbelievers. If it is true, it may mean that agnosticism must necessarily remain the recourse of an intellectual elite. H. L. Mencken affirmed that the agnostic's "doubts, if they are real, undoubtedly tend to make him uneasy, and hence unhappy," but he counters that with these doubts comes a "pride in his capacity to face them." But it is an open question whether this pride is truly restricted only to the select few: the great majority of religious believers, even fundamentalists, are manifestly afflicted with the same doubts that agnostics face daily, and it is by no means clear that their religion provides them today the comforts that it did when it was less subject to scientific, philosophical, moral, and social criticism. In this sense, there is every reason to believe that a substantial number of believers are themselves agnostics who are unwilling or unable to face up to the doubts that plague them on all sides.

NOTES

1. Antony Flew, *A Dictionary of Philosophy* (New York: St. Martin's Press, 1979), p. 291.

2. H. P. Lovecraft, Letter to Robert E. Howard (August 16, 1932), in *Selected Letters 1932–1934* (Sauk City, WI: Arkham House, 1976), p. 57.

3. Charles Darwin, *Autobiography* (1876); excerpts reprinted in *Atheism: A Reader*, ed. S. T. Joshi (Amherst, NY: Prometheus Books, 2000), p. 198.

4. See the selection from G. W. Foote's *Secularism the True Philosophy of Life*, n. 16 (p. 361).

5. On this point, see my *God's Defenders: What They Believe and Why They Are Wrong* (Amherst, NY: Prometheus Books, 2003), pp. 183–206.

Part I.
SOME OVERVIEWS

1

AGNOSTICISM AND CHRISTIANITY

Thomas Henry Huxley

[Thomas Henry Huxley (1825–1895), British naturalist and philosopher, studied medicine at London University, then sailed aboard the H.M.S. *Rattlesnake* as a surgeon; his important observations of flora and fauna in the southern hemisphere established his early scientific reputation. Huxley was greatly influenced by Darwin's *Origin of Species*, earning the nickname "Darwin's bulldog" for his vigorous advocacy of evolution. But he differed from Darwin in several important particulars, downplaying the element of natural selection and expressing skepticism of Darwin's theory of the gradual evolution of species. Although he made several notable contributions in biology and physiology, Huxley gained greatest celebrity as a popularizer of science, especially in such works as *Evidences as to Man's Place in Nature* (1863), *Science and Culture* (1881), and *Evolution and Ethics* (1893). In 1869 he coined the term "agnosticism," claiming

Thomas Henry Huxley, "Agnosticism and Christianity" (1889), *Science and Christian Tradition* (New York: D. Appleton, 1894), pp. 309–47.

that the advance of science had rendered many religious conceptions of the universe invalid or at best highly unlikely. This stance embroiled Huxley in numerous controversies with theologians, into which he entered with vigor and enthusiasm. His writings on the subject are found in *Science and Hebrew Tradition* (1894) and *Science and Christian Tradition* (1894). His *Scientific Memoirs* (1898–1903; 5 vols.), *Life and Letters* (1900; 2 vols.), and *Autobiography and Selected Essays* (1909) appeared posthumously. In the following extract from "Agnosticism and Christianity" (first published in the anthology *Christianity and Agnosticism: A Controversy* [1889] and reprinted in *Science and Christian Tradition*), Huxley defends his essay "Agnosticism" from numerous critics and attacks other theological commentators (notably John Henry Newman), stating that a belief in Christianity necessarily encompasses a belief in demonology and that the miracles attested in the Gospels are no more or less likely than those in later Christian epochs or the miracles put forth by spiritualists.]

Nemo ergo ex me scire quaerat, quod me nescire scio, nisi forte ut nescire discat.
—Augustinus, *De Civ. Dei*, xii. 7.[1]

The present discussion has arisen out of the use, which has become general in the last few years, of the terms "Agnostic" and "Agnosticism."

The people who call themselves "Agnostics" have been charged with doing so because they have not the courage to declare themselves "Infidels." It has been insinuated that they have adopted a new name in order to escape the unpleasantness which attaches to their proper denomination. To this wholly erroneous imputation, I have replied by showing that the term "Agnostic" did, as a matter of fact, arise in a manner which negatives it; and my statement has not been, and cannot be, refuted. Moreover, speaking for myself, and without impugning the right of any other person to use the term in another sense, I further say that Agnosticism is not properly described as a "negative" creed, nor indeed as a creed of any kind, except in so far as it expresses absolute faith in the validity of a principle, which is as much ethical as intellectual. This principle may be stated in various ways, but they all amount to this: that it is wrong for a man to say that he is certain of the objective truth of any proposition unless he can produce evidence which logically justifies that certainty. This is what Agnosticism asserts; and, in my opinion, it is all that is essential to Agnosticism. That which Agnostics deny and repudiate, as immoral, is the contrary doctrine, that there are propositions which men ought to believe, without logically satisfactory evidence; and that reprobation ought to attach to the profession of disbelief in such inadequately supported propositions. The justification of the Agnostic principle lies in the success which follows upon its application, whether in the field of natural, or in that of civil, history; and in the fact that, so far as these topics are concerned, no sane man thinks of denying its validity.

Still speaking for myself, I add that though Agnosticism is not, and cannot be, a creed, except in so far as its general principle is concerned; yet that the application of that principle results in the denial of, or the suspension of judgment concerning, a number of propositions respecting which our contemporary ecclesiastical "gnostics" profess entire certainty. And, in so far as these ecclesiastical persons can be justified in their old-established custom (which many nowadays think more honoured in the breach than the observance) of using opprobrious names to those who differ from them, I fully admit their right to call me and those who think with me "Infidels"; all I have ventured to urge is that they must not expect us to speak of ourselves by that title.

The extent of the region of the uncertain, the number of the problems the investigation of which ends in a verdict of not proven, will vary according to the knowledge and the intellectual habits of the individual Agnostic. I do not very much care to speak of anything as "unknowable."[2] What I am sure about is that there are many topics about which I know nothing; and which, so far as I can see, are out of reach of my faculties. But whether these things are knowable by any one else is exactly one of those matters which is beyond my knowledge, though I may have a tolerably strong opinion as to the probabilities of the case. Relatively to myself, I am quite sure that the region of uncertainty—the nebulous country in which words play the part of realities—is far more extensive than I could wish. Materialism and Idealism; Theism and Atheism; the doctrine of the soul and its mortality or immortality—appear in the history of philosophy like the shades of Scandinavian heroes, eternally slaying one another and eternally coming to life again in a metaphysical "Nifelheim."[3] It is getting on for twenty-five centuries, at least, since mankind began seriously to give their minds to these topics. Generation after generation, philosophy has been doomed to roll the stone uphill; and, just as all the world swore it was at the top, down it has rolled to the bottom again. All this is written in innumerable books; and he who will toil through them will discover that the stone is just where it was when the work began. Hume saw this; Kant saw it; since their time, more and more eyes have been cleansed of the films which prevented them from seeing it; until now the weight and number of those who refuse to be the prey of verbal mystifications has begun to tell in practical life.

It was inevitable that a conflict should arise between Agnosticism and Theology; or rather, I ought to say, between Agnosticism and Ecclesiasticism. For Theology, the science, is one thing; and Ecclesiasticism, the championship of a foregone conclusion as to the truth of a particular form of Theology,[4] is another. With scientific Theology, Agnosticism has no quarrel. On the contrary, the Agnostic, knowing too well the influence of prejudice and idiosyncrasy, even on those who desire most earnestly to be impartial, can wish for nothing more urgently than that the scientific theologian should not only be at perfect liberty to thresh out the matter in his own fashion; but that he should, if he can, find flaws in the Agnostic position; and, even if demonstration is not to be had, that he should put, in their full force, the grounds of the conclusions he thinks probable. The scientific theologian admits the Agnostic principle, however widely his results may differ from those reached by the majority of Agnostics.

But, as between Agnosticism and Ecclesiasticism, or, as our neighbours across the Channel call it, Clericalism, there can be neither peace nor truce. The Cleric asserts that it is morally wrong not to believe certain propositions, whatever the results of a strict scientific investigation of the evidence of these propositions. He tells us "that religious error is, in itself, of an immoral nature."[5] He declares that he has prejudged certain conclusions, and looks upon those who show cause for arrest of judgment as emissaries of Satan. It necessarily follows that, for him, the attainment of faith, not the ascertainment of truth, is the highest aim of mental life. And, on careful analysis of the nature of this faith, it will too often be found to be, not the mystic process of unity with the Divine, understood by the religious enthusiast; but that which the candid simplicity of a Sunday scholar once defined it to be. "Faith," said this unconscious plagiarist of Tertullian, "is the power of saying you believe things which are incredible."[6]

Now I, and many other Agnostics, believe that faith, in this sense, is an abomination; and though we do not indulge in the luxury of self-righteousness so far as to call those who are not of our way of thinking hard names, we do not feel that the disagreement between ourselves and those who hold this doctrine is even more moral than intellectual. It is desirable there should be an end of any mistakes on this topic. If our clerical opponents were clearly aware of the real state of the case, there would be an end of the curious delusion, which often appears between the lines of their writings, that those whom they are so fond of calling "Infidels" are people who not only ought to be, but in their hearts are, ashamed of themselves. It would be discourteous to do more than hint the antipodal opposition of this pleasant dream of theirs to facts.

The clerics and their lay allies commonly tell us, that if we refuse to admit that there is good ground for expressing definite convictions about certain topics, the bonds of human society will dissolve and mankind lapse into savagery. There are several answers to this assertion. One is that the bonds of human society were formed without the aid of their theology; and, in the opinion of not a few competent judges, have been weakened rather than strengthened by a good deal of it. Greek science, Greek art, the ethics of old Israel, the social organisation of old Rome, contrived to come into being, without the help of any one who believed in a single distinctive article of the simplest of the Christian creeds. The science, the art, the jurisprudence, the chief political and social theories, of the modern world have grown out of those of Greece and Rome—not by favour of, but in the teeth of, the fundamental teachings of early Christianity, to which science, art, and any serious occupation with the things of this world, were alike despicable.

Again, all that is best in the ethics of the modern world, in so far as it has not grown out of Greek thought, or Barbarian manhood, is the direct development of the ethics of old Israel. There is no code of legislation, ancient or modern, at once so just and so merciful, so tender to the weak and poor, as the Jewish law; and, if the Gospels are to be trusted, Jesus of Nazareth himself declared that he taught nothing but that which lay implicitly, or explicitly, in the religious and ethical system of his people.

> And the scribe said unto him, Of a truth, Teacher, thou hast well said that he is one; and there is none other but he, and to love him with all the heart, and with all the understanding, and with all the strength, and to love his neighbour as himself, is much more than all whole burnt offerings and sacrifices. (Mark xii. 32, 33.)

Here is the briefest of summaries of the teaching of the prophets of Israel of the eighth century; does the Teacher, whose doctrine is thus set forth in his presence, repudiate the exposition? Nay; we are told, on the contrary, that Jesus saw that he "answered discreetly," and replied, "Thou art not far from the kingdom of God" [Mark 12:34].

So that I think that even if the creeds, from the so-called "Apostles," to the so-called "Athanasian," were swept into oblivion; and even if the human race should arrive at the conclusion that, whether a bishop washes a cup or leaves it unwashed, is not a matter of the least consequence, it will get on very well. The causes which have led to the development of morality in mankind, which have guided or impelled us all the way from the savage to the civilised state, will not cease to operate because a number of ecclesiastical hypotheses turn out to be baseless. And, even if the absurd notion that morality is more the child of speculation than of practical necessity and inherited instinct, had any foundation; if all the world is going to thieve, murder, and otherwise misconduct itself as soon as it discovers that certain portions of ancient history are mythical, what is the relevance of such arguments to any one who holds by the Agnostic principle?

Surely, the attempt to cast out Beelzebub by the aid of Beelzebub is a hopeful procedure as compared to that of preserving morality by the aid of immorality. For I suppose it is admitted that an Agnostic may be perfectly sincere, may be competent, and may have studied the question at issue with as much care as his clerical opponents. But, if the Agnostic really believes what he says, the "dreadful consequence" argufier (consistently, I admit, with his own principles) virtually asks him to abstain from telling the truth, or to say what he believes to be untrue, because of the supposed injurious consequences to morality. "Beloved brethren, that we may be spotlessly moral, before all things let us lie," is the sum total of many an exhortation addressed to the "Infidel." Now, as I have already pointed out, we cannot oblige our exhorters. We leave the practical application of the convenient doctrines of "Reserve" and "Non-natural interpretation" to those who invented them.

I trust that I have now made amends for any ambiguity, or want of fulness, in my previous exposition of that which I hold to be the essence of the Agnostic doctrine. Henceforward, I might hope to hear no more of the assertion that we are necessarily Materialists, Idealists, Atheists, Theists, or any other *ists*, if experience had led me to think that the proved falsity of a statement was any guarantee against its repetition. And those who appreciate the nature of our position will see, at once, that when Ecclesiasticism declares that we ought to believe this, that, and the other, and are very wicked if we don't, it is impossible for us to give any answer but this: We have not the slightest objection to believe anything you like, if you will give us good grounds for belief; but, if you cannot, we must respectfully refuse, even if that refusal should wreck mortality and insure our own damnation several times over. We are quite content to leave that to the decision of the future. The course of the past has impressed us with the firm conviction that no good ever comes of falsehood, and we feel warranted in refusing even to experiment in that direction.

In the course of the present discussion it has been asserted that the "Sermon on the Mount" and the "Lord's Prayer" furnish a summary and condensed view of the essentials of the teaching of Jesus of Nazareth, set forth by himself. Now this supposed *Summa* of Nazarene theology distinctly affirms the existence of a spiritual world, of a Heaven, and of a Hell of fire; it teaches the Fatherhood of God and the malignity of the Devil, it declares the superintending providence of the former and our need of deliverance from the machinations of the latter; it affirms the fact of demoniac possession and the power of casting out devils by the faithful. And from these premises, the conclusion is drawn, that those Agnostics who deny that there is any evidence of such a character as to justify certainty, respecting the existence and the nature of the spiritual world, contradict the express declarations of Jesus. I have replied to this argumentation by showing that there is strong reason to doubt the historical accuracy of the attribution to Jesus of either the "Sermon on the Mount" or the "Lord's Prayer"; and, therefore, that the conclusion in question is not warranted, at any rate, on the grounds set forth.

But, whether the Gospels contain trustworthy statements about this and other alleged historical facts or not, it is quite certain that from them, taken together with the other books of the New Testament, we may collect a pretty complete exposition of that theory of the spiritual world which was held by both Nazarenes and Christians; and which was undoubtedly supposed by them to be fully sanctioned by Jesus, though it is just as clear that they did not imagine it contained any revelation by him of something heretofore unknown. If the pneumatological doctrine which pervades the whole New Testament is nowhere systematically stated,[7] it is everywhere assumed. The writers of the Gospels and of the Acts take it for granted, as a matter of common knowledge; and it is easy to gather from these sources a series of propositions, which only need arrangement to form a complete system.

In this system, Man is considered to be a duality formed of a spiritual element, the soul; and a corporeal element,[8] the body. And this duality is repeated in the Universe, which consists of a corporeal world embraced and interpenetrated by a spiritual world. The former consists of the earth, as its principal and central constituent, with the subsidiary sun, planets, and stars. Above the earth is the air, and below is the watery abyss. Whether the heaven, which is conceived to be above the air, and the hell in, or below, the subterranean deeps, are to be taken as corporeal or incorporeal is not clear. However this may be, the heaven and the air, the earth and the abyss, are peopled by innumerable beings analogous in nature to the spiritual element in man, and these spirits are of two kinds, good and bad. The chief of the good spirits, infinitely superior to all the others, and their creator, as well as the creator of the corporeal world and of the bad spirits, is God. His residence is heaven, where he is surrounded by the ordered hosts of good spirits; his angels, or messengers, and the executors of his will throughout the universe.

On the other hand, the chief of the bad spirits is Satan, the devil *par excellence*. He and his company of demons are free to roam through all parts of the universe, except the heaven. These bad spirits are far superior to man in power and subtlety; and their whole energies are devoted to bringing physical and moral evils upon him, and to thwarting, so far as his power goes, the benevolent intentions of the Supreme Being. In fact, the souls and bodies of men form both the theatre and the prize of an incessant warfare between the good and the evil spirits—the powers of light and the powers of darkness. By leading Eve astray, Satan brought sin and death upon mankind. As the gods of the heathen, the demons are the founders and maintainers of idolatry; as the "powers of the air" they afflict mankind with pestilence and famine; as "unclean spirits" they cause disease of mind and body.

The significance of the appearance of Jesus, in the capacity of the Messiah, or Christ, is the reversal of the satanic work by putting an end to both sin and death. He announces that the kingdom of God is at hand, when the "Prince of this world" shall be finally "cast out" (John xii. 31) from the cosmos, as Jesus, during his earthly career, cast him out from individuals. Then will Satan and all his devilry, along with the wicked whom they have seduced to their destruction, be hurled into the abyss of unquenchable fire—there to endure continual torture, without a hope of winning pardon from the merciful God, their Father; or of moving the glorified Messiah to one more act of pitiful intercession; or even of interrupting, by a momentary sympathy with their wretchedness, the harmonious psalmody of their brother angels and men, eternally lapped in bliss unspeakable.

The straitest Protestant, who refuses to admit the existence of any source of Divine truth, except the Bible, will not deny that every point of the pneumatological theory here set forth has ample scriptural warranty. The Gospels, the Acts, the Epistles, and the Apocalypse assert the existence of the devil, of his demons and of Hell, as plainly as they do that of God and his angels and Heaven. It is plain that the Messianic and the Satanic conceptions of the writers of these books are the obverse and the reverse of the same intellectual coinage. If we turn from Scripture to the traditions of the Fathers and the confessions of the Churches, it will appear that, in this one particular, at any rate, time has brought about no important deviation from primitive belief. From Justin onwards,[9] it may often be a fair question whether God, or the devil, occupies a larger share of the attention of the Fathers. It is the devil who instigates the Roman authorities to persecute; the gods and goddesses of paganism are devils, and idolatry itself is an invention of Satan; if a saint fall away from grace, it is by the seduction of the demon; if heresy arises, the devil has suggested it; and some of the Fathers go so far as to challenge the pagans to a sort of exorcising match,[10] by way of testing the truth of Christianity. Mediaeval Christianity is at one with patristic, on this head. The masses, the clergy, the theologians, and the philosophers alike, live and move and have their being in a world full of demons, in which sorcery and possession are everyday occurrences. Nor did the Reformation make any difference. Whatever else Luther assailed, he left the traditional demonology untouched; nor could any one have entertained a more hearty and uncompromising belief in the devil, than he and, at a later period, the Calvinistic fanatics of New England did. Finally, in these last years of the nineteenth century, the demonological hypotheses of the first century are, explicitly or implicitly, held and occasionally acted upon by the immense majority of Christians of all confessions.

Only here and there has the progress of scientific thought, outside the ecclesiastical world, so far affected Christians, that they and their teachers fight shy of the demonology of their creed. They are fain to conceal their real disbelief in one half of Christian doctrine by judicious silence about it; or by flight to those refuges for the logically destitute, accommodation or allegory. But the faithful who fly to allegory in order to escape absurdity resemble nothing so much as the sheep in the fable who—to save their lives—jumped into the pit. The allegory pit is too commodious, is ready to swallow up so much more than one wants to put into it. If the story of the temptation is an allegory; if the early recognition of Jesus as the Son of God by the demons is an allegory; if the plain declaration of the writer of the first Epistle of John (iii. 8), "To this end was the Son of God manifested, that He might destroy the works of the devil," is allegorical, then the Pauline version of the Fall may be allegorical, and still more the words of consecration of the Eucharist, or the promise of the second coming; in fact, there is not a dogma of ecclesiastical Christianity the scriptural basis of which may not be whittled away by a similar process.

As to accommodation, let any honest man who can read the New Testament ask himself whether Jesus and his immediate friends and disciples can be dishonoured more grossly than by the supposition that they said and did that which is attributed to them; while, in reality, they disbelieved in Satan and his demons, in possession and in exorcism?

An eminent theologian has justly observed that we have no right to look at the propositions of the Christian faith with one eye open and the other shut. (Tract 85, p. 29.) It really is not permissible to see, with one eye, that Jesus is affirmed to declare the personality and the Fatherhood of God, His loving providence and His accessibility to prayer; and to shut the other to the no less definite teaching ascribed to Jesus, in regard to the personality and the misanthropy of the devil, his malignant watchfulness, and his subjection to exorcistic formulae and rites. Jesus is made to say that the devil "was a murderer from the beginning" (John viii. 44) by the same authority as that upon which we depend for his asserted declaration that "God is a spirit" (John iv. 24).

To those who admit the authority of the famous Vincentian dictum that the doctrine which has been held "always, everywhere, and by all" is to be received as authoritative,[11] the demonology must possess a higher sanction than any other Christian dogma, except, perhaps, those of the Resurrection and of the Messiahship of Jesus; for it would be difficult to name any other points of doctrine on which the Nazarene does not differ from the Christian, and the different historical stages and contemporary subdivisions of Christianity from one another. And, if the demonology is accepted, there can be no reason for rejecting all those miracles in which demons play a part. The Gadarene story fits into the general scheme of Christianity, and the evidence for "Legion" and their doings is just as good as any other in the New Testament for the doctrine which the story illustrates.

It was with the purpose of bringing this great fact into prominence; of getting people to open both their eyes when they look at Ecclesiasticism; that I devoted so much space to that miraculous story which happens to be one of the best types of its class.[12] And I could not wish for a better justification of the course I have adopted, than the fact that my heroically consistent adversary has declared his implicit belief in the Gadarene story and (by necessary consequence) in the Christian demonology as a whole. It must be obvious, by this time, that, if the account of the spiritual world given in the New Testament, professedly on the authority of Jesus, is true, then the demonological half of that account must be just as true as the other half. And, therefore, those who question the demonology, or try to explain it away, deny the truth of what Jesus said, and are, in ecclesiastical terminology, "Infidels" just as much as those who deny the spirituality of God. This is as plain as anything can well be, and the dilemma for my opponent was either to assert that the Gadarene pig-bedevilment actually occurred, or to write himself down an "Infidel." As was to be expected, he chose the former alternative; and I may express my great satisfaction at finding that there is one spot of common ground on which both he and I stand. So far as I can judge, we are agreed to state one of the broad issues between the consequences of agnostic principles (as I draw them), and the consequences of ecclesiastical dogmatism (as he accepts it), as follows.

Ecclesiasticism says: The demonology of the Gospels is an essential part of that account of that spiritual world, the truth of which it declares to be certified by Jesus.

Agnosticism (*me judice*) says: There is no good evidence of the existence of a demoniac spiritual world, and much reason for doubting it.

Hereupon the ecclesiastic may observe: Your doubt means that you disbelieve Jesus; therefore you are an "Infidel" instead of an "Agnostic." To which the agnostic may reply: No; for two reasons: first, because your evidence that Jesus said what you say he said is worth very little; and secondly, because a man may be an agnostic, in the sense of admitting he has no positive knowledge, and yet consider that he has more or less probable ground for accepting any given hypothesis about the spiritual world. Just as a man may frankly declare that he has no means of knowing whether the planets generally are inhabited or not, and yet may think one of the two possible hypotheses more likely than the other, so he may admit that he has no means of knowing anything about the spiritual world, and yet may think one or other of the current views on the subject, to some extent, probable.

The second answer is so obviously valid that it needs no discussion.

I draw attention to it simply in justice to those agnostics who may attach greater value than I do to any sort of pneumatological speculations; and not because I wish to escape the responsibility of declaring that, whether Jesus sanctioned the demonological part of Christianity or not, I unhesitatingly reject it. The first answer, on the other hand, opens up the whole question of the claim of the biblical and other sources, from which hypotheses concerning the spiritual world are derived, to be regarded as unimpeachable historical evidence as to matters of fact.

Now, in respect of the trustworthiness of the Gospel narratives, I was anxious to get rid of the common assumption that the determination of the authorship and of the dates of these works is a matter of fundamental importance. That assumption is based upon the notion that what contemporary witnesses say must be true, or, at least, has always a *primâ facie* claim to be so regarded; so that if the writers of any of the Gospels were contemporaries of the events (and still more if they were in the position of eye-witnesses) the miracles they narrate must be historically true, and, consequently, the demonology which they involve must be accepted. But the story of the "Translation of the blessed martyrs Marcellinus and Petrus," and the other considerations (to which endless additions might have been made from the Fathers and the mediaeval writers) set forth in a preceding essay, yield, in my judgment, satisfactory proof that, where the miraculous is concerned, neither considerable intellectual ability nor undoubted honesty, nor knowledge of the world, nor proved faithfulness as civil historians, nor profound piety, on the part of eye-witnesses and contemporaries, affords any guarantee of the objective truth of their statements, when we know that a firm belief in the miraculous was ingrained in their minds, and was the pre-supposition of their observations and reasonings.[13]

Therefore, although it be, as I believe, demonstrable that we have no real knowledge of the authorship, or of the date of composition of the Gospels, as they have come down to us, and that nothing better than more or less probable guesses can be arrived at on that subject, I have not cared to expend any space on the question. It will be admitted, I suppose, that the authors of the works attributed to

Matthew, Mark, Luke, and John, whoever they may be, are personages whose capacity and judgment in the narration of ordinary events are not quite so well certified as those of Eginhard; and we have seen what the value of Eginhard's evidence is when the miraculous is in question.

I have been careful to explain that the arguments which I have used in the course of this discussion are not new; that they are historical and have nothing to do with what is commonly called science; and that they are all, to the best of my belief, to be found in the works of theologians of repute.

The position which I have taken up, that the evidence in favour of such miracles as those recorded by Eginhard, and consequently of mediaeval demonology, is quite as good as that in favour of such miracles as the Gadarene, and consequently of Nazarene demonology, is none of my discovery. Its strength was, wittingly or unwittingly, suggested, a century and a half ago, by a theological scholar of eminence; and it has been, if not exactly occupied, yet so fortified with bastions and redoubts by a living ecclesiastical Vauban,[14] that, in my judgment, it has been rendered impregnable. In the early part of the last century, the ecclesiastical mind in this country was much exercised by the question, not exactly of miracles, the occurrence of which in biblical times was axiomatic, but by the problem: When did miracles cease? Anglican divines were quite sure that no miracles had happened in their day, nor for some time past; they were equally sure that they happened sixteen or seventeen centuries earlier. And it was a vital question for them to determine at what point of time, between this *terminus a quo* and that *terminus ad quem*, miracles came to an end.

The Anglicans and the Romanists agreed in the assumption that the possession of the gift of miracle-working was *primâ facie* evidence of the soundness of the faith of the miracle-workers. The supposition that miraculous powers might be wielded by heretics (though it might be supported by high authority) led to consequences too frightful to be entertained by people who were busied in building their dogmatic house on the sands of early Church history. If, as the Romanists maintained, an unbroken series of genuine miracles adorned the records of their Church, throughout the whole of its existence, no Anglican could lightly venture to accuse them of doctrinal corruption. Hence, the Anglicans, who indulged in such accusations, were bound to prove the modern, the mediaeval Roman, and the later Patristic miracles false; and to shut off the wonder-working power from the Church at the exact point of time when Anglican doctrine ceased and Roman doctrine began. With a little adjustment—a squeeze here and a pull there—the Christianity of the first three or four centuries might be made to fit, or seem to fit, pretty well into the Anglican scheme. So the miracles, from Justin say to Jerome,[15] might be recognised; while, in later times, the Church having become "corrupt"—that is to say, having pursued one and the same line of development further than was pleasing to Anglicans—its alleged miracles must needs be shams and impostures.

Under these circumstances, it may be imagined that the establishment of a scientific frontier between the earlier realm of supposed fact and the later of asserted delusion, had its difficulties; and torrents of theological special pleading about the subject flowed from clerical pens, until that learned and acute Anglican divine, Conyers Middleton, in his "Free Inquiry,"[16] tore the sophistical web they had laboriously woven to pieces, and demonstrated that the miracles of the patristic age, early and late, must stand or fall together, inasmuch as the evidence for the later is just as good as the evidence for the earlier wonders. If the one set are certified by contemporaneous witnesses of high repute, so are the other; and, in point of probability, there is not a pin to choose between the two. That is the solid and irrefragable result of Middleton's contribution to the subject. But the Free Inquirer's freedom had its limits; and he draws a sharp line of demarcation between the patristic and the New Testament miracles—on the professed ground that the accounts of the latter, being inspired, are out of the reach of criticism.

A century later, the question was taken up by another divine, Middleton's equal in learning and acuteness, and far his superior in subtlety and dialectic skill; who, though an Anglican, scorned the name of Protestant; and, while yet a Churchman, made it his business to parade, with infinite skill, the utter hollowness of the arguments of those of his brother Churchmen who dreamed that they could be both Anglicans and Protestants. The argument of the "Essay on the Miracles recorded in the Ecclesiastical History of the Early Ages" by the present [1889] Roman Cardinal,[17] but then Anglican Doctor, John Henry Newman, is compendiously stated by himself in the following passage:—

> If the miracles of Church history cannot be defended by the argu-
> ments of Leslie, Lyttleton, Paley, or Douglas, how many of the
> Scripture miracles satisfy their conditions? (p. cvii).

And, although the answer is not given in so many words, little doubt is left on the mind of the reader, that, in the mind of the writer, it is: None. In fact, this conclusion is one which cannot be resisted, if the argument in favour of the Scripture miracles is based upon that which laymen, whether lawyers, or men of science, or historians, or ordinary men of affairs, call evidence. But there is something really impressive in the magnificent contempt with which, at times, Dr. Newman sweeps aside alike those who offer and those who demand such evidence.

> Some infidel authors advise us to accept no miracles which would
> not have a verdict in their favour in a court of justice; that is, they
> employ against Scripture a weapon which Protestants would confine
> to attacks upon the Church; as if moral and religious questions
> required legal proof, and evidence were the test of truth (p. cvii).[18]

"As if evidence were the test of truth"!—although the truth in question is the occurrence, or the non-occurrence, of certain phenomena, at a certain time and in a certain place. This sudden revelation of the great gulf fixed between the ecclesiastical and the scientific mind is enough to take away the breath of any one unfamiliar with the clerical organon. As if, one may retort, the assumption that miracles may, or have, served a moral or a religious end, in any way alters the fact that they profess to be historical events, things that actually happened; and, as such, must needs be exactly those subjects about which evidence is appropriate and legal proofs (which are such merely because they afford adequate evidence) may be justly demanded. The Gadarene miracle either happened, or it did not. Whether the Gadarene "question" is moral or religious, or not, has nothing to do with the fact that it is a purely historical question whether the demons said what they are declared to have said, and the devil-possessed pigs did, or did not, rush over the heights bounding the Lake of Gennesaret on a certain day of a certain year, after A.D. 26 and before A.D. 36; for vague and uncertain as New Testament chronology is, I suppose it may be assumed that the event in question, if it happened at all, took place during the procuratorship of Pilate. If that is not a matter about which evidence ought to be required, and not only legal, but strict scientific proof demanded by sane men who are asked to believe the story—what is? Is a reasonable being to be seriously asked to credit statements which, to put the case gently, are not exactly probable, and on the acceptance or rejection of which his whole view of life may depend, without asking for as much "legal" proof as would send an alleged pickpocket to gaol, or as would suffice to prove the validity of a disputed will?

"Infidel authors" (if, as I am assured, I may answer for them) will decline to waste time on mere darkenings of counsel of this sort; but to those Anglicans who accept his premises, Dr. Newman is a truly formidable antagonist. What, indeed, are they to reply when he puts the very pertinent question:—

whether persons who not merely question, but prejudge the Ecclesiastical miracles on the ground of their want of resemblance, whatever that be, to those contained in Scripture—as if the Almighty could not do in the Christian Church what He had not already done at the time of its foundation, or under the Mosaic Covenant— whether such reasoners are not siding with the sceptic,

and

whether it is not a happy inconsistency by which they continue to believe the Scriptures while they reject the Church. (p. liii).[19]

Again, I invite Anglican orthodoxy to consider this passage:—

> the narrative of the combats of St. Anthony with evil spirits, is a development rather than a contradiction of revelation, viz. of such texts as speak of Satan being cast out by prayer and fasting. To be shocked, then, at the miracles of Ecclesiastical history, or to ridicule them for their strangeness, is no part of a scriptural philosophy. (pp. liii–liv).

Further on, Dr. Newman declares that it has been admitted

> that a distinct line can be drawn in point of character and circumstance between the miracles of Scripture and of Church history; but this is by no means the case (p. lv) . . . specimens are not wanting in the history of the Church, of miracles as awful in their character and as momentous in their effects as those which are recorded in Scripture. The fire interrupting the rebuilding of the Jewish temple, and the death of Arius, are instances, in Ecclesiastical history, of such solemn events. On the other hand, difficult instances in the Scripture history are such as these: the serpent in Eden, the Ark, Jacob's vision for the multiplication of his cattle, the speaking of Balaam's ass, the axe swimming at Elisha's word, the miracle on the swine, and various instances of prayers or prophecies, in which, as in that of Noah's blessing and curse, words which seem the result of private feeling are expressly or virtually ascribed to a Divine suggestion. (p. lvi).

Who is to gainsay our ecclesiastical authority here? "Infidel authors" might be accused of a wish to ridicule the Scripture miracles by putting them on a level with the remarkable story about the fire which stopped the rebuilding of the Temple, or that about the death of Arius—but Dr. Newman is above suspicion. The pity is that his list of what he delicately terms "difficult" instances is so short. Why omit the manufacture of Eve out of Adam's rib, on the strict historical accuracy of which the chief argument of the defenders of an iniquitous portion of our present marriage law depends? Why leave out the account of the "Bene Elohim" and their gallantries, on which a large part of the worst practices of the mediaeval inquisitors into witchcraft was based? Why forget the angel who wrestled with Jacob, and, as the account suggests, somewhat over-stepped the bounds of fair play, at the end of the struggle? Surely, we must agree with Dr. Newman that, if all these camels have gone down, it savours of affectation to strain at such gnats as the sudden ailment of Arius in the midst of his deadly, if prayerful,[20] enemies; and the fiery explosion which stopped the Julian building operations. Though the *words* of the "Conclusion" of the "Essay on Miracles" may, perhaps, be quoted against me, I may express my satisfaction at finding myself in substantial accordance with a theologian above all suspicion of heterodoxy. With all my heart, I can declare my belief that there is just as good reason for believing in the miraculous slaying of the man who fell short of the Athanasian power of affirming contradictories, with respect to nature of the Godhead, as there is for believing in the stories of the serpent and the ark told in Genesis, the speaking of Balaam's ass in Numbers, or the floating of the axe, at Elisha's order, in the second book of Kings.

It is one of the peculiarities of a really sound argument that it is susceptible of the fullest development; and that it sometimes leads to conclusions unexpected by those who employ it. To my mind, it is impossible to refuse to follow Dr. Newman when he extends his reasoning, from the miracles of the patristic and mediaeval ages backward in time, as far as miracles are recorded. But, if the rules of logic are valid, I feel compelled to extend the argument forwards to the alleged Roman miracles of the present day, which Dr. Newman might not have admitted, but which Cardinal Newman may hardly reject. Beyond question, there is as good, or perhaps better, evidence for the miracles worked by our Lady of Lourdes, as there is for the floating of Elisha's axe, or the speaking of Balaam's ass. But we must go still further; there is a modern system of thaumaturgy and demonology which is just as well certified as the ancient.[21] Veracious, excellent, sometimes learned and acute persons, even philosophers of no mean pretensions, testify to the "levitation" of bodies much heavier than Elisha's axe; to the existence of "spirits" who, to the mere tactile sense, have been indistinguishable from flesh and blood; and, occasionally, have wrested with all the vigour of Jacob's opponent; yet, further, to the speech, in the language of raps, of spiritual beings, whose discourses, in point of coherence and value, are far inferior to that of Balaam's humble but sagacious steed. I have not the smallest doubt that, if these were persecuting times, there is many a worthy "spiritualist" who would cheerfully go to the stake in support of his pneumatological faith; and furnish evidence, after Paley's own heart, in proof of the truth of his doctrines.[22] Not a few modern divines, doubtless struck by the impossibility of refusing the spiritualist evidence, if the ecclesiastical evidence is accepted, and deprived of any *a priori* objection by their implicit belief in Christian Demonology, show themselves ready to take poor Sludge seriously, and to believe that he is possessed by other devils than those of need, greed, and vainglory.

Under these circumstances, it was to be expected, though it is none the less interesting to note the fact, that the arguments of the latest school of "spiritualists" present a wonderful family likeness to those which adorn the subtle disquisitions of the advocate of ecclesiastical miracles of forty years ago. It is unfortunate for the "spiritualists" that, over and over again, celebrated and trusted media, who really, in some respects, call to mind the Montanist and gnostic seers of the second century,[23] are either proved in courts of law to be fraudulent impostors; or, in sheer weariness, as it would seem, of the honest dupes who swear by them, spontaneously confess their long-continued iniquities, as the Fox women did the other day in New York.[24] But, whenever a catastrophe of this kind takes place, the believers are no wise dismayed by it. They freely admit that not only the media, but the spirits whom they summon, are sadly apt to lose sight of the elementary principles of right and wrong; and they triumphantly ask: How does the occurrence of occasional impostures disprove the genuine manifestations (that is to say, all those which have not yet been proved to be impostures or delusions)? And, in this, they unconsciously plagiarise from the churchman, who just as freely admits that many ecclesiastical miracles may have been forged; and asks, with calm contempt, not only of legal proofs, but of common-sense probability, Why does it follow that none are to be supposed genuine? I must say, however, that the spiritualists, so far as I know, do not venture to outrage right reason so boldly as the ecclesiastics. They do not sneer at "evidence"; nor repudiate the requirement of legal proofs. In fact, there can be no doubt that the spiritualists produce better evidence for their manifestations than can be shown either for the miraculous death of Arius, or for the Invention of the Cross.[25]

From the "levitation" of the axe at one end of a period of near three thousand years to the "levitation" of Sludge & Co. at the other end, there is a complete continuity of the miraculous, with every gradation, from the childish to the stupendous, from the gratification of a caprice to the illustration of sublime truth. There is no drawing a line in the series that might be set out of plausibly attested cases of spiritual intervention. If one is true, all may be true; if one is false, all may be false.

This is, to my mind, the inevitable result of that method of reasoning which is applied to the confutation of Protestantism, with so much success, by one of the acutest and subtlest disputants who have ever championed Ecclesiasticism—and one cannot put his claims to acuteness and subtlety higher.

> . . . the Christianity of history is not Protestantism. If ever there were a safe truth it is this. . . . "To be deep in history is to cease to be a Protestant."[26]

I have not a shadow of doubt that these anti-Protestant epigrams are profoundly true. But I have as little that, in the same sense, the "Christianity of history is not" Romanism; and that to be deeper in history is to cease to be a Romanist. The reasons which compel my doubts about the compatibility of the Roman doctrine, or any other form of Catholicism, with history, arise out of exactly the same line of argument as that adopted by Dr. Newman in the famous essay which I have just cited. If, with one hand, Dr. Newman has destroyed Protestantism, he has annihilated Romanism with the other; and the total result of his ambidextral efforts is to shake Christianity to its foundations. Nor was any one better aware that this must be the inevitable result of his arguments—if the world should refuse to accept Roman doctrines and Roman miracles—than the writer of Tract 85.

Dr. Newman made his choice and passed over to the Roman Church half a century ago. Some of those who were essentially in harmony with his views preceded, and many followed him. But many remained; and, as the quondam Puseyite and present Ritualistic party,[27] they are continuing that work of sapping and mining the Protestantism of the Anglican Church which he and his friends so ably commenced. At the present time, they have no little claim to be considered victorious all along the line. I am old enough to recollect the small beginnings of the Tractarian party; and I am amazed when I consider the present position of their heirs. Their little leaven has leavened if not the whole, yet a very large lump of the Anglican Church; which is now pretty much of a preparatory school for Papistry. So that it really behoves Englishmen (who, as I have been informed by high authority, are all legally, members of the State Church, if they profess to belong to no other sect) to wake up to what that powerful organization is about, and whither it is tending. On this point, the writings of Dr. Newman, while he still remained within the Anglican fold, are a vast store of the best and the most authoritative information. His doctrines on Ecclesiastical miracles and on Development are the cornerstones of the Tractarian fabric. He believed that his arguments led either Romeward, or to what ecclesiastics call "Infidelity," and I call Agnosticism. I believe that he was quite right in this conviction; but while he chooses the one alternative, I choose the other; as he rejects Protestantism on the ground of its incompatibility with history, so, *a fortiori*, I conceive that Romanism ought to be rejected; and that an impartial consideration of the evidence must refuse the authority of Jesus to anything more than the Nazarenism of James and Peter and John. And let it not be supposed that this is a mere "infidel" perversion of the facts. No one has more openly and clearly admitted the possibility that they may be fairly interpreted in this way than Dr. Newman. If, he says, there are texts which seem to show that Jesus contemplated the evangelisation of the heathen:

> . . . Did not the Apostles hear our Lord? and what was their impression from what they heard? Is it not certain that the Apostles did not gather this truth from His teaching? (Tract 85, p. 63)
>
> He said, "Preach the Gospel to every creature." These words *need* have only meant "Bring all men to Christianity through Judaism." Make them Jews, that they may enjoy Christ's privileges, which are lodged in Judaism; teach them those rites and ceremonies, circumcision and the like, which hitherto have been dead ordinances, and now are living; and so the Apostles seem to have understood them. (*ibid.* p. 65)

So far as Nazarenism differentiated itself from contemporary orthodox Judaism, it seems to have tended towards a revival of the ethical and religious spirit of the prophetic age, accompanied by the belief in Jesus as the Messiah, and by various accretions which had grown round Judaism subsequently to the exile. To these belong the doctrines of the Resurrection, of the Last Judgment, of Heaven and Hell; of the hierarchy of good angels; of Satan and the hierarchy of evil spirits. And there is very strong ground for believing that all these doctrines, at least in the shapes in which they were held by the post-exilic Jews, were derived from Persian and Babylonian sources,[28] and are essentially of heathen origin.

How far Jesus positively sanctioned all these indrainings of circumjacent Paganism into Judaism; how far any one has a right to declare, that the refusal to accept one or other of these doctrines, as ascertained verities, comes to the same thing as contradicting Jesus, it appears to me not easy to say. But it is hardly less difficult to conceive that he could have distinctly negatived any of them; and, more especially, that demonology which has been accepted by the Christian Churches, in every age and under all their mutual antagonisms. But, I repeat my conviction that, whether Jesus sanctioned the demonology of his time and nation or not, it is doomed. The future of Christianity, as a dogmatic system and apart from the old Israelitish ethics which it has appropriated and developed, lies in the answer which mankind will eventually give to the question, whether they are prepared to believe such stories as the Gadarene and the pneumatological hypotheses which go with it, or not. My belief is they will decline to do anything of the sort, whenever and wherever their minds have been disciplined by science. And that discipline must, and will, at once follow and lead the footsteps of advancing civilisation.

NOTES

1. ["Therefore, no one should ask of me that I know what I know I do not know, unless by chance he wishes to learn not to know." St. Augustine (354–430), *The City of God*, 12.7.]

2. I confess that, long ago, I once or twice made this mistake; even to the waste of a capital "U."

3. [More properly, Niflheim, the underworld in Norse mythology.]

4. "Let us maintain, before we have proved. This seeming paradox is the secret of happiness" (Dr. Newman: Tract 85, p. 85). [John Henry Newman (1801–1890), British theologian who was brought up in the Anglican church but later converted to Roman Catholicism, becoming a cardinal. He discussed this transformation in *Essay on the Development of Christian Doctrine* (1845). Newman wrote many of the *Tracts for the Times* (1833–41), a series of popular expositions of religious doctrine, although these were written before his conversion.]

5. Dr. Newman, *Essay an Development*, p. 357.

6. [Cf. Tertullian (160?–225?), African Church father who wrote in Latin. The reference is to his celebrated utterance *Certum est quia impossibile est* (*De Carne Christi* 5), "It is certain because it is impossible"; often misquoted as *Credo quia impossibile* [or *incredibile*] *est* ("I believe because it is impossible [or incredible]").]

7. [Huxley refers to the doctrine of a spiritual existence or spiritual entities, from the Greek *pneuma* ("breath" or "spirit").]

8. It is by no means to be assumed that "spiritual" and "corporeal" are exact equivalents of "immaterial" and "material" in the minds of ancient speculators on these topics. The "spiritual body" of the risen dead (1 Cor. xv.) is not the "natural" "flesh and blood" body. Paul does not teach the resurrection of the body in the ordinary sense of the word "body"; a fact, often overlooked, but pregnant with many consequences.

9. [Justin Martyr (100?–165?), early Christian apologist who wrote defenses of Christianity in the face of persecution by the Romans.]

10. Tertullian (*Apolog. Adv. Gentes*, cap. xxiii) thus challenges the Roman authorities: let them bring a possessed person into the presence of a Christian before their tribunal, and if the demon does not confess himself to be such, on the order of the Christian, let the Christian be executed out of hand.

11. [A reference to the Vincentian canon, a threefold test of Catholicism devised by St. Vincent de Lérins (d. before 450) in his *Commonitorium* (2.3).]

12. [Huxley refers to his essay "The Keepers of the Herd of Swine" (*Nineteenth Century*, December 1890), part of his long-running dispute with former British prime minister William Ewart Gladstone about the truth of the miracles in the Bible.]

13. [Huxley refers to a story told by Eginhard (more properly Einhard, 770?–840), a Frankish historian who claimed to have personally witnessed a number of miracles relating to the remains of saints Marcellus and Petrus. Huxley discusses the matter at length in "The Value of Witness to the Miraculous" (1889; in *Science and Christian Tradition*).]

14. [Sebastian le Prestre Vauban (1633–1713), a French economist known for his use of statistics. By citing him, Huxley is alluding to John Henry Newman.]

15. [St. Jerome (345?–420), celebrated Roman biblical scholar who translated the Bible into Latin (the Vulgate).]

16. [Conyers Middleton (1683–1750), British theologian and author of *A Free Inquiry into the Miraculous Powers Which Are Supposed to Have Existed in the Christian Church through Several Successive Ages* (1748), in which he largely rejected the evidence for ecclesiastical miracles.]

17. I quote the first edition (1849). A second edition appeared in 1870. Tract 85 of the *Tracts for the Times* should be read with this *Essay*. If I were called upon to compile a Primer of "Infidelity," I think I should save myself trouble by making a selection from these works, and from the *Essay on Development* by the same author.

18. Yet, when it suits his purpose, as in the Introduction to the *Essay on Development*, Dr. Newman can demand strict evidence in religious questions as sharply as any "infidel author"; and he can even profess to yield to its force (*Essay on Miracles*, 1870; note, p. 391).

19. Compare Tract 85, p. 110: "I am persuaded that were men but consistent who oppose the Church doctrines as being unscriptural, they would vindicate the Jews for rejecting the Gospel."

20. According to Dr. Newman. "This prayer [that of Bishop Alexander, who begged God to 'take Arius away'] is said to have been offered about 3 P. M. on the Saturday; that same evening Arius was in the great square of Constantine, when he was suddenly seized with indisposition" (p. clxx). The "infidel" Gibbon seems to have dared to suggest that "an option between poison and miracle" is presented by this case; and, it must be admitted, that, if the Bishop had been within the reach of a modern police magistrate, things might have gone hardly with him. Modern "Infidels," possessed of a slight knowledge of chemistry, are not unlikely, with no less audacity, to suggest an "option between fire-damp and miracle" in seeking for the cause of the fiery outburst at Jerusalem.

21. A writer in a spiritualist journal takes me roundly to task for venturing to doubt the historical and literal truth of the Gadarene story. The following passage in his letter is worth quotation: "Now to the materialistic and scientific mind, to the uninitiated in spiritual verities, certainly this story of the Gadarene or Gergesene swine presents insurmountable difficulties; it seems grotesque and nonsensical. To the experienced, trained, and cultivated Spiritualist this miracle is, as I am prepared to show, one of the most instructive, the most profoundly useful, and the most beneficent which Jesus ever wrought in the whole course of His pilgrimage of redemption on earth." Just so. And the first page of this same journal presents the following advertisement, among others of the same kidney:

"To WEALTHY SPIRITUALISTS—A Lady Medium of tried power wishes to meet with an elderly gentleman who would be willing to give her a comfortable home and maintenance in Exchange for her Spiritualistic services, as her guides consider her health is too delicate for public sittings: London preferred.—Address 'Mary,' Office of *Light*."

Are we going back to the days of the Judges, when wealthy Micah set up his private ephod, teraphim, and Levite?

22. [For Paley, see n. 7 to Charles Watts's "What Is Agnosticism?"]

23. Consider Tertullian's "sister" ("hodie apud nos"), who conversed with angels, saw and heard mysteries, knew men's thoughts, and prescribed medicine for their bodies (*De Anima*, cap. 9). Tertullian tells us that this woman saw the soul as corporeal, and described its colour and shape. The "infidel" will probably be unable to refrain from insulting the memory of the ecstatic saint by the remark, that Tertullian's known views about the corporeality of the soul may have had something to do with the remarkable receptive powers of the Montanist medium, in whose revelations of the spiritual world he took such profound interest. [Montanism was an apocalyptic movement in the latter half of the second century CE, led by Montanus, a Phrygian prophet. The movement believed in the imminent outpouring of the Holy Spirit in the church.]

24. See the New York *World* for Sunday, 21st October, 1888; and the *Report of the Seybert Commission*, Philadelphia, 1887. [The Fox sisters, Kate (1841–1892) and Margaretta (1838-1893), were pioneers of modern spiritualism, living in Hydesville, N.Y. They denounced spiritualism in a letter to the *New York Herald* (May 27, 1888).]

25. Dr. Newman's observation that the miraculous multiplication of the pieces of the true cross (with which "the whole world is filled," according to Cyril of Jerusalem; and of which some say there are enough extant to build a man-of-war) is no more wonderful than that of the loaves and fishes, is one that I do not see my way to contradict. See *Essay on Miracles*, 2d ed. p. 163.

26. *An Essay on the Development of Christian Doctrine*, by J. H. Newman, D. D., pp. 7 and 8. (1878.)

27. [The Puseyites were followers of Edward Pusey (1800–1882), a leader of the Tractarian party (an early name for the Oxford Movement, which sought to restore the Church of England to the high-church policies of the seventeenth century). He wrote several of the most important *Tracts for the Times* (see n. 4 above).]

28. Dr. Newman faces this question with his customary ability. "Now, I own, I am not at all solicitous to deny that this doctrine of an apostate Angel and his hosts was gained from Babylon: it might still be Divine nevertheless. God who made the prophet's ass speak, and thereby instructed the prophet, might instruct His Church by means of heathen Babylon" (Tract 85, p. 83). There seems to be no end to the apologetic burden that Balaam's ass may carry.

2

AGNOSTICISM

Edgar Fawcett

[Edgar Fawcett (1847–1904), American poet, novelist, and playwright, was born of an English father. He received his B.A. and M.A. from Columbia College. A prolific author, he produced thirty-five novels over his career, many of which are satires of New York social life, such as *Purple and Fine Linen* (1873) and *The Adventures of a Widow* (1884). He spent his later years in London. In "Agnosticism," Fawcett expresses doubts about the truth of Christianity and other religions because of the large amount of misery in the world, considers the immortality of the soul an untenable doctrine, and refutes the charge that agnostics are not prominent in charitable and social work.]

Rationalism owes a debt of gratitude to him who coined the word "agnostic." Previously there had been only "infidel" and "atheist," and one or two other similar terms, all irate bayonets pointed

Henry Fawcett, "Agnosticism," in *Agnosticism and Other Essays* (New York: Bedford, Clarke, 1889), pp. 25–47, 49–55, 60–63.

at the very teeth of orthodoxy. They were words, too, that had attained a kind of rowdy, buccaneering prominence; they appeared to prowl, like verbal guerrillas, upon the outskirts of accepted vocabularies. Besides, they failed clearly to express, in many cases, the mental attitudes of those to whom they were applied. A good many sensible and moral people abode in the world who felt as averse to denying the existence of a deity as they did to affirming it. They resembled, to a certain degree, the chancellor in Tennyson's "Sleeping Beauty," who diplomatically

"Dallied with his golden chain and smiling put the question by."[1]

Still, about the real agnostic spirit there is much more sincerity than diplomacy. It means, in its finest sense, a courageous envisaging of the awful problems of life and death, and an admission of their total insolubility. It might almost, in particular temperaments and personalities, be said to have become a sort of new religion by itself, simpler than that of Comte, with his complex and deliberated apings of Christian forms, and yet capable in some respects of being classed with Positivism. At the same time, a very large majority of agnostics are quite without the reverential sense. "I do not know" precludes in them all tendency to "divine" or to "feel." Nor should they be blamed for this indifference, reluctance, or whatever it may be called. Emotion and reason have an arctic and antarctic divergence.

The average type of agnostic has reached his present position through the help of reason, and therefore he cannot be expected to abandon the power which has made him what he is. That power would not desert him, indeed, even if he should try to exorcise it. He recognizes this truth and so patiently accepts the ally with which destiny has provided him. If he leans toward absolute atheism—toward a denial of any conscious and intelligent ruler of the universe—he does so because vast weight of evidence impels him in that direction, while a comparatively small influence lures him in another. Not long ago an eminent thinker said to me, in a moment of colloquial confidence:

"Truly, the most extraordinary idea which ever entered the brain of man is that of a personal, overwatching deity." Most modern agnostics may be said to hold precisely this amazed view of the case. And yet they will not deny the deity either of ecclesiastic faith or of operative imagination. No one has ever seen the other side of the moon, and if you were to tell an agnostic that you felt sure this concealed lunar hemisphere was blazing with active volcanoes he would not consider himself authorized to deny your statement. He might seriously doubt it, but he would not deny it. His quarrel with the atheist is not bitter, but it is appreciable. The latter declares "There is no god," but the former, firmly as he may believe so, scorns assertion based upon partial proof. "Until I have solved the secret of the universe," says the agnostic, "I shall forbear from stating how, why or by whom it was created." He realizes just how potent an Œdipus is requisite to make the Sphinx cast herself into the sea.[2]

What, may be asked, are the causes which lead agnosticism to doubt that an almighty, tutelary and merciful power dwells behind the manifestations of nature? In the first place one might almost affirm that the good and evil which we see around us make any kind of conscious beneficent power beyond them a self-contradiction if not a nullity. For it is hard to conceive of a virtuous and omnipotent god permitting misery such as that with which our planet teems, and it is equally hard to conceive of a diabolic and omnipotent god not stamping out the happiness which also certainly abounds upon earth. John Stuart Mill has suggested the possibility of there being two gods forever at war with one another, from whose perpetual contest all admirable and deplorable things result;[3] but this acute English thinker has touched upon the idea of such a celestial antagonism with a delicacy that might be defined as the irony of metaphysics, and no one more clearly apprehended than did he the complete idleness of mere *a priori* speculation. Again, agnosticism has to-day convinced itself that all religions bear the sure evidence of having originated solely in man's intercourse with his fellow-men. At the root of all worship lies one element—that of fear, and the fear-begotten desire to propitiate some hostile though viewless agency. Christianity, and other creeds dependent upon a so-called "revelation," have never produced a single authentic proof of their validity. Waiving members of the Brahmin, the Buddhist, the Mohammedan, the Parsee, and of other noteworthy faiths, no Christian would at the present time accept for an instant as credible any fact so faintly supported by historic *data* as that of the alleged miraculous birth of Christ, not to mention his having turned water into wine, his having caused a dead man to live again, or his having defied the laws of gravitation by floating up into the sky and so disappearing before the gaze of a multitude. But the Christian insists upon accepting as facts these follies redolent of the grossest ignorance and superstition. The Christian unhesitatingly asserts, too, that morality is a product of direct revelation from some sort of anthropomorphic spirit to mankind, instead of having been gradually evolved through slow stages of civilization, which began at a condition lower than barbarism or cannibalism. The Christian clings to this astonishing tenet in the face of all that science has so ably and amply taught him to the contrary. And yet he by no means rejects the copious and precious teachings of science. He respects them, indeed, with all the practical ardor of an agnostic. If the wind blows harsh from the east he does not content himself with praying to his god that it may fail to inflict pneumonia upon his favorite child. He bids that child button stout wraps about the person and avoid breathing too deeply the icy air. No amount of trust in "providence" would induce him to let a bushel of rotting vegetables pollute his cellar for a single day. When he or any one dear to him is ill, he seeks physician and not parson. Even if he be a Roman Catholic, he gives the calomel or the quinine, the nux vomica or the bismuth, full curative scope, before he welcomes the hollow mummery of extreme unction. In all his goings and comings, among all the details of his daily routine, the Christian is quite as much a servant and devotee of scientific discovery and testimony as the most pronounced agnostic who ever smiled at the absurdities of an Adam, an Eve and an Eden. He will tell you one minute that a benign tenderness and compassion are forever invisibly befriending him, and he will refer, the next, to having taken passage for Europe on a particular line of steamers because that is notoriously the safest. If his house be insufficiently guarded against lightning and yet be struck some day without injury resulting to any of its occupants, he will fall on his knees, most probably, in heartfelt thanksgiving to a kindly and protective personality whose august will forges the thunderbolt and determines its flight. But on the following day he will be sure, if he can afford it, to have the whole house well-equipped with lightning-rods.

From proofs like these the agnostic finds himself arguing that the Christian does not believe half so implicitly as he is under the impression that he believes. For, if his belief were absolute, he would ignore his natural environment a great deal more than he already does, in a fixed certainty that what was to be would be, and that from first to last his mortal career was under a clement and sympathizing guardianship. Or, if it were really credited by the Christian that human ills befall the faithful as blessings in disguise, then he would nerve himself to receive such apparent disasters with ten times that stoicism which we now see him exhibit.

That any other than a god of exquisite cruelty should inflict these disasters upon mankind while the centuries continue to roll along, puzzles the agnostic in marked degree. Nothing is more common than to hear, from enthusiastic Christians, words that express passionate encomium of the grandeur and splendor of creation. "How could all this beauty and magnificence exist," they cry, "unless a god of surpassing worth and wisdom produced them?" But they forget that for every agreeable or alluring feature there is one correspondingly odious and repellent. If the rose blooms, the poisonous plant thrives as well. If the sky bends blue and lucid above us, the tempest, with shafts of death and hurricanes of ruin, also has his reign there. If health glows in certain faces, disease ravages others. If sanity is the blessed endowment of many minds, madness is to many a curse and bane. If sexual love finds often its rightful and genial gratification, often it finds a terrible discontent, an agonizing repulse. If there are the buoyancy and gladness of youth, so are there the decrepitude and pathos of old age. If there is the joy of perfect marriage, so is there the sorrow of the widower and the widow—or, perhaps even worse, the troublous disunion of ill-mated pairs. And thus the chain of contrast might be extended, until we have seen that, link by link, it all means just so much happiness for just so much distress, just so much light for just so much darkness.

Now, if an affectionate god is the author of all that we term good, we cannot deny his accountability for all that we term evil. If he made the lily, in its chaste and odorous loveliness, he made the cancer, a flower of hideous petal and mephitic exhalation. Nor will it serve us to affirm that all baleful things in life are the offspring of a hidden, inscrutable charity toward the race. It is within the limit of every man's imagination to picture himself as realizing, in some *post-mortem* state, that all afflictions poured upon humanity have indeed been "for the best." But even if he were then to concede that this had been wholly true, he could never fairly avoid the declaration that anguish and calamity are, here and now, persecutions and martyrdoms ruthlessly wreaked upon his living earthly kindred. He must always have that quarrel with any god he might meet outside of the flesh from which he has escaped. To *le grand peutêtre* he must always be ready to present *le grand pourquoi*.[4] At least, he must do so if we can speak of a disembodied soul as an entity to be dealt with by laws of human consciousness. And how else can we possibly deal with such an entity?

But, on the other hand, can we deal with it at all? Do we know, even in the vaguest way, what the words 'a disembodied soul' mean? They, and the melodious polysyllable, 'immortality,' pass glibly enough from the lips. A great many estimable people are quite sure that they know precisely what is meant in the utterance of them. But in reality these expressions are quite wild and void. It will not do to say that the Bible has told us what they mean, for even admitting that the Bible be not a book wrought by excessively ignorant and superstitious men from material in part if not wholly fabulous, the information which it conveys on subjects of a supernatural import is of no more real value than a tale like that of Leda and the Swan or any of the thousand myths embedded amid other creeds. There is not the slightest reason why we should look upon the chronicle of either Jeremiah or St. Matthew, of either Samuel or St. Mark, as veracious. No historian of the least real repute would, at the present day, affirm them to be so. The very existence of that particular Christ whose life and death are recorded in the New Testament is by no means a proven fact. The ridiculous story that he was born of a virgin is scarcely less to be respected by unbiassed judges than the story that he was ever born at all. He is a figure not a whit more actual than Helen of Sparta, Achilles or Hector, and the entire legend of his crucifixion has no more historic weight than that of the siege of Troy.

But there probably was an Achilles, a siege of Troy, and there probably was a Christ, a crucifixion. No proof that his Messiah was divine seems to the Christian a stronger one than such reported words and deeds as those of the four gospels. Yet here are both words and deeds which often partake rather of the anchorite's austere self-mortification and asceticism than of the liberal and virile philanthropist's doctrines and axioms. The character of Christ, as his apostles depict it, is that of a sweet-souled, pure-minded communist, yet it is also an individuality filled with impracticable meekness and a tendency toward beautiful yet dangerous kindliness in its dealings with the frailties, crimes and sins of society. The best and purest of modern Christians could not conscientiously endorse the pardoning posture shown by this Christ whom he so adores. It is one thing to worship such an unflawed spirit as an ideal of mildness and compassion; it is another to approve measures of lowlihead and amiability which, if carried out in the government of multitudes by an executive, would entail anarchy of the worst license. We cannot tell hardened culprits to go and sin no more; they are always glad enough to "go," but their wrongdoing is not half so easy of dismissal. To be roughly assaulted by some miscreant and to bid him assault us again—to turn the other cheek toward him after he has smitten us upon one—is a personal revelation of self-control commendable only within the limits of Christ's especial disposition:—that of altruistic goodfellowship, equally wide and indulgent.

But if we overlook the question of slighted self-respect, how can we approve, in this connection, a course so fatally destructive to all true social order as that of forgiveness for wrong and outrage unaccompanied by the least thought of corrective discipline and punishment? Christ, during the brief period that he is said to have appeared before men, preached a theory which would have flung open the doors of prisons and set loose upon cities and communities the most depraved desperadoes whom iron cages ever sought to detain. And this form of counsel in him his worshippers have admired as a piece of poetic abstraction alone. They have no more made it the actual rule of their lives than they have thus made the socialistic "leave all and follow me" of his other celebrated sayings.

But while agnosticism of to-day recoils from much that Christ has been accredited with stating and desiring as devoid of due dignity for the individual and without proper adhesive effect upon society at large, it still fails to see in surrounding nature even a vague confirmation of the promise which this lovely and smooth-voiced prophet so perpetually gives us of a life after death. That wittiest and occasionally saddest of writers, Dumas the younger, is said to have inscribed these words in the album of a friend who solicited some sentiment over his autograph: *"L'espoir qu'a l'homme de la vie immortelle lui vient de son désespoir de se trouver mortel dans celui-ci."*[5] Here, one might say, lies the whole pith and marrow of modern if not ancient religion. Our despair of being mortal in this world prompts us to fabricate for ourselves an eternal duration in some other! And yet the epigram of Dumas has not touched the entire truth. Epigrams rarely do that; they are fire-flies glittering in dark places but not illuminating them, and they show us little except their own transitory brightness. He neglects that impulse of hope in every healthful human breast—that "will to live," which is the one solid grain of truth in Schopenhauer's and Von Hartmann's brilliant though faulty philosophies.[6] The vast majority of mankind cannot help believing in a future existence, because for men not to have hope is either to be the victim of distemper or else to verge upon death itself. Forms of insanity called melancholia and suicidal mania show a complete collapse of this energy; the skilled physician knows well these symptoms in his demented patient, unless it may be that their sudden manifestation defeats his most wary vigilance. Yet agnosticism, which insists upon regarding facts and rejecting such fanciful ghosts of them as strut in their borrowed robes, has clearly taught itself that our hopes of immortality bear an exact analogous relation to our yearnings and desires in all affairs of a more restricted yet equally pungent kind. Supposing that we are in a state of ordinary health, we wake at a certain hour of the morning after a fairly restful sleep. Our pulse is firm; our liver acts; the machinery of vitality does not falter. Immediately, as soon as we are well awake, we begin plans for the day, we bethink ourselves of engagements made on the day previous, we wish to enter upon one more diurnal routine of employment, duty and diversion. Agnostics or Christians, we have this same quiet, automatic longing. And yet the extreme futility of all human endeavor, the evanescence of all we purpose and perform, may be and often is inexorably clear to the agnostic, while he himself would nevertheless be the first to admit that a strenuous force which he cannot explain forever lifts and buoys him. But with the ill or ailing man how different it is! A pessimist might maintain that the jaundiced eyes of such a man often behold us as the masque of shadows we really are. To his despondent brain life will sometimes appear as arid and wearisome as a burnt prairie under a sky of slate. The concept of an immortality for the human soul will seem to him like some remote conjecture born of a fanatic's revery.

And such it really deserves to be called. The agnostic, though he may hope to win it or though he may prefer the nepenthean boon of complete annihilation, sees that, for all he can possibly learn to the contrary, it shines the *ignis fatuus* which must perpetually evade philosophic grasp. With wings wrought from rainbows, and eyes from stars, it is but the intangible child of story, song and dream. Like the κλῖτι μοι of Homeric text,[7] reference to it constantly recurs on page after page of the immense book of life. The tale of no nation could be adequately told without it, and whenever fancy has conspired with faith to achieve the most madcap results of illusion, we are confronted by its Elysiums, Valhallas and Nirwanas. But the agnostic well understands that the species of theological ecstasy which has always surrounded it conduces ill toward a proper logical survey. "Refrain," says Herbert Spencer, in his great 'Psychology,' "from rendering your terms into ideas, and you may reach any conclusion whatever. 'The whole is equal to its part' is a proposition that may be quite comfortably entertained, so long as neither wholes nor parts are imagined."[8] It will probably be many centuries before mankind at length abandons all belief in immortality. Resembling not a few similar delusions, it possesses undeniable charm, and has that sort of beauty which the astute Mr. Lecky tells us that religious ideas,[9] like a dying sun, expend their last rays in creating.

Agnosticism finds little rebuff nowadays for its lack of conventional belief. The pulpiteers make "infidelity" their texts, it is true, but it takes a very ardent church-goer, among really intelligent classes of church-goers, not to compare the keen, limpid reasoning of our modern scientific writers with the mystic, turgid, involved utterances of the Bible greatly to the latter's disadvantage. There is more moral profit in half-a-dozen pages of Herbert Spencer's "Data of Ethics" or "Social Statics" than in all the statements of Paul, vague, problematic, transcendental. And yet the accusation of unmoral apathy and indifference is often brought against agnosticism. "It builds no hospitals," cry its foes; "it endows no charities; it is pagan in its unconcern for the sufferings of humanity. It is so occupied in sneering at Holy Writ that it forgets the sweet lessons of loving-kindness and of devotion to an unstained ideal with which those deathless leaves abound." Now, agnosticism forgets nothing of the sort, and is willing to give the New Testament credit for every line and word of sound ethics contained there, just as it is unsparing in its denunciation and disgust when asked an opinion of those crimes and horrors with which the records of the Old Testament teem, and of that bloody, vengeful Jehovah who makes up for not possessing the sensualism and lust of Jupiter by exhibiting ten times more of his deliberate cruelty and hatred. Agnosticism is very far, moreover, from the callous indifference with which it is so frequently charged. If it has not erected many charitable institutions and has headed few eleemosynary lists, we must remember that it has not, like Christianity, almost two thousand years behind it. There have been a great many lukewarm Christians, if almsgiving is a test of the finer devotedness. But already agnosticism has made, in this respect, an excellent showing, when we consider its youth as a modern movement—a nineteenth-century wave of tendency—apart from earlier unorthodox growths. Professor Felix Adler has deeply and valuably interested himself in tenement-house reform,[10] and many another New York citizen (to say nothing of those in London) yearly gives large sums to the poor, unstimulated by any expectation of receiving angelic compound interest hereafter upon his earthly loan. Indeed, I learned, not long ago, that the English poet, Mr. William Morris, had expended a large fortune in aiding what he believed to be the cause of the poor against the rich.[11] Mr. Morris's motives may be declared socialistic rather than simply and humanely generous; but they nevertheless afford one more instance of a rationalist and freethinker who does not live in selfish disregard of his fellow-men. In fact this fling at agnosticism as being so cold-bloodedly epicurean resembles the absurd rumors which were set afloat after the deaths of Voltaire and Thomas Paine. It is probable that these two famous infidels died very much the same as ordinary mortals die, though a few random, delirious murmurs may have been readily misinterpreted by partisan listeners. Not long ago we had occasion to see with what sweet and sublime courage a freethinker could breathe his last, when Courtlandt Palmer summoned wife and children to his bedside and addressed them in words full of the gentlest and most fearless tranquillity.[12] And yet if Palmer's mind had wandered, at the last, and some grisly hallucination had chanced to usurp it, how probable that there would have been somebody—a servant, perhaps, or one of the country-folk in that quiet Vermont retreat where his death occurred—who would have asserted monstrous things about his final "remorseful agonies"!

As for charitable inclination on the part of agnosticism, it is just as certain to augment with increasing years as frigid avarice is certain to develop. There was never a more preposterous statement than that the religion of Christ brought humanitarianism into the world. Man's pity for his fellow-man existed a thousand years previously in India, where hospitals were among the comforts of civilization. Very possibly the standard of physical health in Greece and Rome was far above ours, and hence hospitals were not required in either nation. If it were true, as so often has been affirmed, that the Romans exposed their old people to die on an island in the Tiber, then such action (grossly inconsistent with the splendid morality of the race previous to its downfall) must be explained as the deed perpetrated by a clique rather than a class—and a most depraved and vagabond one at that. And even in the latter case these exposed persons were probably slaves. Both Rome and Greece, the countries that produced Caesar and Themistocles, Cicero and Aristotle, were cursed by slavery. So was the United States, until a few years ago. Who shall presume to say that in this highly Christian country cruelties have not taken place that might bring envious glitters into the eyes of a Caligula? And if agnosticism had been a prevailing characteristic of the populace south of Mason and Dixon's line, how easy to have held it blamable for the brutalities of the whipping-post, the drunken overseer, the hideous auction and the pursuant bloodhound! In the days of their real glory Greece and Rome were marked by a phenomenal refinement and a morale of surpassing integrity. Christianity, which may be said to have bathed Europe in bloodshed, brought also the impassioned zealot with his dreams of heavenly bliss and the martyr with his unflinching gaze at the fagots which were to consume him. But there are no grander examples in mediaeval times of unswerving adherence to duty at the price of absolute self-sacrifice and self-immolation than those given us in ancient times by such men as Brutus and Virginius.[13] And if agnosticism should wish to point toward a man of unparalleled probity, consistency and bravery as its representative, what figure could more sufficiently stand for these qualities than that intrepid and picturesque one of Giordano Bruno?[14] When we consider the superb intellectual heights which were attained by Athens, how nonsensical seems the claim that Christianity bore civilization in its wake, or that what we call European civilization was anything except that evolutional result of cerebral and climatic conditions indicated so competently by Buckle, Draper and writers of their forceful calibre![15] Full as many sins as virtues have been committed in the name of the Cross. The inquisition, the Massacre of St. Bartholomew, the slaughter of the Albigenses, the appalling persecutions of the Jews, all should now belong to the very alphabet of juvenile instruction. But alas! it is not every child who is permitted to profit by such historic truths in their candid nakedness. Happily, the children of agnostics are always allowed this privilege. [. . .]

There is, Matthew Arnold long ago declared, a "power not ourselves which makes for righteousness,"[16] and it has always seemed to me that just such enemies as this talented and facile writer are at once the most polite and most irritating of any with whom agnosticism is called upon to deal. Matthew Arnold belonged to that type of essayist and controversialist who is wrecked and enfeebled by the very "culture" of which he is so impassioned a convert. He diluted his own abilities into feebleness by mixing them with dilettanteism. It might be said of him that his future fame, unlike Keats's, has been written not so much in water as in Arnold-and-water. Born under the Oxonian shadow of episcopacy, possessing a father whom his "Literature and Dogma" must have struck as the riot and carnival of heterodoxy, Matthew Arnold was never able to welcome those honest doubts which his own width of intellect had summoned. The age forced him to weigh, to sift, to investigate reverend things; but he did so *à contre coeur*,[17] and always with vivid memories of how his youth had treasured their sacredness. Agnosticism, pure and simple, had for him a violence of emphasis that set his teeth on edge. It was extremely unfortunate for the gentleman's teeth—rather more so than for agnosticism. He was a man born either too early or too late. Perhaps it had best be said of him that he was born too late, for, taking him all in all, he would have made a much better Church of England dignitary than the agnostic he is sometimes incorrectly called.

To state that there is a "power not ourselves which makes for right-eousness" is to postulate the undemonstrable. It has always been the favorite method of Matthew Arnold and men who resemble him, to let sentiment pose on the pedestals of their overthrown gods. If there be such a power, what is it? Does it really exist outside the consciousness of man? If so, can its existence be proven, or partly proven, or even vaguely revealed? Provided my neighbor and I choose to live an upright and sinless life, what is the power *not ourselves* that leads us to do so? Is not the power essentially of and in ourselves? Is it not a result of our respective relationships with the men and women around us? Imagine that the planet contained but a single human being, and lo, the moral or unmoral acts that he could commit would be reduced to almost a min-imum! Even suicide would not be criminal, for in putting an end to his solitary life this lone creature would wound no kinsman or friend, he would break no dear ties, deal grief to no loving hearts, bring shame upon no house or clan. But give this lonely denizen of earth a single companion, and at once new moral and unmoral conditions arise. Say that his companion is feminine, and that the Adam who now finds him-self in the society of an Eve is called upon to perform a hundred little acts of protective kindliness which she in turn reciprocates by gentle sympathies peculiar to her sex. Of necessity a new order of moral con-duct has been established. There are acts good and evil which this pair can mutually wreak upon one another. And then, if we increase our duo by one, two, three, or say ten individuals, how complicated the relations will become! We have the beginning of a society; and in a society all virtue and all wrongdoing must depend upon the aidful or deterrent relations between its members.

Here, then, is where the pseudo-liberalism of such thinkers as Matthew Arnold, after leaving the beaten path of Christianity, swings back to its monotheism and its pietism by another route. This is what Robert Elsmere does in the engaging novel of that name.[18] He confuses his desire for a celestial and infinite Friend (whom he has accepted in the place of a lost Christ) with the meagre and insufficient proofs afforded by nature and all ethnologic history that any such occult potency lives outside of space and time. Other men as brave and fine as he have had the same desire and yet have separated it from the perceptive push of their brains as they would winnow chaff from wheat. Experience is forever teaching us that the gulf between what we want and what we get here below the visiting moon is indeed abysmal. Into that abyss the real agnostic unflinchingly gazes. Elsmere had so gazed as well, but had grown foolishly fascinated by the bodiless and tricksy sprites that seemed to float through its uncharted vacuum.

An objection often made to agnosticism by persons of penetration and scholarship is that it destroys without replacing, and that he only destroys who can replace. In other words, religion, as these excellent people claim, is mutable but ineradicable; you cannot take it away from the human race in one form without substituting it in another. Worship has always been and will always be. Agnosticism is not worship, but simply negation. It can never satisfy the cravings of mortality; it can never be made to stand for the rolling organ, the stately altar, the chanted hymn, the curling incense, the prayerful genuflection. . . . Now, the truth is, all such dissent is founded upon a single error—that of supposing mankind has any natural tendency to worship at all. In his barbarous conditions his worship is grovelling, and shows clearly the terrorism which has induced it. Afterward fear changes to awe, and with many impressionable persons (these being chiefly women) a kind of love is generated, perfervid, idolatrous, tinged by hysteria. But let us imagine that all religious people in the world could to-morrow become absolutely certain this god whom they venerate was himself but a portion of nature, subject to its laws and powerless to alter them by the least fraction of an infringement. What would then result? Would not all this zealous 'love' depart on the instant? Would not the monk slip off his shirt of serge, and the nun forego her fasts?

'God is love,' say the churchmen. It would be equally true, judging from what life shows us, to declare that 'God is hate.' But truer than either would it be to maintain that 'God is fear.' We cannot really love an incorporeal dream, a fantasy impalpable as moonlight. We may love the idea of loving it, and cultivate in ourselves that delicate or robust sort of frenzy which is to all religion what its greenness is to a leaf; but the effort of evolution is rather to produce in man a complete discontinuance of prostration before unknowable finalities. A man's home is all the church he needs. Wife and children make charming choristers and acolytes. He can find plenty of spiritual elevation, if so disposed, in ministering to the needs and comforts of his fellows. There is more merit and import in one charitable act than in the hallelujahs and hosannas of a mighty concourse. Prayer is merely a refinement of fetishism. Herbert Spencer says that volumes could be written on the impiety of the pious; he might have added that volumes could also be written on the idiocy of prayer. To call god omniscient, omnipotent, an all-loving and all-merciful father, one moment, and the next, perhaps, implore him to save a treasured child in the agonies of croup or meningitis—who is there that does not see the mockery of such a contradiction? [. . .]

To state that [agnosticism] must replace what it has destroyed is idle verbiage, for to require that it shall replace one superstition by another would mean that it should bring the recurrence of captivity instead of a new and unique liberation. If I tell my friend that he has in his pocket a counterfeit banknote I am not compelled to give him genuine money as the price of my news. The great mistake of those who condemn and oppose agnosticism is their stubborn insistence that it shall build some sort of new church, establish some sort of new priesthood. This mistake is natural enough, and quite pardonable considering its source. Agnosticism pretends to be nothing in the way of a new religion; you might as well ask it to explain itself as ask the sunshine that pierces a cloud-swathed sky after days of gloom and storm. It is the reasoning faculty of humanity grown an assertion instead of an abnegation, a sound instead of a silence, a courage instead of a cowardice. Such writers as Mr. Frederic Harrison, Mr. W. H. Mallock,[19] and others of either a sentimental or an infatuated turn, wholly fail to comprehend that the sense of being free from all codes and restrictions invented by human credulity alone, is at once exhilarant and fortifying. It may be said that certain minds cannot do without the religions of churches; if so, there is no objection to the possessors of these minds continuing to thumb prayer-books. But others of hardier mould, of firmer fibre, will prefer the one large republic of rationalism to the little monarchies and duchies of orthodoxy. Professor Huxley has well called this latter "the Bourbon of thought." And he adds: "It learns not, neither can it forget; and though at present bewildered and afraid to move, it is as willing as ever to insist that the first chapter of Genesis contains the beginning and the end of sound science, and to visit with such petty thunderbolts as its half-paralyzed hands can hurl those who refuse to degrade nature to the level of primitive Judaism."

We near the birth of a new century, and it may be true that before the world is a hundred years older marvellous effects will have accrued from the persistent and undaunted efforts of science. Possibly agnosticism will then almost have changed into a certain kind of gnosticism; before many more centuries have elapsed we are led to trust that it will surely have so changed. If the denizens of Mars were actually signalling to us, as that Italian astronomer is reported not long ago to have claimed that they are, and if anything like interplanetary communication were established between Mars and ourselves, this event would really be no more extraordinary than others brought about by men like Newton, Franklin, Fulton or Edison. If our descendants master the secret of death and wring immortality from nature, these acts will be only analogous to what man is already doing. Toward such a millennial result every loyal agnostic will have given his share. He who has lifted but a single stone of it still helps to build the pyramid. What a debt do we owe to the ancestors that freed us from superstition's trammelling tyrannies! A like debt will our successors owe to us in the ages unborn. This realization must content the agnostic. It is a lofty one, and it is chastely unselfish as well. He cannot say that he has no good cause for thanks; he has been saved from temporizing and makeshift; he has escaped the silliness of Theosophy, "Christian Science," "spiritualism," and like tawdry lures to the fancy and the senses; he has stooped his lips to the crystal waters of pure knowledge and found there a draught far wholesomer and more flavorous than any sacramental wine ever served by foolish priests!

NOTES

1. [Alfred, Lord Tennyson, *The Day-Dream* (1830–42), "The Revival," ll. 31–32.]

2. [In Greek myth, the Sphinx (a hybrid creature, part woman and part lion) was said to ask an insoluble riddle to any who approached her. But Oedipus answered her riddle, causing her to throw herself into the sea.]

3. [See the essay "Theism" in *Three Essays on Religion* (1874), by British philosopher John Stuart Mill (1806–1873).]

4. [*Le grand peutêtre* ("the great perhaps"); *le grand pourquoi* ("the great why").]

5. ["The hope that a man has for immortal life comes to him from his despair at finding himself mortal in this life."]

6. [For Schopenhauer, see p. 233. Karl Robert Eduard von Hartmann (1842–1906) was a German philosopher and pessimist in the tradition of Schopenhauer.]

7. ["Listen to me," an oft-recurring phrase in the Homeric epics.]

8. [See *The Principles of Psychology* (1855), by British philosopher Herbert Spencer (1820–1903).]

9. [For W. E. H. Lecky, see p. 273.]

10. [Felix Adler (1851–1933), German-born social reformer who, although trained to be a rabbi, rejected theism and helped establish the New York Society for Ethical Culture. He gave attention to several social problems, including tenement slums, child labor, and gambling.]

11. [William Morris (1834–1896), celebrated British poet who espoused socialism.]

12. [Courtlandt Palmer (1800–1874), a wealthy real estate owner in New York City.]

13. [Fawcett refers to legendary stories of early Rome found in Livy's *History of Rome*. L. Iunius Brutus murdered his own daughter, Lucretia, after she had been defiled by the tyrant Sextus Tarquinius; he later overthrow the tyrant. Lucius Virginius, a centurion, murdered his daughter, Virginia, who had been enslaved by L. Icilius.]

14. [Giordano Bruno (1548–1600), pioneering Italian mathematician and astronomer, propounded the heliocentric theory, suggested that the universe was infinite and contained countless worlds similar to those in our solar

system, and believed that the Bible should not be followed in astronomical matters. When brought to trial before the Inquisition, he refused to renounce these beliefs, and he was burned alive.]

15. [Henry Thomas Buckle (1821–1862), British historian and author of *History of Civilization in England* (1857–61), which emphasized the role of secularism in the development of English society. For Draper, see p. 169.]

16. [Matthew Arnold (1822–1888), celebrated British critic and poet. The quotation (actually a paraphrase) is from *Literature and Dogma* (1873), chap. 1, sec. 3. The book rejected the notion of an anthropomorphic god but nevertheless asserted the existence of a divine immanence in the universe.]

17. ["Grudgingly."]

18. [Mrs. Humphry (Mary Augusta) Ward (1851–1920), author of the best-selling novel *Robert Elsmere* (1888), about an Anglican parson whose scientific studies gradually lead him to abandon his faith in miracles and in Jesus Christ as anything more than a symbol; he subsequently devotes himself to social work.]

19. [Frederic Harrison (1871–1923) was a British positivist philosopher and author of *The Positive Evolution of Religion*. W. H. Mallock (1849–1923) was a British thinker and writer best known for *The New Republic* (1877), a dialogue in which Mallock sympathizes with the views of religious exponents such as John Ruskin against such freethinkers as Thomas Henry Huxley and Walter Pater.]

3

WHY I AM AN AGNOSTIC

Clarence Darrow

[Clarence Darrow (1847–1938), American lawyer and essayist, gained his greatest celebrity as the defense lawyer in the Scopes evolution trial in 1925. But he had been a well-known figure since the 1890s, when he assisted Judge John Peter Altgeld in seeking amnesty for the defendants in the Haymarket riots in Chicago, who had been falsely branded as anarchists and revolutionaries. He also defended Nathan Leopold and Richard Loeb, two University of Chicago students who killed a fourteen-year-old, in the infamous murder trial of 1924, saving them from execution. Darrow was a prolific writer on a wide variety of subjects, and he frequently spoke out against religious orthodoxy. With Wallace Rice he edited *Infidels and Heretics: An Agnostic's Anthology* (1929). He also spoke eloquently of his secularism in his autobiography, *The Story of My Life* (1932). For a recent collection that includes many of Darrow's writings on

Clarence Darrow, "Why I Am an Agnostic" (1929), in *Why I Am an Agnostic and Other Essays* (Amherst, NY: Prometheus Books, 1995), pp. 11–19.

religion, see *Closing Arguments: Clarence Darrow on Religion, Law, and Society* (Ohio University Press, 2005). In the following essay, included in the anthology *Why I Am an Agnostic*, edited by E. Haldeman-Julius (1929), Darrow outlines his reasons for agnosticism in the simple, elegant, and occasionally sarcastic prose that typifies his writing.]

An agnostic is a doubter. The word is generally applied to those who doubt the verity of accepted religious creeds or faiths. Everyone is an agnostic as to the beliefs or creeds they do not accept. Catholics are agnostic to the Protestant creeds, and the Protestants are agnostic to the Catholic creed. Anyone who thinks is an agnostic about something, otherwise he must believe that he is possessed of all knowledge. And the proper place for such a person is in the madhouse or the home for feeble-minded. In a popular way, in the Western world, an agnostic is one who doubts or disbelieves the main tenets of the Christian faith.

I would say that belief in at least three tenets is necessary to the faith of a Christian: a belief in God, a belief in immortality, and a belief in a supernatural book. Various Christian sects require much more, but it is difficult to imagine that one could be a Christian, under any intelligent meaning of the word, with less. Yet there are some people who claim to be Christians who do not accept the literal interpretation of all the Bible, and who give more credence to some portions of the book than to others.

I am an agnostic as to the question of God. I think that it is impossible for the human mind to believe in an object or thing unless it can form a mental picture of such object or thing. Since man ceased to worship openly an anthropomorphic God and talked vaguely and not intelligently about some Force in the universe, higher than man, that is responsible for the existence of man and the universe, he cannot be said to believe in God. One cannot believe in a force excepting as a force that pervades matter and is not an individual entity. To believe in a thing, an image of the thing must be stamped on the mind. If one is asked if he believes in such an animal as a camel, there immediately arises in his mind an image of the camel. This image has come from experience or knowledge of the animal gathered in some way or other. No such image comes, or can come, with the idea of a God who is described as a force.

Man has always speculated upon the origin of the universe, including himself. I feel, with Herbert Spencer, that whether the universe had an origin—and if it had—what the origin is will never be known by man. The Christian says that the universe could not make itself, that there must have been some higher power to call it into being. Christians have been obsessed for many years by Paley's argument that a person passing through a desert should find a watch and spring, its hands, its case and its crystal, he would at once be satisfied that some intelligent being capable of design had made the watch. No doubt this is true. No *civilized* man would question that someone made the watch. The reason he would not doubt it is because he is familiar with watches and other appliances made by man. The savage was once unfamiliar with a watch and would have had no idea upon the subject. There are plenty of crystals and rocks of natural formation that are as intricate as a watch, but even to intelligent men they carry no implication because no one has any knowledge or experience of someone having made these natural objects which everywhere abound. To say that God made the universe gives us no explanation of the beginning of things. If we are told that God made the universe, the question immediately arises: Who made God? Did he always exist, or was there some power back of that? Did he create matter out of nothing, or is his existence coextensive with matter? The problem is still there. What is the origin of it all? If, on the other hand, one says that the universe was not made by God, that it always existed, he has the same difficulty to confront. To say that the universe was here last year, or millions of years ago, does not explain its origin. This is still a mystery. As to the question of the origin of things, many can only wonder and doubt and guess.

As to the existence of the soul, all people may either believe or disbelieve. Everyone knows the origin of the human being. They know that it came from a single cell in the body of the mother, and that the cell was one out of ten thousand in the mother's body. Before gestation the cell must have been fertilized by a spermatozoon from the body of the father. This was one out of perhaps a billion spermatozoa that was the capacity of the father. When the cell is fertilized a chemical process begins. The cell divides and multiplies and increases into millions of cells, and finally a child is born. Cells die and are born during the life of the individual until they finally drop apart, and this is death.

If there is a soul, what is it, and where did it come from, and where does it go? Can anyone who is guided by his reason possibly imagine a soul independent of a body, or the place of its residence, or the character of it, or anything concerning it? If man is justified in any belief or disbelief on any subject, he is warranted in the disbelief in a soul. Not one scrap of evidence exists to prove any such impossible thing.

Many Christians base the belief of a soul and God upon the Bible. Strictly speaking, there is no such book. To make the Bible sixty-six books are bound into one volume. These books were written by many people at different times, and no one knows the time or the identity of any author. Some of the books were written by several authors at various times. These books contain all sorts of contradictory concepts of life and morals and the origin of things. Between the first and the last nearly a thousand years intervened; a longer time than has passed since the discovery of America by Columbus.

When I was a boy the theologians used to assert that the proof of the divine inspiration of the Bible rested on miracles and prophecies. But a miracle means a violation of a natural law, and there can be no proof imagined that could be sufficient to show the violation of a natural law; even though proof seemed to show violation, it would only show that we were not acquainted with *all* natural laws. One believes in the truthfulness of a man because of his long experience with the man, and because the man has always told a consistent story. But no man has told so consistent a story as nature.

If one should say that the sun did not rise, to use the ordinary expression, on the day before, his hearer would not believe it, even though he had slept all day and knew that his informant was a man of the strictest veracity. He would not believe it because the story is inconsistent with the conduct of the sun in all the ages past.

Primitive and even civilized people have grown so accustomed to believing in miracles that they often attribute the simplest manifestation of nature to agencies of which they know nothing. They do this when the belief is utterly inconsistent with knowledge and logic. They believe in old miracles and new ones. Preachers pray for rain, knowing full well that no such prayer was ever answered. When a politician is sick, they pray for God to cure him, and the politician almost invariably dies. The modern clergyman who prays for rain and for the health of the politician is no more intelligent in this matter than the primitive man who saw a separate miracle in the rising and setting of the sun, in the birth of an individual, in the growth of a plant, in the stroke of lightning, in the flood, in every manifestation of nature and life.

As to prophecies, intelligent writers gave them up long ago. In all prophecies facts are made to suit the prophecy, or the prophecy was made after the facts, or the events have no relation to the prophecy. Weird and strange and unreasonable interpretations are used to explain simple statements, that a prophecy may be claimed.

Can any rational person believe that the Bible is anything but a human document? We now know pretty well where the various books came from, and about when they were written. We know that they were written by human beings who had no knowledge of science, little knowledge of life, and were influenced by the barbarous morality of primitive times, and were grossly ignorant of most things that men know today. For instance, Genesis says that God made the earth, and he made the sun to light the day and the moon to light the night, and in one clause disposes of the stars by saying that "he made the stars also" [Gen. 1:16]. This was plainly written by someone who had no conception of the stars. Man, by the aid of his telescope, has looked out into the heavens and found stars whose diameter is as great as the distance between the earth and the sun. We now know that the universe is filled with stars and suns and planets and systems. Every new telescope looking further into the heavens only discovers more and more worlds and suns and systems in the endless reaches of space. The men who wrote Genesis believed, or course, that this tiny speck of mud that we call the Earth was the center of the universe, the only world in space, and made for man who was the only being worth considering. These men believed that the stars were only a little way above the earth, and were set in the firmament for man to look at, and for nothing else. Everyone today knows that this conception is not true.

The origin of the human race is not as blind a subject as it once was. Let alone God creating Adam out of hand, from the dust of the earth, does anyone believe that Eve was made from Adam's rib:—that the snake walked and spoke in the Garden of Eden—that he tempted Eve to persuade Adam to eat an apple; and that it is on that account that the whole human race was doomed to hell:—that for four thousand years there was no chance for any human to be saved, though none of them had anything whatever to do with the temptation; and that finally men were saved only through God's son dying for them, and that unless human beings believed this silly, impossible and wicked story they were doomed to hell? Can anyone with intelligence really believe that a child born today should be doomed because the snake tempted Eve and Eve tempted Adam? To believe that is not God-worship; it is devil-worship.

Can anyone call this scheme of creation and damnation moral? It defies every principle of morality, as man conceives morality. Can anyone believe today that the whole world was destroyed by flood, save only Noah and his family and a male and female of each species of animal that entered the Ark? There are almost a million species of insects alone. How did Noah match these up and make sure of getting male and female to reproduce life in the world after the flood had spent its force? And why should all the lower animals have been destroyed? Were they included in the sinning of man? This is a story which could not beguile a fairly bright child of five years of age today.

Do intelligent people believe that the various languages spoken by man on earth came from the confusion of tongues at the Tower of Babel, some four thousand years ago? Human languages were dispersed all over the face of the earth long before that time. Evidences of civilizations are in existence now that were old long before the date that romancers fix for the building of the Tower, and even before the date claimed for the flood.

Do Christians believe that Joshua made the sun stand still, so that the day could be lengthened, that a battle might be finished? What kind of person wrote that story, and what did he know about astronomy? It is perfectly plain that the author thought that the earth was the center of the universe and stood still in the heavens, and that the sun either went around it or was pulled across its path each day, and that the stopping of the sun would lengthen the day. We know now that had the sun stopped when Joshua commanded it, and had stood still until now, it would not have lengthened the day. We know that the day is determined by the rotation of the earth upon its axis, and not by the movement of the sun. Everyone knows that this story simply is not true, and not many even pretend to believe the childish fable.

What of the tale of Balaam's ass speaking to him, probably in Hebrew? Is it true, or is it a fable? Many asses have spoken, and doubtless some in Hebrew, but they have not been that breed of asses. Is salvation to depend on a belief in a monstrosity like this?

Above all the rest, would any human being today believe that a child was born without a father? Yet this story was not at all unreasonable in the ancient world; at least three or four miraculous births are recorded in the Bible, including John the Baptist, and Samson. Immaculate conceptions were common in the Roman world at the time and at the place where Christianity really had its nativity. Women were taken to the temples to be inoculated of God so that their sons might be heroes, which meant, generally, wholesale butchers. Julius Caesar was a miraculous conception—indeed they were common all over the world. How many miraculous-birth stories is a Christian now expected to believe?

In the days of the formation of the Christian religion, disease meant the possession of human beings by devils. Christ cured a sick man by casting out the devils, who ran into the swine, and the swine ran into the sea. Is there any question but that was simply the attitude and belief of a primitive people? Does anyone believe that sickness means the possession of the body by devils, and that the devils must be cast out of the human being that he may be cured? Does anyone believe that a dead person can come to life? The miracles recorded in the Bible are not the only instances of dead men coming to life. All over the world one finds testimony of such miracles; miracles which no person is expected to believe, unless it is his kind of a miracle. Still at Lourdes today, and all over the present world, from New York to Los Angeles and up and down the lands, people believe in miraculous occurrences, and even in the return of the dead. Superstition is everywhere prevalent in the world. It has been so from the beginning, and most likely will be so unto the end.

The reasons for agnosticism and skepticism are abundant and compelling. Fantastic and foolish and impossible consequences are freely claimed for the belief in religion. All the civilization of any period is put down as a result of religion. All the cruelty and error and ignorance of the period has no relation to religion. The truth is that the origin of what we call civilization is not due to religion, but to skepticism. So long as men accepted miracles without question, so long as they believed in original sin and the road to salvation—so long as they believed in a hell where man would be kept for eternity on account of Eve, there was no reason whatever for civilization; life was short, and eternity was long, and the business of life was preparation for eternity. When every event was a miracle, when there was no order or system or law, there was no occasion for studying any subject, or being interested in anything except a religion which took care of the soul. As man doubted the primitive conceptions about religion, and no longer accepted the literal, miraculous teachings of ancient books, he set himself to understand nature. We no longer cure disease by casting out devils. Since that time, men have studied the human body, have built hospitals and treated illness in a scientific way. Science is responsible for the building of railroads and bridges, of steamships, of telegraph lines, of cities, towns, large buildings and small, plumbing and sanitation, of the food supply, and the countless thousands of useful things that we now deem necessary to life. Without skepticism and doubt, none of these things could have been given to the world.

The fear of God is not the beginning of wisdom. The fear of God is the death of wisdom. Skepticism and doubt lead to study and investigation, and investigation is the beginning of wisdom.

The modern world is the child of doubt and inquiry, as the ancient world was the child of fear and faith.

4

WHAT IS AN AGNOSTIC?

Bertrand Russell

[Bertrand Russell (1872–1970), British mathematician and philosopher, studied mathematics at Trinity College, Cambridge, and later took up a fellowship there. He began writing in the 1890s, and his *Principles of Mathematics* (1903) is a landmark work in the philosophy of mathematics. The brief paper "On Denoting" (1905) created a revolution in philosophy, especially in the realms of epistemology and the philosophy of language; it was followed by such works as *Our Knowledge of the External World* (1914), *An Inquiry into Meaning and Truth* (1940), and *Human Knowledge: Its Scope and Limits* (1948). Russell eventually came to believe that scientific knowledge must be the basis of both philosophical inquiry and of human conduct. A prolific writer, Russell also espoused numerous social and political causes: in his long life, he protested both World War I and the Vietnam War. He frequently criticized orthodox religion, thereby becoming embroiled

Bertrand Russell, "What Is an Agnostic?" (1953), in *The Collected Papers of Bertrand Russell*, ed. John G. Slater and Peter Köllner (London: Routledge, 1997), 11: 550–57.

in a widely publicized controversy in 1940—his appointment as a visiting lecturer at City College, New York, was withdrawn as a result of protests from Catholics who believed Russell to be an atheist and proponent of free love (a view arrived at by misreadings of such books as *Marriage and Morals*, 1929). Ten years later, he was awarded the Nobel Prize for literature. Some of Russell's writings on religion can be found in *Sceptical Essays* (1928), *Unpopular Essays* (1950), and *Why I Am Not a Christian* (1957). In the following interview, first published in *Look* (November 3, 1953), Russell answers questions posed by the magazine's editors regarding the nature of agnosticism, its relation to ethics and society, and analogous issues.]

1. WHAT IS AN AGNOSTIC?

An agnostic is a man who thinks that it is impossible to know the truth in the matters such as God and a future life with which the Christian religion and other religions are concerned. Or, if not for ever impossible, at any rate impossible at present.

2. ARE AGNOSTICS ATHEISTS?

No. An atheist, like a Christian, holds that we can know whether or not there is a God. The Christian holds that we can know there is a God, the atheist that we can know there is not. The agnostic suspends judgment, saying that there are not sufficient grounds either for affirmation or for denial. At the same time, an agnostic may hold that the existence of God, though not impossible, is very improbable; he may even hold it so improbable that it is not worth considering in practice. In that case, he is not far removed from atheism. His attitude may be that which a careful philosopher would have towards the gods of ancient Greece. If I were asked to prove that Zeus and Poseidon and Hera and the rest of the Olympians do not exist, I should be at a loss to find conclusive arguments. An agnostic may think the Christian God as improbable as the Olympians; in that case, he is, for practical purposes, at one with the atheists.

3. SINCE YOU DENY "GOD'S LAW," WHAT AUTHORITY DO YOU ACCEPT AS A GUIDE TO CONDUCT?

An agnostic does not accept any "authority" in the sense in which religious people do. He holds that a man should think out questions of conduct for himself. Of course he will seek to profit by the wisdom of others, but he will have to select for himself the people he is to consider wise, and he will not regard even what they say as unquestionable. He will observe that what passes as "God's law" varies from time to time. The Bible says both that a woman must not marry her deceased husband's brother, and that in certain circumstances she must do so. If you have the misfortune to be a childless widow with an unmarried brother-in-law, it is logically impossible for you to avoid disobeying "God's law."

4. HOW DO YOU KNOW WHAT IS GOOD AND WHAT IS EVIL? WHAT DOES AN AGNOSTIC CONSIDER A SIN? DOES AN AGNOSTIC DO WHATEVER HE PLEASES?

The agnostic is not quite so certain as some Christians are as to what is good and what is evil. He does not hold, as most Christians in the past held, that people who disagree with the Government on abstruse points of theology ought to suffer a painful death. He is against persecution, and rather chary of moral condemnation.

As for "sin," he thinks it not a useful notion. He admits, of course, that some kinds of conduct are desirable and some undesirable, but he holds that the punishment of undesirable kinds is only to be commended when it is deterrent or reformatory, not when it is inflicted because it is thought a good thing on its own account that the wicked should suffer. It was this belief in vindictive punishment that made men accept Hell. This is part of the harm done by the notion of "sin."

Does an agnostic do whatever he pleases? In one sense, no; in another sense, every one does whatever he pleases. Suppose, for example, you hate some one so much that you would like to murder him. Why do you not do so? You may reply: "Because religion tells me that murder is a sin." But as a statistical fact agnostics are not more prone to murder than other people, in fact rather less so. They have the same motives for abstaining from murder as other people have. Far and away the most powerful of these motives is the fear of punishment. In lawless conditions, such as a gold rush, all sorts of people will commit crimes, although in ordinary circumstances they would have been law-abiding. There is not only actual legal punishment; there is the discomfort of dreading discovery, and the loneliness of knowing that, to avoid being hated, you must wear a mask even with your closest intimates. And there is also what may be called "conscience": if you ever contemplated a murder, you would dread the horrible memory of your victim's last moments or lifeless corpse. All this, it is true, depends upon your living in a law-abiding community, but there are abundant secular reasons for creating and preserving such a community.

I said that there is another sense in which every man does as he pleases. No one but a fool indulges every impulse, but what holds a desire in check is always some other desire. A man's anti-social wishes may be restrained by a wish to please God, but they may also be restrained by a wish to please his friends, or to win the respect of his community, or to be able to contemplate himself without disgust.

But if he has no such wishes, the mere abstract precepts of morality will not keep him straight.

5. HOW DOES AN AGNOSTIC REGARD THE BIBLE?

An agnostic regards the Bible exactly as enlightened clerics regard it. He does not think that it is divinely inspired; he thinks its early history legendary, and no more exactly true than that in Homer; he thinks its moral teaching sometimes good, but sometimes very bad. For example: Samuel ordered Saul, in a war, to kill not only every man, woman, and child of the enemy, but also all the sheep and cattle. Saul, however, let the sheep and cattle live, and for this we are told to condemn him. I have never been able to admire Elisha for cursing the children who laughed at him, or to believe (what the Bible asserts) that a benevolent Deity would send two she-bears to kill the children.

6. HOW DOES AN AGNOSTIC REGARD JESUS, THE VIRGIN BIRTH, AND THE HOLY TRINITY?

Since an agnostic does not believe in God, he cannot think that Jesus was God. Most agnostics admire the life and moral teaching of Jesus as told in the gospels, but not necessarily more than those of some other men. Some would place on an equality with him Buddha, some Socrates, and some Abraham Lincoln. Nor do they think that what He said is not open to question, since they do not accept any authority as absolute.

They regard the Virgin Birth as a doctrine taken over from pagan mythology, where such births were not uncommon. (Zoroaster was said to have been born of a virgin; Ishtar, the Babylonian goddess, is called the Holy Virgin.) They cannot give any credence to it, or to the doctrine of the Trinity, since neither is possible without belief in God.

7. CAN AN AGNOSTIC BE A CHRISTIAN?

The word "Christian" has had various different meanings at different times. Throughout most of the centuries since the time of Christ, it has meant a person who believed in God and immortality and held that Christ was God. But Unitarians call themselves Christians, although they do not believe in the divinity of Christ, and many people nowadays use the word God in a much less precise sense than that which it used to bear. Many people who say they believe in God no longer mean a person, or a trinity of persons, but only a vague tendency or power or purpose immanent in evolution. Others, going still further, mean by "Christianity" merely a system of ethics which, since they are ignorant of history, they imagine to be characteristic of Christians only. When, in a recent book, I said that what the world needs is "love, Christian love, or compassion," many people thought that this showed some change in my views although, in fact, I might have said the same thing at any time. If you mean by a "Christian" a man who loves his neighbour, who has wide sympathy with suffering and who ardently desires a world freed from the cruelties and abominations which at present disfigure it, then, certainly, you will be justified in calling me a Christian. And, in this sense, I think you will find more "Christians" among agnostics than among the orthodox. But, for my part, I cannot accept such a definition. Apart from other objections to it, it seems rude to Jews, Buddhists, Mohammedans, and other non-Christians, who, so far as history shows, have been at least as apt as Christians to practise the virtues which some modern Christians arrogantly claim as distinctive of their own religion. I think also that all who called themselves Christians in an earlier time and a great majority of those who do so at the present day, would consider that belief in God and immortality is essential to a Christian. On these grounds I should not call myself a Christian, and I should say that an agnostic cannot be a Christian. But, if the word "Christianity" comes to be generally used to mean merely a kind of morality, then it will certainly be possible for an agnostic to be a Christian.

8. DOES AN AGNOSTIC DENY THAT MAN HAS A SOUL?

This question has no precise meaning unless we are given a definition of the word "soul." I suppose what is meant is, roughly, something non-material which persists throughout a person's life and even, for those who believe in immortality, throughout all future time. If this is what is meant, an agnostic is not likely to believe that man has a soul. But I must hasten to add that this does not mean that an agnostic must be a materialist. Many agnostics (including myself) are quite as doubtful of the body as they are of the soul, but this is a long story taking one into difficult metaphysics. Mind and matter alike, I should say, are only convenient symbols in discourse, not actually existing things.

9. DOES AN AGNOSTIC BELIEVE IN A HEREAFTER, IN HEAVEN OR HELL?

The question whether people survive death is one as to which evidence is possible. Psychical research and spiritualism are thought by many to supply such evidence. An agnostic, as such, does not take a view about survival unless he thinks that there is evidence one way or the other. For my part, I do not think there is any good reason to believe that we survive death, but I am open to conviction if adequate evidence should appear.

Heaven and Hell are a different matter. Belief in Hell is bound up with the belief that the vindictive punishment of sin is a good thing, quite independently of any reformative or deterrent effect that it may have. Hardly any agnostic believes this. As for Heaven, there might conceivably some day be evidence of its existence through spiritualism, but most agnostics do not think that there is such evidence, and therefore do not believe in Heaven.

10. ARE YOU NEVER AFRAID OF GOD'S JUDGMENT IN DENYING HIM?

Most certainly not. I also deny Zeus and Jupiter and Odin and Brahma, but this causes me no qualms. I observe that a very large portion of the human race does not believe in God and suffers no visible punishment in consequence. And if there were a God, I think it very unlikely that He would have such an uneasy vanity as to be offended by those who doubt His existence.

11. HOW DO AGNOSTICS EXPLAIN THE BEAUTY AND HARMONY OF NATURE?

I do not understand where this "beauty" and "harmony" are supposed to be found. Throughout the animal kingdom, animals ruthlessly prey upon each other. Most of them are either cruelly killed by other animals or slowly die of hunger. For my part, I am unable to see any very great beauty or harmony in the tape-worm. Let it not be said that this creature is sent as a punishment for our sins, for it is more prevalent among animals than among humans. I suppose the questioner is thinking of such things as the beauty of the starry heavens. But one should remember that stars every now and again explode and reduce everything in their neighbourhood to a vague mist. Beauty, in any case, is subjective and exists only in the eye of the beholder.

12. HOW DO AGNOSTICS EXPLAIN MIRACLES AND OTHER REVELATIONS OF GOD'S OMNIPOTENCE?

Agnostics do not think that there is any evidence of "miracles" in the sense of happenings contrary to natural law. We know that faith-healing occurs and is in no sense miraculous. At Lourdes certain diseases can be cured and others cannot. Those that can be cured at Lourdes, can probably be cured by any doctor in whom the patient has faith. As for the records of other miracles, such as Joshua commanding the sun to stand still, the agnostic dismisses them as legends and points to the fact that all religions are plentifully supplied with such legends. There is just as much miraculous evidence for the Greek Gods in Homer, as for the Christian God in the Bible.

13. THERE HAVE BEEN BASE AND CRUEL PASSIONS, WHICH RELIGION OPPOSES. IF YOU ABANDON RELIGIOUS PRINCIPLES, COULD MANKIND EXIST?

The existence of base and cruel passions is undeniable, but I find no evidence in history that religion has opposed these passions. On the contrary, it has sanctified them, and enabled people to indulge them without remorse. Cruel persecutions have been commoner in Christendom than anywhere else. What appears to justify persecution is dogmatic belief. Kindliness and tolerance only prevail in proportion as dogmatic belief decays. In our day a new dogmatic religion, namely Communism, has arisen. To this, as to other systems of dogma, the agnostic is opposed. The persecuting character of present-day Communism is exactly like the persecuting character of Christianity in earlier centuries. In so far as Christianity has become less persecuting, this is mainly due to the work of freethinkers who have made dogmatists rather less dogmatic. If they were as dogmatic now as in former times, they would still think it right to burn heretics at the stake. The spirit of tolerance which some modern Christians regard as essentially Christian is, in fact, a product of the temper which allows doubt and is suspicious of absolute certainties. I think that anybody who surveys past history in an impartial manner will be driven to the conclusion that religion has caused more suffering than it has prevented.

14. WHAT IS THE MEANING OF LIFE TO THE AGNOSTIC?

I feel inclined to answer by another question: What is the meaning of "the meaning of life"? I suppose what is intended is some general purpose. I do not think that life in general has any purpose. It just happened. But individual human beings have purposes, and there is nothing in agnosticism to cause them to abandon these purposes. They cannot, of course, be certain of achieving the results at which they aim; but you would think ill of a soldier who refused to fight unless victory was certain. The person who needs religion to bolster up his own purposes is a timorous person, and I cannot think as well of him as of the man who takes his chances, while admitting that defeat is not impossible.

15. DOES NOT THE DENIAL OF RELIGION MEAN THE DENIAL OF MARRIAGE, CHASTITY AND OTHER ASPECTS OF CHRISTIAN VIRTUE?

Here again one must reply by another question: Does the man who asks this question believe that marriage and chastity contribute to earthly happiness here below, or does he think that, while they cause misery here below, they are to be advocated as means of getting to Heaven? The man who takes the latter view, will no doubt expect agnosticism to lead to a decay of what he calls virtue, but he will have to admit that what he calls virtue is not what ministers to the happiness of the human race while on earth. If, on the other hand, he takes the former view, namely that there are terrestrial arguments in favour of marriage and chastity, he must also hold that these arguments are such as should appeal to an agnostic. Agnostics, as such, have no distinctive views about sexual morality. Some of them think one thing, and some another. But most of them would admit that there are valid arguments against the unbridled indulgence of sexual desires. They would derive these arguments, however, from terrestrial sources and not from supposed divine commands.

16. IS NOT FAITH IN REASON ALONE A DANGEROUS CREED? IS NOT REASON IMPERFECT AND INADEQUATE WITHOUT SPIRITUAL AND MORAL LAWS?

No sensible man, however agnostic, has "faith in reason alone." Reason is concerned with matters of fact, some observed, some inferred. The question whether there is a future life and the question whether there is a God, concern matters of fact, and the agnostic will hold that they should be investigated in the same way as the question, "will there be an eclipse of the moon tomorrow?" But matters of fact alone are not sufficient to determine action, since they do not tell us what ends we ought to pursue. In the realm of ends we need something other than reason. The agnostic will find his ends in his own heart and not in an external command. Let us take an illustration: suppose you wish to travel by train from New York to Chicago, you will use reason to discover when the trains run, and a person who thought that there was some faculty of insight or intuition enabling him to dispense with the time-table would be thought rather silly. But no time-table will tell him that it is wise to travel to Chicago. No doubt, in deciding that it is wise, he will have to take account of further matters of fact; but behind all the matters of fact there will be the ends that he thinks fitting to pursue, and these, for an agnostic as for other men, belong to a realm which is not that of reason, though it should be in no degree contrary to it. The realm I mean is that of emotion and feeling and desire.

17. DO YOU REGARD ALL RELIGIONS AS FORMS OF SUPERSTITION OR DOGMA? WHICH OF THE EXISTING RELIGIONS DO YOU MOST RESPECT, AND WHY?

All the great organized religions that have dominated large populations have involved a greater or less amount of dogma, but "religion" is a word of which the meaning is not very definite. Confucianism, for instance, might be called a religion, although it involves no dogma. And in some forms of liberal Christianity the element of dogma is reduced to a minimum. Of the great religions of history, I prefer Buddhism, especially in its earliest forms, because it has had the smallest element of persecution.

18. COMMUNISM LIKE AGNOSTICISM OPPOSES RELIGION. ARE AGNOSTICS COMMUNISTS?

Communism does not oppose religion. It merely opposes the Christian religion, just as Mohammedanism does. Communism, at least in the form advocated by the Soviet Government and the Communist Party, is a new system of dogma of a peculiarly virulent and persecuting sort. Every genuine agnostic must therefore be opposed to it.

19. DO AGNOSTICS THINK THAT SCIENCE AND RELIGION ARE IMPOSSIBLE TO RECONCILE?

The answer turns upon what is meant by "religion." If it means merely a system of ethics, it can be reconciled with science. If it means a system of dogma, regarded as unquestionably true, it is incompatible with the scientific spirit, which refuses to accept matters of fact without evidence, and also holds that complete certainty is hardly ever attainable.

20. WHAT KIND OF EVIDENCE *COULD* CONVINCE YOU THAT GOD EXISTS?

I think that if I heard a voice from the sky predicting all that was going to happen to me during the next twenty-four hours, including events that would have seemed highly improbable, and if all these events then proceeded to happen, I might perhaps be convinced at least of the existence of some super-human intelligence. I can imagine other evidence of the same sort which might convince me, but so far as I know no such evidence exists.

Part II.

THE CRITICAL STUDY OF RELIGION

5

THE LIFE OF JESUS CRITICALLY EXAMINED

David Friedrich Strauss

[David Friedrich Strauss (1808–1874), German theologian, studied with F. C. Baur, a leading exponent of the Higher Criticism, at the seminary at Blaubauren. He then went to the Tübingen Stift, where he studied with F. D. E. Schleiermacher, another pioneering biblical scholar. In 1835 he issued his most celebrated work, *Das Leben Jesu*, which applied myth theory to the life of Jesus, denying all historical foundation for the supernatural elements in the Gospels, which Strauss believed to be the product of myth-making by early Christians of the first and second centuries CE. The work aroused a storm of protest and led to Strauss's dismissal from the University of Tübingen, where he had been teaching. His next work, *Die christliche Glaubenslehre* (1840–41; Christian Religious Dogma) is a history of Christian doctrine. In 1864 he published a somewhat tempered version of his life of Jesus, *Das Leben Jesu für das deutsche Volk,*

David Friedrich Strauss, *The Life of Jesus Critically Examined*, trans. Marian Evans (1846), 4th ed. (New York: Calvin Blanchard, 1860), pp. 47–49, 53, 54–61, 64–69.

and the next year he issued *Der Christus des Glaubens und der Jesus der Geschichte* (usually translated as *The Christ of Faith and the Jesus of History*), in which he repudiated Schleiermacher's attempts to harmonize the historical Jesus with the "Christ" of dogma. In his final work, *Der alte und der neue Glaube* (1872; translated as *The Old Faith and the New*), Strauss repudiated Christianity altogether. In the following extract from the introduction to *Das Leben Jesu*, translated by Marian Evans (the real name of the British novelist George Eliot) as *The Life of Jesus Critically Examined*, Strauss outlines his notion of "mythi" (myths) that have encrusted around the life of Jesus, rendering the Bible no more "true" than the mythologies of any other religion. Strauss's footnotes have been omitted.]

The assertion that the Bible contains mythi is, it is true, directly opposed to the convictions of the believing Christian. For if his religious view be circumscribed within the limits of his own community, he knows no reason why the things recorded in the sacred books should not literally have taken place; no doubt occurs to him, no reflection disturbs him. But, let his horizon be so far widened as to allow him to contemplate his own religion in relation to other religions, and to draw a comparison between them, the conclusion to which he then comes is that the histories related by the heathens of their deities, and by the Mussulman of his prophet, are so many fictions, whilst the accounts of God's actions, of Christ and other God-like men contained in the Bible are, on the contrary, true. Such is the general notion expressed in the theological position: that which distinguishes Christianity from the heathen religions is this, they are mythical, it is historical.

But this position, thus stated without further definition and proof, is merely the product of the limitation of the individual to that form of belief in which he has been educated, which renders the mind incapable of embracing any but the affirmative view in relation to its own creed, any but the negative in reference to every other—a prejudice devoid of real worth, and which cannot exist in conjunction with an extensive knowledge of history. For let us transplant ourselves among other religious communities; the believing Mohammedan is of opinion that truth is contained in the Koran alone, and that the greater portion of our Bible is fabulous; the Jew of the present day, whilst admitting the truth and divine origin of the Old Testament, rejects the New; and the same exclusive belief in the truth of their own creed and the falsity of every other was entertained by the professors of most of the heathen religions before the period of the Syncretism. But which community is right? Not all, for this is impossible, since the assertion of each excludes the others. But which particular one? Each claims for itself the true faith. The pretensions are equal; what shall decide? The origin of the several religions? Each lays claim to a divine origin. Not only does the Christian religion profess to be derived from the Son of God, and the Jewish from God himself, through Moses; the Mohammedan religion asserts itself to be founded by a prophet immediately inspired by God; in like manner the Greeks attributed the institution of their worship to the gods.

"But in no other religion," it is urged, "are the vouchers of a divine origin so unequivocal as in the Jewish and the Christian. The Greek and Roman mythologies are the product of a collection of unauthenticated legends, whilst the Bible history was written by eye-witnesses; or by those whose connexion with eye-witnesses afforded them opportunities of ascertaining the truth; and whose integrity is too apparent to admit of a doubt as to the sincerity of their intentions." It would most unquestionably be an argument of decisive weight in favour of the credibility of the biblical history, could it indeed be shown that it was written by eye-witnesses, or even by persons nearly contemporaneous with the events narrated. For though errors and false representations may glide into the narrations even of an eye-witness, there is far less probability of unintentional mistake (intentional deception may easily be detected) than where the narrator is separated by a long interval from the facts he records, and is obliged to derive his materials through the medium of transmitted communications.

But this alleged ocular testimony, or proximity in point of time of the sacred historians to the events recorded, is mere assumption, an assumption, originating from the titles which the biblical books bear in our Canon. Those books which describe the departure of the Israelites from Egypt, and their wanderings through the wilderness, bear the name of Moses, who being their leader would undoubtedly give a faithful history of these occurrences, unless he designed to deceive; and who, if his intimate connexion with Deity described in these books be historically true, was likewise eminently qualified, by virtue of such connexion, to produce a credible history of the earlier periods. In like manner, of the several accounts of the life and fate of Jesus, the superscriptions assign one to Matthew and one to John: two men who having been eye-witnesses of the public ministry of Jesus from its commencement to its close were particularly capable of giving a report of it; and who, from their confidential intercourse with Jesus and his mother, together with that supernatural aid which, according to John, Jesus promised to his disciples to teach them and bring all things to their remembrance, were enabled to give information of the circumstances of his earlier years; of which some details are recorded by Matthew.

But that little reliance can be placed on the headings of ancient manuscripts, and of sacred records more especially, is evident, and in reference to biblical books has long since been proved. In the so-called books of Moses mention is made of his death and burial: but who now supposes that this was written beforehand by Moses in the form of prophecy? Many of the Psalms bear the name of David which presuppose an acquaintance with the miseries of the exile; and predictions are put into the mouth of Daniel, a Jew living at the time of the Babylonish captivity, which could not have been written before the reign of Antiochus Epiphanes.[1] It is an incontrovertible position of modern criticism that the titles of the Biblical books represent nothing more than the design of their author, or the opinion of Jewish or Christian antiquity respecting their origin; points the first of which proves nothing: and as to the second every thing depends upon the following considerations: 1. the date of the opinion and the authority on which it rests; 2. the degree of harmony existing between this opinion and the internal character of the writings in question. The first consideration includes an examination of the external, the second of the internal grounds of evidence respecting the authenticity of the biblical books. To investigate the internal grounds of credibility in relation to each detail given in the Gospels, (for it is with them alone we are here concerned) and to test the probability or improbability of their being the production of eye-witnesses, or of competently informed writers, is the sole object of the present work. [. . .]

Th[e] most ancient testimonies tell us, firstly, that an apostle, or some other person who had been acquainted with an apostle, wrote a Gospel history; but not whether it was identical with that which afterwards came to be circulated in the church under his name; secondly, that writings similar to our Gospels were in existence; but not that they were ascribed with certainty to any one individual apostle or companion of an apostle. Such is the uncertainty of these accounts, which after all do not reach further back than the third or fourth decade of the second century. According to all the rules of probability, the Apostles were all dead before the close of the first century; not excepting John, who is said to have lived till A. D. 100; concerning whose age and death, however, many fables were early invented. What an ample scope for attributing to the Apostles manuscripts they never wrote! The Apostles, dispersed abroad, had died in the latter half of the first century; the Gospel became more widely preached throughout the Roman empire, and by degrees acquired a fixed form in accordance with a particular type. It was doubtless from this orally circulated Gospel that the many passages agreeing accurately with passages in our Gospels, which occur without any indication of their source in the earliest ecclesiastical writers, were actually derived. Before long this oral traditionary Gospel became deposited in different manuscripts: this person or that, possibly an apostle, furnishing the principal features of the history. But these manuscripts were not at first compiled according to a particular form and order, and consequently had to undergo many revisions and re-arrangements, of which we have an example in the Gospel of the Hebrews and the citations of Justin. It appears that these manuscripts did not originally bear the names of their compilers, but either that of the community by whom they were first read as the Gospel of Hebrews, or that of the Apostle or disciple after whose oral discourses or notes some other person had composed a connected history. The latter seems to have been the original meaning attached to the word *kata*;[2] as in the title to our first Gospel. Nothing however was more natural than the supposition which arose among the early Christians, that the histories concerning Jesus which were circulated and used by the churches had been written by his immediate disciples. Hence the ascription of the gospel writings generally to the apostles by Justin and by Celsus;[3] and also of particular gospels to those particular apostles and disciples, whose oral discourses or written notes might possibly have formed the groundwork of a gospel manuscript, or who had perhaps been particularly connected with some certain district, or had been held in especial esteem by some particular community. [. . .]

Admitting however that we do not possess the immediate record of an eye-witness in any one of the four Gospels, it is still very incomprehensible, replies the objector, how in Palestine itself, and at a time when so many eye-witnesses yet lived, unhistorical legends and even collections of them should have been formed. But, in the first place, the fact that many such compilations of narratives concerning the life of Jesus were already in general circulation during the lifetime of the Apostles, and more especially that any one of our gospels was known to an Apostle and acknowledged by him, can never be proved. With respect to insolated anecdotes, it is only necessary to form an accurate conception of Palestine and of the real position of the eye-witnesses referred to, in order to understand that the origination of legends, even at so early a period, is by no means incomprehensible. Who informs us that they must necessarily have taken root in that particular district of Palestine where Jesus tarried longest, and where his actual history was well known? And with respect to eye-witnesses, if by these we are to understand the Apostles, it is to ascribe to them absolute ubiquity, to represent them as present here and there, weeding out all the unhistorical legends concerning Jesus in whatever places they had chanced to spring up and nourish. Eye-witnesses in the more extended sense, who had only seen Jesus occasionally and not been his constant companions, must, on the contrary, have been strongly tempted to fill up their imperfect knowledge of his history with mythical representations.

But it is inconceivable, they say, that such a mass of mythi should have originated in an age so historical as that of the first Roman emperors. We must not however be misled by too comprehensive a notion of an historical age. The sun is not visible at the same instant to every place on the same meridian at the same time of year; it gleams upon the mountain summits and the high plains before it penetrates the lower valleys and the deep ravines. No less true is it that the historic age dawns not upon all people at the same period. The people of highly civilized Greece, and of Rome the capital of the world, stood on an eminence which had not been reached in Galilee and Judaea. Much rather may we apply to this age an expression become trite among historians, but which seems in the present instance willingly forgotten: namely, that incredulity and superstition, scepticism and fanaticism go hand in hand.

But the Jews, it is said, had long been accustomed to keep written records; nay, the most flourishing period of their literature was already past, they were no longer a progressing and consequently a productive people, they were a nation verging to decay. But the fact is, the pure historic idea was never developed among the Hebrews during the whole of their political existence; their latest historical works, such as the Books of the Maccabees, and even the writings of Josephus,[4] are not free from marvellous and extravagant tales. Indeed no just notion of the true nature of history is possible, without a perception of the inviolability of the chain of finite causes, and of the impossibility of miracles. This perception which is wanting to so many minds of our own day was still more deficient in Palestine, and indeed throughout the Roman empire. And to a mind still open to the reception of the marvellous, if it be once carried away by the tide of religious enthusiasm, all things will appear credible, and should this enthusiasm lay hold of a yet wider circle, it will awaken a new creative vigour, even in a decayed people. To account for such an enthusiasm it is by no means necessary to presuppose the gospel miracles as the exciting cause. This may be found in the known religious dearth of that period, a dearth so great that the cravings of the mind after some religious belief excited a relish for the most extravagant forms of worship; secondly in the deep religious satisfaction which was afforded by the belief in the resurrection of the deceased Messiah, and by the essential principles of the doctrine of Jesus.

Seeing from what has already been said that the external testimony respecting the composition of our Gospels, far from forcing upon us the conclusion that they proceeded from eye-witnesses or well-informed contemporaries, leaves the decision to be determined wholly by internal grounds of evidence, that is, by the nature of the Gospel narratives themselves: we might immediately proceed from this introduction to the peculiar object of the present work, which is an examination of those narratives in detail. It may however appear useful, before entering upon this special inquiry, to consider the general question, how far it is consistent with the character of the Christian religion that mythi should be found in it, and how far the general construction of the Gospel narratives authorises us to treat them as mythi. Although, indeed, if the following critical examination of the details be successful in proving the actual existence of mythi in the New Testament, this preliminary demonstration of their possibility becomes superfluous.

If with this view we compare the acknowledged mythical religions of antiquity with the Hebrew and Christian, it is true that we are struck by many differences between the sacred histories existing in these religious forms and those in the former. Above all, it is commonly alleged that the sacred histories of the Bible are distinguished from the legends of the Indians, Greeks, Romans, etc., by their moral character and excellence. In the latter, the stories of the battles of the gods, the loves of Krishna, Jupiter, etc., contain much which was offensive to the moral feeling even of enlightened heathens, and which is revolting to ours: whilst in the former, the whole course of the narration, offers only what is worthy of God, instructive, and ennobling. To this it may be answered with regard to the heathens, that the appearance of immorality in many of their narratives is merely the consequence of a subsequent misconception of their original meaning: and with regard to the Old Testament, that the perfect moral purity of its history has been contested. Often, indeed, it has been contested without good grounds, because a due distinction is not made between that which is ascribed to individual men, (who, as they are represented, are by no means spotless examples of purity,) and that which is ascribed to God: nevertheless it is true that we have commands called divine, which, like that to the Israelites on their departure out of Egypt to purloin vessels of gold, are scarcely less revolting to an enlightened moral feeling, than the thefts of the Grecian Hermes. But even admitting this difference in the morality of the religions to its full extent, (and it must be admitted at least with regard to the New Testament,) still it furnishes no proof of the historical character of the Bible; for though every story relating to God which is immoral is necessarily fictitious, even the most moral is not necessarily true.

"But that which is incredible and inconceivable forms the staple of the heathen fables; whilst in the biblical history, if we only presuppose the immediate intervention of the Deity, there is nothing of the kind." Exactly, if this be presupposed. Otherwise, we might very likely find the miracles in the life of Moses, Elias, or Jesus, the Theophany and Angelophany of the Old and New Testament, just as incredible as the fables of Jupiter, Hercules, or Bacchus: presuppose the divinity or divine descent of these individuals, and their actions and fate become as credible as those of the biblical personages with the like presupposition. Yet not quite so, it may be returned. Vishnu appearing in his three first avatars as a fish, a tortoise, and a boar; Saturn devouring his children; Jupiter turning himself into a bull, a swan, etc.—these are incredibilities of quite another kind from Jehovah appearing to Abraham in a human form under the terebinth tree, or to Moses in the burning bush. This extravagant love of the marvellous is the character of the heathen mythology. A similar accusation might indeed be brought against many parts of the Bible, such as the tales of Balaam, Joshua, and Samson; but still it is here less glaring, and does not form as in the Indian religion and in certain parts of the Grecian, the prevailing character. What however does this prove? Only that the biblical history might be true, sooner than the Indian or Grecian fables; not in the least that on this account it must be true, and can contain nothing fictitious.

"But the subjects of the heathen mythology are for the most part such, as to convince us beforehand that they are mere inventions: those of the Bible such as at once to establish their own reality. A Brahma, an Ormusd, a Jupiter, without doubt never existed; but there still is a God, a Christ, and there have been an Adam, a Noah, an Abraham, a Moses." Whether an Adam or a Noah, however, were such as they are represented, has already been doubted, and may still be doubted. Just so, on the other side, there may have been something historical about Hercules, Theseus, Achilles, and other heroes of Grecian story. Here, again, we come to the decision that the biblical history might be true sooner than the heathen mythology, but is not necessarily so. This decision, however, together with the two distinctions already made, brings us to an important observation. How do the Grecian divinities approve themselves immediately to us as non-existing beings, if not because things are ascribed to them which we cannot reconcile with our idea of the divine? whilst the God of the Bible is a reality to us just in so far as he corresponds with the idea we have termed of him in our own minds. Besides the contradiction to our notion of the divine involved in the plurality of heathen gods, and the intimate description of their motives and actions, we are at once revolted to find that the gods themselves have a history; that they are born, grow up, marry, have children, work out their purposes, suffer difficulties and weariness, conquer and are conquered. It is irreconcileable with our idea of the Absolute to suppose it subjected to time and change, to opposition and suffering; and therefore where we meet with a narrative in which these are attributed to a divine being, by this test we recognize it as unhistorical or mythical.

It is in this sense that the Bible, and even the Old Testament, is said to contain no mythi. The story of the creation with its succession of each day's labour ending in a rest after the completion of the task; the expression often recurring in the farther course of the narrative, God repented of having done so and so;—these and similar representations cannot indeed be entirely vindicated from the charge of making finite the nature of the Deity, and this is the ground which has been taken by mythical interpreters of the history of the creation. And in every other instance where God is said to reveal himself exclusively at any definite place or time, by celestial apparition, or by miracle wrought immediately by himself, it is to be presumed that the Deity has become finite and descended to human modes of operation. It may however be said in general, that in the Old Testament the divine nature does not appear to be essentially affected by the temporal character of its operation, but that the temporal shows itself rather as a mere form, an unavoidable appearance, arising out of the necessary limitation of human, and especially of uncultivated powers of representation. It is obvious to every one, that there is something quite different in the Old Testament declarations, that God made an alliance with Noah, and Abraham, led his people out of Egypt, gave them laws, brought them into the promised land, raised up for them judges, kings, and prophets, and punished them at last for their disobedience by exile;—from the tales concerning Jupiter, that he was born of Rhea in Crete, and hidden from his father Saturn in a cave; that afterwards he made war upon his father, freed the Uranides, and with their help and that of the lightning with which they furnished him, overcame the rebellious Titans, and at last divided the world amongst his brothers and children. The essential difference between the two representations is, that in the latter, the Deity himself is the subject of progression, becomes another being at the end of the process from what he was at the beginning, something being effected in himself and for his own sake: whilst in the former, change takes place only on the side of the world; God remains fixed in his own identity as the I AM, and the temporal is only a superficial reflection cast back upon his acting energy by that course of mundane events which he both originated and guides. In the heathen mythology the gods have a history: in the Old Testament, God himself has none, but only his people: and if the proper meaning of mythology be the history of gods, then the Hebrew religion has no mythology.

From the Hebrew religion, this recognition of the divine unity and immutability was transmitted to the Christian. The birth, growth, miracles, sufferings, death, and resurrection of Christ, are circumstances belonging to the destiny of the Messiah, above which God remains unaffected in his own changeless identity. The New Testament therefore knows nothing of mythology in the above sense. The state of the question is however somewhat changed from that which it assumed in the Old Testament: for Jesus is called the Son of God, not merely in the same sense as kings under the theocracy were so called, but as actually begotten by the divine spirit, or from the incarnation in his person of the divine *logos*. Inasmuch as he is one with the Father, and in him the whole fullness of the godhead dwells bodily, he is more than Moses. The actions and sufferings of such a being are not external to the Deity: though we are not allowed to suppose a theopaschitic union with the divine nature, yet still, even in the New Testament, and more in the later doctrine of the Church, it is a divine being that here lives and suffers, and what befalls him has an absolute worth and significance. Thus according to the above accepted notion of the mythus, the New Testament has more of a mythical character than the Old. But to call the history of Jesus mythical in this sense, is as unimportant with regard to the historical question as it is unexceptionable; for the idea of God is in no way opposed to such an intervention in human affairs as does not affect his own immutability; so that as far as regards this point, the gospel history, notwithstanding its mythical designation, might be at the same time throughout, historically true.

Admitting that the biblical history does not equally with heathen mythology offend our idea of Deity, and that consequently it is not in like manner characterized by this mark of the unhistorical, however far it be from bearing any guarantee of being historical,—we are met by the further question whether it be not less accordant with our idea of the world, and whether such discordancy may not furnish a test of its unhistorical nature.

In the ancient world, that is, in the east, the religious tendency was so preponderating, and the knowledge of nature so limited, that the law of connexion between earthly finite beings was very loosely regarded. At every link there was a disposition to spring into the Infinite, and to see God as the immediate cause of every change in nature or the human mind. In this mental condition the biblical history was written. Not that God is here represented as doing all and every thing himself:—a notion which, from the manifold direct evidence of the fundamental connexion between finite things, would be impossible to any reasonable mind:—but there prevails in the biblical writers a ready disposition to derive all things down to the minutest details, as soon as they appear particularly important, immediately from God. He it is who gives the rain and sunshine; he sends the east wind and the storm; he dispenses war, famine, pestilence; he hardens hearts and softens them; suggests thoughts and resolutions. And this is particularly the case with regard to his chosen instruments and beloved people. In the history of the Israelites we find traces of his immediate agency at every step: through Moses, Elias, Jesus, he performs things which never would have happened in the ordinary course of nature.

Our modern world, on the contrary, after many centuries of tedious research, has attained a conviction, that all things are linked together by a chain of causes and effects, which suffers no interruption. It is true that single facts and groups of facts, with their conditions and processes of change, are not so circumscribed as to be unsusceptible of external influence; for the action of one existence or kingdom in nature intrenches on that of another: human freedom controls natural development, and material laws react on human freedom. Nevertheless the totality of finite things forms a vast circle, which, except that it owes its existence and laws to a superior power, suffers no intrusion from without. This conviction is so much a habit of thought with the modern world, that in actual life, the belief in a supernatural manifestation, an immediate divine agency, is at once attributed to ignorance or imposture. It has been carried to the extreme in that modern explanation, which, in a spirit exactly opposed to that of the Bible, has either totally removed the divine causation, or has so far restricted it that it is immediate in the act of creation alone, but mediate from that point onwards;—i. e. God operates on the world only in so far as he gave to it this fixed direction at the creation. From this point of view, at which nature and history appear as a compact tissue of finite causes and effects, it was impossible to regard the naratives of the Bible, in which this tissue is broken by innumerable instances of divine interference, as historical.

It must be confessed on nearer investigation, that this modern explanation, although it does not exactly deny the existence of God, yet puts aside the idea of him, as the ancient view did the idea of the world. For this is, as it has been often and well remarked, no longer a God and Creator, but a mere finite Artist, who acts immediately upon his work only during its first production, and then leaves it to itself; who becomes excluded with his full energy from one particular sphere of existence. It has therefore been attempted to unite the two views so as to maintain for the world its law of sequence, and for God his unlimited action, and by this means to preserve the truth of the biblical history. According to this view, the world is supposed to move in obedience to the law of consecutive causes and effects bound up with its constitution, and God to act upon it only mediately: but, in single instances, where he finds it necessary for particular objects, he is not held to be restricted from entering into the course of human changes immediately. This is the view of modern Supranaturalism; evidently a vain attempt to reconcile two opposite views, since it contains the faults of both, and adds a new one in the contradiction between the two ill-assorted principles. For here the consecutiveness of nature and history is broken through as in the ancient biblical view; and the action of God limited as in the contrary system. The proposition that God works sometimes mediately, sometimes immediately, upon the world, introduces a changeableness, and therefore a temporal element, into the nature of his action, which brings it under the same condemnation as both the other systems; that, namely, of distinguishing the maintaining power, in the one case from individual instances of the divine agency, and in the other from the act of creation.

Since then our idea of God requires an immediate, and our idea of the world a mediate divine operation; and since the idea of combination of the two species of action is inadmissible:—nothing remains for us but to regard them both as so permanently and immovably united, that the operation of God on the world continues for ever and every where twofold, both immediate and mediate; which comes just to this, that it is neither of the two, or this distinction loses its value. To explain more closely: if we proceed from the idea of God, from which arose the demand for his immediate operation, then the world is to be regarded in relation to him as a Whole: on the contrary, if we proceed from the idea of the finite, the world is a congeries of separate parts, and hence has arisen the demand for a merely mediate agency of God:—so that we must say—God acts upon the world as a Whole immediately, but on each part only by means of his action on every other part, that is to say, by the laws of nature.

This view brings us to the same conclusion with regard to the historical value of the Bible as the one above considered. The miracles which God wrought for and by Moses and Jesus, do not proceed from his immediate operation on the Whole, but presuppose an immediate action in particular cases, which is a contradiction to the type of the divine agency we have just given. The supranaturalists indeed claim an exception from this type on behalf of the biblical history; a presupposition which is inadmissible from our point of view, according to which the same laws, although varied by various circumstances, are supreme in every sphere of being and action, and therefore every narrative which offends against these laws, is to be recognized as so far unhistorical.

The result, then, however surprising, of a general examination of the biblical history, is that the Hebrew and Christian religions, like all others, have their mythi. [. . .]

It is not however easy to draw a line of distinction between intentional and unintentional fiction. In the case where a fact lay at the foundation, which, being the subject of popular conversation and admiration, in the course of time formed itself into a mythus, we readily dismiss all notion of wilful fraud, at least in its origin, for a mythus of this kind is not the work of one man, but of a whole body of men, and of succeeding generations; the narrative passing from mouth to mouth, and like a snowball growing by the involuntary addition of one exaggerating feature from this, and another from that narrator. In time however these legends are sure to fall into the way of some gifted minds, which will be stimulated by them to the exercise of their own poetical, religious, or didactic powers. Most of the mythical narratives which have come down to us from antiquity, such as the Trojan, and the Mosaic series of legends, are presented to us in this elaborated form. Here then it would appear there must have been intentional deception: this however is only the result of an erroneous assumption. It is almost impossible, in a critical and enlightened age like our own, to carry ourselves back to a period of civilization in which the imagination worked so powerfully, that its illusions were believed as realities by the very minds that created them. Yet the very same miracles which are wrought in less civilized circles by the imagination, are produced in the more cultivated by the understanding. [. . .]

Perhaps it may be admitted that there is a possibility of unconscious fiction, even when an individual author is assigned to it, provided that the mythical consists only in the filling up and adorning some historical event with imaginary circumstances: but that where the whole story is invented, and not any historical nucleus is to be found, this unconscious fiction is impossible. Whatever view may be taken of the heathen mythology, it is easy to show with regard to the New Testament, that there was the greatest antecedent probability of this very kind of fiction having arisen respecting Jesus without any fraudulent intention. The expectation of a Messiah had grown up amongst the Israelitish people long before the time of Jesus, and just then had ripened to full maturity. And from its beginning this expectation was not indefinite, but determined, and characterized by many important particulars. Moses was said to have promised his people a prophet like unto himself (Deut. xviii. 15), and this passage was in the time of Jesus applied to the Messiah (Acts iii. 22; vii. 37). Hence the rabbinical principle; as the first redeemer (Goël), so shall be the second; which principle was carried out into many particulars to be expected in the Messiah after his prototype Moses. Again, the Messiah was to come of the race of David, and as a second David take possession of his throne (Matt. xxii. 42; Luke i. 32; Acts ii. 30): and therefore in the time of Jesus it was expected that he, like David, should be born in the little village of Bethlehem (John vii. 42; Matt. ii. 5 f.). In the above passage Moses describes the supposed Messiah as a prophet; so in his own idea, Jesus was the greatest and last of the prophetic race. But in the old national legends the prophets were made illustrious by the most wonderful actions and destiny. How could less be expected of the Messiah? Was it not necessary beforehand, that his life should be adorned with that which was most glorious and important in the lives of the prophets? Must not the popular expectation give him a share in the bright portion of their history, as subsequently the sufferings of himself and his disciples were attributed by Jesus when he appeared as the Messiah, to a participation in the dark side of the fate of the prophets (Matt. xxiii. 29 ff.; Luke xiii. 33 ff.; compare Matt. v. 12)? Believing that Moses and all the prophets had prophesied of the Messiah (John v. 46; Luke iv. 21; xxiv. 27), it was as natural for the Jews, with their allegorizing tendency, to consider their actions and destiny as types of the Messiah, as to take their sayings for predictions. In general the whole Messianic era was expected to be full of signs and wonders. The eyes of the blind should be opened, the ears of the deaf should be unclosed, the lame should leap, and the tongue of the dumb praise God (Isaiah xxxv. 5 f.; xlii. 7; comp. xxxii. 3, 4). These merely figurative expressions, soon came to be understood literally (Matt. xi. 5; Luke vii. 21 f.), and thus the idea of the Messiah was continually filled up with new details, even before the appearance of Jesus. Thus many of the legends respecting him had not to be newly invented; they already existed in the popular hope of the Messiah, having been mostly derived with various modifications from the Old Testament, and had merely to be transferred to Jesus, and accommodated to his character and doctrines. In no case could it be easier for the person who first added any new feature to the description of Jesus, to believe himself its genuineness, since his argument would be: Such and such things must have happened to the Messiah; Jesus was the Messiah; therefore such and such things happened to him.

Truly it may be said that the middle term of this argument, namely, that Jesus was the Messiah, would have failed in proof to his contemporaries all the more on account of the common expectation of miraculous events, if that expectation had not been fulfilled by him. But the following critique on the Life of Jesus does not divest it of all those features to which the character of miraculous has been appropriated: and besides we must take into account the overwhelming impression which was made upon those around him by the personal character and discourse of Jesus, as long as he was living amongst them, which did not permit them deliberately to scrutinize and compare him with their previous standard. The belief in him as the Messiah extended to wider circles only by slow degrees; and even during his lifetime the people may have reported many wonderful stories of him (comp. Matt. xiv. 2). After his death, however, the belief in his resurrection, however that belief may have arisen, afforded a more than sufficient proof of his Messiahship; so that all the other miracles in his history need not be considered as the foundation of the faith in this, but may rather be adduced as the consequence of it.

It is however by no means necessary to attribute this same freedom from all conscious intention of fiction, to the authors of all those narratives in the Old and New Testament which must be considered as unhistorical. In every series of legends, especially if any patriotic or religious party interest is associated with them, as soon as they become the subject of free poetry or any other literary composition, some kind of fiction will be intentionally mixed up with them. The authors of the Homeric songs could not have believed that every par-

ticular which they related of their gods and heroes had really happened; and just as little could the writer of the Chronicles have been
ignorant that in his deviation from the books of Samuel and of the
Kings, he was introducing many events of later occurrence into an earlier period; or the author of the Book of Daniel that he was modelling
his history upon that of Joseph, and accommodating prophecies to
events already past; and exactly as little may this be said of all the
unhistorical narratives of the Gospels, as for example, of the first
chapter of the third, and many parts of the fourth Gospel. But a fiction,
although not undesigned, may still be without evil design. It is true, the
case is not the same with the supposed authors of many fictions in the
Bible, as with poets properly so called, since the latter write without
any expectation that their poems will be received as history: but still it
is to be considered that in ancient times, and especially amongst the
Hebrews, and yet more when this people was stirred up by religious
excitement, the line of distinction between history and fiction, prose
and poetry, was not drawn so clearly as with us. It is a fact also
deserving attention that amongst the Jews and early Christians, the
most reputable authors published their works with the substitution of
venerated names, without an idea that they were guilty of any falsehood or deception by so doing.

The only question that can arise here is whether to such fictions,
the work of an individual, we can give the name of mythi? If we regard
only their own intrinsic nature, the name is not appropriate; but it is so
when these fictions, having met with faith, come to be received
amongst the legends of a people or religious party, for this is always a
proof that they were the fruit, not of any individual conception, but of
an accordance with the sentiments of a multitude.

A frequently raised objection remains, for the refutation of which
the remarks above made, upon the date of the origin of many of the
gospel mythi, are mainly important: the objection, namely, that the
space of about thirty years, from the death of Jesus to the destruction
of Jerusalem, during which the greater part of the narratives must have
been formed; or even the interval extending to the beginning of the

second century, the most distant period which can be allowed for the origin of even the latest of these gospel narratives, and for the written composition of our gospels;—is much too short to admit of the rise of so rich a collection of mythi. But, as we have shown, the greater part of these mythi did not arise during that period, for their first foundation was laid in the legends of the Old Testament, before and after the Babylonish exile; and the transference of these legends with suitable modifications to the expected Messiah, was made in the course of the centuries which elapsed between that exile and the time of Jesus. So that for the period between the formation of the first Christian community and the writing of the Gospels, there remains to be effected only the transference of Messianic legends, almost all ready formed, to Jesus, with some alterations to adapt them to Christian opinions, and to the individual character and circumstances of Jesus; only a very small proportion of mythi having to be formed entirely new.

NOTES

1. [Antiochus IV (Epiphanes) (215?–164 BCE), Seleucid king who ruled over Hellenic Syria (175–64). He was king during the Jewish revolt led by Judas Maccabeus (166–64).]

2. [*Kata* means "according to." The title of the first gospel is "Kata Matthaion," "[The Gospel] According to Matthew."]

3. [Celsus (2nd century CE), pagan philosopher whose *True Discourse* (c. 178) is the oldest surviving literary attack on Christianity.]

4. [The Four Books of the Maccabees are now relegated to the Apocrypha, although the first three are included in the Canon of the Eastern Church and the first two in that of the Roman Catholic Church. They present a history of the Jews from c. 217 BCE to c. 161 BCE. They were probably written from c. 100 BCE to c. 70 CE. Flavius Josephus (37?–100? CE) was a Jewish historian who wrote *The Jewish War* and *Antiquities of the Jews*; the latter work reputedly contains one of the earliest mentions of Jesus by a non-Christian writer, although the passage in question (18.3.3) is partially corrupt.]

6

PRIMITIVE CULTURE
Edward Burnett Tylor

[Edward Burnett Tylor (1832–1917), pioneering British anthropologist, was raised as a Quaker but later abandoned his faith. Largely self-educated, Tylor was inspired to study anthropology by a trip to Mexico in 1856, where he examined the remains of the Aztec civilization. Influenced by the theory of evolution, he came to adopt a view of culture as a continuum whose roots must be studied to understand later developments. His *Researches into the Early History of Mankind* (1865) embodies these views. The landmark *Primitive Culture* followed in 1871. Its chief notion was the theory of animism (first outlined in the essay "The Religion of Savages," *Fortnightly Review*, 1866)—the idea that primitive peoples' earliest religious conceptions entailed the existence of spirits "animating" natural objects. Tylor proposed that many animistic notions survive in later religious thought. Tylor later wrote *Anthropology* (1881), the first text-

Edward Burnett Tylor, "Animism," in *Primitive Culture* (1871), 4th ed. (London: John Murray, 1903), 1: 424, 425–30, 436–44, 445–52, 453–58.

book on the subject. In his later years, he taught at Oxford and was president of the Anthropological Society. He was knighted in 1912. In the following extract from the chapter called "Animism" in *Primitive Culture*, Tylor discusses the origin of the conception of the soul, derived from primitive attempts to distinguish between living and dead creatures and from attempts to understand the nature of dreams. Tylor's numerous footnotes, most of them citing the scholarly sources for his data, have been omitted.]

The first requisite in a systematic study of the religions of the lower races, is to lay down a rudimentary definition of religion. By requiring in this definition the belief in a supreme deity or of judgment after death, the adoration of idols or the practice of sacrifice, or other partially-diffused doctrines or rites, no doubt many tribes may be excluded from the category of religious. But such narrow definition has the fault of identifying religion rather with particular developments than with the deeper motive which underlies them. It seems best to fall back at once on this essential source, and simply to claim, as a minimum definition of Religion, the belief in Spiritual Beings. [. . .]

I propose here, under the name of Animism, to investigate the deep-lying doctrine of Spiritual Beings, which embodies the very essence of Spiritualistic as opposed to Materialistic philosophy. Animism is not a new technical term, though now seldom used. From its special relation to the doctrine of the soul, it will be seen to have a peculiar appropriateness to the view here taken of the mode in which theological ideas have been developed among mankind. The word Spiritualism, though it may be, and sometimes is, used in a general sense, has this obvious defect to us, that it has become the designation of a particular modern sect, who indeed hold extreme spiritualistic views, but cannot be taken as typical representatives of these views in the world at large. The sense of Spiritualism in its wider acceptation, the general belief in spiritual beings, is here given to Animism.

Animism characterizes tribes very low in the scale of humanity, and thence ascends, deeply modified in its transmission, but from first to last preserving an unbroken continuity, into the midst of high modern culture. Doctrines adverse to it, so largely held by individuals or schools, are usually due not to early lowness of civilization, but to later changes in the intellectual course, to divergence from, or rejection of, ancestral faiths; and such newer developments do not affect the present enquiry as to the fundamental religious condition of mankind. Animism is, in fact, the groundwork of the Philosophy of Religion, from that of savages up to that of civilized men. And although it may at first sight seem to afford but a bare and meagre definition of a minimum of religion, it will be found practically sufficient; for where the root is, the branches will generally be produced. It is habitually found that the theory of Animism divides into two great dogmas, forming parts of one consistent doctrine; first, concerning souls of individual creatures, capable of continued existence after the death or destruction of the body; second, concerning other spirits, upward to the rank of powerful deities. Spiritual beings are held to affect or control the events of the material world, and man's life here and hereafter; and it being considered that they hold intercourse with men, and receive pleasure or displeasure from human actions, the belief in their existence leads naturally, and it might almost be said inevitably, sooner or later to active reverence and propitiation. Thus Animism, in its full development, includes the belief in souls and in a future state, in controlling deities and subordinate spirits, these doctrines practically resulting in some kind of active worship. One great element of religion, that moral element which among the higher nations forms its most vital part, is indeed little represented in the religion of the lower races. It is not that these races have no moral sense or no moral standard, for both are strongly marked among them, if not in formal precept, at least in that traditional consensus of society which we call public opinion, according to which certain actions are held to be good or bad, right or wrong. It is that the conjunction of ethics and Animistic philosophy, so intimate and powerful in the higher culture, seems scarcely yet to have begun in the lower. I propose here hardly to touch upon the purely moral aspects of religion, but rather to study the animism of the world so far as it constitutes, as unquestionably it does constitute, an ancient and world-wide philosophy, of which belief is the theory and worship is the practice. Endeavouring to shape the materials for an enquiry hitherto strangely undervalued and neglected, it will now be my task to bring as clearly as may be into view the fundamental animism of the lower races, and in some slight and broken outline to trace its course into higher regions of civilization. Here let me state once for all two principal conditions under which the present research is carried on. First, as to the religious doctrines and practices examined, these are treated as belonging to theological systems devised by human reason, without supernatural aid or revelation; in other words, as being developments of Natural Religion. Second, as to the connexion between similar ideas and rites in the religions of the savage and the civilized world. While dwelling at some length on doctrines and ceremonies of the lower races, and sometimes particularizing for special reasons the related doctrines and ceremonies of the higher nations, it has not seemed my proper task to work out in detail the problems thus suggested among the philosophies and creeds of Christendom. Such applications, extending farthest from the direct scope of a work on primitive culture, are briefly stated in general terms, or touched in slight allusion, or taken for granted without remark. Educated readers possess the information required to work out their general bearing on theology, while more technical discussion is left to philosophers and theologians specially occupied with such arguments.

The first branch of the subject to be considered is the doctrine of human and other Souls, an examination of which will occupy the rest of the present chapter. What the doctrine of the soul is among the lower races, may be explained in stating the animistic theory of its development. It seems as though thinking men, as yet at a low level of culture, were deeply impressed by two groups of biological processes. In the first place, what is it that makes the difference between a living body and a dead one; what causes waking, sleep, trance, disease, death? In the second place, what are those human shapes which appear in dreams and visions? Looking at these two groups of phenomena, the ancient savage philosophers probably made their first step by the obvious inference that every man has two things belonging to him, namely, a life and a phantom. These two are evidently in close connexion with the body, the life as enabling it to feel and think and act, the phantom as being its image or second self; both, also, are perceived to be things separable from the body, the life as able to go away and leave it, insensible or dead, the phantom as appearing to people at a distance from it. The second step would seem also easy for savages to make, seeing how extremely difficult civilized men have found it to unmake. It is merely to combine the life and the phantom. As both belong to the body, why should they not also belong to one another, and be manifestations of one and the same soul? Let them then be considered as united, and the result is that well-known conception which may be described as an apparitional-soul, a ghost-soul. This, at any rate, corresponds with the actual conception of the personal soul or spirit among the lower races, which may be defined as follows: It is a thin unsubstantial human image, in its nature a sort of vapour, film, or shadow; the cause of life and thought in the individual it animates; independently possessing the personal consciousness and volition of its corporeal owner, past or present; capable of leaving the body far behind, to flash swiftly from place to place; mostly impalpable and invisible, yet also manifesting physical power, and especially appearing to men waking or asleep as a phantasm separate from the body of which it bears the likeness; continuing to exist and appear to men after the death of that body; able to enter into, possess, and act in the bodies of other men, of animals, and even of things. Though this definition is by no means of universal application, it has sufficient generality to be taken as a standard, modified by more or less divergence among any particular people. Far from these world-wide opinions being arbitrary or conventional products, it is seldom even justifiable to consider their uniformity among distant races as proving communication of any sort. They are doctrines answering in the most forcible way to the plain evidence of men's senses, as interpreted by a fairly consistent and rational primitive phi-losophy. So well, indeed, does primitive animism account for the facts of nature, that it has held its place into the higher levels of education. Though classic and mediaeval philosophy modified it much, and modern philosophy has handled it yet more unsparingly, it has so far retained the traces of its original character, that heirlooms of primitive ages may be claimed in the existing psychology of the civilized world. Out of the vast mass of evidence, collected among the most various and distant races of mankind, typical details may now be selected to dis-play the earlier theory of the soul, the relation of the parts of this theory, and the manner in which these parts have been abandoned, modified, or kept up, along the course of culture. [. . .]

The early animistic theory of vitality, regarding the functions of life as caused by the soul, offers to the savage mind an explanation of several bodily and mental conditions, as being effects of a departure of the soul or some of its constituent spirits. This theory holds a wide and strong position in savage biology. The South Australians express it when they say of one insensible or unconscious, that he is "wilya-marraba," i.e., "without soul." Among the Algonquin Indians of North America, we hear of sickness being accounted for by the patient's "shadow" being unsettled or detached from his body, and of the con-valescent being reproached for exposing himself before his shadow was safely settled down in him; where we should say that a man was ill and recovered, they would consider that he died, but came again. Another account from among the same race explains the condition of men lying in lethargy or trance; their souls have travelled to the banks of the River of Death, but have been driven back and return to reani-mate their bodies. Among the Fijians, "when any one faints or dies, their spirit, it is said, may sometimes be brought back by calling after it; and occasionally the ludicrous scene is witnessed of a stout man lying at full length, and bawling out lustily for the return of his own soul." To the negroes of North Guinea, derangement or dotage is caused by the patient being prematurely deserted by his soul, sleep being a more temporary withdrawal. Thus, in various countries, the bringing back of lost souls becomes a regular part of the sorcerer's or priest's profession. The Salish Indians of Oregon regard the spirit as distinct from the vital principle, and capable of quitting the body for a short time without the patient being conscious of its absence; but to avoid fatal consequences it must be restored as soon as possible, and accordingly the medicine-man in solemn form replaces it down through the patient's head. The Turanian or Tatar races of Northern Asia strongly hold the theory of the soul's departure in disease, and among the Buddhist tribes the Lamas carry out the ceremony of soul-restoration in most elaborate form. When a man has been robbed by a demon of his rational soul, and has only his animal soul left, his senses and memory grow weak and he falls into a dismal state. Then the Lama undertakes to cure him, and with quaint rites exorcises the evil demon. But if this fails, then it is the patient's soul itself that cannot or will not find its way back. So the sick man is laid out in his best attire and surrounded with his most attractive possessions, the friends and relatives go thrice round the dwelling, affectionately calling back the soul by name, while as a further inducement the Lama reads from his book descriptions of the pains of hell, and the dangers incurred by a soul which wilfully abandons its body, and then at last the whole assembly declare with one voice that the wandering spirit has returned and the patient will recover. The Karens of Burma will run about pretending to catch a sick man's wandering soul, or as they say with the Greeks and Slavs, his "butterfly" (leip-pya), and at last drop it down upon his head. The Karen doctrine of the "là" is indeed a perfect and well-marked vitalistic system. This là, soul, ghost, or genius, may be separated from the body it belongs to, and it is a matter of the deepest interest to the Karen to keep his là with him, by calling it, making offerings of food to it, and so forth. It is especially when the body is asleep, that the soul goes out and wanders; if it is detained beyond a certain time, disease ensues, and if permanently, then its owner dies. When the "wee" or spirit-doctor is employed to call back the departed shade or life of a Karen, if he cannot recover it from the region of the dead, he will sometimes take the shade of a living man and transfer it to the dead, while its proper owner, whose soul has ventured out in a dream, sickens and dies. Or when a Karen becomes sick, languid and pining from his là having left him, his friends will perform a ceremony with a garment of the invalid's and a fowl which is cooked and offered with rice, invoking the spirit with formal prayers to come back to the patient. This ceremony is perhaps ethnologically connected, though it is not easy to say by what manner of diffusion or when, with a rite still practised in China. When a Chinese is at the point of death, and his soul is supposed to be already out of his body, a relative may be seen holding up the patient's coat on a long bamboo, to which a white cock is often fastened, while a Tauist priest by incantations brings the departed spirit into the coat, in order to put it back into the sick man. If the bamboo after a time turns round slowly in the holder's hands, this shows that the spirit is inside the garment.

Such temporary exit of the soul has a world-wide application to the proceedings of the sorcerer, priest, or seer himself. He professes to send forth his spirit on distant journeys, and probably often believes his soul released for a time from its bodily prison, as in the case of that remarkable dreamer and visionary Jerome Cardan, who describes himself as having the faculty of passing out of his senses as into ecstasy whenever he will, feeling when he goes into this state a sort of separation near the heart as if his soul were departing, this state beginning from his brain and passing down his spine, and he then feeling only that he is out of himself. Thus the Australian native doctor is alleged to obtain his initiation by visiting the world of spirits in a trance of two or three days' duration; the Khond priest authenticates his claim to office by remaining from one to fourteen days in a languid and dreamy state, caused by one of his souls being away in the divine presence; the Greenland angekok's soul goes forth from his body to fetch his familiar demon; the Turanian shaman lies in lethargy while his soul departs to bring hidden wisdom from the land of spirits. The literature of more progressive races supplies similar accounts. A characteristic story from old Scandinavia is that of the Norse chief Ingimund, who shut up three Finns in a hut for three nights, that they might visit Iceland and inform him of the lie of the country where he was to settle; their bodies became rigid, they sent their souls on the errand, and awakening after the three days they gave a description of the Vatnsdael. The typical classic case is the story of Hermotimos, whose prophetic soul went out from time to time to visit distant regions, till at last his wife burnt the lifeless body on the funeral pile, and when the poor soul came back, there was no longer a dwelling for it to animate. A group of the legendary visits to the spirit-world, which will be described in the next chapter, belong to this class. A typical spiritualistic instance may be quoted from Jung-Stilling,[1] who says that examples have come to his knowledge of sick persons who, longing to see absent friends, have fallen into a swoon during which they have appeared to the distant objects of their affection. As an illustration from our own folklore, the well-known superstition may serve, that fasting watchers on St. John's Eve may see the apparitions of those doomed to die during the year come with the clergyman to the church door and knock; these apparitions are spirits who come forth from their bodies, for the minister has been noticed to be much troubled in his sleep while his phantom was thus engaged, and when one of a party of watchers fell into a sound sleep and could not be roused, the others saw his apparition knock at the church door. Modern Europe has indeed kept closely enough to the lines of early philosophy, for such ideas to have little strangeness to our own time. Language preserves record of them in such expressions as "out of oneself," "beside oneself," "in an ecstasy," and he who says that his spirit goes forth to meet a friend, can still realize in the phrase a meaning deeper than metaphor.

This same doctrine forms one side of the theory of dreams prevalent among the lower races. Certain of the Greenlanders, Cranz remarks,[2] consider that the soul quits the body in the night and goes out hunting, dancing, and visiting; their dreams, which are frequent and lively, having brought them to this opinion. Among the Indians of North America, we hear of the dreamer's soul leaving his body and wandering in quest of things attractive to it. These things the waking man must endeavour to obtain, lest his soul be troubled, and quit the body altogether. The New Zealanders considered the dreaming soul to leave the body and return, even travelling to the region of the dead to hold converse with its friends. The Tagals of Luzon object to waking a sleeper, on account of the absence of his soul. The Karens, whose theory of the wandering soul has just been noticed, explain dreams to be what this là sees and experiences in its journeys when it has left the body asleep. They even account with much acuteness for the fact that we are apt to dream of people and places which we knew before; the leip-pya, they say, can only visit the regions where the body it belongs to has been already. Onward from the savage state, the idea of the spirit's departure in sleep may be traced into the speculative philosophy of higher nations, as in the Vedanta system, and the Kabbala. [. . .]

This opinion, however, only constitutes one of several parts of the theory of dreams in savage psychology. Another part has also a place here, the view that human souls come from without to visit the sleeper, who sees them as dreams. These two views are by no means incompatible. The North American Indians allowed themselves the alternative of supposing a dream to be either a visit from the soul of the person or object dreamt of, or a sight seen by the rational soul, gone out for an excursion while the sensitive soul remains in the body. So the Zulu may be visited in a dream by the shade of an ancestor, the itongo, who comes to warn him of danger, or he may himself be taken by the itongo in a dream to visit his distant people, and see that they are in trouble; as for the man who is passing into the morbid condition of the professional seer, phantoms are continually coming to talk to him in his sleep, till he becomes, as the expressive native phrase is, "a house of dreams." In the lower range of culture, it is perhaps most frequently taken for granted that a man's apparition in a dream is a visit from his disembodied spirit, which the dreamer, to use an expressive Ojibwa idiom, "sees when asleep." Such a thought comes out clearly in the Fijian opinion that a living man's spirit may leave the body, to trouble other people in their sleep; or in a recent account of an old Indian woman of British Columbia sending for the medicine-man to drive away the dead people who came to her every night. A modern observer's description of the state of mind of the negroes of West Africa in this respect is extremely characteristic and instructive. "All their dreams are construed into visits from the spirits of their deceased friends. The cautions, hints, and warnings which come to them through this source are received with the most serious and deferential attention, and are always acted upon in their waking hours. The habit of relating their dreams, which is universal, greatly promotes the habit of dreaming itself, and hence their sleeping hours are characterized by almost as much intercourse with the dead as their waking are with the living. This is, no doubt, one of the reasons of their excessive superstitiousness. Their imaginations become so lively that they can scarcely distinguish between their dreams and their waking thoughts, between the real and the ideal, and they consequently utter falsehood without intending, and profess to see things which never existed." [. . .]

The evidence of visions corresponds with the evidence of dreams in their bearing on primitive theories of the soul, and the two classes of phenomena substantiate and supplement one another. Even in healthy waking life, the savage or barbarian has never learnt to make that rigid distinction between subjective and objective, between imagination and reality, to enforce which is one of the main results of scientific education. Still less, when disordered in body and mind he sees around him phantom human forms, can he distrust the evidence of his very senses. Thus it comes to pass that throughout the lower civilization men believe, with the most vivid and intense belief, in the objective reality of the human spectres which they see in sickness, exhaustion, or excitement. As will be hereafter noticed, one main reason of the practices of fasting, penance, narcotising by drugs, and other means of bringing on morbid exaltation, is that the patients may obtain the sight of spectral beings, from whom they look to gain spiritual knowledge and even worldly power. Human ghosts are among the principal of these phantasmal figures. There is no doubt that honest visionaries describe ghosts as they really appear to their perception, while even the impostors who pretend to see them conform to the descriptions thus established; thus, in West Africa, a man's *kla* or soul, becoming at his death a *sisa* or ghost, can remain in the house with the corpse, but is only visible to the wong-man, the spirit-doctor. Sometimes the phantom has the characteristic quality of not being visible to all of an assembled company. Thus the natives of the Antilles believed that the dead appeared on the roads when one went alone, but not when many went together; thus among the Finns the ghosts of the dead were to be seen by the shamans, but not by men generally unless in dreams. Such is perhaps the meaning of the description of Samuel's ghost, visible to the witch of Endor, but not to Saul, for he has to ask her what it is she sees. Yet this test of the nature of an apparition is one which easily breaks down. We know well how in civilized countries a current rumour of some one having seen a phantom is enough to bring a sight of it to others whose minds are in a properly receptive state. The condition of the modern ghost-seer, whose imagination passes on such slight excitement into positive hallucination, is rather the rule than the exception among uncultured and intensely imaginative tribes, whose minds may be thrown off their balance by a touch, a word, a gesture, an unaccustomed noise. Among savage tribes, however, as among civilized races who have inherited remains of early philosophy formed under similar conditions, the doctrine of visibility or invisibility of phantoms has been obviously shaped with reference to actual experience. To declare that souls or ghosts are necessarily either visible or invisible, would directly contradict the evidence of men's senses. But to assert or imply, as the lower races do, that they are visible sometimes and to some persons, but not always or to every one, is to lay down an explanation of facts which is not indeed our usual modern explanation, but which is a perfectly rational and intelligible product of early science.

Without discussing on their merits the accounts of what is called "second sight," it may be pointed out that they are related among savage tribes, as when Captain Jonathan Carver obtained from a Cree medicine-man a true prophecy of the arrival of a canoe with news next day at noon; or when Mr. J. Mason Brown, travelling with two voyageurs on the Coppermine River, was met by Indians of the very band he was seeking, these having been sent by their medicine-man, who, on enquiry, stated that "He saw them coming, and heard them talk on their journey." These are analogous to accounts of the Highland second-sight, as when Pennant heard of a gentleman of the Hebrides, said to have the convenient gift of foreseeing visitors in time to get ready for them, or when Dr. Johnson was told by another laird that a labouring man of his had predicted his return to the island, and described the peculiar livery his servant had been newly dressed in.[3]

As a general rule, people are apt to consider it impossible for a man to be in two places at once, and indeed a saying to that effect has become a popular saw. But the rule is so far from being universally accepted, that the word "bilocation" has been invented to express the miraculous faculty possessed by certain Saints of the Roman Church, of being in two places at once; like St. Alfonso di Liguori, who had the useful power of preaching his sermon in church while he was confessing penitents at home. The reception and explanation of these various classes of stories fit perfectly with the primitive animistic theory of apparitions, and the same is true of the following most numerous class of the second-sight narratives.

Death is the event which, in all stages of culture, brings thought to bear most intensely, though not always most healthily, on the problems of psychology. The apparition of the disembodied soul has in all ages been thought to bear especial relation to its departure from its body at death. This is well shown by the reception not only of a theory of ghosts, but of a special doctrine of "wraiths" or "fetches." Thus the Karens say that a man's spirit, appearing after death, may thus announce it. In New Zealand it is ominous to see the figure of an absent person, for if it be shadowy and the face not visible, his death may ere long be expected, but if the face be seen he is dead already. A party of Maoris (one of whom told the story) were seated round a fire in the open air, when there appeared, seen only by two of them, the figure of a relative left ill at home; they exclaimed, the figure vanished, and on the return of the party it appeared that the sick man had died about the time of the vision. Examining the position of the doctrine of wraiths among the higher races, we find it especially prominent in three intellectual districts, Christian hagiology, popular folklore, and modern spiritualism. St. Anthony saw the soul of St. Ammonius carried to heaven in the midst of choirs of angels, the same day that the holy hermit died five days' journey off in the desert of Nitria; when St. Ambrose died on Easter Eve, several newly-baptized children saw the holy bishop, and pointed him out to their parents, but these with their less pure eyes could not behold him; and so forth. [. . .]

That the apparitional human soul bears the likeness of its fleshly body, is the principle implicitly accepted by all who believe it really and objectively present in dreams and visions. My own view is that nothing but dreams and visions could have ever put into men's minds such an idea as that of souls being ethereal images of bodies. It is thus habitually taken for granted in animistic philosophy, savage or civilized, that souls set free from the earthly body are recognized by a likeness to it which they still retain, whether as ghostly wanderers on earth or inhabitants of the world beyond the grave. Man's spirit, says Swedenborg,[4] is his mind, which lives after death in complete human form, and this is the poet's dictum in "In Memoriam":

> Eternal form shall still divide
> The eternal soul from all beside;
> And I shall know him when we meet.[5]

This world-wide thought, coming into view here in a multitude of cases from all grades of culture, needs no collection of ordinary instances to illustrate it. But a quaint and special group of beliefs will serve to display the thoroughness with which the soul is thus conceived as an image of the body. As a consistent corollary to such an opinion, it is argued that the mutilation of the body will have a corresponding effect upon the soul, and very low savage races have philosophy enough to work out this idea. Thus it was recorded of the Indians of Brazil by one of the early European visitors, that they believe that the dead arrive in the other world wounded or hacked to pieces, in fact just as they left this. Thus, too, the Australian who has slain his enemy will cut off the right thumb of the corpse, so that although the spirit will become a hostile ghost, it cannot throw with its mutilated hand the shadowy spear, and way be safely left to wander, malignant but harmless. The negro fears long sickness before death, such as will send him lean and feeble into the next world. His theory of the mutilation of soul with body could not be brought more vividly into view than in that ugly story of the West India planter, whose slaves began to seek in suicide at once relief from present misery and restoration to their native land; but the white man was too cunning for them, he cut off the heads and hands of the corpses, and the survivors saw that not even death could save them from a master who could maim their very souls in the next world. The same rude and primitive belief continues among nations risen far higher in intellectual rank. The Chinese hold in especial horror the punishment of decapitation, considering that he who quits this world lacking a member will so arrive in the next, and a case is recorded lately of a criminal at Amoy who for this reason begged to die instead by the cruel death of crucifixion, and was crucified accordingly. The series ends as usual in the folklore of the civilized world. The phantom skeleton in chains that haunted the house at Bologna, showed the way to the garden where was buried the real chained fleshless skeleton it belonged to, and came no more when the remains had been duly buried. When the Earl of Cornwall met the fetch of his friend William Rufus carried black and naked on a black goat across the Bodmin moors, he saw that it was wounded through the midst of the breast; and afterwards he heard that at that very hour the king had been slain in the New Forest by the arrow of Walter Tirell. [. . .]

The conception of dreams and visions as caused by present objective figures, and the identification of such phantom souls with the shadow and the breath, has led to the treatment of souls as substantial material beings. Thus it is a usual proceeding to make openings through solid materials to allow souls to pass. The Iroquois in old times used to leave an opening in the grave for the lingering soul to visit its body, and some of them still bore holes in the coffin for the same purpose. The Malagasy sorcerer, for the cure of a sick man who had lost his soul, would make a hole in a burial-house to let out a spirit, which he would catch in his cap and so convey to the patient's head. The Chinese make a hole in the roof to let out the soul at death. And lastly, the custom of opening a window or door for the departing soul when it quits the body is to this day a very familiar superstition in France, Germany, and England. Again, the souls of the dead are thought susceptible of being beaten, hurt and driven like any other living creatures. Thus the Queensland aborigines would beat the air in an annual mock fight, held to scare away the souls that death had let loose among the living since last year. Thus North American Indians, when they had tortured an enemy to death, ran about crying and beating with sticks to scare the ghost away; they have been known to set nets round their cabins to catch and keep out neighbours' departed souls; fancying the soul of a dying man to go out at the wigwam roof, they would habitually beat the sides with sticks to drive it forth; we even hear of the widow going off from her husband's funeral followed by a person flourishing a handful of twigs about her head like a fly-flapper, to drive off her husband's ghost and leave her free to marry again. With a kindlier feeling, the Congo negroes abstained for a whole year after a death from sweeping the house, lest the dust should injure the delicate substance of the ghost; the Tonquinese avoided house-cleaning during the festival when the souls of the dead came back to their houses for the New Year's visit; and it seems likely that the special profession of the Roman "everriatores" who swept the houses out after a funeral, was connected with a similar idea. To this day, it remains a German peasants' saying that it is wrong to slam a door, lest one should pinch a soul in it. The not uncommon practice of strewing ashes to show the footprints of ghosts or demons takes for granted that they are substantial bodies. In the literature of animism, extreme tests of the weight of ghosts are now and then forthcoming. They range from the declaration of a Basuto diviner that the late queen had been bestriding his shoulders, and he never felt such a weight in his life, to Glanvil's story of David Hunter the neatherd, who lifted up the old woman's ghost, and she felt just like a bag of feathers in his arms,[6] or the pathetic German superstition that the dead mother's coming back in the night to suckle the baby she has left on earth, may be known by the hollow pressed down in the bed where she lay, and at last down to the alleged modern spiritualistic reckoning of the weight of a human soul at from 3 to 4 ounces.

Explicit statements as to the substance of soul are to be found both among low and high races, in an instructive series of definitions. The Tongans imagined the human soul to be the finer or more aeriform part of the body, which leaves it suddenly at the moment of death; something comparable to the perfume and essence of a flower as related to the more solid vegetable fibre. The Greenland seers described the soul as they habitually perceived it in their visions; it is pale and soft, they said, and he who tries to seize it feels nothing, for it has no flesh nor bone nor sinew. The Caribs did not think the soul so immaterial as to be invisible, but said it was subtle and thin like a purified body. Turning to higher races, we may take the Siamese as an example of a people who conceive of souls as consisting of subtle matter escaping sight and touch, or as united to a swiftly moving aerial body. In the classic world, it is recorded as an opinion of Epicurus that "they who say the soul is incorporeal talk folly, for it could neither do nor suffer anything were it such." Among the Fathers, Irenaeus describes souls as incorporeal in comparison with mortal bodies, and Tertullian relates a vision or revelation of a certain Montanist prophetess, of the soul seen by her corporeally, thin and lucid, aerial in colour and human in form. For an example of mediaeval doctrine, may be cited a 14th-century English poem, the "Ayenbite of Inwyt" (i.e. "Remorse of Conscience") which points out how the soul, by reason of the thinness of its substance, suffers all the more in purgatory:

> The soul is more tendre and nesche
> Than the bodi that hath bones and fleysche;
> Thanne the soul that is so tendere of kinde,
> Mote nedis hure penaunce hardere y-finde,
> Than eni bodi that evere on live was.

The doctrine of the ethereal soul passed on into more modern philosophy, and the European peasant holds fast to it still; as Wuttke says,[7] the ghosts of the dead have to him a misty and evanescent materiality, for they have bodies as we have, though of other kind: they can eat and drink, they can be wounded and killed. Nor was the ancient doctrine ever more distinctly stated than by a modern spiritualistic writer, who observes that "a spirit is no immaterial substance; on the contrary, the spiritual organization is composed of matter . . . in a very high state of refinement and attenuation."

Among rude races, the original conception of the human soul seems to have been that of ethereality, or vaporous materiality, which has held so large a place in human thought ever since. In fact, the later metaphysical notion of immateriality could scarcely have conveyed any meaning to a savage. It is moreover to be noticed that, as to the whole nature and action of apparitional souls, the lower philosophy escapes various difficulties which down to modern times have perplexed metaphysicians and theologians of the civilized world. Considering the thin ethereal body of the soul to be itself sufficient and suitable for visibility, movement, and speech, the primitive animists required no additional hypotheses to account for these manifestations; they had no place for theories such as detailed by Calmet,[8] as that immaterial souls have their own vaporous bodies, or occasionally have such vaporous bodies provided for them by supernatural means to enable them to appear as spectres, or that they possess the power of condensing the circumambient air into phantom-like bodies to invest themselves in, or of forming from it vocal instruments. It appears to have been within systematic schools of civilized philosophy that the transcendental definitions of the immaterial soul were obtained, by abstraction from the primitive conception of the ethereal-material soul, so as to reduce it from a physical to a metaphysical entity.

Departing from the body at the time of death, the soul or spirit is considered set free to linger near the tomb, to wander on earth or flit in the air, or to travel to the proper region of spirits—the world beyond the grave. The principal conceptions of the lower psychology is to a Future Life will be considered in the following chapters, but for the present purpose of investigating the theory of souls in general, it will be well to enter here upon one department of the subject. Men do not stop short at the persuasion that death releases the soul to a free and active existence, but they quite logically proceed to assist nature, by slaying men in order to liberate their souls for ghostly uses. Thus there arises one of the most widespread, distinct, and intelligible rites of animistic religion—that of funeral human sacrifice for the service of the dead. When a man of rank dies and his soul departs to its own place, wherever and whatever that place may be, it is a rational inference of early philosophy that the souls of attendants, slaves, and wives, put to death at his funeral, will make the same journey and continue their service in the next life, and the argument is frequently stretched further, to include the souls of new victims sacrificed in order that they may enter upon the same ghostly servitude. It will appear from the ethnography of this rite that it is not strongly marked in the very lowest levels of culture, but that, arising in the lower barbaric stage, it develops itself in the higher, and thenceforth continues or dwindles in survival.

NOTES

1. [For Jung-Stilling, see n. 8 to Schopenhauer's "The Christian Religion."]

2. [Tylor quotes from David Cranz, *Historie von Grönland* (1765).]

3. [The reference is to James Boswell's *Journal of a Tour to the Hebrides* (1785), made in the company of Samuel Johnson.]

4. [Emanuel Swedenborg (1688–1772), Swedish mystic who attempted to show that the universe had a fundamentally spiritual structure.]

5. [Alfred, Lord Tennyson, *In Memoriam: A. H. H.* (1850), 47.6–8. The poem was written in memory of a deceased boyhood friend.]

6. [Tylor cites Joseph Glanvil (or Glanvill) (1636–1680), *Saducismus Triumphatus* (1681), a treatise that attempted to prove the reality of witchcraft.]

7. [Tylor cites Adolf Wuttke, *Der deutsche Volksaberglaube der gegenwart* (1860), a book on German folklore and superstition.]

8. [Tylor cites Augustin Calmet, *Dissertation sur les apparitions des anges, des démons et des esprits* (1746), later published as *Traité sur les apparitions des esprits* (1751; 2 vols.).]

7

ABOUT THE HOLY BIBLE

Robert G. Ingersoll

[Robert Green Ingersoll (1833–1899), American lawyer and lecturer, often called "the great agnostic," was the son of a fanatical Presbyterian preacher. He practiced law in Peoria, Illinois, and was for a time attorney general of Illinois; but further political offices were denied him because of prejudice against his antireligious views. He began lecturing in 1877, speaking against religion and promoting humanism, achieving tremendous popularity but also earning the wrath of orthodox religionists. Among his numerous works are *The Ghosts and Other Lectures* (1878), *Some Mistakes of Moses* (1879), and *The Christian Religion* (1882). His *Works* were published in twelve volumes in 1900. Recent editions include *On the Gods and Other Essays* (Prometheus Books, 1990) and *Reason, Tolerance, and Christianity: The Ingersoll Debates* (Prometheus Books, 1993). In the following chapter from *About the Holy Bible* (1894), entitled

Robert G. Ingersoll, *About the Holy Bible* (1894), in *The Works of Robert G. Ingersoll* (New York: Dresden, 1902), 3: 490–502.

"The New Testament," Ingersoll points out obvious discrepancies between the four gospels and asserts that they cannot be considered inspired.]

Who wrote the New Testament?

Christian scholars admit that they do not know.

They admit that, if the four gospels were written by Matthew, Mark, Luke and John, they must have been written in Hebrew. And yet a Hebrew manuscript of any one of these gospels has never been found. All have been and are in Greek. So, educated theologians admit that the Epistles, James and Jude, were written by persons who had never seen one of the four gospels. In these Epistles—in James and Jude—no reference is made to any of the gospels, nor to any miracle recorded in them.

The first mention that has been found of one of our gospels was made about one hundred and eighty years after the birth of Christ, and the four gospels were first named and quoted from at the beginning of the third century, about one hundred and seventy years after the death of Christ.

We now know that there were many other gospels besides our four, some of which have been lost. There were the gospels of Paul, of the Egyptians, of the Hebrews, of Perfection, of Judas, of Thaddeus, of the Infancy, of Thomas, of Mary, of Andrew, of Nicodemus, of Marcion and several others.

So there were the Acts of Pilate, of Andrew, of Mary, of Paul and Thecla and of many others; also a book called the Shepherd of Hermas.

At first not one of all the books was considered as inspired. The Old Testament was regarded as divine; but the books that now constitute the New Testament were regarded as human productions. We now know that we do not know who wrote the four gospels.

The question is, Were the authors of these four gospels inspired?

If they were inspired, then the four gospels must be true. If they are true, they must agree.

The four gospels do not agree.

Matthew, Mark and Luke knew nothing of the atonement, nothing of salvation by faith. They knew only the gospel of good deeds—of charity. They teach that if we forgive others God will forgive us.

With this the gospel of John does not agree.

In that gospel we are taught that we must believe in the Lord Jesus Christ; that we must be born again; that we must drink the blood and eat the flesh of Christ. In this gospel we find the doctrine of the atonement and that Christ died for us and suffered in our place.

This gospel is utterly at variance with the other three. If the other three are true, the gospel of John is false. If the gospel of John was written by an inspired man, the writers of the other three were uninspired. From this there is no possible escape. The four cannot be true.

It is evident that there are many interpolations in the four gospels.

For instance, in the 28th chapter of Matthew is an account to the effect that the soldiers at the tomb of Christ were bribed to say that the disciples of Jesus stole away his body while they, the soldiers, slept.

This is clearly an interpolation. It is a break in the narrative.

The 10th verse should be followed by the 16th. The 10th verse is as follows:

"Then Jesus said unto them, 'Be not afraid; go tell my brethren that they go unto Galilee and there shall they see me.'"

The 16th verse:

"Then the eleven disciples went away unto Galilee into a mountain, where Jesus had appointed them."

The story about the soldiers contained in the 11th, 12th, 13th, 14th and 15th verses is an interpolation—an afterthought—long after. The 15th verse demonstrates this.

Fifteenth verse: "So they took the money and did as they were taught. And this saying is commonly reported among the Jews until this day."

Certainly this account was not in the original gospel, and certainly the 15th verse was not written by a Jew. No Jew could have written this: "And this saying is commonly reported among the Jews until this day."

Mark, John and Luke never heard that the soldiers had been bribed by the priests; or, if they had, did not think it worth while recording. So the accounts of the Ascension of Jesus Christ in Mark and Luke are interpolations. Matthew says nothing about the Ascension.

Certainly there never was a greater miracle, and yet Matthew, who was present—who saw the Lord rise, ascend and disappear—did not think it worth mentioning.

On the other hand, the last words of Christ, according to Matthew, contradict the Ascension: "Lo I am with you always, even unto the end of the world" [Matt. 28:20].

John, who was present, if Christ really ascended, says not one word on the subject.

As to the Ascension, the gospels do not agree.

Mark gives the last conversation that Christ had with his disciples, as follows:

"Go ye into all the world and preach the gospel to every creature. He that believeth and is baptised shall be saved; but he that believeth not shall be damned. And these signs shall follow them that believe: In my name shall they cast out devils; they shall speak with new tongues. They shall take up serpents, and if they drink any deadly thing it shall not hurt them; they shall lay hands on the sick and they shall recover. So, then, after the Lord had spoken unto them, he was received up into heaven and sat on the right hand of God" [Mark 16:15–19].

Is it possible that this description was written by one who witnessed this miracle?

This miracle is described by Luke as follows: "And it came to pass while he blessed them he was parted from them and carried up into heaven" [Luke 24:51].

"Brevity is the soul of wit."[1]

In the Acts we are told that: "When he had spoken, while they beheld, he was taken up, and a cloud received him out of their sight" [Acts 1:9].

Neither Luke, nor Matthew, nor John, nor the writer of the Acts, heard one word of the conversation attributed to Christ by Mark. The fact is that the Ascension of Christ was not claimed by his disciples.

At first Christ was a man—nothing more. Mary was his mother, Joseph his father. The genealogy of his father, Joseph, was given to show that he was of the blood of David.

Then the claim was made that he was the son of God, and that his mother was a virgin, and that she remained a virgin until her death.

Then the claim was made that Christ rose from the dead and ascended bodily to heaven.

It required many years for these absurdities to take possession of the minds of men.

If Christ rose from the dead, why did he not appear to his enemies? Why did he not call on Caiaphas, the high priest? Why did he not make another triumphal entry into Jerusalem?

If he really ascended, why did he not do so in public, in the presence of his persecutors? Why should this, the greatest of miracles, be done in secret, in a corner?

It was a miracle that could have been seen by a vast multitude—a miracle that could not be simulated—one that would have convinced hundreds of thousands.

After the story of the Resurrection, the Ascension became a necessity. They had to dispose of the body.

So there are many other interpolations in the gospels and epistles.

Again I ask: Is the New Testament true? Does anybody now believe that at the birth of Christ there was a celestial greeting; that a star led the Wise Men of the East; that Herod slew the babes of Bethlehem of two years old and under?

The gospels are filled with accounts of miracles. Were they ever performed?

Matthew gives the particulars of about twenty-two miracles, Mark of about nineteen, Luke of about eighteen and John of about seven.

According to the gospels, Christ healed diseases, cast out devils, rebuked the sea, cured the blind, fed multitudes with five loaves and two fishes, walked on the sea, cursed a fig tree, turned water into wine and raised the dead.

Matthew is the only one that tells about the Star and the Wise Men—the only one that tells about the murder of babes.

John is the only one who says anything about the resurrection of Lazarus, and Luke is the only one giving an account of the raising from the dead the widow of Nain's son.

How is it possible to substantiate these miracles?

The Jews, among whom they were said to have been performed, did not believe them. The diseased, the palsied, the leprous, the blind who were cured, did not become followers of Christ. Those that were raised from the dead were never heard of again.

Does any intelligent man believe in the existence of devils? The writer of three of the gospels certainly did. John says nothing about Christ having cast out devils, but Matthew, Mark and Luke give many instances.

Does any natural man now believe that Christ cast out devils? If his disciples said he did, they were mistaken. If Christ said he did, he was insane or an impostor.

If the accounts of casting out devils are false, then the writers were ignorant or dishonest. If they wrote through ignorance, then they were not inspired. If they wrote what they knew to be false, they were not inspired. If what they wrote is untrue, whether they knew it or not, they were not inspired.

At that time it was believed that palsy, epilepsy, deafness, insanity and many other diseases were caused by devils; that devils took possession of and lived in the bodies of men and women. Christ believed this, taught this belief to others, and pretended to cure diseases by casting devils out of the sick and insane. We know now, if we know anything, that diseases are not caused by the presence of devils. We know, if we know anything, that devils do not reside in the bodies of men.

If Christ said and did what the writers of the three gospels say he said and did, then Christ was mistaken. If he was mistaken, certainly he was not God. And if he was mistaken, certainly he was not inspired.

Is it a fact that the Devil tried to bribe Christ?

Is it a fact that the Devil carried Christ to the top of the temple and tried to induce him to leap to the ground?

How can these miracles be established?

The principals have written nothing, Christ has written nothing, and the Devil has remained silent.

How can we know that the Devil tried to bribe Christ? Who wrote the account? We do not know. How did the writer get his information? We do not know.

Somebody, some seventeen hundred years ago, said that the Devil tried to bribe God; that the Devil carried God to the top of the temple and tried to induce him to leap to the earth and that God was intellectually too keen for the Devil.

This is all the evidence we have.

Is there anything in the literature of the world more perfectly idiotic?

Intelligent people no longer believe in witches, wizards, spooks and devils, and they are perfectly satisfied that every word in the New Testament about casting out devils is utterly false.

Can we believe that Christ raised the dead?

A widow living in Nain is following the body of her son to the tomb. Christ halts the funeral procession and raises the young man from the dead and gives him back to the arms of his mother.

This young man disappears. He is never heard of again. No one takes the slightest interest in the man who returned from the realm of death. Luke is the only one who tells the story. Maybe Matthew, Mark and John never heard of it, or did not believe it and so failed to record it.

John says that Lazarus was raised from the dead; Matthew, Mark and Luke say nothing about it.

It was more wonderful than the raising of the widow's son. He had not been laid in the tomb for days. He was only on his way to the grave, but Lazarus was actually dead. He had begun to decay.

Lazarus did not excite the least interest. No one asked him about the other world. No one inquired of him about their dead friends.

When he died the second time no one said: "He is not afraid. He has traveled that road twice and knows just where he is going."

We do not believe in the miracles of Mohammed, and yet they are as well attested as this. We have no confidence in the miracles performed by Joseph Smith, and yet the evidence is far greater, far better.

If a man should go about now pretending to raise the dead, pretending to cast out devils, we would regard him as insane. What, then, can we say of Christ? If we wish to save his reputation we are compelled to say that he never pretended to raise the dead; that he never claimed to have cast out devils.

We must take the ground that these ignorant and impossible things were invented by zealous disciples, who sought to deify their leader.

In those ignorant days these falsehoods added to the fame of Christ. But now they put his character in peril and belittle the authors of the gospels.

Can we now believe that water was changed into wine? John tells of this childish miracle, and says that the other disciples were present, yet Matthew, Mark and Luke say nothing about it.

Take the miracle of the man cured by the pool of Bethseda. John says that an angel troubled the waters of the pool of Bethseda, and that whoever got into the pool first after the waters were troubled was healed.

Does anybody now believe that an angel went into the pool and troubled the waters? Does anybody now think that the poor wretch who got in first was healed? Yet the author of the gospel according to John believed and asserted these absurdities. If he was mistaken about that he may have been about all the miracles he records.

John is the only one who tells about this pool of Bethseda. Possibly the other disciples did not believe the story.

How can we account for these pretended miracles?

In the days of the disciples, and for many centuries after, the world was filled with the supernatural. Nearly everything that happened was regarded as miraculous. God was the immediate governor of the world. If the people were good, God sent seed time and harvest; but if they were bad he sent flood and hail, frost and famine. If anything wonderful happened it was exaggerated until it became a miracle. Of the order of events—of the unbroken and the unbreakable chain of causes and effects—the people had no knowledge and no thought.

A miracle is the badge and brand of fraud. No miracle ever was performed. No intelligent, honest man ever pretended to perform a miracle, and never will.

If Christ had wrought the miracles attributed to him; if he had cured the palsied and insane; if he had given hearing to the deaf, vision to the blind; if he had cleansed the leper with a word, and with a touch had given life and feeling to the withered limb; if he had given pulse and motion, warmth and thought, to cold and breathless clay; if he had conquered death and rescued from the grave its pallid prey—no word would have been uttered, no hand raised, except in praise and honor. In his presence all heads would have been uncovered—all knees upon the ground.

Is it not strange that at the trial of Christ no one was found to say a word in his favor? No man stood forth and said: "I was a leper, and this man cured me with a touch." No woman said: "I am the widow of Nain and this is my son whom this man raised from the dead."

No man said: "I was blind, and this man gave me sight."

All silent.

NOTE

1. Shakespeare, *Hamlet*, 2.2.90.

8

CHRISTIANITY AND MORALS

Edward Westermarck

[Edward Alexander Westermarck (1862–1939), Finnish anthropologist and sociologist, was educated at Helsinki University, where he abandoned his religious beliefs as "unworthy of a thinking human being." Rejecting the German metaphysics that then prevailed in Europe, he was attracted to British empiricism and much influenced by Darwin. All his major works were written in English. The first was *The History of Human Marriage* (1891), a landmark work that traced the evolutionary underpinnings of marriage. Westermarck received a PhD from Helsinki in 1890 and taught there from 1890 to 1897. He subsequently did much traveling for research. In 1904 he gave a series of lectures on sociology at the London School of Economics, and he later accepted a position as professor of sociology, remaining there from 1907 to 1930. He simultaneously taught at Helsinki University (1906–18) and at the Äbo Akademi (1918–32). He

Edward Westermarck, "Summary and Concluding Remarks," *Christianity and Morals* (London: Kegan Paul, Trench, Trübner, 1939), pp. 394–411.

published *The Origin an Development of the Moral Ideas* (1906–08), which propounded a naturalistic and emotive theory of morality; it was followed by *Ethical Relativity* (1932). His last work was *Christianity and Morals* (1939), published a few months before his death. He also wrote the autobiography *Memories of My Life* (1929). In the following, Westermarck points out the differences between the theory of morality espoused by Jesus and that espoused by Paul, and concludes that the influence of Christianity upon morality in Western civilization has been, at best, mixed.]

There would have been no Paul without Christ, but there would have been no Christianity without Paul. The new faith would, no doubt, have merely remained the religion of a Jewish sect destined to pine away, if Paul had not rescued it for history, and made it a religion of the world. He did this by transforming its character. Jesus had taught, in the Sermon on the Mount, that the salvation of any man depended on his own moral conduct, and that the way which led to the kingdom of God was anything but easy. According to Paul, future life was the result of a divine work of redemption, which prepared the salvation for mankind once for all through the death and resurrection of Christ and faith. Christian theologians often tell us that there is no essential difference between the teaching of Jesus and that of Paul. But from the moral point of view the difference is radical.

I have tried to show that the ethics of Jesus were expressions of his moral emotions, and that these were in general agreement with the nature of such emotions when guided by sufficient sympathy and discrimination. This is proved by the great similarities between the teaching of Jesus and that of the world's other great moralists. Moral emotions are disinterested retributive emotions. Personal anger and vindictiveness are strongly condemned by Jesus; and the injunctions of forgiveness and kindness to enemies are also found in the Old Testament and other Jewish writings, in the Koran and the Mohammedan traditions, in Brahmanism,[1] Buddhism, and Chinese ethics; and the principle of forgiveness had advocates in Greece and Rome, as well, the condemnation of anger and resentment being particularly abundant in Stoicism. Quite different from the resentment and retaliation springing from personal motives are moral resentment and the punishment in which it finds expression. These vary indefinitely. The moral indignation of Jesus is often intense, and the future punishment he assigns to unrepentant sinners enormous. This is an unsurmountable stumbling-block for those who insist on the objectivity of the rules of Christian ethics. Nowadays Christians are shocked by the ancient doctrine of hell and make vain attempts to explain it away. But side by side with the doctrine of retribution there is in the gospels the message of forgiveness for the repentant sinner. That repentance is followed by forgiveness is also found in other religions, such as Judaism, Zoroastrianism, Brahmanism, and the Vedic religion. But repentance not only blunts the edge of moral indignation and recommends the offender to mercy: it is also the sole ground on which pardon can be given by a scrupulous judge. When sufficiently guided by deliberation and left to itself without being unduly checked by other emotions, the feeling of moral resentment is apt to last as long as its cause remains unaltered, that is, until the will of the offender has ceased to be offensive; and it ceases to be so only when he acknowledges his guilt and repents. That moral indignation is appeased by repentance, and that repentance is the only proper ground for forgiveness, however, is due, not to the specifically moral character of such indignation, but to its being a form of resentment. This is confirmed by the fact that an angry and revengeful man is apt to be influenced in a similar way by the sincere repentance of the offender.

While Jesus was capable of feeling intense moral indignation, his emotion of moral approval, of which moral praise or reward is the outward manifestation, plays a no less prominent part in his teaching, as is shown by the innumerable cases in which eternal reward is promised for righteousness. Does this imply that Jesus considered hope of reward as an adequate reason for receiving it? We do not feel the emotion of moral approval or retributive kindliness towards a person if we recognise that he does something merely in the selfish hope of being benefited by it; and, like all great moralists, Jesus certainly laid stress on the motives of conduct, on inwardness and purity of heart. But there is no inconsistency between benevolence being the immediate spring of action and the hope of reward being an ultimate motive for it: a person may aim at his own happiness as his ultimate end and at the same time aim sincerely at the happiness of his neighbour as a means to that end. The desire to gain divine favour with everything implied in it must certainly have been regarded by Jesus as a right motive for our conduct.

While Jesus' doctrine of punishment and reward is an outcome of the retributive character of the moral emotions, his teaching also emphasises that disinterestedness which distinguishes them from other, non-moral, retributive emotions. This he does in his enunciation of "the Golden Rule," which, also, is much older than Christianity and, especially in its negative form, widespread. The disinterestedness of the moral emotions, moreover, partly underlies the rule, "Thou shalt love thy neighbour as thyself," which occurs both in the Old Testament and in the three synoptic gospels [Lev. 19:18; Matt. 19:19; Mark 12:31; Luke 10:27]. But this maxim contains much more than the disinterestedness of the conception of duty. When a person pronounces an act right or wrong, it implies that it is so, *ceteris paribus*, whether he does it to another or another does it to him; but this has nothing to do with the particular nature of the act. When my own interests clash with those of my neighbour, I may have the right to prefer my own lesser good to the greater good of another, but only on condition that the other person also, in similar circumstances, is admitted to have the right to prefer his own lesser good to my greater good. No such right to prefer one's own lesser good to the greater good of another is recognised in the precept, "Thou shalt love thy neighbour as thyself"; but this precept owes its origin to the strength of the altruistic sentiment in him who laid down the rule, and not merely to the disinterestedness of his moral emotions. It is another instance of the relative validity of our moral judgments; and so are moral rules relating to different groups of neighbours. They vary indefinitely because the altruistic sentiment varies in expanse as well as in strength. The impartiality of my moral emotions does not prevent me from promoting the welfare of my own family or country in preference to that of other families or countries; but it tells me that I must allow anybody else to show a similar preference for his family or country. Among the positive duties resulting from benevolence almsgiving holds a very prominent position in the teaching of Jesus, as it did in Judaism and particularly in the Old Testament apocrypha and in rabbinical literature.

While his ethics were an expression of intense moral emotions in which both the retributive and the altruistic elements came out very prominently, specific religious and eschatological beliefs were blended with the ideas springing from those emotions. Our duties to neighbours were founded upon our submission to the will of God, and their sanctions were rewards or penalties for obedience or disobedience to his commandments. But those beliefs did not essentially alter the contents of those commandments, as is testified by the innumerable parallels between the teaching of Jesus and that of other great moralists. We also find that certain doctrines which had crept into the moral system of the Jews from their religion, but were alien to the emotional origin of morals, were opposed by Jesus, as was the case with his attitude towards the sabbath.

Among the sayings of Jesus there are injunctions which cannot be meant to be obeyed literally, but are more or less paradoxical, in conformity to the Oriental habit of speaking in proverbs, which stress one side of a case to the exclusion of every other. We must also remember that much of his teaching was conditioned by his belief that the End was at hand; and least of all must we expect his sayings to be applicable to the circumstances of modern life. It may, moreover, be said that Jesus himself somewhat modified his teaching by recognising the existing institutions of the State. There is no hint that he wanted soldiers to abandon their profession, or that he regarded this profession as wrong; his attitude towards the centurion whose servant was sick of the palsy was altogether friendly. And when the Pharisees tried to entangle him in his talk, he told them that they should render unto Caesar the things which were Caesar's, and unto God the things that were God's. This helped Luther to find a compromise between what we should do as members of the kingdom of God and as members of the kingdom of Caesar.[2] Roman Catholicism had found another way of softening the severity of the Sermon on the Mount. The harder sayings came to be reckoned as counsels of perfection, the observance of which implied that the performer did more than was required for his own salvation.

While Jesus was a moralist, Paul was in the first place a theologian. Faith is the keystone of his teaching, faith in the redemption through the crucified and risen Christ. He never speaks of Jesus as a teacher or of his teaching, he extremely seldom appeals to any words of Jesus as a moral norm, he never refers to his example in any concrete situation. "A man is justified by faith without the deeds of the law" [Rom. 3:28]; "To him that worketh not, but believeth on him that justifieth the ungodly, his faith is counted for righteousness" [Rom. 4:5]. Whatever else Paul's conception of faith may imply, it presupposes in the first place the intellectual acceptance of some fact as true; and such a belief cannot be a proper object of moral judgment. But even if the sin of unbelief, as Thomas Aquinas argues,[3] has its cause in the will because it consists in "contrary opposition to the faith, whereby one stands out against the hearing of the faith," it could not be imputed to anybody who never heard of the faith. Moreover, the faith itself is a gift of God: "God hath dealt to every man the measure of faith" [Rom. 12:3]. Salvation depends on an "election of grace": God "hath mercy on whom he will have mercy, and whom he will he hardeneth" [Rom. 9:18]. Yet there is some reason for his mercy. Those who believe are justified by the grace of God "through the redemption that is in Christ Jesus: whom God hath set forth to be a propitiation through faith in his blood, to declare his righteousness for the remission of sins that are past, through the forbearance of God" [Rom.

3:24–25]. Christ "died for all, that they which live should not hence-forth live unto themselves, but unto him which died for them, and rose again" [2 Cor. 5:15]. "Christ our passover is sacrificed for us" [1 Cor. 5:7]. It is thus by the vicarious suffering of Jesus that the wrath of God, aroused by the sin of men, is appeased. "As by one man sin entered into the world, and death by sin" [Rom. 5:12], and "as by the offence of one judgment came upon all men to condemnation; even so by the righteousness of one the free gift came upon all men unto justification of life" [Rom. 5:18].

The idea that all mankind are doomed to death on account of Adam's sin, which Paul had imbibed from his Jewish upbringing, is explicable by the conception of sin as a kind of material substance or infection which is transplanted by propagation. But the Prophets already broke with the old notions of divine vengeance by declaring that "every one shall die for his own iniquity" [Jer. 31:20], and that "the soul that sinneth, it shall die" [Ezek. 18:4]; and Ezekiel added that as the wickedness of the wicked shall be upon him, so also "the right-eousness of the righteous shall be upon him" [Ezek. 18:20]. This is in agreement with the fact that the moral emotions of disapproval and approval, in their capacity of retributive emotions, are hostile or friendly attitudes of mind towards persons conceived as causes of pain or pleasure. They cannot admit that a person is punished or rewarded on account of another person's behaviour. There cannot be either a guilt or a merit by transfer. It is contrary to the fundamental principles of our moral consciousness.

We find, however, also another line of thought in Paul's epistles. He writes not only that a man is justified by faith without the deeds of the law, but sometimes also that God will show himself as a righteous judge, "who will render to every man according to his deeds" [Rom. 2:6], or that "every man shall receive his own reward according to his own labour" [1 Cor. 3:8]. In various passages he expresses the idea that faith produces obedience to the law and charity, and it may be argued that if a person is justified by faith, which is a gift of God, and good deeds are manifestations of it, his "reward" for them is really due to the faith which God has given him, and that the damnation of a person who has done evil is due to the fact that he has not received the gift of faith from God; whereas if he receives such a gift, and is justified thereby, he will do no evil again. Such a conclusion might be drawn from one of his sayings. But Paul was not a consistent thinker. On the one hand he teaches that justification depends upon faith alone, that faith is a gift of God, that man's work really is God's work, nay that it even was God who gave Israel "the spirit of slumber, eyes that they should not see, and ears that they should not hear" [Rom. 11:8]; but on the other hand he also looks upon the activity of the human will as a factor of importance. When he speaks of the retribution for good and evil deeds, he is evidently moved by his moral consciousness, which repeatedly finds expression without any reference to justification by faith. He refers to "conscience" and speaks of the "witness" it bears, and finds a conscience not only among the Christians, but in every man. "When the Gentiles, which have not the law, do by nature the things contained in the law, these, having not the law, are a law unto themselves: which shew the work of the law written in their hearts" [Rom. 2:14].

The antithesis between the moralistic teaching of Jesus as reported in the synoptic gospels and Paul's formula of justification by faith, alternated in the early Church. But through Augustine Paulinism got the upper hand, though a Paulinism modified by popular Catholic elements. To him the object of the faith which is necessary for salvation was the truth guaranteed by the Church, which he regarded as infallible in consequence of its authority as based on apostolicity. But the faith which saves is only the faith that works in love—faith, love, and merit being successive steps in the way to final salvation. This also became the view of the Catholic Church. The conception of merits, which had been current in her from earlier days, was accepted by Augustine, but was reconciled with the doctrine of grace. Faith and love and merits are all God's gifts, and "no one is saved except by undeserved mercy, and no one is condemned except by a deserved judgment." As Paul taught, the elect are saved because God, in virtue of his eternal decree of salvation, has predestinated, chosen, called,

justified, sanctified, and preserved them. All men are by nature children of wrath, and are burdened by original sin and their own sins.
Therefore a mediator was necessary who should appease that wrath by
presenting a unique sacrifice. That this was done constitutes the grace
of God through Jesus Christ, who by submitting to death without com-
pulsion became a sacrifice for sin, representing our sin in the flesh in
which he was crucified, "that in some way he might die to sin, in dying
to the flesh," and from the resurrection might seal our new life.

From the moral point of view the relation between the grace of
God and the faith, love, and merit of man in Augustine's doctrine of
salvation is an absurdity. If the latter are gifts of God he rewards man
with eternal felicity for what he himself has given him. That God has
predestinated some persons to salvation and others to damnation
makes moral responsibility impossible, since moral judgments, owing
to their very nature, are passed on persons conceived as the cause of a
certain mode of conduct which is directly or indirectly attributed to
their own will. Nor can Augustine's conception of original sin satisfy
even the most elementary moral claim. The punishment for Adam's
disobedience was inflicted not only on himself but on his descendants
as well; and at the same time they had also to pay for the sin contracted
by their parents producing them in sinful lust.

Augustinianism was accepted by the Western Church, though with
the secret reservation that it was to be moulded by its own mode of
thought when it did not harmonise with the tendencies of the Church.
Its greatest and most influential champion was Thomas Aquinas, particularly with regard to its doctrines of God, predestination, sin, and
grace. But in spite of his ardent adherence to Augustinianism we find
in him a timid revision of it in a moralistic direction. Although he
makes an earnest endeavour to assert the sole efficacy of divine grace,
his line of statement takes ultimately a different direction. While man
cannot merit eternal life without grace, there must for justification co-
operate a movement of free will, a movement of faith, and a hatred of
sin; in other words, there is an intermingling of grace and self-action,
and only then justification takes place. Thus, according to Thomas, the

process of grace realises itself with the consent of free will, even though this consent is at the same time the effect of grace. The doctrine that eternal salvation must be merited by good works is common to all the mediaeval Schoolmen, and the Council of Trent stamped it with its approval.[4]

This doctrine of grace culminates in the "evangelical counsels." Thomas points out, as others had done before him, that there are both precepts and counsels. A precept is compulsory, whereas a counsel is dependent on the option of him to whom it was given. The observance of precepts is necessary, but also sufficient, for the gaining of eternal life; but there are counsels "regarding those things by which man can attain the appointed end better and more readily." This distinction between command and counsel, between a higher and a lower Christian life, was supported by Paul's saying that the virgin state is superior to the married one, but that he who marries has not sinned. The distinction in question has certainly a solid foundation in our moral consciousness, in so far that a command implies the concept of duty, which is based on the emotion of disapproval, and a counsel implies the concept of goodness, which derives its origin from the emotion of moral approval. It is obvious that if a course of conduct which is not regarded as a duty is held to be meritorious, it is *ipso facto* admitted that a man can do more than his duty. This is denied both by those who derive goodness from duty and consider that what is good is what ought to be done, and by those who derive duty from goodness and consider that everybody ought to do the best he is able to do. Duty, which is the minimum of morality, in so far that it implies that the opposite mode of conduct is wrong, is identified with the supreme moral ideal, which requires the best possible conduct for its realisation. This rigorism may be traced either to the direct or indirect influence of Protestant theology with its denial of all works of supererogation, or to the endeavour of normative moralists to preach the most elevated kind of morality they can conceive. It is certainly not supported by our practical moral judgments, and I do not see how such a doctrine could serve any useful purpose at all. It is nowadays a recognised principle in legislation that a law loses much of its weight if it cannot be enforced. If the realisation of the highest moral ideal is commanded by a moral law, such a law will always remain a dead letter, and morality will gain nothing. It seems to me that far above the anxious effort to fulfil the commandments of duty stands the free and lofty aspiration to live up to an ideal, which, unattainable as it may be, threatens neither with blame nor remorse him who fails to reach its summits.

At the same time there are in the Roman Catholic doctrine of merit certain very objectionable features. It implies that a good deed stands in the same relation to a bad deed as a claim to a debt; that the claim is made on the same person to whom the debt is due, that is God, even though it only be by his mercy; and that the debt consequently may be compensated for in the same way as the infliction of a loss or damage may be compensated for by the payment of an indemnity. This doctrine of reparation comes inevitably to attach badness and goodness to external acts rather than to mental facts. No reparation can be given for badness. It can only be forgiven, and moral forgiveness can only be granted on condition that the agent's mind has undergone a radical alteration for the better, that the badness of the will has given way to repentance. This point was certainly not overlooked by the Catholic moralists, but even the most ardent apology cannot explain away the idea of reparation in the Catholic conception of the justification of man. Moreover, the ethical value of the theory of "good works" is much reduced when merit is particularly ascribed to works which our moral consciousness is apt to regard as indifferent or even to disapprove of, namely, ascetic practices, not in the sense of strict self-discipline but of relinquishing worldly pleasures and enjoyments and of deliberate maltreatment of the body. Finally, vicarious efficacy is attributed to good deeds. It is argued that Christ has done more by his suffering than was necessary for redemption, and that also many saints have performed meritorious deeds which God's grace rewards; and that this surplus merit, or "treasury of supererogatory works," must necessarily fall to the benefit of the Church, since neither Christ nor the saints derive further advantage from it.

The question how Christ's suffering and death can be a means of justification called for an answer. According to Augustine it was a ransom paid to the devil, who has acquired a legal claim on men—a theory which had previously been set forth by Origen[5]—and this explanation was accepted by most of the Western Fathers. It did not, however, exclude the old idea that Christ's suffering and death constituted a sacrifice presented by him to God in order to propitiate him. This has remained the most popular view, although rival explanations have also been suggested, and there is an increasing number of disbelievers. Moral justification is claimed for it. In the recent Report of the Anglican Commission on Christian Doctrine we are told that "the Cross is a satisfaction for sin so far as the moral order of the universe makes it impossible that human souls should be redeemed from sin except at a cost. . . . The redeeming love of God, through the life of Jesus Christ sacrificially offered in death upon the Cross, acted with cleansing power upon a sin-stained world, and so enables us to be cleaned."[6] To me it seems that even the slightest degree of reflection should show how incompatible the infliction of punishment on an innocent person in place of the culprit is with the very nature of our moral consciousness, moral indignation being a hostile attitude of mind towards an individual conceived as a cause of pain.

The Reformation implied an Augustinian reaction and a restoration of Paulinism. It substituted the Bible for the authority of the Church, and to Luther in particular the kernel and marrow of the Bible was the epistles of Paul. We are justified by faith alone. The Schoolmen had developed the hint contained in Paul's expression "faith working by love,"[7] and distinguished between an "unformed" faith—a mere intellectual belief—and a "formed" faith, which includes love, and which alone justifies and saves. According to Luther, on the other hand, "we can be saved without charity," but not without pure doctrine and faith. "No good work can profit an unbeliever to justification and salvation; and, on the other hand, no evil work makes him an evil and condemned person, but that unbelief, which makes the person and the tree bad, makes his works evil and condemned." Luther even denied that we can do any good work at all; among the famous ninety-five theses which he nailed on the church door of Wittenberg there was the assertion that "the just man sins in every good work." It is true that in his more moderate statements he can declare that the sanctifying grace given after the man has been justified by faith enables him to do good works, nay that good works will necessarily follow his faith; but then the good works are not really done by him but by God. As Luther grew older, his conception of faith became more and more intellectual, till at last it comprised little beyond the assent of mind to certain articles of an orthodox creed. "One little point of doctrine," he says, "is of more value than heaven and earth; therefore we do not suffer it (*i.e.* doctrine) to be injured in the smallest particular. But at errors of life we may very well connive."

Although Luther would not hear of any human merit, he believed in the merit of Christ, who, as the Confession of Augsburg put it, "suffered and died that he might reconcile the Father to us, and be a sacrifice, not only for original guilt, but also for all actual sins of men."[8] Christ's righteousness is imputed to us. Our faith in him makes his piety ours, and makes our sins his. He was the greatest of all sinners, because he assumed in his body the sins we had committed, to make satisfaction for them on the cross; "he was crucified and died for us, and offered up our sins in his own body." And Christ is represented by Luther as not merely dying instead of us, but also as keeping the law instead of us. "This is the gospel . . . that the law has been fulfilled, that is, by Christ, so that it is not necessary for us to fulfil it, but only to adhere and to be conformed to him who fulfils it." The denial of all human merit in conjunction with the belief in the saving efficacy of the vicarious merit of Christ seems to be the climax of the antimoralism of Christian theology.

The other Reformers were, generally, in substantial agreement with Luther. Zwingli likewise substituted the authority of the Bible for the authority of the Church, and preached the justification by faith alone.[9] But he did not so exclusively as Luther take his gospel from Paul's epistles and then read it into the whole Bible. He was much more than Luther a humanist, and more a moralist as well. He wrote that "it is the part of a Christian man not to talk magnificently of doctrines, but always, with God to do great and hard things." Like Luther, Calvin was an Augustinian in assuming the absolute foreknowledge and determining power of God, the servitude of the human will, the corruption and incapacity of man's nature.[10] But to him the main thing was not the sinner's personal relation to Christ and his appropriation of the Saviour's work, but the awful omnipotence of the divine decree fixing the unalterable succession of events and shutting out all co-operation of the human will. God predestinated certain individuals to salvation from eternity by his gratuitous mercy, and consigned the remainder to eternal damnation, by "a just and irreprehensible, but incomprehensible judgment." To apply earthly standards of justice to his sovereign decrees is meaningless and an insult to his majesty. To assume that human merit and guilt play a part in determining the destiny of men, would be to think of God's absolutely free decrees, which have been settled from eternity, as subject to change by human influence—an impossible contradiction. Yet however useless good works might be as a means of attaining salvation, they are nevertheless indispensable as a sign of election. They are the technical means, not of purchasing salvation, but of getting rid of the fear of damnation.

Reformation was a protest not only against doctrines taught by the Catholic Church, but also against moral abuses practised in its name, such as benefactions being accepted in atonement for flagrant sin, and escape from purgatory being bought in any market-place. But at the same time the Reformers rejected the sound moral principles which were defiled by such corrupt practices, when they denied the value of good deeds however sincere, and the different degrees of sinfulness of which the doctrine of purgatory is an expression. This doctrine, which had been suggested by Augustine and generally accepted by the Schoolmen, had mitigated the monstrosity of the teaching of eternal tortures by intercalating a place between heaven and hell, where those who have been accepted for a blessed state but are only partially prepared for it are subjected to a painful discipline. Its existence had been inferred indirectly from Matthew (xii. 31) and the First Epistle to the Corinthians (iii. 12 sq.); but the Protestants declared it to be, in the words of the Anglican Article XXII., "a fond thing vainly invented, and grounded upon no warranty of Scripture, but rather repugnant to the word of God." The shocking abuses which were connected with the belief in purgatory—even in the decree of the Council of Trent relating to it there is an allusion to "base gain, scandals, and stumbling-blocks for the faithful"—cannot disguise the fact that the doctrine itself has a moral foundation.

Something similar may be said of the sacrament of penance, the starting-point of which is the contrition, or at any rate attrition, of the penitent, though the real sacrament is the external acts of him and the priest. The satisfaction preceding the absolution, or priestly declaration of forgiveness of sins, became a sheer travesty through the practice of indulgences, which implied the exchange of more arduous penitential acts for very small performances, such as the payment of penance money, with the result that the Church dispensed from the temporal pains of purgatory all, whether living or departed, who either themselves or vicariously performed those ecclesiastical exercises. The practice and theory of indulgences was vehemently attacked by Luther, who substituted repentance alone, which he conceived of as the crushed feeling about sin awakened by faith. But his own doctrine that only such repentance as springs from faith has value before God is also open to criticism, though of a different kind. It alienates repentance widely from the sphere of morality, and is fraught with serious consequences. It makes it as constant as faith. The first of Luther's ninety-five theses runs: "Our Lord and Master Jesus Christ in saying, 'Repent ye,' etc., intended that the whole life of believers should be penitence." Harnack remarks that if men are told that they must constantly repent, and that particular acts of repentance are of no use, there are few who will ever repent.[11]

Whatever importance has been attached either to merits or to faith, the doctrine of salvation has at the same time been influenced by the belief in a mystical efficacy of the sacraments of baptism and the

Eucharist, which are common both to Catholics and Protestants. The former is regarded as a bath of regeneration, by which sins are blotted out, and as a necessary means of salvation. According to Thomas Aquinas it is the indispensable medicine for the consequences of the Fall, which abolishes the guilt both of original sin and of all committed sins without exception; and in the Confession of Augsburg the Lutherans asserted the absolute necessity of baptism quite as emphatically as the Catholics. In Catholicism, however, the notion that unbaptised children will be tormented gradually gave way to a more humane opinion, according to which there is a place, called *limbus*, or *infernus puerorum*, where unbaptised infants will dwell without being subject to torture. But the older view was again set up by the Protestants, who generally maintained that the due punishment of original sin is, in strictness, damnation in hell, although many of them were inclined to think that if a child dies by misfortune before it is baptised, the parents' sincere intention of baptising it, together with their prayers, will be accepted with God for the deed. The Confession of Augsburg emphatically condemns the doctrine of the Anabaptists that children are saved without baptism. So also the damnation of infants who die unbaptised was an acknowledged belief of Calvinism, although an exception was made for the children of pious parents, provided "there is neither sloth, nor contempt, nor negligence."

The Eucharist, which like the baptism evidently owes its sacramental character to Paul, was looked upon by him as a mystical re-enactment of the death and resurrection of Christ through which the believer participates in his immortality, the bread and wine being an incarnation of his body and blood. Aquinas says of the effects of the Eucharist that it conveys grace, gives aid for eternal life, blots out venial sins but not mortal sins, and guards against future transgressions. Luther maintained that both the Eucharist and baptism, which were the only sacraments recognised by him, work forgiveness of sin and thereby procure life and blessedness, but not without faith; he insisted that the sacraments do not become efficacious in their being celebrated, but in their being believed in. In any case they are rooted in magical ideas, and the efficacy attributed to them has always retained a magical character. For the supposed saving effect of baptism and the Eucharist there is no moral justification whatever. A righteous God does not forgive a sinner unless he repents, and if he repents he is forgiven without any external rite. Repentance is not much spoken of in connection with those sacraments. In the case of baptism it was formerly expected of converts; but when infant baptism was introduced it ceased even nominally to be required of him who was going to be baptised.

From this survey of Christian ethics as expressed in theories of salvation and of the agreement or disagreement of these theories with the nature of our moral emotions we now come to the question, how far they may be supposed to have influenced the morality of human conduct. The belief in a god who acts as a guardian of worldly morality undoubtedly gives emphasis to its rules. To the social and legal sanctions a new one is added, which derives particular strength from the supernatural power and knowledge of the deity. The divine avenger can punish those who are beyond the reach of human justice and those whose secret wrongs escape the censure of their fellowmen; and the righteous god can also reward goodness which receives no other reward. Among the early Christians the hope of future blessedness and especially the fear of eternal punishment must have exercised a powerful effect in connection with their belief in the imminence of the millennium. Fear of divine wrath is often known to have impelled men to conversion.[12] It was an element in the conversion of Paul, and entered into that of Luther, and revivalists like Jonathan Edwards and Wesley often appeal to the emotion of crude fear.[13] Wesley wrote in one of his letters: "My chief motive, to which all the rest are subordinate, is the hope of saving my own soul."[14] William James observes that the "old-fashioned hell-fire Christianity well knew how to extract from fear its full conversion value."[15] As late as the middle of the nineteenth century, General Booth could write: "Nothing moves people like the terrific. They must have hell-fire flashed before their faces, or they will not move."[16] But in that century, at last, a considerable number of Christians began to feel shocked by the ancient doctrine of eternal punishment. Nowadays, according to Dr. Major,[17] the general belief in the English Church is, that "the soul at death passes into the spirit world, and never again has anything to do with its fleshy integument, which has been deposited in the grave"; and a conviction has grown up that heaven and hell are thought of not as localities but as personal states, and that there is every degree of purgatory between them. Dr. Inge does not think that in our own time at any rate self-regarding motives, based on a calculation of future happiness or misery, have much influence.[18] For those who accept the view expressed in the recent Report of the Commission on Christian Doctrine appointed by the English Archbishops, that the essence of hell is merely exclusion from the fellowship of God, there cannot be much fear of it. At the same time acts which originally were prompted by hope or fear may leave behind habits for which there is no longer any such motive. Moreover, sincere devotion to a divine law-giver may lead to a perfectly unselfish desire to obey his will.

As for the doctrine that a man is justified by faith without the deeds of the law, it may be asserted unhesitatingly that it has proved to exercise an evil influence upon the morality of conduct. While to an ecstatic convert like Paul faith may seem a sufficient source of good deeds as its fruits, the faith of the ordinary believer may fail entirely to produce similar effects. It was already found in the Apostolic age that the formula about salvation by faith alone was taken advantage of as a cloak of laxity; it was argued that one may have the true faith, although in this case faith remained dead or was combined with immorality. James evidently saw this danger when he wrote in his epistle: "What doth it profit, my brethren, though a man may say he hath faith, and have not works? can faith save him? . . . Faith without works is dead" [James 2:14]. Ordinary men are not mystics; and ecstatic converts are dangerous founders of religious creeds. The demoralising effect of the teaching of justification by faith was again testified by its revival at the Reformation. There remain a series of painful confessions of disappointment with the moral results of their work on the part of the Reformers themselves. Sometimes the devil is called in to account for so painful and perplexing a state of things. But it is significant that Luther himself does not altogether acquit the doctrine of justification—though in his view misapprehended—of blame in this matter. It may be worth while to repeat the verdict of Harnack, the great Lutheran theologian: "The holding to the 'faith alone' ('fides sola') necessarily resulted in dangerous laxity. What would really have been required here would have been to lead Christians to see that only the 'fides caritate formata' has a real value before God. . . . If one has persuaded himself that everything that suggests 'good works' must be dropped out of the religious sequence, there ultimately remains over only the readiness to subject one's self to faith, *i.e.*, to the pure doctrine. . . . The Lutheran Church had to pay dearly for turning away from 'legal righteousness,' 'sacrifice,' and 'satisfactions.' Through having the resolute wish to go back to *religion* and to it alone, it neglected far too much the moral problem, the 'Be ye holy, for I am holy.'"[19] But the faith which is required for salvation may also in another respect be a danger to morality. The Socinians argued that the doctrine of vicarious suffering blunts the conscience and leads easily to moral slackness. And the doctrine of the vicarious merit of Christ may have a similar effect.[20]

But worse things may be said of the doctrine of justification by faith. In Catholicism the faith required is that recognised by the Catholic Church, which is looked upon as the guarantor of the truth of her doctrines; while the Protestants hold that the faith of their own Church, or at any rate faith in Christ, is necessary for salvation. Even in the case of Christians errors in the belief on such subjects as the Trinity, original sin, and predestination have been declared to expose the guilty to eternal damnation. This led to those terrific persecutions of heretics which occurred on an enormous scale in Catholicism, but also were advocated and practised by Protestants. Luther's intolerance chiefly spends itself in violent words, and he objects to inflicting capital punishment in cases of heresy. Melanchthon was less merciful, and Calvin lays down with great distinctness the duty of repressing heresy by force. And even Zwingli, who once spoke of a heaven in which

Christians may expect to meet the wise and good of heathen antiquity, approved of putting false teachers to death. In England Presbyterians, through a long succession of reigns, were imprisoned, branded, mutilated, scourged, and exposed in pillory; many Catholics under false pretences were tortured and hung; Anabaptists and Arians were burnt alive. When Reformation triumphed in Scotland, one of its first fruits was a law which declared that whoever either said mass, or was present while it was said, should for the first offence lose his goods, for the second offence be exiled, and for the third offence be put to death.

There has been religious persecution outside Christendom, but then there were mostly political reasons for it.[21] In Christianity, too, such reasons have not been wanting. Another reason was greed; and an ecclesiastical motive was undoubtedly that the cohesion and power of the Church depended upon a strict adherence to its doctrines. But the principal reason was undoubtedly the doctrine of exclusive justification by faith. Thus Paul, who before his conversion had been persecuting Christians, became afterwards the indirect cause of religious persecution on an infinitely greater scale. It is significant that the reviver of Paulinism, Augustine, also was the spiritual father of persecution.

The persecutions were by no means ineffective. Before operating in any district the inquisitors used to make a proclamation offering pardon under certain conditions to those who confessed and retracted their heresies within thirty or forty days. We are told that when such a proclamation was made on the first establishment of the Inquisition in Andalusia, 17,000 recantations followed. This was presumably regarded as a triumph of truth; but it was scarcely a triumph of truthfulness. Augustine himself writes that we must avoid the lie, and even when we err in our thought, must always say what we think.

But it is not only by persecutions that the Christian Churches have impaired the spirit of truth. They have also done it by softer means— by inducing the State to make the profession of a certain creed, or at any rate the performance of certain religious rites, a condition of the enjoyment of full civic rights. And this is what even Protestant countries have been doing up to our own time. In the case of the clergy, too, there is considerable inducement to insincerity. Dean Rashdall remarks that the most deadly result of the doctrine of justification by faith is that it has fostered the belief that honest thinking is sinful and blind credulity meritorious.[22] "It deters the clergy from study, from thought, and from openly teaching what they themselves really believe."

The highest regard for truth is not to profess it, but to seek for it. In this respect the Christian Churches have been lamentably deficient. While the knowledge of religious truth has been held to be a necessary requirement of salvation, all other knowledge was for a long time regarded not only as valueless but even as sinful. "The wisdom of this world," says Paul, "is foolishness with God" [1 Cor. 3:19]; and Tertullian expresses the ecclesiastical contempt of scientific knowledge in the famous formula, "I believe because it is impossible."[23] It has been truly said that "there is scarcely a disposition that marks the love of abstract truth, and scarcely a rule which reason teaches as essential for its attainment, that theologians did not for centuries stigmatise as offensive to the Almighty." We are told that Europe was at last rescued from this frightful condition by the intellectual influences that produced the Reformation. This may be true in a manner, but it was not the Reformation itself that marked the change. With Luther reason and faith were deadly enemies: what Scripture imposes upon us was precisely what reason would bid us to reject. "All the articles of our Christian faith," he writes, "which God has revealed to us in his Word are in presence of reason sheerly impossible"; and when his natural reason rebelled against the violence offered to it, the revolt was ascribed to the direct agency of the devil.

The patient and impartial search after hidden truth, for the sake of truth alone, which constitutes the essence of scientific research, is of course the very opposite of that ready acceptance of a revealed truth for the sake of eternal salvation, which has been insisted on by the Churches. Nevertheless we are told, even by highly respectable writers, that the modern world owes its scientific spirit to the extreme importance which Christianity assigned to the possession of truth, of *the* truth. This statement is a curious instance of the common tendency to attribute to the influence of the Christian religion almost any good which may be found among Christian peoples. This is particularly prevalent in the case of morals. It has been claimed that "Christianity has proved itself the highest ethical force in the history of man"; that all virtue and good conduct in mankind owes its origin to the Christian religion; that it has been the main source of the moral development of Europe. I have examined the influence which Christianity has exercised both on morals in general and within various departments of social and moral life, and arrived at different conclusions. It is interesting to note that even a theological writer, like Dr. Inge, says "it is disquieting for Christians to have to admit that the growth of humanity, in the sense of humaneness, does not owe much to the Churches."[24]

My criticism has not been based on any standard of "moral objectivity," because I maintain that there is no such standard, moral judgments being ultimately based upon emotions, which necessarily vary in different individuals. It has been said that Christianity lifts morality out of mere relativity, and that "the Christian point of view gives to conduct an absolute value"; but, as we have seen, there are in Christianity many different points of view. At the same time there are certain general characteristics which belong to the very nature of our moral consciousness and show a considerable uniformity, especially when the moral judgments are guided by sufficient sympathy and intellectual discernment. These have also within Christianity proved to be important correctives of old dogmas. Professor Sasse writes: "For modern Protestantism, as it has been defined by the Age of Enlightenment, the Lamb of God who bears the sins of the world no longer exists at all. . . . Christ has become merely a new law-giver, a second Moses, who left behind him a moral and religious teaching. And then the salvation or damnation of man depends solely upon the obedience or disobedience to these laws."[25] Yet there are also Protestants who still adhere to Luther's anti-moralism.[26] To me it seems that all believers in a righteous God, who has implanted a moral consciousness in the human mind, have to admit that no religious doctrines which conflict with its principles can have a divine revelation as its source.

NOTES

1. [I.e., Hinduism.]

2. See N. Söderblom, *Jesu bärgspredikan och vår tid* (Stockholm, 1899), p. 56 sqq.

3. [Thomas Aquinas (1225?–1274), Dominican philosopher and theologian whose views dominated the Christian Church for centuries.]

4. [The Council of Trent (1545–63) was convened by the Catholic Church to combat the spread of Protestantism in Europe; it became the focal point of the Counter-Reformation.]

5. [Origen (185?–254?), Alexandrian biblical scholar who wrote in Greek.]

6. [*Doctrine in the Church of England: The Report of the Commission on Christian Doctrine Appointed by the Archbishops of Canterbury and York in 1922* (London: Society for Promoting Christian Knowledge, 1938).]

7. [A paraphrase of Gal. 5:6.]

8. [The Lutheran confession of faith, prepared in 1530, mainly by Philipp Melanchthon, but with Martin Luther's approval.]

9. [Ulrich Zwingli (1484–1531), Swiss religious figure and leader of the Reformation in Switzerland.]

10. [John Calvin (1509–1564), French theologian who led the Reformation, largely in the city of Geneva, although his influence extended throughout Europe.]

11. [Adolf Harnack (1851–1930), German church historian and author of *Lehrbuch der Dogmengeschichte* (1886–89; translated as *History of Dogma*) and *Das Wesen des Christentums* (1900; translated as *What Is Christianity?*).]

12. A. C. Underwood, *Conversion: Christian and Non-Christian* (London, 1925), p. 134 sqq.

13. [Jonathan Edwards (1703–1758), American Calvinist theologian who became notorious for his "fire-and-brimstone" sermons. John Wesley (1703–1791), British founder of Methodism.]

14. Wesley, quoted in *The Times Literary Supplement*, May 21, 1938.

15. [William James (1842–1910), *The Varieties of Religious Experience* (1902).]

16. [William Booth (1829–1912), British founder and first "General" of the Salvation Army (1865).]

17. [Henry Dewsbury Alves Major (1871–1961), British theologian and a leading exponent of Modernist theology, which sought to eliminate or downplay the claims of miracles and other supernatural phenomena in Christian doctrine. He was the founder and editor of the influential journal *Modern Churchman* (1911–56).]

18. W. R. Inge, *Christian Ethics and Moral Problems* (London, 1932), p. 74. [William Ralph Inge (1860–1954), dean of St. Paul's and a leading Anglican thinker of his day.]

19. ["Faith formed by charity."]

20. [Socinianism is a religious movement associated with Lelio Francesco Maria Sozini (1525–1562) and his nephew, Fausto Paolo Sozini (1539–1604), who denied the Trinity, the essential divinity of Jesus, and the natural immortality of human beings.]

21. Max Weber, "Die protestantische Ethik und der Geist des Kapitalismus," in *Gesammelte Aufsätze zur Religionssoziologie* (Tübingen, 1922), p. 132 n.

22. [Hastings Rashdall (1858–1924), British theologian and philosopher who taught at Oxford (1888–1917) and delivered the Bampton Lectures for 1915, *The Idea of Atonement in Christian Theology* (1919). He emphasized the role of reason in ascertaining the "truth" of religion.]

23. [See n. 6 to Huxley's "Agnosticism and Christianity."]

24. Inge, op. cit. p. 281.

25. H. Sasse, "Luther and the Teaching of the Reformation," in B. G. Selwyn, *History of Christian Thought* (London, 1937), p. 122.

26. See G. Aulén, "Kravet på dogmhistorisk revision," in *Svensk teologisk kvartalskriff*, ix (Lund, 1933).

Part III.

AGNOSTICISM
AND SCIENCE

HISTORY OF THE CONFLICT BETWEEN RELIGION AND SCIENCE

John William Draper

[John William Draper (1811–1882), American scientist and historian, was born in England, the son of a Methodist minister. He emigrated to the United States in 1832, becoming a professor of chemistry at Hampden-Sydney College in Virginia. He taught at the University of the City of New York (later New York University), helping found its medical college. He wrote numerous treatises on chemistry, physiology, and other subjects, but he then broadened his interests to write *A History of the Intellectual Development of Europe* (1862) and *History of the American Civil War* (1867–70), the first serious study of that conflict. In 1874 he published *History of the Conflict Between Religion and Science*, the first of several works by various writers on this subject in the later nineteenth century. In this work Draper maintained that the history of science is not merely the accumulation of isolated facts but the formation of a worldview opposed to the

John William Draper, "Conflict Respecting the Nature of the World," in *History of the Conflict Between Religion and Science* (1874; repr. London: Watts, 1927), pp. 152–67.

supernaturalism of religion. Although in part marred
by prejudice against the Catholic Church, the work
was immensely popular and retains value today.
Draper later became the first president of the American
Chemistry Society (1876) and a member of the
National Academy of Sciences (1877). In the following, Draper traces the development of an accurate
conception of the universe, established by such
thinkers as Copernicus, Kepler, and Galileo, in the
face of continual opposition from the Church.]

An uncritical observation of the aspect of Nature persuades us
that the earth is an extended level surface which sustains the
dome of the sky, a firmament dividing the waters above from the
waters beneath; that the heavenly bodies—the sun, the moon, the
stars—pursue their way, moving from east to west, their insignificant
size and motion round the motionless earth proclaiming their inferi-
ority. Of the various organic forms surrounding man none rival him in
dignity, and hence he seems justified in concluding that every thing
has been created for his use—the sun for the purpose of giving him
light by day, the moon and stars by night.

Comparative theology shows us that this is the conception of
Nature universally adopted in the early phase of intellectual life. It is
the belief of all nations in all parts of the world in the beginning of
their civilization: geocentric, for it makes the earth the centre of the
universe; anthropocentric, for it makes man the central object of the
earth. And not only is this the conclusion spontaneously come to from
inconsiderate glimpses of the world; it is also the philosophical basis
of various religious revelations, vouchsafed to man from time to time.
These revelations, moreover, declare to him that above the crystalline
dome of the sky is a region of eternal light and happiness—heaven—
the abode of God and the angelic hosts, perhaps also his own abode
after death; and beneath the earth a region of eternal darkness and

misery, the habitation of those that are evil. In the visible world is thus seen a picture of the invisible.

On the basis of this view of the structure of the world great religious systems have been founded, and hence powerful material interests have been engaged in its support. These have resisted, sometimes by resorting to bloodshed, attempts that have been made to correct its incontestable errors—a resistance grounded on the suspicion that the localization of heaven and hell and the supreme value of man in the universe might be affected.

That such attempts would be made was inevitable. As soon as men began to reason on the subject at all, they could not fail to discredit the assertion that the earth is an indefinite plane. No one can doubt that the sun we see to-day is the self-same sun that we saw yesterday. His reappearance each morning irresistibly suggests that he has passed on the underside of the earth. But this is incompatible with the reign of night in those regions. It presents more or less distinctly the idea of the globular form of the earth.

The earth cannot extend indefinitely downward; for the sun cannot go through it, nor through any crevice or passage in it, since he rises and sets in different positions at different seasons of the year. The stars also move under it in countless courses. There must, therefore, be a clear way beneath.

To reconcile revelation with these innovating facts, schemes, such as that of Cosmas Indicopleustes in his Christian Topography,[1] were doubtless often adopted. To this in particular we have had occasion on a former page to refer. It asserted that in the northern parts of the flat earth there is an immense mountain, behind which the sun passes, and thus produces night.

At a very remote historical period the mechanism of eclipses had been discovered. Those of the moon demonstrated that the shadow of the earth is always circular. The form of the earth must therefore be globular. A body which in all positions cast a circular shadow must itself be spherical. Other considerations, with which every one is now familiar, could not fail to establish that such is her figure.

But the determination of the shape of the earth by no means deposed her from her position of superiority. Apparently vastly larger than all other things, it was fitting that she should be considered not merely as the centre of the world, but, in truth, as—the world. All other objects in their aggregate seemed utterly unimportant in comparison with her.

Though the consequences flowing from an admission of the globular figure of the earth affected very profoundly existing theological ideas, they were of much less moment than those depending on a determination of her size. It needed but an elementary knowledge of geometry to perceive that correct ideas on this point could be readily obtained by measuring a degree on her surface. Probably there were early attempts to accomplish this object, the results of which have been lost. But Eratosthenes executed one between Syene and Alexandria, in Egypt, Syene being supposed to be exactly under the tropic of Cancer. The two places are, however, not on the same meridian, and the distance between them was estimated, not measured. Two centuries later Posidonius made another attempt between Alexandria and Rhodes; the bright star Canopus just grazed the horizon at the latter place, at Alexandria it rose 7½°. In this instance, also, since the direction lay across the sea, the distance was estimated, not measured. Finally, as we have already related, the Khalif Al-Mamun made two sets of measures—one on the shore of the Red Sea; the other near Cufa, in Mesopotamia. The general result of these various observations gave for the earth's diameter between seven and eight thousand miles.

This approximate determination of the size of the earth tended to depose her from her dominating position, and gave rise to very serious theological results. In this the ancient investigations of Aristarchus of Samos, one of the Alexandrian school, 280 B.C., powerfully aided. In his treatise on the magnitudes and distances of the sun and moon he explains the ingenious though imperfect method to which he had resorted for the solution of that problem. Many ages previously a speculation had been brought from India to Europe by Pythagoras. It presented the sun as the centre of the system. Around him the planets revolved in circular orbits, their order of position being Mercury,

Venus, Earth, Mars, Jupiter, Saturn, each of them being supposed to rotate on its axis as it revolved round the sun. According to Cicero, Nicetas suggested that, if it were admitted that the earth revolves on her axis, the difficulty presented by the inconceivable velocity of the heavens would be avoided.

There is reason to believe that the works of Aristarchus, in the Alexandrian Library, were burnt at the time of the fire of Caesar. The only treatise of his that has come down to us is that above mentioned, on the size and distance of the sun and moon.

Aristarchus adopted the Pythagorean system as representing the actual facts. This was the result of a recognition of the sun's amazing distance, and therefore of his enormous size. The heliocentric system, thus regarding the sun as the central orb, degraded the earth to a very subordinate rank, making her only one of a company of six revolving bodies.

But this is not the only contribution conferred on astronomy by Aristarchus, for, considering that the movement of the earth does not sensibly affect the apparent position of the stars, he inferred that they are incomparably more distant from us than the sun. He, therefore, of all the ancients, as Laplace remarks, had the most correct ideas of the grandeur of the universe. He saw that the earth is of absolutely insignificant size, when compared with the stellar distances. He saw, too, that there is nothing above us but space and stars.

But the views of Aristarchus, as respects the emplacement of the planetary bodies, were not accepted by antiquity; the system proposed by Ptolemy, and incorporated in his *Syntaxis*, was universally preferred. The physical philosophy of those times was very imperfect, one of Ptolemy's objections to the Pythagorean system being that, if the earth were in motion, it would leave the air and other light bodies behind it. He therefore placed the earth in the central position, and in succession revolved round her the Moon, Mercury, Venus, the Sun, Mars, Jupiter, Saturn; beyond the orbit of Saturn came the firmament of the fixed stars. As to the solid crystalline spheres, one moving from east to west, the other from north to south, these were a fancy of Eudoxus, to which Ptolemy does not allude.

The Ptolemaic system is, therefore, essentially a geocentric system. It left the earth in her position of superiority, and hence gave no cause of umbrage to religious opinions, Christian or Mohammedan. The immense reputation of its author, the signal ability of his great work on the mechanism of the heavens, sustained it for almost fourteen hundred years—that is, from the second to the sixteenth century.

In Christendom the greater part of this long period was consumed in disputes respecting the nature of God, and in struggles for ecclesiastical power. The authority of the Fathers, and the prevailing belief that the Scriptures contain the sum of all knowledge, discouraged any investigation of Nature. If by chance a passing interest was taken in some astronomical question, it was at once settled by a reference to such authorities as the writings of Augustine or Lactantius, not by an appeal to the phenomena of the heavens. So great was the preference given to sacred over profane learning that Christianity had been in existence fifteen hundred years, and had not produced a single astronomer.

The Mohammedan nations did much better. Their cultivation of science dates from the capture of Alexandria, A.D. 638. This was only six years after the death of the Prophet. In less than two centuries they had not only become acquainted with, but correctly appreciated, the Greek scientific writers. As we have already mentioned, by his treaty with Michael III, the Khalif Al-Mamun had obtained a copy of the *Syntaxis* of Ptolemy. He had it forthwith translated into Arabic. It became at once the great authority of Saracen astronomy. From this basis the Saracens had advanced to the solution of some of the most important scientific problems. They had ascertained the dimensions of the earth; they had registered or catalogued all the stars visible in their heavens, giving to those of the larger magnitudes the names they still bear on our maps and globes; they determined the true length of the year, discovered astronomical refraction, invented the pendulum-clock, improved the photometry of the stars, ascertained the curvilinear path of a ray of light through the air, explained the phenomena of the horizontal sun and moon, and why we see those bodies before they have risen and after they have set; measured the height of the atmosphere, determining it to be fifty-eight miles; given the true theory of the twilight, and of the twinkling of the stars. They had built the first observatory in Europe. So accurate were they in their observations that the ablest modern mathematicians have made use of their results. Thus Laplace, in his *Système du Monde*,[2] adduces the observations of Al-Batagni as affording incontestable proof of the diminution of the eccentricity of the earth's orbit. He uses those of Ibn-Junis in his discussion of the obliquity of the ecliptic, and also in the case of the problems of the greater inequalities of Jupiter and Saturn.

These represent but a part, and indeed but a small part, of the services rendered by the Arabian astronomers in the solution of the problem of the nature of the world. Meanwhile, such was the benighted condition of Christendom, such its deplorable ignorance, that it cared nothing about the matter. Its attention was engrossed by image-worship, transubstantiation, the merits of the saints, miracles, shrine-cures.

This indifference continued until the close of the fifteenth century. Even then there was no scientific inducement. The inciting motives were altogether of a different kind. They originated in commercial rivalries, and the question of the shape of the earth was finally settled by three sailors—Columbus, De Gama, and, above all, by Ferdinand Magellan.

The trade of Eastern Asia has always been a source of immense wealth to the Western nations who in succession have obtained it. In the middle ages it had centred in Upper Italy. It was conducted along two lines—a northern, by way of the Black and Caspian Seas, and camel-caravans beyond—the headquarters of this were at Genoa; and a southern, through the Syrian and Egyptian ports, and by the Arabian Sea, the headquarters of this being at Venice. The merchants engaged in the latter traffic had also made great gains in the transport service of the Crusade-wars.

The Venetians had managed to maintain amicable relations with the Mohammedan powers of Syria and Egypt; they were permitted to have consulates at Alexandria and Damascus, and, notwithstanding the military commotions of which those countries had been the scene, the trade was still maintained in a comparatively flourishing condition. But the northern or Genoese line had been completely broken up by the irruptions of the Tartars and the Turks, and the military and political disturbances of the countries through which it passed. The Eastern trade of Genoa was not merely in a precarious condition; it was on the brink of destruction.

The circular visible horizon and its dip at sea, the gradual appearance and disappearance of ships in the offing, cannot fail to incline intelligent sailors to a belief in the globular figure of the earth. The writings of the Mohammedan astronomers and philosophers had given currency to that doctrine throughout Western Europe; but, as might be expected, it was received with disfavour by theologians. When Genoa was thus on the very brink of ruin, it occurred to some of her mariners that, if this view were correct, her affairs might be re-established. A ship sailing through the straits of Gibraltar westward, across the Atlantic, would not fail to reach the East Indies. There were apparently other great advantages. Heavy cargoes might be transported without tedious and expensive land-carriage, and without breaking bulk.

Among the Genoese sailors who entertained these views was Christopher Columbus.

He tells us that his attention was drawn to this subject by the writings of Averroes; but among his friends he numbered Toscanelli, a Florentine, who had turned his attention to astronomy, and had become a strong advocate of the globular form. In Genoa itself Columbus met with but little encouragement. He then spent many years in trying to interest different princes in his proposed attempt. Its irreligious tendency was pointed out by the Spanish ecclesiastics, and condemned by the Council of Salamanca; its orthodoxy was confuted from the Pentateuch, the Psalms, the Prophecies, the Gospels, the Epistles, and the writings of the Fathers—St. Chrysostom, St. Augustine, St. Jerome, St. Gregory, St. Basil, St. Ambrose.

At length, however, encouraged by the Spanish Queen Isabella, and substantially aided by a wealthy seafaring family, the Pinzons of

Palos, some of whom joined him personally, he sailed on August 3, 1492, with three small ships, from Palos, carrying with him a letter from King Ferdinand to the Grand-Khan of Tartary, and also a chart, or map, constructed on the basis of that of Toscanelli. A little before midnight, October 11, 1492, he saw from the forecastle of his ship a moving light at a distance. Two hours subsequently a signal-gun from another of the ships announced that they had descried land. At sunrise Columbus landed in the New World.

On his return to Europe it was universally supposed that he had reached the eastern parts of Asia, and that therefore his voyage had been theoretically successful. Columbus himself died in that belief. But numerous voyages which were soon undertaken made known the general contour of the American coast-line, and the discovery of the Great South Sea by Balboa revealed at length the true facts of the case, and the mistake into which both Toscanelli and Columbus had fallen, that in a voyage to the West the distance from Europe to Asia could not exceed the distance passed over in a voyage from Italy to the Gulf of Guinea—a voyage that Columbus had repeatedly made.

In his first voyage, at nightfall on September 13, 1492, being then two and a half degrees east of Corvo, one of the Azores, Columbus observed that the compass needles of the ships no longer pointed a little to the east of north, but were varying to the west. The deviation became more and more marked as the expedition advanced. He was not the first to detect the fact of variation, but he was incontestably the first to discover the line of no variation. On the return voyage the reverse was observed; the variation westward diminished until the meridian in question was reached, when the needles again pointed due north. Thence, as the coast of Europe was approached, the variation was to the east. Columbus, therefore, came to the conclusion that the line of no variation was a fixed geographical line, or boundary, between the Eastern and Western Hemispheres. In the bull of May, 1493, Pope Alexander VI accordingly adopted this line as the perpetual boundary between the possessions of Spain and Portugal, in his settlement of the disputes of those nations. Subsequently, however, it was discovered that the line was moving eastward. It coincided with the meridian of London in 1662.

By the papal bull the Portuguese possessions were limited to the east of the line of no variation. Information derived from certain Egyptian Jews had reached that government that it was possible to sail round the continent of Africa, there being at its extreme south a cape which could be easily doubled. An expedition of three ships under Vasco de Gama set sail, July 9, 1497; it doubled the cape on November 20th, and reached Calicut, on the coast of India, May 19, 1498. Under the bull, this voyage to the East gave to the Portuguese the right to the India trade.

Until the cape was doubled, the course of De Gama's ships was in a general manner southward. Very soon it was noticed that the elevation of the pole-star above the horizon was diminishing, and soon after the equator was reached that star had ceased to be visible. Meantime other stars, some of them forming magnificent constellations, had come into view—the stars of the Southern Hemisphere. All this was in conformity to theoretical expectations founded on the admission of the globular form of the earth.

The political consequences that at once ensued placed the Papal Government in a position of great embarrassment. Its traditions and policy forbade it to admit any other than the flat figure of the earth, as revealed in the Scriptures. Concealment of the facts was impossible; sophistry was unavailing. Commercial prosperity now left Venice as well as Genoa. The front of Europe was changed. Maritime power had departed from the Mediterranean countries, and passed to those upon the Atlantic coast.

But the Spanish Government did not submit to the advantage thus gained by its commercial rival without an effort. It listened to the representations of one Ferdinand Magellan, that India and the Spice Islands could be reached by sailing to the west, if only a strait or passage through what had now been recognized as "the American Continent" could be discovered; and, if this should be accomplished, Spain, under the papal bull, would have as good a right to the India trade as

Portugal. Under the command of Magellan, an expedition of five ships, carrying two hundred and thirty-seven men, was dispatched, from Seville, August 10, 1519.

Magellan at once struck boldly for the South American coast, hoping to find some cleft or passage through the continent by which he might reach the great South Sea. For seventy days he was becalmed on the line; his sailors were appalled by the apprehension that they had drifted into a region where the winds never blew and that it was impossible for them to escape. Calms, tempests, mutiny, desertion, could not shake his resolution. After more than a year he discovered the strait which now bears his name, and, as Pigafetti, an Italian, who was with him, relates, he shed tears of joy when he found that it had pleased God at length to bring him where he might grapple with the unknown dangers of the South Sea, "the Great and Pacific Ocean."

Driven by famine to eat scraps of skin and leather with which his rigging was here and there bound, to drink water that had gone putrid, his crew dying of hunger and scurvy, this man, firm in his belief of the globular figure of the earth, steered steadily to the north-west, and for nearly four months never saw inhabited land. He estimated that he had sailed over the Pacific not less than twelve thousand miles. He crossed the equator, saw once more the pole-star, and at length made land— the Ladrones. Here he met with adventurers from Sumatra. Among these islands he was killed, either by the savages or by his own men. His lieutenant, Sebastian d'Elcano, now took command of the ship, directing her course for the Cape of Good Hope, and encountering frightful hardships. He doubled the cape at last, and then for the fourth time crossed the equator. On September 7, 1522, after a voyage of more than three years, he brought his ship, the *San Vittoria*, to anchor in the port of St. Lucar, near Seville. She had accomplished the greatest achievement in the history of the human race. She had circumnavigated the earth.

The *San Vittoria*, sailing westward, had come back to her starting-point. Henceforth the theological doctrine of the flatness of the earth was irretrievably overthrown.

Five years after the completion of the voyage of Magellan, was made the first attempt in Christendom to ascertain the size of the earth. This was by Fernel,[3] a French physician, who, having observed the height of the pole at Paris, went thence northward until he came to a place where the height of the pole was exactly one degree more than at that city. He measured the distance between the two stations by the number of revolutions of one of the wheels of his carriage, to which a proper indicator had been attached, and came to the conclusion that the earth's circumference is about twenty-four thousand four hundred and eighty Italian miles.

Measures executed more and more carefully were made in many countries: by Snell in Holland; by Norwood between London and York in England; by Picard, under the auspices of the French Academy of Sciences, in France.[4] Picard's plan was to connect two points by a series of triangles, and, thus ascertaining the length of the arc of a meridian intercepted between them, to compare it with the difference of latitudes found from celestial observations. The stations were Malvoisine in the vicinity of Paris, and Sourdon near Amiens. The difference of latitudes was determined by observing the zenith-distances of δ Cassiopeia. There are two points of interest connected with Picard's operation: it was the first in which instruments furnished with telescopes were employed; and its result, as we shall shortly see, was to Newton the first confirmation of the theory of universal gravitation.

At this time it had become clear from mechanical considerations, more especially such as had been deduced by Newton, that, since the earth is a rotating body, her form cannot be that of a perfect sphere, but must be that of a spheroid, oblate or flattened at the poles. It would follow, from this, that the length of a degree must be greater near the poles than at the equator.

The French Academy resolved to extend Picard's operation, by prolonging the measures in each direction, and making the result the basis of a more accurate map of France. Delays, however, took place, and it was not until 1718 that the measures, from Dunkirk on the north to the southern extremity of France, were completed. A discussion arose as to the interpretation of these measures, some affirming that they indicated a prolate, others an oblate spheroid. The former figure may be popularly represented by a lemon; the latter by an orange. To settle this, the French Government, aided by the Academy, sent out two expeditions to measure degrees of the meridian—one under the equator, the other as far north as possible; the former went to Peru, the latter to Swedish Lapland. Very great difficulties were encountered by both parties. The Lapland commission, however, completed its observations long before the Peruvian, which consumed not less than nine years. The results of the measures thus obtained confirmed the theoretical expectation of the oblate form. Since that time many extensive and exact repetitions of the observation have been made, among which may be mentioned those of the English in England and in India, and particularly that of the French on the occasion of the introduction of the metric system of weights and measures. It was begun by Delambre and Mechain, from Dunkirk to Barcelona, and thence extended, by Biot and Arago, to the island of Formentera near Minorca.[5] Its length was nearly twelve and a half degrees.

Besides this method of direct measurement, the figure of the earth may be determined from the observed number of oscillations made by a pendulum of invariable length in different latitudes. These, though they confirm the foregoing results, give a somewhat greater ellipticity to the earth than that found by the measurement of degrees. Pendulums vibrate more slowly the nearer they are to the equator. It follows, therefore, that they are there farther from the centre of the earth. From the most reliable measures that have been made, the dimensions of the earth may be thus stated:—

Greater or equatorial diameter	7,925	miles
Less or polar diameter	7,899	"
Difference or polar compression	26	"

Such was the result of the discussion respecting the figure and size of the earth. While it was yet undetermined, another controversy arose, fraught with even more serious consequences. This was the conflict respecting the earth's position with regard to the sun and the planetary bodies.

Copernicus, a Prussian, about the year 1507, had completed a book "On the Revolutions of the Heavenly Bodies." He had journeyed to Italy in his youth, had devoted his attention to astronomy, and had taught mathematics at Rome. From a profound study of the Ptolemaic and Pythagorean systems, he had come to a conclusion in favour of the latter, the object of his book being to sustain it. Aware that his doctrines were totally opposed to revealed truth, and foreseeing that they would bring upon him the punishments of the Church, he expressed himself in a cautious and apologetic manner, saying that he had only taken the liberty of trying whether, on the supposition of the earth's motion, it was possible to find better explanations than the ancient ones of the revolutions of the celestial orbs; that in doing this he had only taken the privilege that had been allowed to others, of feigning what hypothesis they chose. The preface was addressed to Pope Paul III.

Full of misgivings as to what might be the result, he refrained from publishing his book for thirty-six years, thinking that "perhaps it might be better to follow the examples of the Pythagoreans and others, who delivered their doctrine only by tradition and to friends." At the entreaty of Cardinal Schomberg he at length published it in 1543. A copy of it was brought to him on his death-bed. Its fate was such as he had anticipated. The Inquisition condemned it as heretical. In their decree, prohibiting it, the Congregation of the Index denounced his system as "that false Pythagorean doctrine utterly contrary to the Holy Scriptures."

Astronomers justly affirm that the book of Copernicus, *De Revolutionibus*, changed the face of their science. It incontestably established the heliocentric theory. It showed that the distance of the fixed stars is infinitely great, and that the earth is a mere point in the heavens. Anticipating Newton, Copernicus imputed gravity to the sun, the moon, and heavenly bodies; but he was led astray by assuming that the celestial motions must be circular. Observations on the orbit of

Mars, and his different diameters at different times, had led Copernicus to his theory.

In thus denouncing the Copernican system as being in contradiction to revelation, the ecclesiastical authorities were doubtless deeply moved by inferential considerations. To dethrone the earth from her central dominating position, to give her many equals and not a few superiors, seemed to diminish her claims upon the Divine regard. If each of the countless myriads of stars was a sun, surrounded by revolving globes, peopled with responsible beings like ourselves, if we had fallen so easily and had been redeemed at so stupendous a price as the death of the Son of God, how was it with them? Of them were there none who had fallen or might fall like us? Where, then, for them could a Saviour be found?

During the year 1608 one Lippershey, a Hollander, discovered that by looking through two glass lenses, combined in a certain manner together, distant objects were magnified and rendered very plain. He had invented the telescope. In the following year Galileo, a Florentine, greatly distinguished by his mathematical and scientific writings, hearing of the circumstance, but without knowing the particulars of the construction, invented a form of the instrument for himself. Improving it gradually, he succeeded in making one that could magnify thirty times. Examining the moon, he found that she had valleys like those of the earth, and mountains casting shadows. It had been said in the old times that in the Pleiades there were formerly seven stars, but a legend related that one of them had mysteriously disappeared. On turning his telescope toward them, Galileo found that he could easily count not fewer than forty. In whatever direction he looked, he discovered stars that were totally invisible to the naked eye.

On the night of January 7, 1610, he perceived three small stars in a straight line, adjacent to the planet Jupiter, and, a few evenings later, a fourth. He found that these were revolving in orbits round the body of the planet, and, with transport, recognized that they presented a miniature representation of the Copernican system.

The announcement of these wonders at once attracted universal attention. The spiritual authorities were not slow to detect their tendency, as endangering the doctrine that the universe was made for man. In the creation of myriads of stars, hitherto invisible, there must surely have been some other motive than that of illuminating the nights for him.

It had been objected to the Copernican theory that, if the planets Mercury and Venus move round the sun in orbits interior to that of the earth, they ought to show phases like those of the moon; and that in the case of Venus, which is so brilliant and conspicuous, these phases should be very obvious. Copernicus himself had admitted the force of the objection, and had vainly tried to find an explanation. Galileo, on turning his telescope to the planet, discovered that the expected phases actually exist; now she was a crescent, then half-moon, then gibbous, then full. Previously to Copernicus, it was supposed that the planets shine by their own light, but the phases of Venus and Mars proved that their light is reflected. The Aristotelian notion, that celestial differ from terrestrial bodies in being incorruptible, received a rude shock from the discoveries of Galileo, that there are mountains and valleys in the moon like those of the earth, that the sun is not perfect, but has spots on his face, and that he turns on his axis instead of being in a state of majestic rest. The apparition of new stars had already thrown serious doubts on this theory of incorruptibility.

These and many other beautiful telescopic discoveries tended to the establishment of the truth of the Copernican theory, and gave unbounded alarm to the Church. By the low and ignorant ecclesiastics they were denounced as deceptions or frauds. Some affirmed that the telescope might be relied on well enough for terrestrial objects, but with the heavenly bodies it was altogether a different affair. Others declared that its invention was a mere application of Aristotle's remark that stars could be seen in the daytime from the bottom of a deep well. Galileo was accused of imposture, heresy, blasphemy, atheism. With a view of defending himself, he addressed a letter to the Abbé Castelli, suggesting that the Scriptures were never intended to be a scientific authority, but only a moral guide. This made matters worse. He was summoned before the Holy Inquisition, under an accusation of having taught that the earth moves round the sun—a doctrine "utterly contrary to the Scriptures." He was ordered to renounce that heresy, on pain of being imprisoned. He was directed to desist from teaching and advocating the Copernican theory, and pledge himself that he would neither publish nor defend it for the future. Knowing well that Truth has no need of martyrs, he assented to the required recantation, and gave the promise demanded.

For sixteen years the Church had rest. But in 1632 Galileo ventured on the publication of his work entitled *The System of the World*, its object being the vindication of the Copernican doctrine. He was again summoned before the Inquisition at Rome, accused of having asserted that the earth moves round the sun. He was declared to have brought upon himself the penalties of heresy. On his knees, with his hand on the Bible, he was compelled to abjure and curse the doctrine of the movement of the earth. What a spectacle! This venerable man, the most illustrious of his age, forced by the threat of death to deny facts which his judges as well as himself knew to be true! He was then committed to prison, treated with remorseless severity during the remaining ten years of his life, and was denied burial in consecrated ground. Must not that be false which requires for its support so much imposture, so much barbarity? The opinions thus defended by the Inquisition are now objects of derision to the whole civilized world.

One of the greatest of modern mathematicians, referring to this subject, says that the point here contested was one which is for mankind of the highest interest, because of the rank it assigns to the globe that we inhabit. If the earth be immovable in the midst of the universe, man has a right to regard himself as the principal object of the care of Nature. But if the earth be only one of the planets revolving round the sun, an insignificant body in the solar system, she will disappear entirely in the immensity of the heavens, in which this system, vast as it may appear to us, is nothing but an insensible point.

The triumphant establishment of the Copernican doctrine dates from the invention of the telescope. Soon there was not to be found in all Europe an astronomer who had not accepted the heliocentric theory with its essential postulate, the double motion of the earth—a movement of rotation on her axis, and a movement of revolution round the sun. If additional proof of the latter were needed, it was furnished by Bradley's great discovery of the aberration of the fixed stars[6]—an aberration depending partly on the progressive motion of light, and partly on the revolution of the earth. Bradley's discovery ranked in importance with that of the precession of the equinoxes, Roemer's discovery of the progressive motion of light, though denounced by Fontenelle as a seductive error, and not admitted by Cassini, at length forced its way to universal acceptance.[7]

Next it was necessary to obtain correct ideas of the dimensions of the solar system, or, putting the problem under a more limited form, to determine the distance of the earth from the sun.

In the time of Copernicus it was supposed that the sun's distance could not exceed five million miles, and indeed there were many who thought that estimate very extravagant. From a review of the observations of Tycho Brahe, Kepler, however, concluded that the error was actually in the opposite direction, and that the estimate must be raised to at least thirteen million. In 1670 Cassini showed that these numbers were altogether inconsistent with the facts, and gave as his conclusion eighty-five million.

The transit of Venus over the face of the sun, June 3, 1769, had been foreseen, and its great value in the solution of this fundamental problem in astronomy appreciated. With commendable alacrity various governments contributed their assistance in making observations, so that in Europe there were fifty stations, in Asia six, in America seventeen. It was for this purpose that the English Government dispatched Captain Cook on his celebrated first voyage. He went to Otaheite.[8] His voyage was crowned with success. The sun rose without a cloud, and the sky continued equally clear throughout the day. The transit at Cook's station lasted from about half-past nine in the morning until about half-past three in the afternoon, and all the observations were made in a satisfactory manner.

But, on the discussion of the observations made at the different stations, it was found that there was not the accordance that could have been desired—the result varying from eighty-eight to one hundred and nine million. The celebrated mathematician, Encke,[9] therefore reviewed them in 1822–'24, and came to the conclusion that the sun's horizontal parallax—that is, the angle under which the semi-diameter of the earth is seen from the sun—is 8 576/1000 seconds; this gave as the distance 95,274,000 miles. Subsequently the observations were reconsidered by Hansen,[10] who gave as their result 91,659,000 miles. Still later Leverrier made it 91,750,000.[11] Airy and Stone,[12] by another method, made it 91,400,000; Stone alone, by a revision of the old observations, 91,730,000; and finally, Foucault and Fizeau,[13] from physical experiments, determining the velocity of light, and therefore in their nature altogether differing from transit observations, 91,400,000. Until the results of the transit of next year (1874) are ascertained, it must therefore be admitted that the distance of the earth from the sun is somewhat less than ninety-two million miles.

This distance once determined, the dimensions of the solar system may be ascertained with ease and precision. It is enough to mention that the distance of Neptune from the sun, the most remote of the planets at present known, is about thirty times that of the earth.

By the aid of these numbers we may begin to gain a just appreciation of the doctrine of the human destiny of the universe—the doctrine that all things were made for man. Seen from the sun, the earth dwindles away to a mere speck, a mere dust-mote glistening in his beams. If the reader wishes a more precise valuation, let him hold a page of this book a couple of feet from his eye; then let him consider one of its dots or full-stops; that dot is several hundred times larger in surface than is the earth as seen from the sun!

Of what consequence, then, can such an almost imperceptible particle be? One might think that it could be removed or even annihilated, and yet never be missed. Of what consequence is one of those human monads, of whom more than a thousand millions swarm on the surface of this all but invisible speck, and of a million of whom scarcely one will leave a trace that he has ever existed? Of what consequence is man, his pleasures or his pains?

Among the arguments brought forward against the Copernican system at the time of its promulgation, was one by the great Danish astronomer, Tycho Brahe, originally urged by Aristarchus against the Pythagorean system, to the effect that, if, as was alleged, the earth moves round the sun, there ought to be a change of the direction in which the fixed stars appear. At one time we are nearer to a particular region of the heavens by a distance equal to the whole diameter of the earth's orbit than we were six months previously, and hence there ought to be a change in the relative position of the stars. They should seem to separate as we approach them, and to close together as we recede from them; or, to use the astronomical expression, these stars should have a yearly parallax.

The parallax of a star is the angle contained between two lines drawn from it—one to the sun, the other to the earth.

At that time the earth's distance from the sun was greatly under-estimated. Had it been known, as it is now, that that distance exceeds ninety million miles or that the diameter of the orbit is more than one hundred and eighty million, that argument would doubtless have had very great weight.

In reply to Tycho, it was said that, since the parallax of a body diminishes as its distance increases, a star may be so far off that its parallax may be imperceptible. This answer proved to be correct. The detection of the parallax of the stars depended on the improvement of instruments for the measurement of angles.

The parallax of α Centauri, a fine double star of the Southern Hemisphere, at present considered to be the nearest of the fixed stars, was first determined by Henderson and Maclear at the Cape of Good Hope in 1832–'33.[14] It is about nine-tenths of a second. Hence this star is almost two hundred and thirty thousand times as far from us as the sun. Seen from it, if the sun were even large enough to fill the whole orbit of the earth, or one hundred and eighty million miles in diameter, he would be a mere point. With its companion, it revolves round their common centre of gravity in eighty-one years, and hence it would seem that their conjoint mass is less than that of the sun.

The star 61 Cygni is of the sixth magnitude. Its parallax was first found by Bessel in 1838,[15] and is about one-third of a second. The distance from us is, therefore, much more than five hundred thousand times that of the sun. With its companion, it revolves round their common centre of gravity in five hundred and twenty years. Their conjoint weight is about one-third that of the sun.

There is reason to believe that the great star Sirius, the brightest in the heavens, is about six times as far off as α Centauri. His probable diameter is twelve million miles, and the light he emits two hundred times more brilliant than that of the sun. Yet, even through the telescope, he has no measurable diameter; he looks merely like a very bright spark.

The stars, then, differ not merely in visible magnitude, but also in actual size. As the spectroscope shows, they differ greatly in chemical and physical constitution. That instrument is also revealing to us the duration of the life of a star, through changes in the refrangibility of the emitted light. Though, as we have seen, the nearest to us is at an enormous and all but immeasurable distance, this is but the first step—there are others the rays of which have taken thousands, perhaps millions, of years to reach us! The limits of our own system are far beyond the range of our greatest telescopes; what, then, shall we say of other systems beyond? Worlds are scattered like dust in the abysses in space.

Have these gigantic bodies—myriads of which are placed at so vast a distance that our unassisted eyes cannot perceive them—have these no other purpose than that assigned by theologians, to give light to us? Does not their enormous size demonstrate that, as they are centres of force, so they must be centres of motion—suns for other systems of worlds?

While yet these facts were very imperfectly known—indeed, were rather speculations than facts—Giordano Bruno, an Italian, born seven years after the death of Copernicus, published a work on the *Infinity of the Universe and of Worlds*. He was also the author of *Evening Con-*

versations on Ash-Wednesday, an apology for the Copernican system, and of *The One Sole Cause of Things*. To these may be added an allegory published in 1584, *The Expulsion of the Triumphant Beast*. He had also collected, for the use of future astronomers, all the observations he could find respecting the new star that suddenly appeared in Cassiopeia, A.D. 1572, and increased in brilliancy, until it surpassed all the other stars. It could be plainly seen in the daytime. On a sudden, November fifth, it was as bright as Venus at her brightest. In the following March it was of the first magnitude. It exhibited various hues of colour in a few months, and disappeared in March, 1574.

The star that suddenly appeared in Serpentarius, in Kepler's time (1604), was at first brighter than Venus. It lasted more than a year, and, passing through various tints of purple, yellow, red, became extinguished.

Originally Bruno was intended for the Church. He had become a Dominican, but was led into doubt by his meditations on the subjects of transubstantiation and the immaculate conception. Not caring to conceal his opinions, he soon fell under the censure of the spiritual authorities, and found it necessary to seek refuge successively in Switzerland, France, England, Germany. The cold-scented sleuthhounds of the Inquisition followed his track remorselessly, and eventually hunted him back to Italy. He was arrested in Venice, and confined in the Piombi for six years, without books, or paper, or friends.

In England he had given lectures on the plurality of worlds, and in that country had written, in Italian, his most important works. It added not a little to the exasperation against him that he was perpetually declaiming against the insincerity, the impostures, of his persecutors—that wherever he went he found scepticism varnished over and concealed by hypocrisy; and that it was not against the belief of men, but against their pretended belief, that he was fighting; that he was struggling with an orthodoxy that had neither morality nor faith.

In his *Evening Conversations* he had insisted that the Scriptures were never intended to teach science, but morals only—and that they cannot be received as of any authority on astronomical and physical subjects. Especially must we reject the view they reveal to us of the constitution of the world; that the earth is a flat surface, supported on pillars; that the sky is a firmament—the floor of heaven. On the contrary, we must believe that the universe is infinite, and that it is filled with self-luminous and opaque worlds, many of them inhabited; that there is nothing above and around us but space and stars. His meditations on these subjects had brought him to the conclusion that the views of Averroes are not far from the truth—that there is an Intellect which animates the universe, and of this Intellect the visible world is only an emanation or manifestation, originated and sustained by force derived from it; and, were that force withdrawn, all things would disappear. This ever-present, all-pervading Intellect is God, who lives in all things, even such as seem not to live; that every thing is ready to become organized, to burst into life. God is, therefore, "the One Sole Cause of Things," "the All in All."

Bruno may hence be considered among philosophical writers as intermediate between Averroes and Spinoza. The latter held that God and the Universe are the same—that all events happen by an immutable law of Nature by an unconquerable necessity; that God is the Universe, producing a series of necessary movements or acts, in consequence of intrinsic, unchangeable, and irresistible energy.

On the demand of the spiritual authorities, Bruno was removed from Venice to Rome, and confined in the prison of the Inquisition, accused not only of being a heretic, but also a heresiarch, who had written things unseemly concerning religion; the special charge against him being that he had taught the plurality of worlds, a doctrine repugnant to the whole tenour of Scripture and inimical to revealed religion, especially as regards the plan of salvation. After an imprisonment of two years he was brought before his judges, declared guilty of the acts alleged, excommunicated, and on his nobly refusing to recant, was delivered over to the secular authorities to be punished "as mercifully as possible, and without the shedding of his blood," the horrible formula for burning a prisoner at the stake. Knowing well that, though his tormentors might destroy his body, his thoughts would still live among men, he said to his judges: "Perhaps it is with greater fear that you pass the sentence upon me than I receive it." The sentence was carried into effect, and he was burnt at Rome, February 16th, A.D. 1600.

No one can recall without sentiments of pity the sufferings of those countless martyrs, who first by one party, and then by another, have been brought for their religious opinions to the stake. But each of these had in his supreme moment a powerful and unfailing support. The passage from this life to the next, though through a hard trial, was the passage from a transient trouble to eternal happiness—an escape from the cruelty of earth to the charity of heaven. On his way through the dark valley the martyr believed that there was an invisible hand that would lead him, a friend that would guide him all the more gently and firmly because of the terrors of the flames. For Bruno there was no such support. The philosophical opinions, for the sake of which he surrendered his life, could give him no consolation. He must fight the last fight alone. Is there not something very grand in the attitude of this solitary man, something which human nature cannot help admiring, as he stands in the gloomy hall before his inexorable judges? No accuser, no witness, no advocate is present; but the familiars of the Holy Office, clad in black, are stealthily moving about. The tormentors and the rack are in the vaults below. He is simply told that he has brought upon himself strong suspicions of heresy, since he has said that there are other worlds than ours. He is asked if he will recant and abjure his error. He cannot and will not deny what he knows to be true, and per- haps—for he had often done so before—he tells his judges that they, too, in their hearts are of the same belief. What a contrast between this scene of manly honour, of unshaken firmness, of inflexible adherence to the truth, and that other scene which took place more than fifteen centuries previously by the fireside in the hall of Caiaphas, the high- priest, when the cock crew, and "the Lord turned and looked upon Peter" (Luke xxii. 61)! And yet it is upon Peter that the Church has grounded her right to act as she did to Bruno.

But perhaps the day approaches when posterity will offer an expi- ation for this great ecclesiastical crime, and a statue of Bruno be unveiled under the dome of St. Peter's at Rome.

NOTES

1. [Cosmas Indicopleustes (whose name means "Cosmas the Indian navigator"), Alexandrian monk and author of a *Christian Topography* (c. 547), which attacked the Ptolemaic system as inconsistent with a literal reading of the Bible.]

2. [Pierre Simon, marquis de Laplace (1749–1827), French astronomer and author of the *Exposition du système du monde* (1796), which propounded the nebular hypothesis that dominated astronomical thought until the 20th century.]

3. [Jean François Fernel (1497?–1558), French physician. His theories on the size of the earth are found in his *Cosmotheoria* (1528).]

4. [Willebrod Snel (1580–1626), Dutch mathematician and astronomer. Richard Norwood (1590–1665), British mathematician and surveyor. Jean Picard (1620–1682), French astronomer and author of *La Mesure de la terre* (1671).]

5. [Jean-Baptiste Joseph Delambre (1749–1822), French astronomer. Pierre-François-André Méchain (1744–1804), French astronomer. Jean-Baptiste Biot (1774–1862), French physicist. Dominique François Jean Arago (1786–1853), French physicist and astronomer.]

6. [James Bradley (1693–1762), British astronomer.]

7. [Ole Christensen Römer (1644–1710), Danish astronomer. Bernard le Bouyer Fontenelle (1657–1757), French mathematician and philosopher. Gian Domenico Cassini (1625–1712), Italian astronomer.]

8. [I.e., Tahiti.]

9. [Johann Franz Encke (1791–1865), German astronomer.]

10. [Peter Andreas Hansen (1795–1874), German astronomer.]

11. [Urbain Jean Joseph Le Verrier (1811–1877), French astronomer and meteorologist.]

12. [The British astronomers George Biddell Airy (1801–1892) and Edward James Stone (1831–1897).]

13. [The French physicists Jean Bernard Léon Foucault (1819–1868) and Armand-Hippolyte-Louis Fizeau (1819–1896).]

14. [Draper refers to the Scottish astronomers Thomas Henderson (1798–1844) and Thomas Maclear (1794–1879).]

15. [Friedrich Wilhelm Bessel (1784–1846), German astronomer and mathematician.]

10

THE PRE-DARWINITE AND POST-DARWINITE WORLD

Moncure Daniel Conway

[Moncure Daniel Conway (1832–1907), American reformer and author, graduated from Dickinson College, becoming caught up in a Methodist revival there. In 1851 he became a circuit-riding Methodist minister in rural Maryland but soon grew disenchanted with Methodism. He later received a degree from Harvard Divinity School and became a Unitarian minister, campaigning vigorously against slavery. While at a congregation in Cincinnati, he denounced New Testament miracles and the divinity of Jesus Christ. During the Civil War, he wrote several anti-slavery tracts, but the horrific killing of the war depressed him, and he left the United States in 1863, settling in London. There he evolved from theism to agnosticism as a celebrated minister at the South Place Chapel (1864–84). He returned to the United States in 1885, produced a biography of the freethinker Thomas Paine (1892), and edited Paine's collected writings (1894–96; 4 vols.).

Moncure Daniel Conway, "The Pre-Darwinite and Post-Darwinite World," in *Idols and Ideals; with an Essay on Christianity* (New York: Henty Holt, 1877), pp. 79–95, 98–102.

He wrote one of the most noteworthy nineteenth-century American memoirs, the immense *Autobiography, Memories and Experiences* (1904). Among his other works are *Demonology and Devil-Lore* (1879) and a life of Nathaniel Hawthorne (1890). In the following essay, Conway discusses the effects of the theory of evolution upon religion and morality, denying that the notion of the "survival of the fittest" reduces humanity to a level of savagery and brute force.]

I.

In estimating the general bearings of a purely scientific statement it is first of all necessary to know just what that statement is; and, secondly, it is necessary to translate it into the largest expression of which it admits.

The doctrine of evolution, as interpreted and applied by the man whose name is now preeminently associated with it, is the consummate result to which the great highways of discovery had long tended before they converged. Over one hundred years ago the ancient speculations were recalled by Buffon, who said, "There is but one animal."[1] This grew through Buffon's pupil Lamarck to the theory of an evolution by fits and starts, something like that popularised in England in the book entitled "The Vestiges of Creation."[2] It gained a more scientific expression with Geoffroy Saint-Hilaire, who affirmed the unity of all parts of the animal body, and indicated that "balance of organs" by which each form was shown to be only another transformation of the common type.[3] That all bones are vertebrae was discovered by Oken, who also demonstrated, in 1805, that all animals are built up out of vesicles or cells.[4] Bichat was engaged in the work of showing the bearing of these facts upon the structure of man when unhappily his life terminated in 1771.[5] Goethe extended the same principle to the morphology of plants. In England Dr. Erasmus Darwin struck the theme somewhat poetically, which his famous grandson has made into the great scientific generalisation of our time.[6] Thus the Darwinian theory of evolution had great forerunners. It is no empyrical speculation, no isolated or eccentric fancy. It is the apex of a great pyramid of facts and researches resting solidly and squarely upon the graduated formations of knowledge in all time, and built up by the certain method of science.

Nor, in saying this, do I detract from the just fame of the man who has summed up and named the great series of preceding discoveries. The finest genius can do no greater work for us than that of filtrating, combining, and organising the mass of facts, and of applying to the full extent methods which had hitherto been doing but slight and partial service. That the telegraph was used in a German lecture-room long before it was known to society, does not detract from the grandeur of the achievement which has made it flash the thought of man through sea and mountain round the world. The great man does not create the laws of nature: he discovers them, he studies them, he applies them, he obeys them. Nor is he less a discoverer who discerns where a principle may be truly applied, and so recovers from chaos a realm of knowledge, than he who originally discovered the principle. Darwin inherited the principle of evolution, but he discovered that form of it through which alone it could simplify, revise, and harmonise every branch of human knowledge. He merits, therefore, the acknowledgment I once heard expressed by a distinguished American, that he had restored to England the intellectual sceptre of Europe. That sceptre had passed to the hand of Germany, but now every civilised nation looks again to England, as it looked in the days of Bacon and in those of Newton.

II.

What, then, is the Darwinian theory? It is that all the organic forms around us, from lowest to highest, have been evolved the one from the other by means of the principle of natural selection. Natural selection is the obvious law that every power or trait which better adapts an animal to live amid its surroundings enables that animal to survive another which has not the same power or trait. The fit outlive the unfit. And because they outlive their inferiors they will propagate their species more freely. Their offspring will inherit their advantages; by the laws of heredity will still further improve upon them; and thus there will be a cumulative storing up of such advantages established. Each form less furnished with resources to maintain itself is crowded out before the increase of forms which are better supplied with hereditary abilities. A sufficient accumulation of slight advantages amount in the end to a new form or species. An accumulation of specific advantages will be summed up in a new genus.

And thus, as Emerson has said—

> Striving to be man, the worm
> Mounts through all the spires of form.[7]

Now, to the merely scientific mind evolution is simply a scientific generalisation. In its light he beholds the sprouting leaf hardening to a stem, unpacking itself to a blossom, swelling again to the pulpy leaf, called fruit. He inspects the crustacean egg; sees the trilobite in the embryo stretching into a tiny lobster, shortening into a crab; and says, trilobite, lobster and crab pass from one to the other in this little egg-world, as the new theory shows they did in the big world. He will be interested to find out the intervening steps of improvement between one form and another, and will fix upon this or that animal as the one from which a consummate species budded. But, as I have stated, a truth in any one department of knowledge is capable of being translated into every other. We are already familiar with a popular translation of the Darwin theory in the phrase which explains it as meaning that men are descended from monkeys. And by this common interpretation many conclude that it implies a degradation of the human species. But that phrase does not convey the truth of the theory any more than if a rough pediment in the museum were declared to be the splendid temple of Diana of Ephesus. For behind each one of the forms evolving higher, there stretch the endless lines and processions of the forms which combined to produce it. The ape may appear ugly seen as he is among us, detached from his environment, when contrasted with man; but he is royal when contrasted with a worm in the mud. But neither worm nor ape can be truly seen when detached from the cosmical order and beauty. It matters little what rude form sheathed the first glory of a human brain. It does not rob the opal of its beauty that its matrix was common flint, nor does it dim the diamond's lustre that it crystallised out of charcoal. The ape may be the jest of the ignorant, but the thinker will see behind him the myriad beautiful forms which made him possible. What wondrous forests of fern and vine grew in voiceless ages, clothing the hard primaeval rock, what flowers rich and rare broidered the raiment of the earth! What bright insects flashed through their green bowers, what gorgeous birds lit up the deep solitudes with torch-like plumage! Through a thousand ages the shining swimmers darted through pool or air; for unnumbered generations star-gemmed creatures, lithe and beautiful, sprang through jungle and forest: they browse peacefully on hill and meadow; they slake their thirst at crystal streams; they pursue their savage loves in wood and vale; with mighty roar, with sweetest melody, they chant the music by which the world marches onward and upward,—onward and upward for ever! Millions pass away—millions advance: from every realm of nature they come to add their fibre of strength or tint of beauty to the rising form; beneath every touch, with every tribute it ascends,—till at last, lodged for a moment in some rugged humanlike form for combination, the selected concentred powers expand into man—the sum of every creature's best!

The right translation of this theory for us is, then, that it shows man to be the offspring, not of an ape, but of the animated universe; the heir of its richest bounties; the consummate work of a matchless Artist, a figure of which all preceding forms were but sketches and studies. Admitting—though it is an extreme and questionable concession—that the theory has not yet fortified itself completely by demonstrations in detail of the connecting links between species, yet it has certainly shown such an immense balance of probabilities in its favour as to command the adhesion of the scientific world to a greater extent than the Newtonian theory of gravitation did within the same time after its discovery. It may be affirmed that there is now not a single great man of science in the world who does not maintain that in one way or another species were continuously evolved.

III.

But what effect has this theory on religion or moral philosophy? We all know that it has awakened earnest controversies. There are several ways in which it has been regarded. One class of religious teachers, seeing that the verdict of the scientific world in its favour is beyond appeal, have been assuring us that it can have no effect upon religion whatever. Dean Stanley,[8] too liberal and scholarly not to recognise the facts, recently admonished an audience that it mattered nothing at all to them whether it should turn out that man is descended from the animal world, or lower still, as the Bible said, from the inanimate dust of the earth, for right would still be right, and wrong, wrong; and we should still feel that we are individual souls. What he said was true, but the tone of his remark was that this is a question quite aside from the great religious problems of our time.

They who indulge this hope will very soon find it delusive. It has never been the case that a great scientific generalisation has failed to be reflected in the religious and moral convictions of mankind. The instinctive horror which priesthoods have of science has been developed by a long experience of the certainty with which theological changes have followed scientific discoveries. If any one will study the conditions of religious thought in this country before and after the discoveries of Newton, he will see that by those discoveries the whole controversy was shifted, theology was revolutionised; old questions died, new problems arose; nay, theology itself declined in England from that day. When I have had the pleasure of sitting in the historic Abbey of Westminster and listening to such rationalism from its Dean as would have sent a preacher in old times to the stake, I have reflected that beneath that floor lies the dust of Isaac Newton. And when England had advanced sufficiently to bury in the shrine of her best and greatest that scientific revolutioniser of thought, himself a Unitarian (Sir Charles Lyell),[9] there was planted another of the seeds that have flowered into the rationalism which inspires her most venerable and powerful pulpit. The Dean himself is the best answer to his own suggestion, that religion can stand still while science moves. It cannot stand still. And the reason is plain: that which represents religion in Europe is a set of dogmas based upon the Bible, and the Bible is not only a religious but a scientific book; it contains a system of theories as to the origin and the facts of nature. This system was the speculation of an ignorant tribe in an ignorant age of the world. Yet theology blended its religious dogmas with these scientific speculations; and as, in the progress of knowledge, these crude fancies of the infant world about nature are necessarily set aside by successive discoveries, the dogmas must go with them. Insensibly men feel that a tribe so mistaken about visible nature, must naturally have been mistaken about invisible nature. The people find that they have been deceived by their religious teachers,—deceived about the sky, about the earth, and their own origin,—and they imbibe a suspicion of those teachers. An atmosphere of suspicion settles around every church and priest. Universal scepticism prevails. It is that scepticism which in England has quenched the fires of Smithfield, abolished tithes, opened Universities to heresy, and which steadily severs Church from State.

IV.

On the other hand there are theologians who instead of indulging the dream that the Darwinian theory will leave religion just where it was before, announce that it is cutting the faith of man up by the roots. They declare that it abolishes God, destroys the hope of immortality, and resolves morality itself into a mere mechanic force.

Such phantoms are familiar, but they become more thin with each reappearance. Our fathers heard that the pillars of the universe had fallen again and again, when it only turned out that somebody's little idol had collapsed. "The giving up of the sun's motion is giving up the foundation of religion," said they who burned the book of Copernicus and the body of Bruno. "The giving up of witchcraft is giving up the Bible," said Sir Matthew Hale.[10] We have grown accustomed to such alarms, and can consider such things with the assured calmness of long experience.

Unquestionably a revolution has occurred. No one can peruse the common literature of the day without recognising that the theory of Darwin has given the world new eyes with which to look at nearly everything. Each truth is a mother-truth, and brings forth a family of other truths. The faculties of man, too, are a fraternity, and what comes to one passes to all the rest. If we examine the mental condition of the world before this theory was impressed upon it, we shall find even advanced and liberal men taking views of the nature of things which now seem antiquarian. Take the pre-Darwinite rationalist; what did he believe? He did not believe the miracles of the Bible, nor modern superstitions; but the supernaturalist could easily press him into a corner by compelling him to admit that the world began by a miracle, that man began by a miracle, and that each star in the sky, each animal on earth, was formed from nothing by the creative fiat of the deity. The theist repeated as often as the orthodox the words—"God said, Let there be light, and there was light" [Gen. 1:3]; "God made man in his own image" [Gen. 1:26]. Then the pre-Darwinite rationalist easily conceded that Milton's version was true,—and that the first man and woman sprang from the hand of God in all perfection of intelligence and beauty, and able to speak a perfect language. There were, of course, exceptions. Some did not believe in any God at all, but the average rationalist of our memory, who still held to a God, thus conceived of him as an Almighty Mechanic and Contriver. Upon the moral world he looked with awe, seeing in it a chaos over which the principles—Good and Evil—perpetually struggled. His great problem was as to free will or necessity; his hope, that by the divine will good would finally triumph over evil.

Then Darwinism came and gave every department of inquiry a new point of departure, and a new theorem. It was found that even the blind elements had shaped themselves in accordance with principles of adaptation to necessary circumstances; that life had begun everywhere in the feeblest and lowest forms; that the first man and woman were savages but little raised above the brute; that there was no evidence whatever of any such Creation as was represented in the old belief in an original vacuum; but, on the contrary, every probability that the substance of things had always existed and would exist. The philologists proved that language, instead of being a miraculous gift, had grown up like—perhaps out of—the cries of animals. In a word, the idea of a Mighty Mechanic, a Supreme Wonder-worker, was driven out of the conception of the rationalist.

V.

And what has thereby been lost? Nothing whatever, I contend, which could be of the slightest advantage to the religious nature of man but much that hampered and misdirected it. For this conception of an arbitrary Creator involved the notion of a gigantic man,—a will like our own, though much more powerful. And this notion involved the darkest of problems—why this Omnipotent Maker did not make things better? Why did he create a world full of imperfections and bitter pains and evils? The orthodox could explain these evils by declaring all nature to be under a curse, but the rationalist was simply left in a cloud.

But does the doctrine of natural selection, then, expel God from the universe? Does it imply that in all these fair worlds, amid all this beauty, there is no intimation of a divine Being? By no means. It has simply broken up an old belief as to the relation of that Being to the universe. As theology had in the far past narrowed him to the seven-planet theory, or again fancied that the sun rose every morning because God waked it up, and declared in each case that God was driven from the universe whenever a law was substituted for his immediate action, so now we see the infirmity of mind which can see no God except as prisoned in its crude notion. Darwinism simply says to the human mind—Once more you have been found wrong in your speculations as to God's relation to this universe. Once more you are proved unable to comprehend the Incomprehensible. Once more you are taught to abstain from dogmatising where you cannot know, and to learn humility!

But still, above our crumbled creeds and vanished speculations the ancient heavens declare a divine glory; still day speaketh unto day, and night unto night showeth knowledge; and man may still reverently raise his reason to contemplate order and beauty in the universe. Out of decay and death springs the flower with its breath of love, and over earthly ruin bends the tender sky. There is nothing whatever in this theory which veils to man a single expression of wisdom, or love shining through the mystery around him.

Nay, on the contrary, I will maintain that this theory has added fresh tints of love, brighter beams of reason to the universe by opening our eyes to new aspects of it. It has illuminated for the first time the dreary track of pain and wrong. The pre-Darwinite might say to the suffering, "I hope and trust your pain is for some good end"; but the post-Darwinite can say with confidence, "I know and see that pain is a beneficent agent. Pain has been the spur under which the whole world has progressed. To escape danger, to survive pain, every form has gained its fleetness, its skill, its power: the hardships of nature gave man his arts to conquer it; the cruel elements built his home; and in the black ink of sin were written the laws of morality and civilisation."

And if this theory has for the first time taught man the sublime uses of evil, none the less has it harmonised nature with the laws of his reason. For in their best statement the old pre-Darwinite views of nature made it discordant with the intellectual history of man. History shows us a continuous moral, mental, and religious development of humanity. The theories, the philosophies, the creeds of mankind have not been distinct and isolated creations; they have been an unbroken series of religions, schools, ideas, each growing out of one preceding, giving birth to another, so that step by step we trace philosophy back from Huxley to Moses, or religion from Christendom to Assyria and India. This unbroken evolution of thought in human history we find repeated in the unfolding intellect of every individual being. We do not think one thing, and then a totally different thing, and feel that there is no link binding our days and our purposes together into a life that represents an individuality. Yet we had long been looking out into nature and seeing it as a set of distinct creations; one form made, then another. We may well reverence the great men who have found in the universe one theme with endless variations. They have enabled us to hear a grand music such as Plato dreamed of as the harmony to which the planets moved. Finding now that his moral and intellectual history have in their development repeated in higher series the growth of the physical world that bore him, man takes his own brain as his standpoint, and from the summit of his own thought sees the immeasurable thought reflected in nature so far as his intelligence can reach.

Nor has the post-Darwinite world lost any rational hope held by the pre-Darwinite,—neither for the present or for the future. For rational men, emancipated from fables, immortality has long been a high hope; and a high hope it will remain, untouched by the fact of his birth out of the organic world. So far as that hope rested upon the dignity of the human being, it is increased by a theory which shows that for millions of ages the forms and forces of the world were all employed in preparing and working out the marvel of a human brain. He may well argue that nature will fitly cherish the gem which it cost aeons to produce, and myriads of busy hands to polish.

And as to this world, the new theory has caused a hope to dawn over us so dazzling that our eyes can hardly yet bear it. It has revealed that the force which has built up from a zoophyte the wondrous frame of man, remains still in our hands, ready to lay hold on man himself and build him into a nobler race; to fossilize deformity and liberate every power; ready to apply the omnipotent universe for the culture of man and his dwelling-place, causing social deserts to rejoice and blossom like the rose.

VI.

The history of the world shows that the dreaded discoveries of one age become the cherished beliefs of another. Few men aroused more alarm by discoveries than Newton, yet few other men's names are now oftener uttered with reverence by theologians, and pulpits illustrate by his theories that divine existence they once seemed to imperil. But that is not a healthy moral condition of the world in which truth is always dealt with as an enemy when it first appears, and only treated as a friend after he who discovered it is dead. That is very disheartening to the intellectual world. We shall never have the really great progress in knowledge so long as every youth sees that the prosaic world regards with wrath the messengers that bring tidings of newly-discovered laws and truths.

It is not at all certain that the fault of such a state of things rests exclusively with the world at large. There would seem to be a fault with the men of science also. It may be that it was the long ages of persecution which has driven science into a sort of scholarly hermitage, from which it sends out works so full of hard technical words derived from the dead tongues once made compulsory lest the people should understand them; and it may have been the old theological monopoly of the speculative moral and emotional realms of human interest which originally relegated the *savant* to that hard, unpoetical aspect of his facts from which he so rarely ventures, and even now, it must be admitted, only with risk of stern remand to the valley of dry bones. Whatever may be the reason, it is plain that for lack of more general "scientific use of the imagination," or other cause, some of the most important discoveries are still lingering in fragmentary isolation,—stones of stumbling, because left in the way instead of being fitted into the wall.

I was conversing with some gentlemen on the subject of evolution in its purely scientific aspects. A lady sat listening, and when the others had gone, she remarked to me, "It is a most horrible doctrine." I was startled by her look—there was on it pallor, and an expression of mental suffering. "What is horrible?" I asked. "Why, that doctrine you have been all talking about—the survival of the strongest. It may be that it is the law of nature that the weak should be trampled out by the strong, but it is dreadful." Her eyes were filled with tears. I answered, "I believe in no such doctrine as the survival of the strongest,—nor do those scientific men believe in it. They believe in the survival of the fittest; but mere strength is not fitness. The survival of the strongest were indeed a horrible doctrine; but all nature is against it. Huge monstrous things that were only strong—moving mountains of force, mammoth and megalosaurus—have perished because they were merely strong, and so not fit to survive; the forms of cruelty and brute force have had to give way before things much weaker; the lions have decreased before the lambs; and man, weakest of all animals at birth, has been awarded the sceptre of the world because he was fittest through his power to love, to consider, to deny himself for others."

I had the happiness of witnessing the relief of that young heart when she discovered her mistake,—that the horrible doctrine of the reign of brute force has been especially crushed by that of evolution, which proves the steady triumph of the gentle forces of sympathy and justice. How much misunderstanding of this kind envelopes all great truths when they first ascend the horizon, so that human hearts tremble like the watching shepherds when they saw their star. "The glory of the Lord shone round about them, and they were sore afraid" [Luke 2:9]. 'Tis an old poem, but ever repeated.

It is the very evangel of our time that knowledge is shadowing out the moral essence of the world. It has shown mere physical power steadily decreasing, and the power of thought and love increasing, and it has thus discovered for the humane a new basis for their hope, a new spur for their effort. Ferocity is a weakness; fanaticism is feebleness; selfishness is suicidal: Turkey feels it; Spain feels it; Rome is learning it. Love, justice, knowledge, lead the world, and human hearts may now sing unto their Lord a new song! [. . .]

VII.

The whole tendency and evolution of the world has been to the end of unfolding in man a power to overcome all the selfishness of brute nature. Through ages, by self-seeking the animal has been formed; but now by self-denial the animal reaches a new birth. The impulse to love that which can give no recompense to the lower nature; the power to serve with unwearied devotion the true and right; these are the last and highest forces evolved from nature. They are the first signs of human freedom. For no man is free who is morally fettered by his interests, his fears, or his prejudices. He is a slave to the world. A man is free only when he is able to go against his interests, his fears, and his prejudices. "He is free whom the truth makes free"—the man whom nothing can swerve from that.

Religion—which should be an expression of this consummate force in nature—the power that frees man from low motives and makes his action flow straight from reason and conscience,—must itself be born again. That which is commonly called religion is not the loving service, but servility under threat and bribe,—and these the coarsest. So far the conventional religion is irreligious. There is a healthy fear—the fear of doing wrong. There is a noble hope—the hope that rectitude will bring benefit to all. But that is a base fear, a mean hope, which look merely to personal consequences of animal pain and pleasure. How wild is the unreason that tries by the tremendous menace and promise of eternal anguish and bliss—the most powerful appeals to selfishness—to make men religious, that is unselfish, acting purely from motives of reason and right. That such a religion as this, which has been tried on human nature for ages, has failed, can be matter of surprise to no thinking man.

True, when it was really believed, its threats and bribes availed to conquer some of the ordinary outward effects of selfishness. It led monks and nuns to give up earthly for future gain. It made fanatics frown on human joys to secure celestial delights and escape future torment. For the Puritan it turned the face of nature to stone, like a Medusa, and blighted the sweetest flowers of life. Such men gave up much; but the selfish character remained—nay, it was intensified. The type of character was also as self-righteous and cruel as it was joyless and narrow.

The old so-called religion having failed to produce the perfect love that casteth out fear, the man of perfect truth, whom no menace of deity or devil can turn from his rectitude,—where are we to look for the religion which can lead forth that culminating flower of nature, the perfect character? Only in the high fruition of a religion whose God is Love, to whom the highest service is love, whose law is not sacrifice, but mercifulness. It is a reasonable service, for that which falling on the heart is love, falling on the intellect is reason. It knows no hell but falsehood and wrong, it dreams of no heaven but an eternity of progressive thought and ever-growing harmony. Its power has been manifested in all time in the great lovers and saviours of men, who have consecrated their lives to truth, right and humanity, though denounced to flames on earth and flames in hell. Every rational truth, we hold, has been planted in the earth and nourished with the tears of men who gave their service in purity of love and fidelity to truth. Every divine truth that is to us as a fragrant flower, is crimsoned with the blood of a brave man's heart. They who are free from all authority but truth, are the heirs of their faith and trustees of their example; on them mainly depends whether, in the coming time, the religion of love, reason and right shall more largely manifest its power to conquer selfishness, without terror, and stimulate to high action without any sealed contract for payment in Paradise. To be able to bear on their work, to add to it, and transmit in fuller force to the future, it is not necessary that a man or woman should be eminent, but only that what power they possess should be pure. If a man have within, firmly based, that character which is organised by truth and love, able to obey them and them only, every thought, word and deed of that man will further, though in ways he know not, all right and true things, and his feeble hand become part of the law that upholds the universe.

More than any Sufi does the believer in evolution feel himself walking through life on the perilous scimitar-edged bridge, Al-Sirat;[11] between vast worlds of happiness and misery. On the one side the abyss of animalism, on the other the radiant realm where every aspiring power within him finds its fruition. How often will he turn upon himself and ask, am I yet a real man? Am I acting from high or from low motives? Am I in anything acting from motives of pride, of prejudice, or with a view to mere personal ends? If so, how can I belong to that kingdom of pure truth and perfect rectitude, which is the high and fair religion that the ages have been building? If impelled by passion, how am I better than those lower orders whose natural life is passion? If acting selfishly, what am I but a higher form, perhaps therefore more dangerous, of the creature prowling for its prey? Why, anybody can do that! Any creature can be angry, and obstinate, and forget all but himself; nature abounds in horns and stings. It hasn't required a million ages merely to evolve that type of man that can stick to his wrong and injure others. But nature might well have laboured a myriad ages to produce a man who would rather be injured than injure another, and who is great enough when he is wrong to hold his pride underfoot, and say "I have been wrong." That is greatness.

It is, indeed, a high and steep ladder, that by which a man must climb out of his lower up to his higher nature; one slip towards the false, one backward fall, and he relapses in the scale of moral being, and adds his weight to all the baser forces of the earth. Love and truth alone can save and uplift us. Let none attempt to deny or evade the grave necessity. Moral evolution is not only true, it is a tremendous truth. He who shall realise it will in that instant fall upon his knees in the awful presence of conscience, and there make his solemn vow. To

Truth he will appeal,—"Take me, fill me with thy pure spirit! If to thee I have been at any time disloyal, if I have fostered any conscious error, or practiced any mean concealment, or acted on considerations of mere expediency,—pardon me, thou one only light of mortals, and henceforth witness that I speak and live the simple truth! And thou, spirit of Love, let me come to rest upon thy gentle breast! If I have wandered from thee—have steeled my heart against my brother—forgotten charity—thought only of myself—forgive me, sweetest and best—pardon me, thou Love which alone can make life worth living,—and henceforth may my word and deed be not mine, but proceed from thy pure and perfect heart!"

Anew is the commandment given to us—If any will be great let him serve. Let him seek not to be ministered unto, but to minister. Let him turn his back on self and its low successes: let him trust himself absolutely to love that must prevail, and truth that cannot fail,—and then wherever he may stand, beside him stand the law and the majesty of God.

NOTES

1. [Georges-Louis Leclerc, comte de Buffon (1707–1788), French naturalist whose *Histoire naturelle* (1749–88) presented the history of plant and animal life as part of a coordinated pattern.] Jean-Baptiste de Monet, chevalier de Lamarck (1744–1829), French biologist and proponent of an early version of the theory of evolution, although he asserted the inheritability of acquired traits, a point denied by Darwin.]

2. [Robert Chambers (1802–1871), Scottish author of *Vestiges of the Natural History of Creation* (1844), which presented an early but erroneous theory of evolution.]

3. [Etienne Geoffroy Saint-Hilaire (1772–1844), French zoologist who studied the transformation of species.]

4. [Lorenz Oken (1779–1851), German naturalist and pioneer in the study of protozoa.]

5. [Marie-François-Xavier Bichat (1771–1802), French anatomist. Conway gives his date of birth as the date of death.]

6. [Erasmus Darwin (1731–1802), British physicist, grandfather of Charles Darwin, and author of *The Botanick Garden* (1789–91), a long poem that anticipated the theory of evolution.]

7. [Ralph Waldo Emerson, "May-Day" (1867), ll. 81–82.]

8. [Arthur Penrhyn Stanley (1815–1881), leading British theologian of the period and dean of Westminster (1864–81).]

9. [Sir Charles Lyell (1797–1875), British geologist whose *Principles of Geology* (1830) is the foundation of modern geological thought.]

10. [Sir Mathew Hale (1609–1676), British judge who presided over a witchcraft trial at Bury St. Edmunds in 1662. A similar statement is found in the diary of John Wesley, the founder of Methodism.]

11. [Sufism is an Islamic sect in which devotees seek a direct and personal experience with God.]

11

SCIENCE AND RELIGION

Albert Einstein

[Albert Einstein (1879–1955), German-Swiss physicist and philosopher, was born in Ulm, Germany, and studied mathematics and physics at the Federal Polytechnic Academy in Zürich, becoming a Swiss citizen upon graduating in 1900. In a series of papers in 1905, he propounded the special theory of relativity, revolutionizing humanity's conception of the universe. He expounded the general theory of relativity in 1916. Throughout this period, Einstein was devoted to social and political causes: he was vehemently opposed to World War I and to German militarism and continued to advocate peace for the rest of his life. Relativity was confirmed by eclipse observations in 1919, leading to his receiving the Nobel Prize for physics in 1921. Einstein spent the rest of his life in a futile attempt to identify a unified field theory linking electromagnetism and gravitation—an attempt doomed to failure by his

Albert Einstein, "Science and Religion" (1941), in *Out of My Later Years* (New York: Philosophical Library, 1950), pp. 24–30.

refusal to accept Max Planck's quantum theory and the indeterminacy it introduced.

While disenchanted with humanity's continuing love of violence and warfare, Einstein never became an atheist, adhering to Spinoza's conception of a god that revealed himself in the harmony of nature. Upon the accession of Adolf Hitler in 1833, Einstein moved to the United States, working at the Institute for Advanced Study in Princeton. He later became a US citizen. Hearing of German attempts to split the uranium atom, Einstein urged President Franklin D. Roosevelt to build an atomic bomb ahead of the Germans, although he took no part in the Manhattan Project and did not know of the bomb until it was dropped on Japan. He at once urged all nations to renounce the use of atomic weapons. In the following extract, Einstein believes that there is no true conflict between religion and science as properly understood, but conflicts arise when each encroaches upon the other's domain.]

It would not be difficult to come to an agreement as to what we understand by science. Science is the century-old endeavor to bring together by means of systematic thought the perceptible phenomena of this world into as thoroughgoing an association as possible. To put it boldly, it is the attempt at the posterior reconstruction of existence by the process of conceptualization. But when asking myself what religion is I cannot think of the answer so easily. And even after finding an answer which may satisfy me at this particular moment I still remain convinced that I can never under any circumstances bring together, even to a slight extent, all those who have given this question serious consideration.

At first, then, instead of asking what religion is I should prefer to ask what characterizes the aspirations of a person who has given me the impression of being religious: A person who is religiously enlightened appears to me to be one who has, to the best of his ability, liberated himself from the fetters of his selfish desires and is preoccupied with thoughts, feelings, and aspirations to which he clings because of their super-personal value. It seems to me that what is important is the force of this super-personal content and the depth of the conviction concerning its overpowering meaningfulness, regardless of whether any attempt is made to unite this content with a divine Being, for otherwise it would not be possible to count Buddha and Spinoza as religious personalities. Accordingly, a religious person is devout in the sense that he has no doubt of the significance and loftiness of those super-personal objects and goals which neither require nor are capable of rational foundation. They exist with the same necessity and matter-of-factness as he himself. In this sense religion is the age-old endeavor of mankind to become clearly and completely conscious of these values and goals and constantly to strengthen and extend their effect. If one conceives of religion and science according to these definitions then a conflict between them appears impossible. For science can only ascertain what *is*, but not what *should be*, and outside of its domain value judgments of all kinds remain necessary. Religion, on the other hand, deals only with evaluations of human thought and action: it cannot justifiably speak of facts and relationships between facts. According to this interpretation the well-known conflicts between religion and science in the past must all be ascribed to a misapprehension of the situation which has been described.

For example, a conflict arises when a religious community insists on the absolute truthfulness of all statements recorded in the Bible. This means an intervention on the part of religion into the sphere of science; this is where the struggle of the Church against the doctrines of Galileo and Darwin belongs. On the other hand, representatives of science have often made an attempt to arrive at fundamental judgments with respect to values and ends on the basis of scientific method, and in this way have set themselves in opposition to religion. These conflicts have all sprung from fatal errors.

Now, even though the realms of religion and science in themselves are clearly marked off from each other, nevertheless there exist between the two strong reciprocal relationships and dependencies. Though religion may be that which determines the goal, it has, nevertheless, learned from science, in the broadest sense, what means will contribute to the attainment of the goals it has set up. But science can only be created by those who are thoroughly imbued with the aspiration towards truth and understanding. This source of feeling, however, springs from the sphere of religion. To this there also belongs the faith in the possibility that the regulations valid for the world of existence are rational, that is, comprehensible to reason. I cannot conceive of a genuine scientist without that profound faith. The situation may be expressed by an image: Science without religion is lame, religion without science is blind.

Though I have asserted above that in truth a legitimate conflict between religion and science cannot exist I must nevertheless qualify this assertion once again on an essential point, with reference to the actual content of historical religions. This qualification has to do with the concept of God. During the youthful period of mankind's spiritual evolution human fantasy created gods in man's own image, who, by the operations of their will were supposed to determine, or at any rate to influence the phenomenal world. Man sought to alter the disposition of these gods in his own favor by means of magic and prayer. The idea of God in the religions taught at present is a sublimation of that old conception of the gods. Its anthropomorphic character is shown, for instance, by the fact that men appeal to the Divine Being in prayers and plead for the fulfilment of their wishes.

Nobody, certainly, will deny that the idea of the existence of an omnipotent, just and omnibeneficent personal God is able to accord man solace, help, and guidance; also, by virtue of its simplicity it is accessible to the most undeveloped mind. But, on the other hand, there are decisive weaknesses attached to this idea in itself, which have been painfully felt since the beginning of history. That is, if this being is omnipotent then every occurrence, including every human action, every human thought, and every human feeling and aspiration is also His work; how is it possible to think of holding men responsible for their deeds and thoughts before such an almighty Being? In giving out punishment and rewards He would to a certain extent be passing judgment on Himself. How can this be combined with the goodness and righteousness ascribed to Him?

The main source of the present-day conflicts between the spheres of religion and of science lies in this concept of a personal God. It is the aim of science to establish general rules which determine the reciprocal connection of objects and events in time and space. For these rules, or laws of nature, absolutely general validity is required—not proven. It is mainly a program, and faith in the possibility of its accomplishment in principle is only founded on partial successes. But hardly anyone could be found who would deny these partial successes and ascribe them to human self-deception. The fact that on the basis of such laws we are able to predict the temporal behavior of phenomena in certain domains with great precision and certainty is deeply embedded in the consciousness of the modern man, even though he may have grasped very little of the contents of those laws. He need only consider that planetary courses within the solar system may be calculated in advance with great exactitude on the basis of a limited number of simple laws. In a similar way, though not with the same precision, it is possible to calculate in advance the mode of operation of an electric motor, a transmission system, or of a wireless apparatus, even when dealing with a novel development.

To be sure, when the number of factors coming into play in a phenomenological complex is too large scientific method in most cases fails us. One need only think of the weather, in which case prediction even for a few days ahead is impossible. Nevertheless no one doubts that we are confronted with a causal connection whose causal components are in the main known to us. Occurrences in this domain are beyond the reach of exact prediction because of the variety of factors in operation, not because of any lack of order in nature.

We have penetrated far less deeply into the regularities obtaining within the realm of living things, but deeply enough nevertheless to sense at least the rule of fixed necessity. One need only think of the systematic order in heredity, and in the effect of poisons, as for instance alcohol, on the behavior of organic beings. What is still lacking here is a grasp of connections of profound generality, but not a knowledge of order in itself.

The more a man is imbued with the ordered regularity of all events the firmer becomes his conviction that there is no room left by the side of this ordered regularity for causes of a different nature. For him neither the rule of human nor the rule of divine will exists as an independent cause of natural events. To be sure, the doctrine of a personal God interfering with natural events could never be *refuted*, in the real sense, by science, for this doctrine can always take refuge in those domains in which scientific knowledge has not yet been able to set foot.

But I am persuaded that such behavior on the part of the representatives of religion would not only be unworthy but also fatal. For a doctrine which is able to maintain itself not in clear light but only in the dark, will of necessity lose its effect on mankind, with incalculable harm to human progress. In their struggle for the ethical good, teachers of religion must have the stature to give up the doctrine of a personal God, that is, give that source of fear and hope which in the past placed such vast power in the hands of priests. In their labors they will have to avail themselves of those forces which are capable of cultivating the Good, the True, and the Beautiful in humanity itself. This is, to be sure, a more difficult but all incomparably more worthy task.[1] After religious teachers accomplish the refining process indicated they will surely recognize with joy that true religion has been ennobled and made more profound by scientific knowledge.

If it is one of the goals of religion to liberate mankind as far as possible from the bondage of egocentric cravings, desires, and fears, scientific reasoning can aid religion in yet another sense. Although it is true that it is the goal of science to discover rules which permit the association and foretelling of facts, this is not its only aim. It also seeks to reduce the connections discovered to the smallest possible number of mutually independent conceptual elements. It is in this striving after the rational unification of the manifold that it encounters its greatest successes, even though it is precisely this attempt which causes it to run the greatest risk of falling a prey to illusions. But whoever has undergone the intense experience of successful advances made in this domain, is moved by profound reverence for the rationality made manifest in existence. By way of the understanding he achieves a far-reaching emancipation from the shackles of personal hopes and desires, and thereby attains that humble attitude of mind towards the grandeur of reason incarnate in existence, and which, in its profoundest depths, is inaccessible to man. This attitude, however, appears to me to be religious, in the highest sense of the word. And so it seems to me that science not only purifies the religious impulse of the dross of its anthropomorphism but also contributes to a religious spiritualization of our understanding of life.

The further the spiritual evolution of mankind advances, the more certain it seems to me that the path to genuine religiosity does not lie through the fear of life, and the fear of death, and blind faith, but through striving after rational knowledge. In this sense I believe that the priest must become a teacher if he wishes to do justice to his lofty educational mission.

NOTE

1. This thought is convincingly presented in Herbert Samuel's book *Belief and Action*.

12

IN THE BEGINNING . . .

Isaac Asimov

[Isaac Asimov (1920–1992), American scientist and science fiction writer, was born in Russia of Jewish parents, who emigrated to the United States in 1923. A precocious youth, Asimov graduated from high school at fifteen. He received a degree in chemistry from Columbia College in 1939, followed by an MA (1941) and PhD (1948). Attracted by the burgeoning field of science fiction, Asimov published his first story in 1938. He went on to become a towering figure in the "Golden Age" of science fiction, writing such works as "Nightfall" (1941); *I, Robot* (1950); and the Foundation Trilogy: *Foundation* (1951), *Foundation and Empire* (1952), and *Beyond Foundation* (1953). Asimov also wrote many popularizations of science and other subjects, including *The Intelligent Man's Guide to Science* (1960); *Asimov's Guide to the Bible* (1971); *Science Past, Science Future* (1975); and *Asimov on Physics* (1976). He wrote three autobiogra-

Isaac Asimov, *In the Beginning* . . . (New York: Crown, 1981), pp. 5–15.

phies. In all, he published nearly 500 books, although many of these are anthologies with which he had relatively little involvement. In the following extract, a detailed commentary on Genesis, Asimov discusses the first sentence of Genesis and displays its incongruity with the findings of modern science.]

THE FIRST BOOK OF MOSES,[1] CALLED

GENESIS[2]

CHAPTER 1[3]

1. By ancient tradition, the first five books of the Bible were written by Moses, the folk hero who, according to the account given in the second through fifth books of the Bible, rescued the Israelites from Egyptian slavery.

Modern scholars are convinced that this theory of authorship is not tenable and that the early books of the Bible are not the single work of any man, and certainly not of Moses. Rather, they are a carefully edited compilation of material from a number of sources.

The theory of multiple authorship of the Bible dates only from the nineteenth century, however.

In 1611, when King James I of England appointed fifty-four scholars to produce an English translation of the Bible suitable for English-speaking Protestants, no one questioned the tradition of the Mosaic authorship of the five books. The Bible produced by these scholars is the "Authorized Version" (authorized by the king, that is, in his capacity as head of the Anglican Church). The Authorized Version is commonly referred to as the King James Bible. It is the one I am using in this book because, even today, it is the Bible in the minds of almost all English-speaking people. There have been better translations since, to be sure, but none can match the King James Version for sheer poetry.

In the King James, the initial book of the Bible is referred to as "The First Book of Moses."

2. The First Book of Moses begins, in the original Hebrew, with the word *bereshith*. It was not uncommon in Biblical times to refer to a book by its first word or words. (Papal bulls, to this day, are named for the two Latin words with which they begin.)

The Hebrew name for the First Book of Moses is therefore *Bereshith*. Since the word happens to mean "in the beginning," and since the First Book of Moses starts its tale with the creation of the Universe, it is an apt name. (In fact, I use the phrase as the title for the book you are holding.)

The Bible was first translated into another language, Greek, in the third century B.C. In the Greek version of the Bible, the Hebrew habit of using the first words as the name was not followed, and descriptive names were used instead. The First Book of Moses was named *Genesis*, a Greek word meaning "coming into being." This is also an apt name, and the Greek *Genesis* is commonly used as the title of the first Book of the Bible, even in English translation.

3. Early manuscripts of the Bible did not divide the various books into chapters and verses. It was only little by little that such divisions appeared. The present system of chapters and verses first appeared in an English Bible in 1560.

The divisions are not always logical, but there is no way of abandoning them or changing them, for they have been used in reference, in commentaries, and in concordances for four centuries now, and one cannot wipe out the usefulness of all these books.

In the beginning[4] God[5] created[6] the heaven[7] and the earth.[8]

4. The very first phrase in the Bible states that there was a beginning to things.

Why not? It seems natural. Those objects with which we are familiar have a beginning. You and I were born, and before that we did not exist, at least not in our present form. The same is true of other human beings, of plants and animals and, in fact, of all living things, as far as we know from common observation.

We are surrounded, moreover, by all the works of humanity, and all these were, in one way or another, fashioned by human beings; before that, they did not exist, at least in their fashioned form.

It seems natural to feel that if all things alive and human-fashioned had a beginning, then the rule might be universal, and that things that are neither alive nor human-fashioned might also have had a beginning.

At any rate, primitive attempts to explain the Universe start with an explanation of its beginning. This seems so natural a thing that it is doubtful if anyone ever questioned the concept of a beginning in early times, however much disagreement there may have been over the details.

And in the scientific view, there is also considered to be a beginning, not only for Earth, but for the entire Universe.

Since the Bible and science both state that heaven and earth had a beginning, does this represent a point of agreement between them?

Yes, of course—but it is a trivial agreement. There is an enormous difference between the Biblical statement of beginning and the scientific statement of beginning, which I will explain because it illuminates all subsequent agreements between the Biblical and scientific point of view; and, for that matter, all subsequent disagreements.

Biblical statements rest on authority. If they are accepted as the inspired word of God, all argument ends there. There is no room for disagreement. The statement is final and absolute for all time.

A scientist, on the other hand, is committed to accepting nothing that is not backed by acceptable evidence. Even if the matter in question seems obviously certain on the face of it, it is all the better if it is backed by such evidence.

Acceptable evidence is that which can be observed and measured in such a way that subjective opinion is minimized. In other words, different people repeating the observations and measurements with different instruments at different times and in different places should come to the same conclusion. Furthermore, the deductions made from the observations and measurements must follow certain accepted rules of logic and reason.

Such evidence is "scientific evidence," and ideally, scientific evidence is "compelling." That is, people who study the observations and measurements, and the deductions made therefrom, feel compelled to agree with the conclusions even if, in the beginning, they felt strong doubts in the matter.

One may argue, of course, that scientific reasoning is not the only path to truth; that there are inner revelations, or intuitive grasps, or blinding insights, or overwhelming authority that all reach the truth more firmly and more surely than scientific evidence does.

That may be so, but none of these alternate paths to truth is compelling. Whatever one's internal certainty, it remains difficult to transfer that certainty simply by saying, "But I'm sure of it." Other people very often remain unsure and skeptical.

Whatever the authority of the Bible, there has never been a time in history when more than a minority of the human species has accepted that authority. And even among those who accepted the authority, differences in interpretation have been many and violent, and on every possible point, no one interpretation has ever won out over all others.

So intense have been the differences and so unable has any one group been to impress other groups with its version of the "truth" that force has very often been resorted to. There is no need here to go into the history of Europe's wars of religion or of the burning of heretics, to give examples.

Science, too, has seen its share of arguments, disputes, and polemics; scientists are human, and scientific ideals (like all other ideals) are rarely approached in practice. An extraordinary number of such arguments, disputes, and polemics have been settled on one side or the other, and the general scientific opinion has then swung to that side because of *compelling* evidence.

And yet, no matter how compelling the evidence, it remains true, in science, that more and better evidence may turn up, that hidden errors and false assumptions may be uncovered, that an unexpected incompleteness may make itself visible, and that yesterday's "firm" conclusion may suddenly twist and change into a deeper and better conclusion.

It follows, then, that the Biblical statement that earth and heaven had a beginning is authoritative and absolute, but not compelling; while the scientific statement that earth and heaven had a beginning is compelling, but not authoritative and absolute. There is a disagreement there that is deeper and more important than the superficial agreement of the words themselves.

And even the superficial agreement of the words themselves disappears as soon as we ask a further question.

For instance, if we grant the existence of a beginning, suppose we ask just *when* that beginning took place.

The Bible does not tell us when, directly. Indeed, the Bible does not date a single event in any of the books of the King James Version in any way that would help us tie those events into a specific time in the system of chronology we use.

Nevertheless, the question of when the Creation took place has aroused curiosity, and various Biblical scholars have made every effort to deduce its date by using various statements found in the Bible as indirect evidence.

They did not come to precisely the same answer. The generally accepted conclusion among Jewish scholars, for instance, was that the date of the Creation was October 7, 3761 B.C.

James Ussher, the Anglican archbishop of Armagh, Ireland, decided in 1654, on the other hand, that the Creation took place at 9 A.M. on October 23, 4004 B.C. (Ussher's calculations for this and for the dating of other events in the Bible are usually found in all the page headings of the King James Bible.) Other calculations put the Creation as far back as 5509 B.C.

Thus, the usual estimates for the age of the heaven and earth from Biblical data run from about fifty-seven hundred to seventy-five hundred years. It is over this point that the Biblical conclusions represent an enormous disagreement with the conclusions of science.

The weight of scientific evidence is that Earth, and the solar system generally, came into being in approximately their present form about 4.6 billion years ago. The Universe, generally, came into being, it would seem, about fifteen billion years ago.

The age of Earth, then, according to science, is about six hundred thousand times the age according to the Bible, and the age of the Universe, according to science, is at least two million times the age according to the Bible.

In the light of that discrepancy, the mere agreement between the Bible and science that there was, in fact, a beginning, loses most of its value.

5. God is introduced at once as the motive force behind the Universe. His existence is taken for granted in the Bible, and one might, indeed, argue that the existence of God is self-evident.

Consider: All living things are born through the activities of previous living things. If there were, indeed, a beginning, as the Bible and science both agree, how then did the first living things come into existence?

If there were indeed a beginning, how did all the natural objects— land and sea, hills and valleys, sky and earth—come into being? All artificial objects were fashioned by human beings; who or what then fashioned natural objects?

The usual manner in which this is presented is something like, "A watch implies a watchmaker." Since it is inconceivable that an object as intricate as a watch came into being spontaneously, it must therefore have been fashioned; how much more must something as intricate as the Universe have been fashioned!

In early times, the analogy was drawn much more tightly. Since human beings can, by blowing, create a tiny wind rushing out of their nostrils and mouths, the wind in nature must, by analogy, be the product of a much more powerful being blowing through nostrils and mouth. If a horse-and-chariot is a common way of progressing over land, then a glowing horse-and-chariot must be the means by which the sun is carried over the sky.

In the myths, every natural phenomenon is likely to have a human-like creature performing functions analogous to those of the human actions we know, so that nothing in nature takes place spontaneously.

These myriad specialized divinities were often pictured as at odds with each other and as producing a disorderly Universe. As thought grew deeper, the tendency was to suppose one divine being who is responsible for everything, who directs humanity, Earth, and the whole Universe, combining it all into a harmonious whole directed toward some specific end.

It is this sophisticated picture of a monotheistic God that the Bible presents—but one who constantly engages himself in the minutiae of his creation. Even under a monotheistic religion, popular thought imagines myriad angels and saints taking on specialized functions so that a form of polytheism (under a supreme monarch) exists.

In the last four centuries, however, scientists have built up an alternate picture of the Universe. The sun doesn't move across the sky; its apparent motion is due to Earth's rotation. The wind doesn't have to be produced by giant lungs; its existence arises through the spontaneous action of air subjected to uneven heating by the sun. In other words, a moving sun does not imply a horse-and-chariot, after all; nor does the wind imply the mouth of a blower.

The natural phenomena of Earth and of the Universe have seemed to fall into place bit by bit as behavior that is random, spontaneous, unwilled, and that takes place within the constraints of the "laws of nature."

Scientists grew increasingly reluctant to suppose that the workings of the laws of nature were ever interfered with (something that would be defined as a "miracle"). Certainly, no such interference was ever observed, and the tales of such interferences in the past came to seem increasingly dubious.

In short, the scientific view sees the Universe as following its own rules blindly without either interference or direction.

That still leaves it possible that God created the Universe to begin with and designed the laws of nature that govern its behavior. From this standpoint, the Universe might be viewed as a wind-up toy, which God has wound up once and for all and which is now winding down and working itself out in all its intricacy without having to be touched at all.

If, so, that reduces God's involvement to a minimum and makes one wonder if he is needed at all.

So far, scientists have not uncovered any evidence that would hint that the workings of the Universe require the action of a divine being. On the other hand, scientists have uncovered no evidence that indicates that a divine being does *not* exist.

If scientists have not proven either that God exists or that he does not exist, then, from the scientific viewpoint, are we entitled to believe either alternative?

Not really. It is not reasonable to demand proof of a negative and to accept the positive in the absence of such a proof. After all, if science has not succeeded in proving that God does not exist, neither has it succeeded in proving that Zeus does not exist, or Marduk, or Thoth, or any of the myriads of gods postulated by all sorts of mythmakers. If the failure of proof of nonexistence is taken as proof of existence, then we must conclude that *all* exist.

Yet that leaves us with the final, nagging question: "But where did all this come from? How did the Universe come into being in the first place?"

If one tries to answer, "The Universe was always there; it is eternal," then one comes up against the uncomfortable concept of eternity and the irresistible assumption that everything had to have a beginning.

Out of sheer exhaustion one longs to solve everything by saying, "God made the Universe!" That gives us a start, at least.

But then we find that we have escaped eternity only by postulating

it, for we are not even allowed to ask the question, "Who made God?"
The question itself is blasphemous. God is eternal, by definition.

If, then, we are going to be stuck with eternity in any case, there
seems some advantage to a science that lives by observing and measuring, to choose an eternal something that can at least be observed
and measured—the Universe itself, rather than God.

The notion of an eternal Universe introduces a great many difficulties, some of them apparently (at least in the present state of our
scientific knowledge) insuperable, but scientists are not disturbed by
difficulties—those make up the game. If all the difficulties were gone
and all the questions answered, the game of science would be over.
(Scientists suspect that will never happen.)

There, then, is perhaps the most fundamental disagreement
between the Bible and science. The Bible describes a Universe created
by God, maintained by him, and intimately and constantly directed by
him, while science describes a Universe in which it is not necessary to
postulate the existence of God at all.

This is *not* to say, by the way, that scientists are all atheists or that
any of them must be atheists of necessity. There are many scientists
who are as firmly religious as any nonscientist. Nevertheless, such scientists, if they are competent professionals, must operate on two
levels. Whatever their faith in God in ordinary life, they must leave
God out of account while engaged in their scientific observations.
They can never explain a particular puzzling phenomenon by claiming
it to be the result of God's suspension of natural law.

6. The first act of God recorded in the Bible is that of the creation of
the Universe. But since God is eternal, there must have been an infinitely long period of time before he set our Universe into motion.
What was he doing during that infinitely long period of time?

When St. Augustine was asked that question, he is supposed to
have roared, "Creating Hell for those who ask questions like that!"

Ignoring St. Augustine (if we dare), we might speculate. God
might, for instance, have spent the time creating an endless hierarchy

of angels. For that matter, he might have created an endless number of universes, one after the other, each for its own purpose, with our own being merely the current member of the series, to be followed by an equally endless number of successors. Or God might, until the moment of the Creation, have done nothing but commune with his infinite self.

All possible answers to the question are merely suppositions, however, since there is no evidence for any one of them. There is not only no scientific evidence for them; there is not even any Biblical evidence. The answers belong entirely to the world of legend.

But then if we switch to the world of science and think of an eternal Universe, we must ask what the Universe was like before it took on its present form about fifteen billion years ago. There are some speculations. The Universe may have existed through eternity as an infinitely thin scattering of matter and energy that very slowly coalesced into a tiny dense object, the "cosmic egg," which exploded to form the Universe we now have, a Universe that will expand forever until it is an infinitely thin scattering of matter and energy again.

Or else there is an alternation of expansion and contraction, an endless series of cosmic eggs, each of which explodes to form a Universe. Our own present Universe is only the current member of an endless series.

Science, however, has found no way as yet of penetrating into a time earlier than that of the cosmic egg that exploded to form our Universe. The Bible and science agree in being unable to say anything certainly about what happened before the beginning.

There is this difference. The Bible will never be able to tell us. It has reached its final form, and it simply doesn't say. Science, on the other hand, is still developing, and the time may come when it can answer questions that, at present, it cannot.

7. By heaven, in this verse, is meant the vault of the sky and the permanent objects within it—the sun, moon, planets, and stars. The Bible views this vault as the Babylonians did (and the Egyptians, the Greeks,

and all the early peoples, apparently without exception); that is, as a solid, semicircular dome overspreading Earth. This is the Biblical view throughout. Thus, in Revelation, the last book of the Bible, the final end of the heaven is described thus: "The heaven departed as a scroll when it is rolled together" (Revelation 6:14). This quoted a passage in the Old Testament (Isaiah 34:4) and clearly shows the heaven to have been viewed as no thicker, in proportion to its extent, than a sheet of parchment.

In the scientific view, however, the sky is not a simple vault, but is a vast outstretching of space-time into which our telescopes have probed for distances of ten billion light-years, where each light-year is 5.88 trillion miles long.

8. The "heaven and the earth" form a definite geometrical shape in the Bible. The earth is a flat, probably circular, area of extent large enough to hold those kingdoms known to the Biblical writers. The heaven is a semispherical vault that nestles down over the earth. Human beings, by this picture, seem to live on the floor of a world that is inside a hollow semisphere.

It is so described in the Book of Isaiah: "It is he [God] that sitteth upon the circle of the earth . . . that stretched out the heavens as a curtain, and spreadeth them out as a tent to dwell in" (Isaiah 40:22).

The vault of heaven would require support to keep it from collapsing, if we judge from earthly structures. The support might be a supernatural being (like the Greek myth of Atlas) or something more mechanical. The Bible has a passage that reads, "The pillars of heaven tremble" (Job 26:11).

All this is utterly different from the scientific view of Earth as a sphere, suspended in emptiness, that rotates on its axis, revolves about the sun, takes part in the sun's revolution about the center of the Galaxy, and is surrounded by a largely empty and virtually illimitable Universe.

Part IV.

THE DEFICIENCIES
OF RELIGION

13

THE CHRISTIAN SYSTEM

Arthur Schopenhauer

[Arthur Schopenhauer (1788–1860), German philosopher, studied in Germany, France, and England and was well acquainted with Goethe and the brothers Grimm. His major philosophical work is *Das Welt als Wille und Vorstellung* (1818; usually translated as *The World as Will and Representation*). In this work, Schopenhauer develops the idea of will as the fundamental reality in the universe, equivalent to Kant's thing-in-itself. Human life is dominated by willing and hence is filled with struggle and conflict. Although the "will to live" is universal, the optimum state for human beings is the reduction or elimination of will, achievable only by those who reject desire. Accordingly, Schopenhauer's philosophy is highly pessimistic, and in a succession of essays in the collection *Parerga et Paralipomena* (1851), he advocated universal suicide as the only remedy for the agony of life. These essays were later translated into the volume *Studies in Pes-*

Arthur Schopenhauer, "The Christian System," in *Religion: A Dialogue and Other Essays*, trans. T. Bailey Saunders (London: Swan Sonnenschein, 1889), pp. 105–17.

simism. In "Über das Christentum" (part of the essay Über Religion" in *Parerga et Paralipomena*), translated as "The Christian System," Schopenhauer points out several moral deficiencies in Christian doctrine, especially as pertains to the treatment of animals.]

When the Church says that, in the dogmas of religion, reason is totally incompetent and blind, and its use to be reprehended, it is in reality attesting the fact that these dogmas are allegorical in their nature, and are not to be judged by the standard which reason, taking all things *sensu proprio*,[1] can alone apply. Now the absurdities of a dogma are just the mark and sign of what is allegorical and mythical in it. In the case under consideration, however, the absurdities spring from the fact that two such heterogeneous doctrines as those of the Old and New Testaments had to be combined. The great allegory was of gradual growth. Suggested by external and adventitious circumstances, it was developed by the interpretation put upon them, an interpretation in quiet touch with certain deep-lying truths only half realized. The allegory was finally completed by Augustine, who penetrated deepest into its meaning, and so was able to conceive it as a systematic whole and supply its defects. Hence the Augustinian doctrine, confirmed by Luther, is the complete form of Christianity; and the Protestants of to-day, who take Revelation *sensu proprio* and confine it to a single individual, are in error in looking upon the first beginnings of Christianity as its most perfect expression. But the bad thing about all religions is that, instead of being able to confess their allegorical nature, they have to conceal it; accordingly, they parade their doctrine in all seriousness as true *sensu proprio*, and as absurdities form an essential part of these doctrines, you have the great mischief of a continual fraud. And, what is worse, the day arrives when they are no longer true *sensu proprio*, and then there is an end of them; so that, in that respect, it would be better to admit their allegorical nature at once. But the difficulty is to teach the multitude that something can be both true and untrue at the same time. And as all religions are in a greater or less degree of this nature, we must recognize the fact that mankind cannot get on without a certain amount of absurdity, that absurdity is an element in its existence, and illusion indispensable; as indeed other aspects of life testify.

I have said that the combination of the Old Testament with the New gives rise to absurdities. Among the examples which illustrate what I mean, I may cite the Christian doctrine of Predestination and Grace, as formulated by Augustine and adopted from him by Luther; according to which one man is endowed with grace and another is not. Grace, then, comes to be a privilege received at birth and brought ready into the world; a privilege, too, in a matter second to none in importance. What is obnoxious and absurd in this doctrine may be traced to the idea contained in the Old Testament, that man is the creation of an external will, which called him into existence out of nothing. It is quite true that genuine moral excellence is really innate; but the meaning of the Christian doctrine is expressed in another and more rational way by the theory of metempsychosis, common to Brahmans and Buddhists. According to this theory, the qualities which distinguish one man from another are received at birth, are brought, that is to say, from another world and a former life; these qualities are not an external gift of grace, but are the fruits of the acts committed in that other world. But Augustine's dogma of Predestination is connected with another dogma, namely, that the mass of humanity is corrupt and doomed to eternal damnation, that very few will be found righteous and attain salvation, and that only in consequence of the gift of grace, and because they are predestined to be saved; whilst the remainder will be overwhelmed by the perdition they have deserved, viz., eternal torment in hell. Taken in its ordinary meaning, the dogma is revolting, for it comes to this: it condemns a man, who may be, perhaps, scarcely twenty years of age, to expiate his errors, or even his unbelief, in everlasting torment; nay, more, it makes this almost universal damnation the natural effect of original sin, and therefore the necessary consequence of the Fall. This is a result which must have been foreseen by him who made mankind, and who, in the first place, made them not better than they are, and secondly, set a trap for them into which he must have known they would fall; for he made the whole world, and nothing is hidden from him. According to this doctrine, then, God created out of nothing a weak race prone to sin, in order to give them over to endless torment. And, as a last characteristic, we are told that this God, who prescribes forbearance and forgiveness of every fault, exercises none himself, but does the exact opposite; for a punishment which comes at the end of all things, when the world is over and done with, cannot have for its object either to improve or deter, and is therefore pure vengeance. So that, on this view, the whole race is actually destined to eternal torture and damnation, and created expressly for this end, the only exception being those few persons who are rescued by election of grace, from what motive one does not know.

Putting these aside, it looks as if the Blessed Lord had created the world for the benefit of the devil! It would have been so much better not to have made it at all. So much, then, for a dogma taken *sensu proprio*. But look at it *sensu allegorico*,[2] and the whole matter becomes capable of a satisfactory interpretation. What is absurd and revolting in this dogma is, in the main, as I said, the simple outcome of Jewish theism, with its "creation out of nothing," and really foolish and paradoxical denial of the doctrine of metempsychosis which is involved in that idea, a doctrine which is natural, to a certain extent self-evident, and, with the exception of the Jews, accepted by nearly the whole human race at all times. To remove the enormous evil arising from Augustine's dogma, and to modify its revolting nature, Pope Gregory I., in the sixth century, very prudently matured the doctrine of *Purgatory*, the essence of which already existed in Origen (cf. Bayle's article on Origen, note B.).[3] The doctrine was regularly incorporated into the faith of the Church, so that the original view was much modified, and a certain substitute provided for the doctrine of metempsychosis; for both the one and the other admit a process of purification. To the same end, the doctrine of "the Restoration of all things" αποκατασταί was established, according to which, in the last act of the Human Comedy, the sinners one and all will be reinstated *in integrum*.[4] It is only Protestants, with their obstinate belief in the Bible, who cannot be induced to give up eternal punishment in hell. If one were spiteful, one might say, "much good may it do them," but it is consoling to think that they really do not believe the doctrine; they leave it alone, thinking in their hearts, "It can't be so bad as all that."

The rigid and systematic character of his mind led Augustine, in his austere dogmatism and his resolute definition of doctrines only just indicated in the Bible and, as a matter of fact, resting on very vague grounds, to give hard outlines to these doctrines and to put a harsh construction on Christianity: the result of which is that his views offend us, and just as in his day Pelagianism arose to combat them,[5] so now in our day Rationalism does the same. Take, for example, the case as he states it generally in the *De Civitate Dei*, Bk. xii. ch. 21. It comes to this: God creates a being out of nothing, forbids him some things, and enjoins others upon him; and because these commands are not obeyed, he tortures him to all eternity with every conceivable anguish; and for this purpose, binds soul and body inseparably together, so that, instead of the torment destroying this being by splitting him up into his elements, and so setting him free, he may live to eternal pain. This poor creature, formed out of nothing! At least, he has a claim on his original nothing: he should be assured, as a matter of right, of this last retreat, which, in any case, cannot be a very evil one: it is what he has inherited. I, at any rate, cannot help sympathizing with him. If you add to this Augustine's remaining doctrines, that all this does not depend on the man's own sins and omissions, but was already predestined to happen, one really is at a loss what to think. Our highly educated Rationalists say, to be sure, "It's all false, it's a mere bugbear; we're in a state of constant progress, step by step raising ourselves to ever greater perfection." Ah! what a pity we didn't begin sooner; we should already have been there.

In the Christian system the devil is a personage of the greatest importance. God is described as absolutely good, wise and powerful; and unless he were counterbalanced by the devil, it would be impossible to see where the innumerable and measureless evils, which predominate in the world, come from, if there were no devil to account for them. And since the Rationalists have done away with the devil, the damage inflicted on the other side has gone on growing, and is becoming more and more palpable; as might have been foreseen, and was foreseen, by the orthodox. The fact is, you cannot take away one pillar from a building without endangering the rest of it. And this confirms the view, which has been established on other grounds, that Jehovah is a transformation of Ormuzd, and Satan of the Ahriman who must be taken in connection with him. Ormuzd himself is a transformation of Indra.[6]

Christianity has this peculiar disadvantage, that, unlike other religions, it is not a pure system of doctrine: its chief and essential feature is that it is a history, a series of events, a collection of facts, a statement of the actions and sufferings of individuals: it is this history which constitutes dogma, and belief in it is salvation. Other religions, Buddhism, for instance, have, it is true, historical appendages, the life, namely, of their founders: this, however, is not part and parcel of the dogma but is taken along with it. For example, the Lalitavistara may be compared with the Gospel so far as it contains the life of Sakya-muni,[7] the Buddha of the present period of the world's history: but this is something which is quite separate and different from the dogma, from the system itself: and for this reason; the lives of former Buddhas were quite other, and those of the future will be quite other, than the life of the Buddha of to-day. The dogma is by no means one with the career of its founder; it does not rest on individual persons or events; it is something universal and equally valid at all times. The Lalitavistara is not, then, a gospel in the Christian sense of the word; it is not the joyful message of an act of redemption; it is the career of him who has shown how each one may redeem himself. The historical constitution of Christianity makes the Chinese laugh at missionaries as story-tellers.

I may mention here another fundamental error of Christianity, an error which cannot be explained away, and the mischievous consequences of which are obvious every day: I mean the unnatural distinction Christianity makes between man and the animal world to which he really belongs. It sets up man as all-important, and looks upon animals as merely things. Brahmanism and Buddhism, on the other hand, true to the facts, recognize in a positive way that man is related generally to the whole of nature, and specially and principally to animal nature; and in their systems man is always represented by the theory of metempsychosis and otherwise, as closely connected with the animal world. The important part played by animals all through Buddhism and Brahmanism, compared with the total disregard of them in Judaism and Christianity, puts an end to any question as to which system is nearer perfection, however much we in Europe may have become accustomed to the absurdity of the claim. Christianity contains, in fact, a great and essential imperfection in limiting its precepts to man, and in refusing rights to the entire animal world. As religion fails to protect animals against the rough, unfeeling and often more than bestial multitude, the duty falls to the police; and as the police are unequal to the task, societies for the protection of animals are now formed all over Europe and America. In the whole of uncircumcised Asia, such a procedure would be the most superfluous thing in the world, because animals are there sufficiently protected by religion, which even makes them objects of charity. How such charitable feelings bear fruit may be seen, to take an example, in the great hospital for animals at Surat, whither Christians, Mohammedans and Jews can send their sick beasts, which, if cured, are very rightly not restored to their owners. In the same way when a Brahman or a Buddhist has a slice of good luck, a happy issue in any affair, instead of mumbling a *Te Deum*, he goes to the market-place and buys birds and opens their cages at the city gate; a thing which may be frequently seen in Astrachan, where the adherents of every religion meet together: and so on in a hundred similar ways. On the other hand, look at the revolting ruffianism with which our Christian public treats its animals; killing them for no object at all, and laughing over it, or mutilating or torturing them: even its horses, who form its most direct means of livelihood, are strained to the utmost in their old age, and the last strength worked out of their poor bones until they succumb at last under the whip. One might say with truth, Mankind are the devils of the earth, and the animals the souls they torment. But what can you expect from the masses, when there are men of education, zoologists even, who, instead of admitting what is so familiar to them, the essential identity of man and animal, are bigoted and stupid enough to offer a zealous opposition to their honest and rational colleagues, when they class man under the proper head as an animal, or demonstrate the resemblance between him and the chimpanzee or ourang-outang. It is a revolting thing that a writer who is so pious and Christian in his sentiments as Jung Stilling should use a simile like this, in his *Scenen aus dem Geister-reich.* (Bk. II. sc. I, p. 15.) "Suddenly the skeleton shriveled up into an indescribably hideous and dwarf-like form, just as when you bring a large spider into the focus of a burning glass, and watch the purulent blood hiss and bubble in the heat."[8] This man of God then was guilty of such infamy! or looked on quietly when another was committing it! in either case it comes to the same thing here. So little harm did he think of it that he tells us of it in passing, and without a trace of emotion. Such are the effects of the first chapter of Genesis, and, in fact, of the whole of the Jewish conception of nature. The standard recognized by the Hindus and Buddhists is the Mahavakya (the great word),—"tat-twam-asi" (this is thyself), which may always be spoken of every animal, to keep us in mind of the identity of his inmost being with ours. Perfection of morality, indeed! Nonsense. [. . .]

Whoever seriously thinks that superhuman beings have ever given our race information as to the aim of its existence and that of the world, is still in his childhood. There is no other revelation than the thoughts of the wise, even though these thoughts, liable to error as is the lot of everything human, are often clothed in strange allegories and myths under the name of religion. So far, then, it is a matter of indifference whether a man lives and dies in reliance on his own or another's thoughts; for it is never more than human thought, human opinion, which he trusts. Still, instead of trusting what their own minds tell them, men have as a rule a weakness for trusting others who pretend to supernatural sources of knowledge. And in view of the enormous intellectual inequality between man and man, it is easy to see that the thoughts of one mind might appear as in some sense a revelation to another.

NOTES

1. ["In the proper (or literal) sense."]
2. ["In the allegorical sense."]
3. [Schopenhauer refers to an article by Pierre Bayle (1647–1706) in his *Dictionnaire historique et critique* (1697), a work condemned by the church because of its deliberate attempt to destroy Christian beliefs.]
4. ["Into wholeness."]
5. [Pelagianism is the doctrine that human beings can, by their own efforts, take steps toward their own salvation, apart from divine grace. It was condemned as a heresy in 411 and 418.]
6. [Ormuzd is the principle of good, as opposed to Ahriman, the principle of evil, in Zoroastrianism. Indra is the supreme god of the Indo-Aryans and part of the pre-Hindu religion embodied in the *Rig Veda*.]
7. [The *Lalitavistara* is a Buddhist text of the second century CE that provides a poetical account of the life of the young Buddha. Sayamuni is a title of the Buddha, denoting that he is derived from the Sakya tribe in present-day Nepal.]
8. [Johann Heinrich Jung-Stilling (1740–1817), German mystic and author of *Scenen aus dem Geisterreiche* (1795; Scenes from the World of Spirits), a treatise on spirits from a Christian perspective.]

14

THE ETHICS OF RELIGION

W. K. Clifford

[William Kingdon Clifford (1845–1879), British mathematician and philosopher, studied at King's College, London, and Trinity College, Cambridge, where he became a leading member of the debating club, the Cambridge Apostles. Influenced by readings of Darwin and Spencer, he abandoned his high-church upbringing and became a freethinker. He taught mathematics at University College, London, and became a fellow of the Royal Society. Although afflicted with a pulmonary disease that would result in his early death, Clifford wrote prolifically on mathematics, philosophy, and other subjects. Some of his work was posthumously published as *Mathematical Papers* (1882) and *The Common Sense of the Exact Sciences* (1885). He turned his attention to religion and ethics in the landmark paper "The Ethics of Belief" (1876), which asserted the immorality of believing any proposition on insufficient evidence. His essays on these

W. K. Clifford, "The Ethics of Religion" (1877), in *Lectures and Essays*, ed. Leslie Stephen and Frederick Pollock (London: Macmillan, 1879), 1: 218–28, 237–43.

subjects were gathered by Leslie Stephen and Frederick Pollock in *Lectures and Essays* (1879). In "The Ethics of Religion," first published in the *Fortnightly Review* (July 1877), Clifford notes that many actions by the Christian God represent "a magnified copy of what bad men do."]

L et us enquire [. . .] what morality has to say in regard to religious doctrines. It deals with the *manner* of religious belief directly, and with the *matter* indirectly. Religious beliefs must be founded on evidence; if they are not so founded, it is wrong to hold them. The rule of right conduct in this matter is exactly the opposite of that implied in the two famous texts: "He that believeth not shall be damned" [Mark 16:16], and "Blessed are they that have not seen and yet have believed" [John 20:29]. For a man who clearly felt and recognized the duty of intellectual honesty, of carefully testing every belief before he received it, and especially before he recommended it to others, it would be impossible to ascribe the profoundly immoral teaching of these texts to a true prophet or worthy leader of humanity. It will comfort those who wish to preserve their reverence for the character of a great teacher to remember that one of these sayings is in the well-known forged passage at the end of the second gospel, and that the other occurs only in the late and legendary fourth gospel; both being described as spoken under utterly impossible circumstances. These precepts belong to the Church and not to the Gospel. But whoever wrote either of them down as a deliverance of one whom he supposed to be a divine teacher, has thereby written down himself as a man void of intellectual honesty, as a man whose word cannot be trusted, as a man who would accept and spread about any kind of baseless fiction for fear of believing too little.

So far as to the manner of religious belief. Let us now inquire what bearing morality has upon its matter. We may see at once that this can only be indirect; for the rightness or wrongness of belief in a doctrine depends only upon the nature of the evidence for it, and not upon what the doctrine is. But there is a very important way in which religious doctrine may lead to morality or immorality, and in which, therefore, morality has a bearing upon doctrine. It is when that doctrine declares the character and actions of the Gods who are regarded as objects of reverence and worship. If a God is represented as doing that which is clearly wrong, and is still held up to the reverence of men, they will be tempted to think that in doing this wrong thing they are not so very wrong after all, but are only following an example which all men respect. So says Plato:—[1]

"We must not tell a youthful listener that he will be doing nothing extraordinary if he commit the foulest crimes, nor yet if he chastise the crimes of a father in the most unscrupulous manner, but will simply be doing what the first and greatest of the Gods have done before him. . . .

"Nor yet is it proper to say in any case—what is indeed untrue—that Gods wage war against Gods, and intrigue and fight among themselves; that is, if the future guardians of our state are to deem it a most disgraceful thing to quarrel lightly with one another: far less ought we to select as subjects for fiction and embroidery the battles of the giants, and numerous other feuds of all sorts, in which Gods and heroes fight against their own kith and kin. But if there is any possibility of persuading them that to quarrel with one's fellow is a sin of which no member of a state was ever guilty, such ought rather to be the language held to our children from the first, by old men and old women, and all elderly persons; and such is the strain in which our poets must be compelled to write. But stories like the chaining of Hera by her son, and the flinging of Hephaistos out of heaven for trying to take his mother's part when his father was beating her, and all those battles of the Gods which are to be found in Homer, must be refused admittance into our state, whether they be allegorical or not. For a child cannot discriminate between what is allegory and what is not; and whatever at that age is adopted as a matter of belief has a tendency to become fixed and indelible, and therefore, perhaps, we ought to esteem it of the greatest importance that the fictions which children first hear should be adapted in the most perfect manner to the promotion of virtue."

And Seneca says the same thing, with still more reason in his day and country: "What else is this appeal to the precedent of the Gods for, but to inflame our lusts, and to furnish licence and excuse for the corrupt act under the divine protection?" And again, of the character of Jupiter as described in the popular legends: "This has led to no other result than to deprive sin of its shame in man's eyes, by showing him the God no better than himself." In Imperial Rome, the sink of all nations, it was not uncommon to find the intending sinner addressing to the deified vice which he contemplated a prayer for the success of his design; the adulteress imploring of Venus the favours of her paramour; . . . the thief praying to Hermes Dolios for aid in his enterprise, or offering up to him the first fruits of his plunder; . . . youths entreating Hercules to expedite the death of a rich uncle."[2]

When we reflect that criminal deities were worshipped all over the empire, we cannot but wonder that any good people were left; that man could still be holy, although every God was vile. Yet this was undoubtedly the case; the social forces worked steadily on wherever there was peace and a settled government and municipal freedom; and the wicked stories of theologians were somehow explained away and disregarded. If men were no better than their religions, the world would be a hell indeed.

It is very important, however, to consider what really ought to be done in the case of stories like these. When the poet sings that Zeus kicked Hephaistos out of heaven for trying to help his mother, Plato says that this fiction must be suppressed by law. We cannot follow him there, for since his time we have had too much of trying to suppress false doctrines by law. Plato thinks it quite obviously clear that God cannot produce evil, and he would stop everybody's mouth who ventured to say that he can. But in regard to the doctrine itself, we can only ask, "Is it true?" And that is a question to be settled by evidence. Did Zeus commit this crime, or did he not? We must ask the apologists, the reconcilers of religion and science, what evidence they can produce to prove that Zeus kicked Hephaistos out of heaven. That a doctrine may lead to immoral consequences is no reason for disbelieving it. But whether the doctrine were true or false, one thing does clearly follow from its moral character: namely this, that if Zeus behaved as he is said to have behaved, he ought not to be worshipped. To those who complain of his violence and injustice, it is no answer to say that the divine attributes are far above human comprehension; that the ways of Zeus are not our ways, neither are his thoughts our thoughts. If he is to be worshipped, he must do something vaster and nobler and greater than good men do, but it must be like what they do in its goodness. His actions must not be merely a magnified copy of what bad men do. So soon as they are thus represented, morality has something to say. Not indeed about the fact; for it is not conscience, but reason, that has to judge matters of fact; but about the worship of a character so represented. If there really is good evidence that Zeus kicked Hephaistos out of heaven, and seduced Alkmene by a mean trick, say so by all means; but say also that it is wrong to salute his priests or to make offerings in his temple.

When men do their duty in this respect, morality has a very curious indirect effect on the religious doctrine itself. As soon as the offerings become less frequent, the evidence for the doctrine begins to fade away; the process of theological interpretation gradually brings out the true inner meaning of it, that Zeus did not kick Hephaistos out of heaven, and did not seduce Alkmene.

Is this a merely theoretical discussion about faraway things? Let us come back for a moment to our own time and country, and think whether there can be any lesson for us in this refusal of common-sense morality to worship a deity whose actions are a magnified copy of what bad men do. There are three doctrines which find very wide acceptance among our countrymen at the present day: the doctrines of original sin, of a vicarious sacrifice, and of eternal punishments. We are not concerned with any refined evaporations of these doctrines which are exhaled by courtly theologians, but with the naked state-ments which are put into the minds of children and of ignorant people, which are taught broadcast and without shame in denominational schools. Father Faber, good soul, persuaded himself that after all only a very few people would be really damned, and Father Oxenham gives one the impression that it will not hurt even them very much.[3] But one learns the practical teaching of the Church from such books as "A Glimpse of Hell,"[4] where a child is described as thrown between the bars upon the burning coals, there to writhe for ever. The masses do not get the elegant emasculations of Father Faber and Father Oxenham; they get "a Glimpse of Hell."

Now to condemn all mankind for the sin of Adam and Eve; to let the innocent suffer for the guilty; to keep anyone alive in torture for ever and ever; these actions are simply magnified copies of what bad men do. No juggling with "divine justice and mercy" can make them anything else. This must be said to all kinds and conditions of men: that if God holds all mankind guilty for the sin of Adam, if he has visited upon the innocent the punishment of the guilty, if he is to torture any single soul for ever, then it is wrong to worship him.

But there is something to be said also to those who think that religious beliefs are not indeed true, but are useful for the masses; who deprecate any open and public argument against them, and think that all sceptical books should be published at a high price; who go to church, not because they approve of it themselves, but to set an example to the servants. Let us ask them to ponder the words of Plato, who, like them, thought that all these tales of the Gods were fables, but still fables which might be useful to amuse children with: *"We ought to esteem it of the greatest importance that the fictions which children first hear should be adapted in the most perfect manner to the promotion of virtue."* If we grant to you that it is good for poor people and children to believe some of these fictions, is it not better, at least, that they should believe those which are adapted to the promotion of virtue? Now the stories which you send your servants and children to hear are adapted to the promotion of vice. So far as the remedy is in your own hands, you are bound to apply it; stop your voluntary subscriptions and the moral support of your presence from any place where the criminal doctrines are taught. You will find more men and better men to preach that which is agreeable to their conscience, than to thunder out doctrines under which their minds are always uneasy, and which only a continual self-deception can keep them from feeling to be wicked.

Let us now go on to enquire what morality has to say in the matter of religious *ministrations*, the official acts and the general influence of a priesthood. This question seems to me a more difficult one than the former; at any rate it is not so easy to find general principles which are at once simple in their nature and clear to the conscience of any man who honestly considers them. One such principle, indeed, there is, which can hardly be stated in a Protestant country without meeting with a cordial response; being indeed that characteristic of our race which made the Reformation a necessity, and became the soul of the Protestant movement. I mean the principle which forbids the priest to come between a man and his conscience. If it be true, as our daily experience teaches us, that the moral sense gains in clearness and power by exercise, by the constant endeavour to find out and to see for ourselves what is right and what is wrong, it must be nothing short of a moral suicide to delegate our conscience to another man. It is true that when we are in difficulties and do not altogether see our way, we quite rightly seek counsel and advice of some friend who has more experience, more wisdom begot by it, more devotion to the right than ourselves, and who, not being involved in the difficulties which encompass us, may more easily see the way out of them. But such counsel does not and ought not to take the place of our private judgment; on the contrary, among wise men it is asked and given for the purpose of helping and supporting private judgment. I should go to my friend, not that he may tell me what to do, but that he may help me to see what is right.

Now, as we all know, there is a priesthood whose influence is not to be made light of, even in our own land, which claims to do two things: to declare with infallible authority what is right and what is wrong, and to take away the guilt of the sinner after confession has been made to it. The second of these claims we shall come back upon in connexion with another part of the subject. But that claim is one which, as it seems to me, ought to condemn the priesthood making it in the eyes of every conscientious man. We must take care to keep this question to itself, and not to let it be confused with quite different ones. The priesthood in question, as we all know, has taught that as right which is not right, and has condemned as wrong some of the holiest duties of mankind. But this is not what we are here concerned with. Let us put an ideal case of a priesthood which, as a matter of fact, taught a morality agreeing with the healthy conscience of all men at a given time; but which, nevertheless, taught this as an infallible revelation. The tendency of such teaching, if really accepted, would be to destroy morality altogether, for it is of the very essence of the moral sense that it is a common perception by men of what is good for man. It arises, not in one man's mind by a flash of genius or a transport of ecstasy, but in all men's minds, as the fruit of their necessary intercourse and united labour for a common object. When an infallible authority is set up, the voice of this natural human conscience must be hushed and schooled, and made to speak the words of a formula. Obedience becomes the whole duty of man; and the notion of right is attached to a lifeless code of rules, instead of being the informing character of a nation. The natural consequence is that it fades gradually out and ends by disappearing altogether. I am not describing a purely conjectural state of things, but an effect which has actually been produced at various times and in considerable populations by the influence of the Catholic Church. It is true that we cannot find an actually crucial instance of a pure morality taught as an infallible revelation, and so in time ceasing to be morality for that reason alone. There are two circumstances which prevent this. One is that the Catholic priesthood has always practically taught an imperfect morality, and that it is difficult to distinguish between the effects of precepts which are wrong in themselves, and precepts which are only wrong because of the manner in which they are enforced. The other circumstance is that the priesthood has very rarely found a population willing to place itself completely and absolutely under priestly control. Men must live together and work for common objects even in priest-ridden countries;

and those conditions which in the course of ages have been able to create the moral sense cannot fail in some degree to recall it to men's minds and gradually to reinforce it. Thus it comes about that a great and increasing portion of life breaks free from priestly influences, and is governed upon right and rational grounds. The goodness of men shows itself in time more powerful than the wickedness of some of their religions. [. . .]

I can find no evidence that seriously militates against the rule that the priest is at all times and in all places the enemy of all men—*Sacerdos semper, ubique, et omnibus inimicus*.[5] I do not deny that the priest is very often a most earnest and conscientious man, doing the very best that he knows of as well as he can do it. Lord Amberley is quite right in saying that the blame rests more with the laity than with the priesthood;[6] that it has insisted on magic and mysteries, and has forced the priesthood to produce them. But then, how dreadful is the system that puts good men to such uses!

And although it is true that in its origin a priesthood is the effect of an evil already existing, a symptom of social disease rather than a cause of it, yet, once being created and made powerful, it tends in many ways to prolong and increase the disease which gave it birth. One of these ways is so marked and of such practical importance that we are bound to consider it here: I mean the education of children. If there is one lesson which history forces upon us in every page, it is this: *Keep your children away from the priest, or he will make them the enemies of mankind.* It is not the Catholic clergy and those like them who are alone to be dreaded in this matter; even the representatives of apparently harmless religions may do incalculable mischief if they get education into their hands. To the early Mohammedans the mosque was the one public building in every place where public business could be transacted; and so it was naturally the place of primary education, which they held to be a matter of supreme importance. By-and-by, as the clergy grew up, the mosque was gradually usurped by them, and primary education fell into their hands. Then ensued a "revival of religion"; religion became a fanaticism: books were burnt and universities were closed; the empire rotted away in East and West, until it was conquered by Turkish savages in Asia and by Christian savages in Spain.

The labours of students of the early history of institutions—notably Sir Henry Maine and M. de Laveleye[7]—have disclosed to us an element of society which appears to have existed in all times and places, and which is the basis of our own social structure. The village community, or commune, or township, found in tribes of the most varied race and time, has so modified itself as to get adapted in one place or another to all the different conditions of human existence. This union of men to work for a common object has transformed them from wild animals into tame ones. Century by century the educating process of the social life has been working at human nature; it has built itself into our inmost soul. Such as we are—moral and rational beings—thinking and talking in general conceptions about the facts that make up our life, feeling a necessity to act, not for ourselves, but for Ourself, for the larger life of Man in which we are elements; such moral and rational beings, I say, Man has made us. By Man I mean men organized into a society, which fights for its life, not only as a mere collection of men who must separately be kept alive, but as a society. It must fight, not only against external enemies, but against treason and disruption within it. Hence comes the unity of interest of all its members; each of them has to feel that he is not himself only but a part of all the rest. Conscience—the sense of right and wrong—springs out of the habit of judging things from the point of view of all and not of one. It is Ourself, not ourselves, that makes for righteousness.

The codes of morality, then, which are adopted into various religions, and afterwards taught as parts of religious systems, are derived from secular sources. The most ancient version of the Ten Commandments, whatever the investigations of scholars may make it out to be, originates not in the thunders of Sinai, but in the peaceful life of men on the plains of Chaldaea. Conscience is the voice of Man ingrained into our hearts, commanding us to work for Man.

Religions differ in the treatment which they give to this most sacred heirloom of our past history. Sometimes they invert its precepts—telling men to be submissive under oppression because the powers that be are ordained of God; telling them to believe where they have not seen, and to play with falsehood in order that a particular doctrine may prevail, instead of seeking for truth whatever it may be; telling them to betray their country for the sake of their church. But there is one great distinction to which I wish, in conclusion, to call special attention—a distinction between two kinds of religious emotion which bear upon the conduct of men.

We said that conscience is the voice of Man within us, commanding us to work for Man. We do not know this immediately by our own experience; we only know that something within us commands us to work for Man. This fact men have tried to explain; and they have thought, for the most part, that this voice was the voice of a God. But the explanation takes two different forms: the God may speak in us for Man's sake, or for his own sake. If he speaks for his own sake—and this is what generally happens when he has priests who lay claim to a magical character and powers—our allegiance is apt to be taken away from Man, and transferred to the God. When we love our brother for the sake of our brother, we help all men to grow in the right; but when we love our brother for the sake of somebody else, who is very likely to damn our brother, it very soon comes to burning him alive for his soul's health. When men respect human life for the sake of Man, tranquillity, order, and progress go hand in hand; but those who only respected human life because God had forbidden murder have set their mark upon Europe in fifteen centuries of blood and fire.

These are only two examples of a general rule. Wherever the allegiance of men has been diverted from Man to some divinity who speaks to men for his own sake and seeks his own glory, one thing has happened. The right precepts might be enforced, but they were enforced upon wrong grounds, and they were not obeyed. But right precepts are not always enforced; the fact that the fountains of morality have been poisoned makes it easy to substitute wrong precepts for right ones.

To this same treason against humanity belongs the claim of the priesthood to take away the guilt of a sinner after confession has been made to it. The Catholic priest professes to act as an ambassador for his God, and to absolve the guilty man by conveying to him the forgiveness of heaven. If his credentials were ever so sure, if he were indeed the ambassador of a superhuman power, the claim would be treasonable. Can the favour of the Czar make guiltless the murderer of old men and women and children in Circassian valleys? Can the pardon of the Sultan make clean the bloody hands of a Pasha? As little can any God forgive sins committed against man. When men think he can, they compound for old sins which the God did not like by committing new ones which he does like. Many a remorseful despot has atoned for the levities of his youth by the persecution of heretics in his old age. That frightful crime, the adulteration of food, could not possibly be so common amongst us if men were not taught to regard it as merely objectionable because it is remotely connected with stealing, of which God has expressed his disapproval in the Decalogue; and therefore as quite naturally set right by a punctual attendance at church on Sundays. When a Ritualist breaks his fast before celebrating the Holy Communion, his deity can forgive him if he likes, for the matter concerns nobody else; but no deity can forgive him for preventing his parishioners from setting up a public library and reading-room for fear they should read Mr. Darwin's works in it. That sin is committed against the people, and a God cannot take it away.

I call those religions which undermine the supreme allegiance of the conscience to Man *ultramontane* religions, because they seek their springs of action *ultra montes*, outside of the common experience and daily life of man. And I remark about them that they are especially apt to teach wrong precepts, and that even when they command men to do the right things they put the command upon wrong motives, and do not get the things done.

But there are forms of religious emotion which do not thus undermine the conscience. Far be it from me to undervalue the help and strength which many of the bravest of our brethren have drawn from the thought of an unseen helper of men. He who, wearied or stricken in the fight with the powers of darkness, asks himself in a solitary place, "Is it all for nothing? shall we indeed be overthrown?"—he does find something which may justify that thought. In such a moment of utter sincerity, when a man has bared his own soul before the immensities and the eternities, a presence in which his own poor personality is shrivelled into nothingness arises within him, and says, as plainly as words can say, "I am with thee, and I am greater than thou." Many names of Gods, of many shapes, have men given to this presence; seeking by names and pictures to know more clearly and to remember more continually the guide and the helper of men. No such comradeship with the Great Companion shall have anything but reverence from me, who have known the divine gentleness of Denison Maurice, the strong and healthy practical instinct of Charles Kingsley, and who now revere with all my heart the teaching of James Martineau.[8] They seem to me, one and all, to be reaching forward with loving anticipation to a clearer vision which is yet to come—*tendentesque manus ripae ulterioris amore*.[9] For, after all, such a helper of men, outside of humanity, the truth will not allow us to see. The dim and shadowy outlines of the superhuman deity fade slowly away from before us; and as the mist of his presence floats aside, we perceive with greater and greater clearness the shape of a yet grander and nobler figure—of Him who made all Gods and shall unmake them. From the dim dawn of history, and from the inmost depth of every soul, the face of our father Man looks out upon us with the fire of eternal youth in his eyes, and says, "Before Jehovah was, I am!"

NOTES

1. *Rep.* ii. 378. Tr. Davies and Vaughan. [Clifford refers to a translation of Plato's *Republic* by J. Llewelyn Davies and David James Vaughan (1866).]

2. *North British Review*, 1867, p. 284. [The quotations are from various works by the Roman philosopher Seneca the Younger, as cited in an anonymous article by C. W. Russell reviewing several books on early Christianity in the *North British Review*, December 1867, pp. 257–301.]

3. [Frederick William Faber (1814–1863), British theologian and hymn writer. See his *The Creator and the Creature; or, The Wonders of Divine Love* (1857). Henry Nutcombe Oxenham (1829–1888), British theologian. See *The Catholic Doctrine of the Atonement* (1869).]

4. [Unidentified.]

5. ["The priest is always, everywhere, and to everyone an enemy."]

6. [John Russell, Viscount Amberley (1842–1876), British politician and author of *An Analysis of Religious Belief* (1876). He was the father of Bertrand Russell.]

7. [Sir Henry Maine (1822–1888), British jurist and author of *Ancient Law* (1861), a celebrated treatise on the foundations of law and its evolution in ancient and modern society. Emile Louis Victor de Laveleye (1822–1892), Belgian economist and author of *Essai sur les formes de gouvernement dans les sociétés modernes* (1872) and other works.]

8. [Frederick Denison Maurice (1805–1872), Anglican divine who, in *The Kingdom of Christ* (1838) and other works, challenged religious orthodoxy on several points, including the notion of eternal punishment. Charles Kingsley (1819–1875), Anglican divine who devoted himself to social reform and debated John Henry Newman on points of doctrine. James Martineau (1805–1900), Unitarian divine and philosopher who defended theism in the face of evolution and other scientific advances in *A Study of Religion* (1888) and other works.]

9. ["Holding out hands through love of the farther shore." Virgil, *Aeneid* 6.314. The reference is to the souls of the dead who wish to be conveyed by Charon across the river Styx to the Land of the Blest.]

15

CHRISTIANITY AND CIVILIZATION

Charles T. Gorham

[Very little is known of the life of Charles Turner Gorham (1856–?), British secularist. He was a prolific author, producing a biography of Robert G. Ingersoll (1921) along with such works as *Faith: Its Freaks and Follies* (1902), *God and the War: Some Questions for Christians* (1916), *A Plain Man's Plea for Rationalism* (1919), and *Why We Do Right: A Rational View of Conscience* (1924). In the following chapter titled "The Influence of Religion upon Civilization," Gorham notes that Christianity has frequently hindered the advance of Western civilization, especially in regard to the pursuit of knowledge, the development of religious tolerance, and the alleviation of poverty and other social ills.]

S o far as civilization has any definite aim, that aim must be the increase of human happiness. The means to the attainment of this object are material comfort and prosperity. Man has not yet evolved any completely satisfactory and universally diffused form of

Charles T. Gorham, *Christianity and Civilization* (London: Watts, 1914), pp. 1–19.

social life. He is tending towards it, but the achievement is frustrated mainly by his own folly and ignorance. The removal of ignorance and the growth of knowledge are, therefore, necessary to the development of happiness. It is no doubt true that civilization takes man away from nature, gives rise to artificial needs, and burdens him with sorrows which might be averted by a simpler mode of life. But these inconveniences are more than compensated by the advantages of personal comfort, security for life and property, peaceful industry, and the acquisition of knowledge, which attend, though with many unhappy exceptions, the progress towards ideal social conditions. To assert this is not to glorify basely materialistic views of life; for, speaking broadly, it is on these conditions that the growth of the higher qualities of humanity depends.

Civilization is a state in which human beings live in peaceful intercourse with one another, in which the operations and products of nature are utilized for their benefit, and in which intellectual exertion is combined with observance of the moral laws derived from experience. The object of the present inquiry is to ascertain, if possible, the extent to which the Christian religion has assisted man's efforts to reach the ideal civilization to which as yet he only approximates.

In relation to social progress, the value of religion lies not in its intellectual forms, which are constantly changing and ever becoming discredited by wider knowledge, nor in the spiritual exaltation which leads the mind away from the contemplation of material things, and is usually confined to a small number of exceptional natures. The truth of religious doctrines has always been a matter of speculation; their value depends upon their utility. This value is measurable by practical results rather than by criteria of truth concerning which no generally accepted standard is available. Some distinction has to be observed between the effect which religion exerts upon minds possessing the appropriate sensibility and the effect produced upon natures with which only the inferior elements of religion have any affinity. When religion develops a keener sense of moral obligation, when it makes men and women unselfish, just, and loving, it promotes the growth of civilization by the diffusion of higher ethical conceptions and by stimulating their application to conduct. So far, however, as its precepts fail to govern practice, so far as they are themselves imperfect, religion does little or nothing to forward social improvement.

A large proportion of human misery has resulted from the enforcement of religious doctrines which experience and knowledge have shown to be erroneous or defective, but which have nevertheless been assumed to be of divine and universal obligation. If Christianity is a system of perfect moral purity, it must be explained why it has been so frequently and so seriously misunderstood that zeal on its behalf has led to the violation of the ethical laws which Christianity itself inculcates. In reading history one is constantly perplexed by the bigoted and persecuting spirit which has, generally in all sincerity, based itself upon sanctions alleged to be of divine origin. It is really astonishing that during a long period of European history men should have thought themselves constrained, not merely to ignore, but to reverse the mild and tolerant precepts of a Gospel the truth of which they were so far from doubting that they conceived it their duty to enforce it even at the cost of torture and death. So remarkable a fact may be variously, though never perhaps satisfactorily, accounted for. Ignorance was one of its chief causes; yet lack of knowledge is not an adequate explanation of the neglect of simple moral duties, and many of the persecutors were eminent for learning and wisdom. That the passion of intolerance is natural to imperfectly developed minds helps to explain its prevalence; but it is strange that it should have been assumed to come from the shining courts of heaven, instead of from the smoke of the pit. The indefinable influence termed the "spirit of the age" has been held to excuse the employment of physical coercion to induce psychical changes; but it has still to be explained how the spirit of the age took that particular form. Coercion of opinion was exercised by the Christian Church with a relentless and systematic cruelty never shown by any other of the great religions. Torture was, it is true, employed for judicial purposes by pagan Rome, but the laws imposed strict limits to its use in all cases. "The Church," says an able writer, "not only maintained the institution, but permitted the withdrawal of the limit in two cases—heresy and witchcraft"[1]—besides greatly extending the scope of the practice. Little reflection is needed to show how it must not only have debased human nature, but perverted the justice which it was supposed to promote. Probably the most powerful of all the causes of bigotry, persecution, religious wars, and theological dissension was the notion that in the Christian faith the world had received from God a definite, complete, and final revelation of truth.

If revelation is believed to imply finality, intellectual stagnation is an inevitable consequence. Civilization means progress, and to progress liberty of thought is absolutely essential. When men believe that truth has been received from a source superior to and distinguishable from their own mental activities, they will be content to accept what they are told without examination. In the sphere of religion they will cease to think for themselves; they will bow before authority simply because the claims of authority are put forward. They will accept tradition without inquiry; they will sanctify abuses; they will banish the very thought of improvement. Their intellects will become dormant and incapable of exertion. The valuable discipline of effort will be lost, and contented ignorance will be preferred to advancing knowledge. The blurred features of Error will be deemed the bright countenance of Truth. Under the influence of an authority which it is impious to question, human nature becomes a caricature of its possibilities.

A serious effect of dogmatic religion is that in the long run it depraves the morality almost as much as it benumbs the mind of man. The two elements are more intimately related than is commonly assumed. The virtues most important to progress in civilization are the sentiment of justice and the desire to know what is true. If these are repressed, the free play of the intellect becomes impossible. Truth and justice are not simple ethical emotions, and, although individuals may possess a clear sense of their necessity, their operation is fettered if the mind is ill stored with knowledge. They involve complex reasoning processes, in order that their real nature and their extensive social effects may be perceived.

It would be unjust to contend that Christianity has not in various departments of life exerted a highly beneficial influence. It has, with many lapses from its own ideals, and in spite of its harsher doctrines, stimulated the idea of human equality and given an enhanced value to human life. It has, at least in intention, discouraged the spirit of violence and war. While it has imposed arbitrary ideas concerning the relations between the sexes, it has done something to purify them; it has sought to alleviate human suffering; it has enjoined the spirit of compassion, self-sacrifice, devotion, and unselfishness; it has afforded relief to many minds struggling against the perplexities of life. But, after making the deductions which historical truth compels, it is questionable whether all these benefits are not outweighed by the generally disastrous effect of organized Christianity on intellectual progress. During the greater part of its career Christianity has made a criminal offence of the most undoubted of all natural rights and the first condition of civilization— the free exercise of thought. If it has done something to soften and refine morality, it has effected little to enlarge and strengthen moral ideas. Sincerity is one of the grandest of human qualities. By its insistence on formal religion the Church has so trained men to insincerity that in many epochs hypocrisy has been essential to worldly success, and even to personal safety. A sincere Christian, whether Catholic or Protestant, can hardly read the history of the Church without a deep sense of shame. The feat is accomplished only by dwelling on its nobler activities, its charities, its saints, its martyrs, and excluding all contemplation of its crimes. We cannot judge Christianity by its highest achievements alone. Our estimate must be based on what it has actually done; and if praise is given, blame cannot be withheld. To-day the Christian Church proclaims a faith of comparative purity and spiritual excellence which the majority of its members fail to realize in practice. Its most influential section still demands adherence to a system of religious externalism which the experience of its whole history has proved injurious to spiritual faith. Formal religion is harmful because it attaches merit to the performance of actions in themselves worthless, to the neglect of those impulses of mind and heart which give to religion its social value.

Faith in external rites and ceremonies always issues in intolerance, because where external acts are considered the most essential part of religion there is a natural disposition to regard their non-observance as a wilful neglect of sacred duties. Intolerance springs less from the sway of passions which are evil than from the misdirection of those which are good. A strong assurance of the truth of particular doctrines is commonly formed without that careful examination of their grounds on which alone conviction can properly rest, and apart from which unfamiliar points of view are not perceived. Conscientious examination almost invariably results in some slackening of the tenacity with which doctrines are held, because the advance of knowledge involves a clearer perception of its dependence on objective facts. Religion postulates the action of forces the true nature of which is imperfectly known, and, if investigation of them is forbidden, a receptive instead of an inquisitive habit of mind is induced. In such a mental atmosphere authority is unrestricted and development made difficult in other departments of thought. The use of reason is altogether prohibited, or utilized only so far as it can be made serviceable to faith.

Thus reason is either employed illegitimately to support predetermined conceptions, or debarred from the criticism of religious dogmas. Intolerant religions are specially prone to enlarge the province of belief, and, by making the most indifferent secular concerns a "matter of faith," to impede progress and retain abuses. Any faculty which, like the fabled rod of Aaron, swallows up all its rivals produces deleterious effects by losing the sense of proportion. In this respect faith is at a disadvantage compared with reason, for, while history reveals scarcely any evils as resulting from the excess of reason, the lamentable consequences of religious credulity form the most terrible pages of the human record. It is possible for the exclusive cultivation of the reasoning faculties to deprive their possessor of sweetness, sympathy, and tenderness; but it is not possible to think too rightly or to be too well informed. Faith is peculiarly liable to become narrow, intolerant, and persecuting. An eminent Christian Father may, perhaps, without injury to personal virtue, declare the merit of believing the impossible; but this exaltation of credulity cannot form a universal rule.

Intolerance, then, is the child of ignorance; and ignorance is not likely to frame an impartial estimate of the effects of religious zeal. Strong convictions of the error of aberrations from a particular doctrinal standard merge insensibly into moral disapproval and hatred of their holders. In this attitude, anti-social in proportion to its strength, may be discovered the genesis of religious persecutions and wars. It is not asserted that a pure and enlightened faith is necessarily intolerant but that it tends to become so whenever it disdains the light of reason. That the Christian Church has during many ages enjoined intolerance as a religious duty; that a religion of love has become in practice a religion of hatred, will be shown in the ensuing pages. The idea of the wrongfulness of unfamiliar modes of worship, whether as regards doctrines or ceremonies, indicates the proneness of men to make their own ideas the measure of deity.

Such manifestations of the religious sentiment are in some respects abnormal, because they are inconsistent with the purer elements of the faith professed, and subvert rather than elevate the standard of morals. Yet they are at the same time a perfectly natural development from those sacrificial observances by which primitive man sought to appease the anger of incomprehensible deities—they result from an ignorance that is doubly prejudicial when fostered by those whose office it should be to remove it. The inconsistency appears to arise from the fact that, whatever religious conceptions are propounded, they are insensibly transformed by the mind into a reflection of its own attributes. Human knowledge cannot progress unless it assumes that the laws or sequences of nature operate with unbroken regularity. Belief in God tends to weaken this postulate. A personal Creator must possess the power, if he chooses to exert it, of altering the laws which he has established, and persons trained to bow to that authority are disposed to believe that this power has frequently been exercised in the past and may at any moment be exerted in the future. If, however, it is maintained that God does not interpose to vary the natural order, it must be presumed that he does not consider it necessary to aid humanity in its struggle towards better conditions of existence. Such a conception of a supreme intelligence has never been, and perhaps is not likely to become, so popular as the idea of frequent divine interpositions. The truth of the latter conception was once assumed to be verified in the experience of every believer, though a rigid interpretation of experience might have seriously discredited it had rational tests been applied. Formerly one of the most vital elements of religion, it is now for the most part regarded as a non-essential matter. It is one of the principal difficulties which have impeded the march of secular knowledge.

Thus from a purely humanistic standpoint the idea of a personal deity seems open to grave objections.[2] It implies either indifference to human effort or a certain hostility to it. It transcends normal experience, though claiming to lie within it. While it presumes, not unnaturally, a totally different origin for good and for evil, it is yet unable to deny that both must logically proceed from the one source which alone is assumed to exist. It finds it impossible so to limit in thought the power of God as to admit of independent action by man. It involves a degree of superintendence of the world which cannot be reconciled with the facts of daily experience. Human affairs go on just as if no God existed. All improvement, material, scientific, mental, moral, and social, is, as far as can be seen, gained by the unaided exertions of man. Civilization owes little to even the purest religious ideas, and has certainly been seriously hindered by abuses of them.

This conclusion is strengthened by closer examination. The fundamental attribute which piety ascribes to a supreme being is unlimited power. But, unless men can be certain that it will be exercised in their favour, unlimited power is calculated to awaken dread rather than to create confidence. Fear is one of the primary elements of natural religion, and to a large extent dominates the life and depresses the intellectual activity of undeveloped races. The "fear of the Lord" is inculcated in the Bible as the beginning of wisdom, but is not necessarily its end. A man who fears God is not, for that reason, a craven;

for, assuming God's existence, the emotion seems fully justified, but its general effect is to discourage speculation on the origins of life and of good and evil, as well as the investigation of doctrines said to be divinely revealed. Unlimited power inspires fear by leaving open the possibility that harm may result from scrutiny of its manifestations. It gives rise to the idea that the behaviour of its possessor is incomprehensible, and therefore may exhibit caprice, which is necessarily beyond calculation. If the conduct of a supreme being is unintelligible, it cannot be inferred that it will always be marked by justice. Religion does not set forth God as either invariably kind or invariably malicious, for either supposition would destroy the attribute of incomprehensibility which must always surround a being whose superiority to man is infinite. The faith of the Christian is not untroubled by the perplexities which beset the animism of the savage. The modern believer is tortured by doubts in proportion to his intellectual sensibility and the uncertainty regarding the application to himself personally of the doctrines to which he adheres. He is compelled to believe in the goodness of his deity, but is also compelled by his creed to believe that deity capable of conduct which in man would be revoltingly cruel and immoral. It is suicidal to reply that God's ways may be quite unlike the ways of man, for, if evil is not the same with both, no reason can be shown why good should be the same.

So far as it operates from a logical and doctrinal basis, earnest religious faith usually has the effect of making its professors indifferent to secular relations. Believing that all things are ordained of God, they tend to regard human endeavours towards improvement as contrary to his designs and the effort to understand and apply the laws of nature as an impious disregard of his will. In recent times this tendency has become greatly weakened, but in the past it has placed innumerable obstacles in the path of progress. On authority mistakenly supposed to be infallible the Church has, with sufficient consistency to justify the sceptical, opposed the spread of knowledge, denounced the researches of science, forbidden the exercise of reason, and fostered the evils of superstition. The belief in trial by ordeal was a remarkable instance of this tendency. Although now ranked as a gross superstition, it seems nothing but a logical result of the belief in providential care. If God interferes at all in human affairs, it was, with some plausibility, assumed he would do so when the question of a suspected person's guilt or innocence was at stake. It was supposed that when human endeavours to find out the truth failed, and the matter was expressly referred to his decision, he would not remain inactive and permit guilt to triumph if innocence was wrongfully accused.

Yet experience showed so clearly the error of this assumption that theories of divine interposition had to give way to the logic of facts. Similarly, the belief in witchcraft rested upon a faith in the power and activity of supernatural agencies which was plainly sanctioned by the founder of Christianity, and was supported by the emphatic injunction of the Old Testament that witches should be put to death. Its formal refutation on scriptural grounds was impossible. The superstition faded away in the light of experience and common sense.

Analogous objections may be urged against the practice of prayer. If man can, as he commonly believes, get what he wants by asking for it, as expressly promised in the New Testament, he will be the less inclined to personal exertion. His own efforts are deemed superfluous, and he is reduced to passivity. To assume that divine benefits are conditional on our own exertions can only mean that we must act as if we did not rely upon God to confer them. Our conduct must therefore be the same whether we do or do not expect supernatural aid. Cromwell's advice to "trust in God and keep your powder dry" was radically sceptical, for reliance on human means which would in any case bring about a certain result negates divine means which operate with less certainty. It is clear that the beliefs in divine superintendence and petitionary prayer are harmful to social evolution in proportion to the degree in which they discourage human energy, and, by excluding it from the chain of cause and effect, render the results of its exercise uncertain. The devout Theist regards God as the real author of human civilization, and, if consistent, he leaves God to carry on the work of improvement.

Religious faith tends to enfeeble the judgment, because it looks upon reason as an inferior quality, which, although the gift of God, it is dangerous to cultivate. Civilization owes its origin and extension mainly to those faculties by which man seeks to understand the nature of the universe and to turn its forces to account for the betterment of his condition. When these faculties are weakened faith is given a free and unrestrained course, and, when not checked by reason, merges into that abject credulity of which religious history affords so many saddening examples. As reason is depressed faith is magnified. From this to the subjection of all natural passions and rational sentiments is but a step. The absurdity of the extravagances to which in the Middle Ages the spirit of asceticism gave rise hid from view and almost destroyed the idea of reasonable self-control which they were supposed to represent.

One very important effect of unenlightened faith is that it throws power—temporal as well as spiritual power—into the hands of the priestly caste whose claims and privileges have so greatly hampered the growth of civilization. It is to the interest of this class to exaggerate the guilt of offences against religion and require gifts and penances for their remission, to favour credulity and prevent the acquisition of the knowledge which would remove it, to discourage inquiry into its professional claims, and to assert that the means of communication between God and man are confided to it alone. In every age these claims have been abused, sometimes from conviction of their truth, more often from less creditable motives. A hierarchy may imagine that it is acting solely for the glory of God, but into even the most conscientious aims an element of self-interest not uncommonly obtrudes. It is seldom that a whole class is made up of purely conscientious persons, and when the privileges of the best may be abused by the worst the moral vitality of the entire community is lowered. A priestly caste habitually describes God as of uncertain temper and extreme severity. Its members, as his chosen servants, are able to influence him on behalf of the suppliant and secure for him favours which otherwise he would have to go without. For their good offices a compensation is demanded, which in credulous epochs takes a substantial and excessive form. Hence the system of penances, absolutions, and indulgences, which, during medieval times, was carried to an extremity of superstition that an educated laity would not have permitted. Moral offenders could purchase for money a fallacious pardon which condoned sin and emboldened them to repeat it. Ecclesiasticism created and still facilitates artificial offences which are equally without moral guilt or ill consequences, such as the sin of eating meat on Friday, an offence for which, late in the Middle Ages, a man was burnt alive. Thus even sincere faith is likely to act injuriously on civilization, partly by giving unworthy representations of a supreme being, partly by banning innocent pleasure and so diminishing the general happiness, and partly by the direct depravation of morals which results from the creation of a punitive code that violates justice. To these must be added the stunting of intellectual growth by confining it within the narrow channels of a particular creed. If a comparatively pure religion has this effect, how great must be the evils of ignorant faith!

Christianity has increased human unhappiness and intensified superstition by its terrible doctrine of an everlasting hell. Arising from essentially unworthy conceptions of a supreme being, this idea has, more than any other, perpetuated and extended them by its appeal to the instincts of savagery. In the main the theory of religious persecution was based upon this doctrine, and among its prominent effects have been the lessening of intellectual activity, the degradation of religion, and a startling number of cases of insanity in its most dangerous forms.

An exaggerated fear of death is far more frequently an accompaniment of perplexed faith than of what is termed "infidelity," for, while the unbeliever is hardly likely to be frightened by a hell in which he does not believe, the anxious pietist can seldom be sure that some tincture of sin may not imperil his chance of salvation. The utilization of this fear of hell secured to the medieval Church enormous accessions of wealth. At one time about half the land of England was in its possession, largely owing to the gifts made to it to ensure future salvation.

It is open to serious doubt whether the belief in a future state does, on the whole, conduce to morality, and therefore to civilization. It may do so when held in a spirit of sincerity and of desire for the triumph of good over evil. It should create in the believer a disposition to qualify himself by purity of life for that ideal state which he hopes to enjoy. But the remoteness of the prospect, the tacitly recognized uncertainty of its reality, and our inability to comprehend its conditions, greatly diminish its practical effect on the majority of believers. Apart from the excesses of credulity to which this tenet has led, it becomes, when holding out the certainty of undeserved happiness prolonged throughout eternity, an effective stimulus to selfish desires and a force detrimental to social life in this world. If the desire for immortality were as strong as it logically should be, it would tend to cause neglect of our present temporary state, and so far to discourage secular progress. If life here is but a brief preparation for eternity, worldly prosperity is a fallacious aim. Nor can a future life afford a pleasing prospect unless conceived as a life of bliss. No one desires an eternity of misery, and against the idea of unending joy (perhaps not so great a boon as is assumed) must be set those fears and terrors of future pain which have driven many sensitive natures to madness. On any supposition belief in a future state is environed with perplexities.[3] As commonly held it assumes that disembodied spirits can experience the highest pleasures without becoming wearied by their endless repetition; that they can suffer physical pain; that they can and will continue in sin when the temptations to sin have been removed with the passing of the fleshly nature and the material environment. It assumes that we can continue to think without a brain; that we can grow in knowledge in the absence of both the materials of knowledge and the physical apparatus for utilizing them. It assumes that spiritual beings, devoid of substance and form, can recognize one another and exchange ideas and intercourse. It postulates, in fact, the permanence of conditions which, so far as our knowledge goes, do not exist at all. How can these fantastic notions have a beneficial influence on a civilization based upon physical conditions? And we have to take into account not only religion at its best, but religion at its worst. "Where true religion has prevented one crime false religions have afforded a pretext for a thousand." As false religions, or, at least, inferior conceptions of religion, have been far more common and more influential than faiths of ideal purity, this may be taken as a candid admission that, in its total effects, religion has conferred little or no benefit upon the human race.

It may be rejoined that this contention has no relevance to the pure and beneficent teaching of the New Testament. But this teaching is neither so pure nor so favourable to morals as is commonly supposed. For the time in which it appeared the morality of the Gospels is, on the whole, admirable. But it is not, and could not have been, purely original. If in the softer virtues it excels the conceptions of the great Stoics, in the recognition of justice and reason it falls below them. It can scarcely be denied that even the teachings of Jesus himself, especially in the "Sermon on the Mount," appeal in many points to personal selfishness rather than to universal sympathy. His ethical teaching, in fact, may be termed in some respects detrimental to civilization for two reasons: (1) Because it holds out the hope of his immediate coming again, and therefore was regarded as of temporary application. The continuous effort to which civilization owes its existence—work, thrift, and forethought—were all somewhat discountenanced, family life was little esteemed, and celibacy implicitly favoured. (2) Because it took no account of some of the chief developments of civilized life, such as civic duties, art, science, and literature. Such omissions are perfectly natural if Christianity was a human development, but are not easily explicable on the theory of its divine origin. Civilization is built up by mental alertness and calculation of the future results of actions. But if we obey literally the command to "take no thought for the morrow" [Matt. 6:34] we shall neglect the care and foresight which are necessary for the realization of our aims. Civilization involves a long and arduous struggle against conditions which are in many ways evil; to follow blindly the rule that evil is not to be resisted is to offer facilities for its manifestation, and to deprive the good of its legitimate influence. On the other hand, the recognition by Jesus of human brotherhood, the clear and emphatic injunctions to inward purity as the true spring of right conduct, and the exaltation of love and mercy as controlling sentiments of life, are ideas not only noble in themselves, but among the most valuable aids in the progress of humanity towards better conditions.

NOTES

1. J. McCabe, *The Bible in Europe*, p. 114. [Joseph McCabe (1867–1955), prolific British freethinker.]

2. For a fuller discussion of this question, see *The Existence of God*, by Joseph McCabe (Vol. I. of Inquirer's Library).

3. The character and growth of this doctrine are judicially discussed in *The Belief in Personal Immortality*, by E. S. P. Haynes (Vol. II. of Inquirer's Library).

Part V.

CHRISTIANITY IN DECLINE

16

RATIONALISM IN EUROPE

W. E. H. Lecky

[William Edward Hartpole Lecky (1838–1903), Irish historian, graduated from Trinity College, Dublin. One of his earliest writings was the treatise *The Religious Tendencies of the Age* (1860), which expressed a broad tolerance for the various Christian sects in Britain. Influenced by the work of Henry Thomas Buckle, Lecky produced the pioneering treatise, *History of the Rise and Influence of the Spirit of Rationalism in Europe* (1865), which portrayed the gradual decay of superstition, and religion itself, in the wake of the Reformation and the secularization of politics in the French Revolution. Lecky then wrote another major work, *History of European Morals from Augustus to Charlemagne* (1860), a kind of prequel to his earlier work and showing the gradual evolution of secular ethics. Lecky's last major works were *History of England in the Eighteenth Century* (1878–90; 8 vols.) and *Democracy and Liberty* (1896). He was elected to Par-

W. E. H. Lecky, *History of the Rise and Influence of the Spirit of Rationalism in Europe* (1865; rev. ed., New York: D. Appleton, 1900), 2: 126–36.

liament in 1895, advocating non-denominational education in Ireland and old-age pensions. In the following extract from the chapter entitled "The Secularisation of Politics," Lecky relates the decline of Christianity through the increasing secularization of
Western political systems, noting that the sectarianism
formerly inspired by religious differences has now
been channeled into political differences.]

To those who have appreciated the great truth that a radical
political change necessarily implies a corresponding change in
the mental habits of society, the process which I have traced will furnish a decisive evidence of the declining influence of dogmatic theology. That vast department of thought and action which is comprised
under the name of politics was once altogether guided by its power. It
is now passing from its influence rapidly, universally, and completely.
The classes that are most penetrated with the spirit of special dogmas
were once the chief directors of the policy of Europe. They now form
a baffled and desponding minority, whose most cherished political
principles have been almost universally abandoned, who are struggling faintly and ineffectually against the ever-increasing spirit of the
age, and whose ideal is not in the future but in the past. It is evident
that a government never can be really like a railway company, or a literary society, which only exercises an influence over secular affairs.
As long as it determines the system of education that exists among its
subjects, as long as it can encourage or repress the teaching of particular doctrines, as long as its foreign policy brings it into collision with
governments which still make the maintenance of certain religious
systems a main object of their policy, it will necessarily exercise a
gigantic influence upon belief. It cannot possibly be uninfluential, and
it is difficult to assign limits to the influence that it may exercise. If the
men who compose it (or the public opinion that governs them) be per-
vaded by an intensely-realised conviction that the promulgation of a

certain system of doctrine is incomparably the highest of human interests, that to assist that promulgation is the main object for which they
were placed in the world, and should be the dominant motive of their
lives, it will be quite impossible for these men, as politicians, to avoid
interfering with theology. Men who are inspired by an absorbing passion will inevitably gratify it if they have the power. Men who sincerely desire the happiness of mankind will certainly use to the utter-
most the means they possess of promoting what they feel to be beyond
all comparison the greatest of human interests. If by giving a certain
direction to education they could avert fearful and general physical
suffering, there can be no doubt that they would avail themselves of
their power. If they were quite certain that the greatest possible suffering was the consequence of deviating from a particular class of
opinions, they could not possibly neglect that consideration in their
laws. This is the conclusion we should naturally draw from the nature
of the human mind, and it is most abundantly corroborated by experience.[1] In order to ascertain the tendencies of certain opinions, we
should not confine ourselves to those exceptional intellects who,
having perceived the character of their age, have spent their lives in
endeavouring painfully and laboriously to wrest their opinions in conformity with them. We should rather observe the position which large
bodies of men, governed by the same principles, but living under various circumstances and in different ages, naturally and almost unconsciously occupy. We have ample means of judging in the present case.
We see the general tone which is adopted on political subjects by the
clergy of the most various creeds, by the religious newspapers, and by
the politicians who represent that section of the community which is
most occupied with dogmatic theology. We see that it is a tendency
distinct from and opposed to the tendencies of the age. History tells us
that it was once dominant in politics, that it has been continuously and
rapidly declining, and that it has declined most rapidly and most
steadily in those countries in which the development of intellect has
been most active. All over Europe the priesthood are now associated
with a policy of toryism, of reaction, or of obstruction. All over Europe

the organs that represent dogmatic interests are in permanent opposition to the progressive tendencies around them, and are rapidly sinking into contempt. In every country in which a strong political life is manifested, the secularisation of politics is the consequence. Each stage of that movement has been initiated and effected by those who are most indifferent to dogmatic theology, and each has been opposed by those who are most occupied with theology.[2]

And as I write these words, it is impossible to forget that one of the great problems on which the thoughts of politicians are even now concentrated is the hopeless decadence of the one theocracy of modern Europe, of the great type and representative of the alliance of politics and theology. That throne on which it seemed as though the changeless Church had stamped the impress of her own perpetuity—that throne which for so many centuries of anarchy and confusion had been the Sinai of a protecting and an avenging law—that throne which was once the centre and the archetype of the political system of Europe, the successor of Imperial Rome, the inheritor of a double portion of her spirit, the one power which seemed removed above all the vicissitudes of politics, the iris above the cataract, unshaken amid so much turmoil and so much change—that throne has in our day sunk into a condition of hopeless decrepitude, and has only prolonged its existence by the confession of its impotence. Supported by the bayonets of a foreign power, and avowedly incapable of self-existence, it is no longer a living organism, its significance is but the significance of death. There was a time when the voice that issued from the Vatican shook Europe to its foundations, and sent forth the proudest armies to the deserts of Syria. There was a time when all the valour and all the chivalry of Christendom would have followed the banner of the Church in any field and against any foe. Now a few hundred French, and Belgians, and Irish are all who would respond to its appeal. Its august antiquity, the reverence that centres around its chief, the memory of the unrivalled influence it has exercised, the genius that has consecrated its past, the undoubted virtues that have been displayed by its rulers, were all unable to save the papal government from a decadence the most irretrievable and the most hopeless. Reforms were boldly initiated, but they only served to accelerate its ruin. A repressive policy was attempted, but it could not arrest the progress of its decay. For nearly a century, under every ruler and under every system of policy, it has been hopelessly, steadily, and rapidly declining. At last the influences that had so long been corroding it attained their triumph. It fell before the Revolution, and has since been unable to exist, except by the support of a foreign army. The principle of its vitality has departed.

No human pen can write its epitaph, for no imagination can adequately realise its glories. In the eyes of those who estimate the greatness of a sovereignty, not by the extent of territory, or by the valour of its soldiers, but by the influence which it has exercised over mankind, the papal government has had no rival, and can have no successor. But though we may not fully estimate the majesty of its past, we can at least trace the causes of its decline. It fell because it neglected the great truth that a government to be successful must adapt itself to the ever-changing mental condition of society; that a policy which in one century produces the utmost prosperity, in another leads only to ruin and to disaster. It fell because it represented the union of politics and theology, and because the intellect of Europe has rendered it an anachronism by pronouncing their divorce. It fell because its constitution was essentially and radically opposed to the spirit of an age in which the secularisation of politics is the measure and the condition of all political prosperity.

The secularisation of politics is, as we have seen, the direct consequence of the declining influence of dogmatic theology. I have said that it also reacts upon and influences its cause. The creation of a strong and purely secular political feeling diffused through all classes of society, and producing an ardent patriotism, and a passionate and indomitable love of liberty, is sufficient in many respects to modify all the great departments of thought, and to contribute largely to the formation of a distinct type of intellectual character.

It is obvious, in the first place, that one important effect of a purely secular political feeling will be to weaken the intensity of sectarianism. Before its existence sectarianism was the measure by which all things and persons were contemplated. It exercised an undivided control over the minds and passions of men, absorbed all their interests, and presided over all their combinations. But when a purely political spirit is engendered, a new enthusiasm is introduced into the mind, which first divides the affections and at last replaces the passion that had formerly been supreme. Two different enthusiasms, each of which makes men regard events in a special point of view, cannot at the same time be absolute. The habits of thought that are formed by the one, will necessarily weaken or efface the habits of thought that are formed by the other. Men learn to classify their fellows by a new principle. They become in one capacity the cordial associates of those whom in another capacity they had long regarded with unmingled dislike. They learn to repress and oppose in one capacity those whom in another capacity they regard with unbounded reverence. Conflicting feelings are thus produced which neutralise each other; and if one of the two increases, the other is proportionately diminished. Every war that unites for secular objects nations of different creeds, every measure that extends political interests to classes that had formerly been excluded from their range, has therefore a tendency to assuage the virulence of sects.

Another consequence of the intellectual influence of political life is a tendency to sacrifice general principles to practical results. It has often been remarked that the English constitution, which is commonly regarded as the most perfect realisation of political freedom, is beyond all others the most illogical, and that a very large proportion of those measures which have proved most beneficial, have involved the grossest logical inconsistencies, the most partial and unequal applications of some general principle. The object of the politician is expediency, and his duty is to adapt his measures to the often crude, undeveloped, and vacillating conceptions of the nation. The object, on the other hand, of the philosopher is truth, and his duty is to push every principle which he believes to be true to its legitimate consequences, regardless of the results which may follow. Nothing can be more fatal in politics than a preponderance of the philosophical, or in philosophy than a preponderance of the political spirit. In the first case, the ruler will find himself totally incapable of adapting his measures to the exigencies of exceptional circumstances; he will become involved in inextricable difficulties by the complexity of the phenomena he endeavours to reduce to order; and he will be in perpetual collision with public opinion. In the second case, the thinker will be continually harassed by considerations of expediency which introduce the bias of the will into what should be a purely intellectual process, and impart a timidity and a disingenuousness to the whole tone of his thoughts. There can, I think, be little doubt that this latter influence is at present acting most unfavourably upon speculative opinion in countries where political life is very powerful. A disinterested love of truth can hardly coexist with a strong political spirit. In all countries where the habits of thought have been mainly formed by political life, we may discover a disposition to make expediency the test of truth, to close the eyes and turn away the mind from any arguments that tend towards a radical change, and above all to make utilitarianism a kind of mental perspective according to which the different parts of belief are magnified or diminished. All that has a direct influence upon the well-being of society is brought into clear relief; all that has only an intellectual importance becomes unrealised and inoperative. It is probable that the capacity for pursuing abstract truth for its own sake, which has given German thinkers so great an ascendency in Europe, is in no slight degree to be attributed to the political languor of their nation.

This predisposition acts in different ways upon the progress of Rationalism. It is hostile to it on account of the intense conservatism it produces, and also on account of its opposition to that purely philosophical spirit to which Rationalism seeks to subordinate all departments of speculative belief. It is favourable to it, inasmuch as it withdraws the minds of men from the doctrinal aspect of their faith to concentrate them upon the moral aspect, which in the eyes of the politician as of the rationalist is infinitely the most important.

But probably the most important, and certainly the most beneficial, effect of political life is to habituate men to a true method of enquiry. Government in a constitutional country is carried on by debate, all the arguments on both sides are brought forward with unrestricted freedom, and every newspaper reports in full what has been said against the principles it advocates by the ablest men in the country. Men may study the debates of Parliament under the influence of a strong party bias, they may even pay more attention to the statements of one party than to those of the other, but they never imagine that they can form an opinion by an exclusive study of what has been written on one side. The two views of every question are placed in juxtaposition, and every one who is interested in the subject examines both. When a charge is brought against any politician, men naturally turn to his reply before forming an opinion, and they feel that any other course would be not only extremely foolish, but also extremely dishonest. This is the spirit of truth as opposed to the spirit of falsehood and imposture, which in all ages and in all departments of thought has discouraged men from studying opposing systems, lamented the circulation of adverse arguments, and denounced as criminal those who listen to them. Among the higher order of intellects, the first spirit is chiefly cultivated by those philosophical studies which discipline and strengthen the mind for research. But what philosophy does for a very few, political life does, less perfectly, indeed, but still in a great degree, for the many. It diffuses abroad not only habits of acute reasoning, but also, what is far more important, habits of impartiality and intellectual fairness, which will at last be carried into all forms of discussion, and will destroy every system that refuses to accept them. Year after year, as political life extends, we find each new attempt to stifle the expression of opinion received with an increased indignation, the sympathies of the people immediately enlisted on behalf of the oppressed teacher, and the work which is the object of condemnation elevated in public esteem often to a degree that is far greater than it deserves. Year after year the conviction becomes more general that a provisional abnegation of the opinions of the past and a resolute and unflinching impartiality are among the highest duties of the enquirer, and that he who shrinks from such a research is at least morally bound to abstain from condemning the opinions of his neighbour.

If we may generalise the experience of modern constitutional governments, it would appear that this process must pass through three phases. When political life is introduced into a nation that is strongly imbued with sectarianism, this latter spirit will at first dominate over political interests, and the whole scope and tendency of government will be directed by theology. After a time the movement I have traced in the present chapter will appear. The secular element will emerge into light. It will at length obtain an absolute ascendency, and, expelling theology successively from all its political strongholds, will thus weaken its influence over the human mind. Yet in one remarkable way the spirit of sectarianism will still survive: it will change its name and object, transmigrate into political discussion, and assume the form of an intense party-spirit. The increasing tendency, however, of political life seems to be to weaken or efface this spirit, and in the more advanced stages of free government it almost disappears. A judicial spirit is fostered which leads men both in politics and theology to eclecticism, to judge all questions exclusively on the ground of their intrinsic merits, and not at all according to their position in theological or political systems. To increase the range and intensity of political interests is to strengthen this tendency; and every extension of the suffrage thus diffuses over a wider circle a habit of thought that must eventually modify theological belief. If the suffrage should ever be granted to women, it would probably, after two or three generations, effect a complete revolution in their habits of thought, which by acting upon the first period of education would influence the whole course of opinion.

NOTES

1. This has been very clearly noticed in one of the ablest modern books in defence of the Tory theory. "At the point where Protestantism becomes

vicious, where it receives the first tinge of latitudinarianism, and begins to join hands with infidelity by superseding the belief of an objective truth in religion, necessary for salvation; at that very spot it likewise assumes an aspect of hostility to the union of Church and State." (Gladstone, on *Church and State*, p. 188.) [Lecky refers to William Ewart Gladstone's *The State in Its Relations with the Church* (1838; rev. ed. 1841).]

2. The evidence of the secularisation of politics furnished by the position of what is called "the religious press," is not confined to England and France. The following very remarkable passage was written by a most competent observer in 1858, when Austria seemed the centre of religious despotism: "Tous les intérêts les plus chétifs ont des nombreux organes dans la presse périodique et font tons de bonnes affaires. La religion, le premier et le plus grand de tous les intérêts, n'en a qu'un nombre presque imperceptible et qui a bien de la peine à vivre. Dans la Catholique Autriche sur 135 journaux il n'y a qu'un seul consacré aux intérêts du Christianisme, et il laisse beaucoup à désirer sous le rapport de l'orthodoxie. . . . La vérité est que décidément l'opinion publique ainsi que l'intérêt publique ont cessé d'être Chrétiens en Europe." (Ventura, *Le Pouvoir Chrétien en Politique*, p. 139.) ["All the most trivial interests have several organs in the periodical press and all are doing well. Religion, the first and greatest of all the interests, has a scarcely imperceptible number and these struggle to survive. In Catholic Austria, out of 135 journals there is hardly one devoted to Christian interests, and it leaves much to be desired in terms of orthodoxy. . . . The truth is that, emphatically, public opinion as well as public interest has ceased to be Christian in Europe." Gioacchino Ventura, *Le Pouvoir politique chrétien* (1858).]

17

ARE WE CHRISTIANS?

Leslie Stephen

[Leslie Stephen (1832–1904), British essayist, critic, and father of Virginia Woolf, was among the leading British intellectuals of his time. He was educated at Trinity Hall, Cambridge, where he later received a fellowship as a tutor. One requirement of the position was that he take holy orders within a year, and accordingly he became an ordained deacon in 1855. But his readings of John Stuart Mill, Auguste Comte, and Immanuel Kant led him to reject the historical bases of Christianity, and he resigned his tutorship. Stephen went on to write pioneering works of literary criticism, notably *Hours in a Library* (1874–79) and *History of English Thought in the Eighteenth Century* (1876), as well as biographies of Samuel Johnson, Alexander Pope, Jonathan Swift, George Eliot, and Thomas Hobbes for the English Men of Letters series. He was knighted in 1902. His numerous essays on religion were gathered in *Essays on Freethinking and Plain-*

Leslie Stephen, "Are We Christians?" *Fortnightly Review* 19 (March 1873): 281–91, 295–303.

speaking (1873) and *An Agnostic's Apology and Other Essays* (1893). In the following essay, Stephen ponders whether the decreasing emphasis on doctrine and dogma in the wake of advancing knowledge has rendered many Christians unwitting agnostics or skeptics.]

Are we still Christians? is the question recently propounded by Strauss.[1] The answer which he gives has startled Mr. Gladstone into a pathetic appeal to the schoolboys of Liverpool.[2] The Premier advises the youth of England to rest content with the decisions pronounced some centuries ago by the Council of Nice.[3] The advice is amiable, if perhaps a little singular from the leader of the party of progress, and let us hope that it will bring peace to the schoolboy mind. Regarded from the point of view of pure logic, such a reply can scarcely be considered effective as against Strauss and modern criticism. Strauss, indeed, is not writing for schoolboys. The "we" of whom he speaks belong to the class—a class, he adds, no longer to be counted by thousands—to whom the old faith and the old church can no longer offer a weatherproof refuge. The majority even of this class would be content to lop off the decayed bough, trusting that there is yet vital power in the trunk. But there is a minority, and it is in their name that Strauss speaks, who think that in giving up the old supernaturalism, they must also take final leave of the worship to which it alone could give enduring power over the souls of men. Taking the "we" in this limited sense, there can be but one answer to the question. That answer is given by Strauss in the most unequivocal terms, and at times with some unnecessary asperity. Passing in review the most essential articles of the Christian creed, and the practices founded upon them, Strauss declares that for "us" they can have no meaning. The attempts to effect a compromise between Christianity and Rationalism are nothing but a lamentable waste of human ingenuity. And thus he replies to his own question: emphatically, no. To be a Christian, a modern thinker must be dull or dishonest; he must palter with his own convictions, or with the world. "We," if we would be true to ourselves or to mankind, must abandon our ancient dwelling-place. Let us shake the dust off our feet, and taking reason for our guide, and Mr. Darwin for the best modern expounder of the universe, go boldly forwards to whatever may be in store for us.

That such a question should be so put, and so answered, is clearly a noteworthy phenomenon even to men who are not perorating to schoolboys. That Strauss speaks in the name of a numerous and an intellectually powerful class is undeniable. Whether, in fact, a love of truth bids us abandon all those beliefs which alone rendered the world beautiful or even tolerable to the good and to the wise of former generations, is one of the most important questions that can be asked, and one, it need not be said, infinitely too wide to be considered here. Another analogous question is suggested by Strauss's inquiry. What of the vast "we" who lie outside the little band of true believers; the "we" upon whom the sun of science has not arisen, and who lie in the dim twilight, or even in the tenfold shades of night cast by the ancient superstitions not yet dispersed by its rays? It is long, as Mr. Tennyson tells, before—

> The sunrise creeping down,
> Flood with full day-light glebe and town.[4]

The mountain-tops may be glowing, but centuries may pass before the valleys partake of that brilliant illumination. The ordinary phrases about the development of thought refer only to a select few. It is but a numerically insignificant minority which has broken the old chains, and seen through the old fallacies. The emancipation of masses at the other extremity of the social scale, if it is to be called emancipation, is of a purely negative character. The thinking class is analogous to the brain of Hobbes's Leviathan; but the analogy must be made to fit, by assuming that Leviathan resembles some monstrous whale, in whom the propagation of impulses from the brain to the extremities takes a perceptible time, and whose organization includes a number of subsidiary ganglia which can imperfectly discharge the cerebral functions. When a living idea no longer dominates the brain, the extremities are the first to feel the loss of its vital power. The intermediate parts of the body continue to work in the old fashion by a sort of blind spontaneity which yet lingers in the secondary organs. When a church loses its hold on the intellectual classes, it can no longer maintain its sway over the "proletariate"; but the great bulk of the nation continues to think or to fancy it thinks in the old formulae, though conscious that a strange numbness is creeping over its faculties. What, then, is the state of mind of that great bulk of Englishmen who have neither listened to Strauss nor to Mr. Bradlaugh;[5] who have neither positively revolted nor unconsciously fallen away; whose intellects are not active enough to care for scientific impulse, and yet too active to be content with a pure absence of ideas? Assuming for the moment that Strauss speaks truly as to his own "we," what of the next of the concentric social circles?

As the new doctrines filter downwards, they exercise a strange and, it almost seems, a capricious effect upon the lower strata of belief. Here and there old creeds are dissolved, leaving incoherent fragments behind them. Sometimes the destruction of later incrustations of doctrines only brings to light ancient forms of superstition, which we supposed to have vanished long ago from the world. The ancient gods of the heathen survived, as we know, to become the devils of Christian nations. Beliefs, instead of being abandoned, are transformed, and adapt themselves by slight modifications to the new atmosphere. Half understood fragments of the new theories work strange havoc with the older systems of thought. Ignorant people, it may be, see only the destructive side of rationalist teaching, and with their belief in the old sanctions lose their belief in the permanence of all morality. Or, taking fright at the prospect before them, they plunge back into the ancient superstitions. Or, catching at the scientific jargon, they dress up new idols, whose worship, to say the least of it, is not less degrading than that of their predecessors. And thus we have a blundering system of chaotic beliefs, of which it is difficult to render any coherent account, or to detect the animating principle. Strauss we know, and Dr.

Newman we know; but what of all these singular phantoms which are moving, and to all appearance living, in the world? Which doctrines are mere shadowy ghosts, and which have some solid core of genuine belief? When a man boasts of his implicit faith, is he really avowing utter scepticism or profound conviction? The old method of arguing from creeds to genuine beliefs, from what men say to what they think, has become a mere byeword. Were it applicable we should have to suppose that some people still believe the Athanasian Creed.[6] If we could conceive the old formulae to be suddenly blotted out of existence, and men to endeavour to express their creeds in the simplest words that occurred to them, we should have a strange substitute for the Thirty-nine Articles.[7] Cross-examine the simple-minded believer, and you will find him quite unconsciously avowing the most startling tactics. In spite of the rash assertions of metaphysicians, mutually contradictory propositions lie side by side in his mind in perfect harmony. Perhaps he will seldom assert blankly that A is at once B and not B; but if those statements be a little disguised, he will produce them alternately, or even simultaneously, with the utmost complacency. He has no trouble in holding the premises of a syllogism, and denying its conclusion; and still less in asserting a general proposition whilst denying every particular statement that it includes. What—to take an obvious example—is commoner than to find a zealot who vigorously asserts a belief in hell, and is yet shocked at the opinion that anybody will be damned? A place of eternal torture eternally untenanted seems to be no very useful article of faith, and yet it is perhaps the nearest expression of the ordinary opinion on the subject. The statement, indeed, must be made with diffidence, for to discover by any direct inquiry what people really think on that most tremendous subject is one of the most hopeless of tasks.

Indeed it may be said, with little exaggeration, not only that there is no article in the creeds which may not be contradicted with impunity, but that there is none which may not be contradicted in a sermon calculated to win the reputation of orthodoxy, and be regarded as a judicious bid for a bishopric. The popular state of mind seems to be typified in the well-known anecdote of the cautious churchwarden, who, whilst commending the general tendency of his incumbent's sermon, felt bound to hazard a protest upon one point. "You see, sir," as he apologetically explained, "I think there be a God." He thought it an error of taste, or perhaps of judgment, to hint a doubt as to the first article of the creed. Undoubtedly, any one who should say in plain terms "I am an Atheist," would be in danger, not indeed of persecution, but of some social inconvenience. He would be wanting in good manners, though not a criminal. For is it not a wanton insult to our neighbours to contradict their harmless prejudices, when we can so easily reduce them to a mere verbal difference? What else is the good of metaphysics? Is it not the art of identifying "is" and "is not," and of repelling the profane vulgar by the terrors of a mysterious jargon, whilst you propound what views you please to esoteric disciples? May you not say, in language strong enough to satisfy a Positivist,[8] that the human mind can form no conception of Divinity; that good and merciful, applied to the Almighty, mean no more than wrathful and jealous, or even than epithets implying corporeal attributes, and say it all amidst general applause so long as your assault is ostensibly directed against the presumptuous deist, and not against Moses or St. Paul? A grateful clergy will applaud you for wielding weapons so unfamiliar to them, and so steadily associated with the adversary, and will take your word for it that you mean well. To repudiate Christianity in express terms would, of course, be inadmissible for a sound divine; but dexterously soften away the old doctrines, explain that there is a divine element in all men as well as in Christ, interpret the true meaning of his mission upon earth, and the means of salvation for fallen man in terms of modern philosophy instead of the old theological phraseology, and nothing is easier than to show, and to win the credit of a pious motive for showing, that the one central event round which, as old believers thought, the whole universe revolved, is nothing but an ancient legend, more touching perhaps, but not more vitally important to human beings, than the death of Socrates.

But why insist on facts so notorious? Do not all sections of

Churchmen lament or exult over the marvellous elasticity of the ancient formulae? In truth, shifts of this kind are scarcely adapted for the vulgar. They belong either to the outward circle of Strauss's "we"; to those who live in the penumbra, not in the outer darkness, who fancy that they can allow the decayed branches to fall of themselves, without laying the axe to the root of the tree. Plainer minds are perplexed by such manifestations, and cannot put up with a creed where, for the old formula, "I believe," they are requested to read, "I am on the whole inclined to believe," or to say more positively, "I firmly believe in a general stream of tendency." They want some more tangible grip of substantial realities, not these shadowy phantoms of opinion, changeable and bodiless as a morning mist. To discover the belief of the half educated, which includes ninety-nine in a hundred of the so-called educated classes, we must not look to sermons—if, indeed, sermons reveal to us anybody's belief, and not rather blind gropings after something that will serve as a stop-gap for belief. Even those popular preachings which are modelled to suit the popular taste, fail to give us any very trustworthy indications. They are sometimes seasoned more highly to suit a decaying palate. Shall we look then to those popular platitudes which bring down the applauses of crowded audiences, and sell cheap newspapers by the hundred thousand? From them we may learn, for example, that the British workman will not have the Bible excluded from his schools, and will not have the Sunday desecrated. Certainly these are two of the most definite points in the popular creed. Our reverence for the Bible is, as Dr. Newman tells us, the strong point of Protestantism; and our observance of Sunday is the one fact which tells a foreigner that we have a religious faith. No one, whatever his opinions, should undervalue those beliefs, or, if so, they must be called superstitions. An English Sunday, with all its gloom and with all its drunkenness, is a proof that we do in fact worship something besides our stomachs. Familiarity with the Bible, slavish and dull as is our reverence for the letter, affords almost the only means by which the imagination of the people is cultivated, and some dim perception maintained of a divine meaning in the universe.

But then these two sentiments do not make a creed. Sunday is cherished by those who never enter a church, and the Bible may be a symbol of every creed that has existed in Europe for eighteen hundred years. Inquiring a little further, we probably come upon the statement that the people of England believe in unsectarian Christianity. There is a whole armoury of popular platitudes used to stimulate our enthusiasm in this noble cause. Platforms ring with its praises, and articles are published about it on Good Friday, which, if sincere—as we must hope they are—should have melted their authors to tears.

If we brutally put such statements to the torture, and persist in crushing them in a logical mill, they can have but one meaning. They simply amount to scepticism in a gushing instead of a cynical form. Unsectarian Christianity can no more exist than there can be a triangle which is neither scalene nor isosceles nor equilateral. All Christians might conceivably be converted to one sect; but if you strip off from the common creed all the matters which are in dispute between them, the residuum is at most the old-fashioned deism, if, indeed, it amounts to that. Nor is this mere logic chopping. The more we look into the question, the plainer is the answer. Christianity, as it is understood by ultramontanes or by ultra-Protestants, implies a body of beliefs of unspeakable importance to the world. They may be true or they may be false, but they cannot be set aside as perfectly indifferent. Man is or is not placed here for a brief interval, which is to decide his happiness or his misery throughout all eternity. His situation does or does not depend upon his allegiance to the Church, or upon his undergoing a certain spiritual change. Christ came or did not come from God, and died or did not die to reconcile man to his Maker. An infidel is a man who accepts the negative of those propositions; a Christian is one who takes the affirmative; an unsectarian Christian, if he has any belief at all, is one who says that they may or may not be true, and that it does not much matter. If that is a roundabout way of expressing agreement with the infidel, the statement is intelligible, though its sincerity is questionable. But, taking it literally, it is surely the most incredible of all the assertions that a human being can possibly put forward. Can it possibly be a matter of indifference whether or not hell is gaping for me, and heaven opening its doors? whether or not there is only one means provided by my Creator of escape from the dangers that environ us, and whether or not I avail myself of them? Dogmas, you say, matter nothing; charity and purity are everything. But to say that such dogmas matter nothing is to imply that they are not true; for the only alternative is the blasphemous proposition that God Almighty sent his Son upon earth to proclaim to his creatures the awful realities of their position; to tell them how to escape his wrath and how to do his will; and that, for all practical purposes, He might as well have let it alone. The dogmas are true, or they are immoral; for they tend to alter radically our whole conception of the world and of our position in it. They give us the chart by which to direct our course over the mysterious ocean to the unknown shore. It cannot be a matter of indifference whether the dangers which they indicate, and the harbour to which they would direct us, have or have not a real existence.

It is out of place, it may be urged, to apply serious reasoning to such vague aspirations. Rather let us admit that, flimsy as is the popular rhetoric, disgusting to all who ask for grain instead of chaff as is the unctuous sentimentalism in which it wraps itself, it contains a sort of meaning not devoid of value. By Christianity, in such phrases, is chiefly meant, so far as can be guessed, a few maxims from the sermon on the mount. The sturdy old Scotchwoman who complained of the "cauld morality" of that document, had still a theology; but her sentiments are thoroughly out of fashion. The ordinary mind is rather shocked than otherwise by the statement that our faith means anything more than a command to do to others as we would that they should do to us; and a belief that the character of Christ is a perfect embodiment of the virtues of benevolence and humility. The creed is a simple one, and not a bad one as far as it goes. Some exceptions might be taken to the type of character which it is calculated to develop. People who use the phrase have a peculiar Manichaeism of their own. The evil principle is represented by Malthus, working by the "inexorable laws" of supply and demand; and the good principle by spasmodic outbursts of "genial" sentimentalism. At one moment the poor are to be improved by allowing them to starve; at another, by giving them plenty of plum-pudding and milk-punch at Christmas. But, be this as it may, the doctrine, turn it how you will, is essentially sceptical. It is Strauss translated into the popular tongue; for it amounts to saying that the doctrines which were the very life-blood of the old creeds which once stirred men's hearts to flame are to be respectfully and civilly shelved, and that morality can do very well without them. It is the product of intellectual indolence, though not of active intellectual revolt. We have not the courage to say that the Christian doctrines are false, but we are lazy enough to treat them as irrelevant. We shut our eyes to the Christian theory of the universe, and fix them exclusively upon those moral precepts which are admittedly common to Buddhists and Mahomedans, to Stoics and to Positivists, though, it may be, most forcibly expressed by Christians. To proclaim unsectarian Christianity is, in circuitous language, to proclaim that Christianity is dead. The love of Christ, as representing the ideal perfection of human nature, may indeed be still a powerful motive, and powerful whatever the view which we take of Christ's character. The advocates of the doctrine in its more intellectual form represent this passion as the true essence of Christianity. They assert with obvious sincerity of conviction that it is the leverage by which alone the world can be moved. But, as they would themselves admit, this conception would be preposterous if, with Strauss, we regard Christ as a mere human being. Our regard for Him might differ in degree, but would not differ in kind, from our regard for Socrates or for Pascal. It would be impossible to consider it as an overmastering and all-powerful influence. The old dilemma would be inevitable; he that loves not his brother whom he hath seen, how can he love Christ whom he hath not seen? A mind untouched by the agonies and wrongs which invest London hospitals and lanes with horror, could not be moved by the sufferings of a single individual, however holy, who died eighteen centuries ago. No! the essence of the belief is the belief in the divinity of Christ. But accept that belief; think for a moment of all that it implies; and you must admit that your Christianity becomes dogmatic in the highest degree. Our conception of the world and its meaning are more radically changed than our conceptions of the material universe, when the sun instead of the earth became its centre. Every view of history, every theory of our duty, must be radically transformed by contact with that stupendous mystery. Whether you accept or reject the special tenets of the Athanasian Creed is an infinitesimal trifle. You are bound to assume that every religion which does not take this dogma into account is without true vital force. Infidels, heathens, and Unitarians reject the single influence which alone can mould our lives in conformity with the everlasting laws of the universe. Of course, there are tricks of logical sleight of hand by which the conclusion is evaded. It would be too long and too trifling to attempt to expose them. Unsectarian Christianity consists in shirking the difficulty without meeting it, and trying hard to believe that the passion can survive without its essential basis. It proclaims the love of Christ as our motive, whilst it declines to make up its mind whether Christ was God or man; or endeavours to escape a categorical answer under a cloud of unsubstantial rhetoric. But the difference between man and God is infinite; and no effusion of superlatives will disguise the plain fact from honest minds. To be a Christian in any real sense, you must start from a dogma of the most tremendous kind, and an undogmatic creed is as senseless as a statue without shape or a picture without colour. Unsectarian means unchristian.

Are we, then, to assume that with averted eyes and hesitating steps men are abandoning, or have already substantially abandoned, the old creeds, and quietly preserved the name whilst tacitly adding a neutralizing epithet? If some facts might be alleged in favour of that view, there are not wanting many which may be advanced on the opposite side. The preachers who lament over the progress of infidelity, boast also of the revival which has passed over all creeds within the present century. The old trunk continues to put out fresh shoots. Churches have risen all over the land; schools have been built; priests are supported; and the increase of the spiritual provision is overtaking the increase of the population. The cold breath of the eighteenth-century scepticism has passed away. Voltaire has done his worst; Darwinism and the other agencies of which Strauss speaks have destroyed the outworks instead of the citadel; and the reconciliation of faith and reason, distant as it may still appear, is beginning dimly to shadow itself forth on the far horizon. Which is the main stream and which the eddy? The great protest against the old dogmatism has liberated the intellect from obsolete fetters; but may it not turn out that the intellect will itself frame laws substantially identical with the old? Some obvious deductions must indeed be made. Church building is a very pretty amusement for rich men. There has been an immensely increased expenditure upon all kinds of luxury, and ecclesiastical luxury has of course increased with the rest. There is a taste for painted windows as there is a taste for Venetian glass; and perhaps the tithe which rich men pay to religious purposes has not increased in proportion to their expenditure on purposes of a purely selfish kind. Antiquarianism has become a popular amusement, instead of being confined to a few. We have the South Kensington Museum instead of the few petty collections of which Strawberry Hill was the most prominent example.[9] We have built real churches, and put in them real priests in real vestments, instead of running up a few sham ruins like our respected grandfathers. The restoration, as we are pleased to call it, of a modern cathedral, provides some pleasant excitement for the surrounding nobility and gentry; and the only misfortune is that our toy is too big to be put in a museum. And then, too, the expenditure on religious institutions is part of the insurance which we all have to pay against "blazing principles." What with communists and members of the International, we are too much in the position of people sitting on a powder magazine to be quite comfortable. It pays from a purely commercial point of view to support the Establishment. We send out our "black dragoons" into every parish, agents of social order, whose duty it is to assure agricultural peasants and others—first, that they are very comfortable; secondly, that submission is a Christian duty; and finally, that they ought to set their affections on things above, and not upon houses and lands which belong to other people. The Christian religion, as some people seem to think, had an uncomfortable dash of socialism in its early ages, but has now become an excellent bulwark to the rights of property. It provides a harmless vent for a good deal of ugly enthusiasm; a dissenting hymn, aesthetically objectionable, is a much safer expression of sentiment than the Marseillaise; and the wild rant about hell fire is more convenient than allusions to the incendiary properties of petroleum. Indeed, we are sincere enough. We have been to the brink of the volcano, and we did not like the glimpses we caught of the seething masses of inflammatory matter at the bottom. The effect was fairly to startle us back into any old creed which led to less disastrous results. The Pope, or the Archbishop of Canterbury, or even Mr. Spurgeon,[10] are much more satisfactory guides than the prophets of the revolution, and we may willingly swallow a few dogmas in which we do not quite believe, to secure the alliance of powerful manifestations of popular impulses. Even Gibbon, when he saw the outbreak of the first French revolution, became an admirer of the Church of England. To decide for how much motives of this kind may count in the general movement is of course impossible. Every strong current of feeling is derived from complex sources, and the base and selfish interests have their part in it as well as the noblest. Indeed, it would be absurd to stigmatise as essentially ignoble all that we call the purely reactionary or even the purely dilettante elements of the new-born zeal. Their existence is a proof how much remains to be done before the subversive school can satisfy men's imaginations, and provide a bond capable of holding society together with its ancient solidity. It would be equally foolish and cynical, even in those who have most distinctly parted company with the old beliefs, to overlook the generosity and the sincerity displayed by the loyal adherents of the dying cause. In that, as in all other movements which stir men's souls profoundly, there must undoubtedly be a groundwork of true faith and heroism. The difficulty is to decide how far the impulse comes from external contagion, and how far it is derived from the native and unexhausted forces of the ancient creeds. The flame of zeal lighted up by the heretics spreads also to their antagonists. When, from any causes, a vigorous stimulant is acting upon the world, a more rapid current of circulation is driven through the old channels as well as through the new. The phenomenon is by itself ambiguous. A stronger sense of the necessity of social revolutions may take the form of increased religious enthusiasm, though at bottom it may have little enough to do with renewed faith in the ancient dogmas. The same impulse may strengthen the hands both of the Positivist and of the Romish priest, and it can only be decided by experiment which provides the best expression for the new emotions that are stirring the foundations of society. That a creed may be permanent, it must satisfy the intellect; but the first impulse comes from the passions, and therefore a revival of belief may be due much more to a change in social conditions than to any process of logical conviction.

Thus the problem of determining what are our genuine beliefs cannot be decided by simply counting congregations, or adding up subscription lists, any more than by a simple inspection of creeds. Some means must be discovered of testing the true significance of the evidence. Somewhere under all the mass of loud profession and ambiguous rhetoric there must be a genuine core of belief. If we probe deep enough and long enough, we must, or so we fancy, come in the end to something sound and solid. No one but a practised metaphysician can succeed in balancing his mind for any length of time in an attitude of sceptical equilibrium. Few people, it is true, think coherently, or push their doubts home. They are in one state of mind on Sunday and in another on Monday; they have different religions for their shops and their domestic houses; and yet, chaotic as is the intellectual furniture of most minds, one may find in them some little stock of cherished opinion, or at least of prejudice, which supplies a more or less solid standing ground. There have been periods at which one might say that a man believed what he would fight for; but there are two difficulties in the way of applying such a test now, namely, that we very seldom fight for anything; and, still more, that when we do, we do not generally know for what we are fighting. An Irishman may fancy that he is fighting for the Pope, when he is really fighting from hatred of the Saxon, or from an abstract love of fighting for its own sake; and a clergyman that he is fighting for the Athanasian Creed, when he is really animated by a wholesome jealousy of Dissenters. The only available method would seem to be an indirect one. A living creed is distinguished from a dead creed by this—that it is constantly germinating and associating itself with all our modes of thought, and therefore one may sometimes find out what a man believes, not by asking him, point-blank, "Will you subscribe to such or such an Article?" but by taking him unawares, and judging whether he keeps his dogma in a pigeon-hole, to be exhibited on proper occasions, or applies it spontaneously to any task in hand. [. . .]

The question, however, remains, What effect does this indefinable state of mind produce upon our lives? Does it entitle us to be called, in any intelligible sense, Christians? Does that inarticulate conviction give so firm a standing-ground as materially to affect our conduct, or is it merely retained because some sense of awful mystery is necessary to the imagination? Are we like men whose guiding star has become indistinct and shadowy, but yet serves to direct their course; or are we conscious of its light merely as a diffused glow, colouring the bare world with a magical harmony, but affording no indication to impel us in any definite direction? If our hopes of immortality be unfounded, says St. Paul, then are we of all men the most miserable.[11] The statement is susceptible of an unpleasant interpretation; for it may easily be pressed into the service of people who hold that the only object of being virtuous is to win a pension in this world or the next; but in a less literal sense it must be true of every revealed religion. What could be more cruel to the most unselfish hero than to find that his whole scheme of life had been laid out on a false hypothesis, and that he had been guiding his followers into the wilderness instead of the promised land? To have erased from St. Paul's creed his faith in a future world, would have been to destroy the thread which alone held together the whole network of interwoven beliefs. It would at once have fallen into a hopelessly intricate tangle. The universe would have appeared to him as a blind jumble of incoherent forces. He would not have felt that his loss was confined simply to the weakening of one motive to virtue, but rather that his whole system of thought was, as it were, dislocated and paralysed. The belief in the life beyond the grave is in some creeds merely a beautiful and elevating, but, in the strict sense, a superfluous corollary from the other doctrines. Its loss would be sensibly felt, but it would not change the practical lessons of life. In others it is the base, which cannot be removed without bringing down the whole super-structure in ruin. Which is the case with ourselves?

We may judge by trying to place ourselves for a moment in the position of men who really believe in some of the old doctrines now repeated so glibly, because with so little meaning. To them the present world appears to be a scene of misery; its pleasures are empty delusions; to partake of them is to run the risk of sullying our souls, and he is best who yields least to the temptations of the senses. Marriage is not the natural state of man, but a concession to our baser passions, mercifully granted to avoid worse evils. The virgin life is the highest, and to mortify the flesh and wean ourselves from the world the only course that can entitle us to eternal rewards. We are sojourners here, and properly denizens of a purer abode, from which we have been exiled for a time, and which the corruption of our natures prevents us from distinctly viewing with our earthly vision. Our best hope is that the whole visible framework of the universe may be dissolved, and a new heaven and new earth be revealed to our wayworn souls. The spirit of man is clogged and debased by the vile clay with which it is mixed, and the whole purpose of the world is, by some supernatural chemistry, to extract the finer essence from the alloy into which it has been plunged. Such a doctrine is, of course, only tenable if the future life appears to be as real as the present, or, indeed, to have a more intense reality. In the lower forms of the creed, the belief is necessary, because otherwise we could never be repaid for the tortures which we have undergone; it is equally necessary in the higher forms, because otherwise our whole activity has been directed to a chimerical aim. A lifelong and internecine struggle with the elements of which this life is composed, is nonsensical if this life be all, and our power necessarily limited to making the best of the world as it is.

The creed of the genuine ascetic, even where it is most vigorously entertained, does not, of course, produce a corresponding effect upon men's lives. The ties by which we are bound to the world and the flesh are infinitely too strong to be broken by any imaginative doctrine. Divines of all classes, Roman Catholic priests, and Dissenting ministers, strain their powers to give form and colouring to the scenes which are to terrify or to allure us. With eternity and infinite power to draw upon, it is their own fault if the picture be not sufficiently brilliant.

> The weariest and most loathed worldly life
> That age, ache, penury, and imprisonment
> Can lay on nature, is a paradise
> To what we fear of death.[12]

For the fears have been stimulated by the simple process of taking all that is most horrible in this world, and conceiving it as multiplied in intensity and duration till the imagination faints under the burden. The result does not correspond to the benevolent intentions of the artists, partly because the imagination is sluggish, and a tacit revolt is produced by too exorbitant drafts upon our powers of belief, and partly too because the artists themselves are compelled to devise modes of escape from the horrors which they have depicted. The power of the Church to remit the penalties, or of some change in the individual to avoid them, grows in proportion to the rigour of the penalties themselves, and the terms of escape are arranged in such a way as not to bear too hardly upon human weakness. All bad men, it is proclaimed, will be damned; but we, it is whispered, possess the key to some convenient back-door which will enable you to slink into paradise without too great a sacrifice of your natural passions.

It would be absurd, therefore, to measure the vitality of the creed by the degree in which it actually produces the effect at which it is ostensibly aimed. The vilest licentiousness constantly exists in the very places where its consequences are believed, in all sincerity, to be most unspeakably momentous. Indeed, to condemn all human passions is to lower the moral tone of those who cannot quench them; for stringency encourages immorality, just as it encourages smuggling. But wherever such a creed is powerful, the moral standard of the believers will be altered, though not their lives. An ascetic nation will not produce a whole nation of ascetics, and it may at times exist in a whole nation of voluptuaries; but it will show itself in the moral type which they admire. Their saints, real or imaginary, will be men who have issued from the world and its cares to cultivate the spiritual faculties. The criterion of virtue will not be the tendency of actions to improve this life, but to encourage indifference to temporal interests. Charity will be admirable, not in so far as it tends to eradicate poverty, but in so far as it imposes sacrifices upon the benevolent; and a man will be admired if, without directly contributing to the happiness of others, he has deliberately made himself miserable during his earthly pilgrimage.

What, then, is the ordinary creed of our modern society upon these points of morals? Is the ascetic or the utilitarian code of morality most in harmony with our practice, or rather with our theories? What type of virtue would an average Englishman or American most admire?— that which is embodied in an inmate of the Chartreuse,[13] who slowly and silently tortures himself to death on the summit of a bleak mountain; or that in a clergyman, with a wife and twelve children, good clothes and kitchen, and even a tolerable cellar of wine, who yet does his duty manfully, like the hard-working doctor or lawyer who lives next door, and who succeeds in diminishing drunkenness and in increasing the deposits in the savings bank of the neighbourhood? If virtue is to be measured by the extent of the victory won over natural passions, the monk has of course an indefinite superiority; if by the degree in which a man's activity is subservient to the welfare of his fellow-man, the balance inclines as decidedly in the opposite direction. The monk may be thoroughly and grossly selfish, for he may be calculating on a tenfold repayment; and the clergyman may have acted in every case upon the most chivalrous motives. His marriage may have been a great act of self-denial; and he may sincerely hold even that the comfort in which he lives is necessary to fit his children to play their parts as refined and accomplished members of the class to which they belong. The ultimate motives are beyond our judgment; but we may ask which type of humanity is most likely to flourish in the soil of modern society? Nor can the answer be for a moment doubtful. Those who hate most and those who most admire the tendencies summed up in what we call progress, are pretty well agreed as to some of the characteristics implied. An observer, for example, like Tocqueville is never tired of writing upon the passion for material well-being,[14] which, according to him, is the distinguishing mark of modern democracy. To fit people for this world rather than for the next seems to be the sole object of modern philanthropists and statesmen. If we wish to denounce the dominant tendencies of the age, we call them materialising, and argue that Christianity is more than ever necessary to save us from the grovelling worship of the almighty dollar. If we approve of them, we urge that a religion which confines itself to condemning the world cannot really leaven it with higher influences. The heat of pious enthusiasm which, under the old forms of belief, radiated into the void of infinite space, must be retained within our atmosphere to give light and warmth on earth. Religion, to retain its vitality, must sanctify the ordinary passions of men, and not fruitlessly aim at their extirpation. Can the motives provided by Christianity receive this application? That was no doubt the opinion of the benevolent persons who, some years ago, invented the name of Christian socialism; and it is implied in the various attempts of the Church of Rome to form an alliance between the priests and the populace. Why should not Christianity, as of old, be the great force for the upheaval of society? Is not the alliance between the Church and the ancient political framework merely a temporary accident; and may not the principles of Christian morality be represented as identical with those of a modern radical? The revolutionists, who repudiated the old faith along with the old rulers, were perhaps rejecting the force which could alone have given them the necessary consistency for winning a final victory. The intellectual difficulties which have alienated the class represented by Strauss's "we," have little significance for the lowest social stratum. A New York Irishman or a Belgian peasant is not much affected by the results of historical criticism and scientific discovery. Why then should there be any mutual repulsion between the modern democrats and those who boast of a succession from the ancient fishermen of Galilee? The Founder of our religion was called the first *sans culotte*; and passing over the irreverence of the phrase, it expressed an important analogy. The sentiments to which the early Christians appealed were in many respects the same as those to which our modern socialists owe their strength.

The fundamental difficulty in the way to such an alliance lies in the difference of the remedy suggested. The doctrine of the early Christians proceeded from men who renounced the world as the scene of a brutal tyranny, but looked for safety to passive submission, instead of active revolt. They accepted poverty and suffering as inevitable, and sought for a refuge in the hopes of another world, or of a millennium to be brought about by miraculous agencies. The modern socialist aspires to conquer the world, instead of withdrawing from it, and would extirpate rather than idealise poverty. His millennium is to be won by his own efforts, and he contemplates entrance into Utopia instead of heaven. The promised land to which he looks forward is not an eternity of happiness, where he will be freed from the body and its cares, but an indefinite vista of material and social progress. He will not walk with saints and angels, and sing hymns of praise to his Creator throughout all ages; but he anticipates a time when capital will be the servant instead of the master of labour; when every man will have a fair day's wages for a fair day's work; when intelligent co-operation will be substituted for blind competition, and the crushing burden of poverty which now bends him to the earth will be finally removed. The vision is less splendid, for he has no longer an unbounded field for his imagination; but it is more tangible. It must be gained, not by prayer and fasting, but by the sweat of his brow, and it must be the reward of the industrial and not of the ascetic virtues. A belief in immortality is not incompatible with such a view of man's destiny and purposes; nay, it is easy to maintain that it is essential in order to balance the neutralising tendencies of the doctrine; but the hope of immortality expresses a different set of sentiments. To a Christian of the old type the vision of heaven and hell must be as vivid as possible, in order to express his abhorrence of the existing order. There must be some place where Lazarus could be made equal with Dives; for in this world he could only look forward to a life of hopeless bondage. But when Lazarus expects to compel Dives to share his wealth with his humbler brethren, a change comes over the spirit of his dream. He conceives of the next life, so far as he cares to conceive of it at all, rather as a prolongation of this than as a contrast to it. He cannot bear to think that all the kindly affections which run so cruelly to waste in this world—the love for the dead who have been taken from us, the noble aspirations that never meet with any adequate fulfilment—should be entirely dispersed without any adequate satisfaction. But he has a strong enough hope of good being ultimately realised here not to feel the necessity of a heaven to make the thought of the universe endurable. In spite of his discontent with the existing order of things, he is on the whole in too good humour with himself and the world to feel any great need of a hell. When brutal tyranny is no longer definitely triumphant, he does not wish to punish his oppressors with eternal torments. Progress, though a vague enough word, means the hope that things will somehow right themselves on earth in the course of time, and it is no longer necessary to throw out the present misery of the good and the past happiness of the wicked against a background in which their future positions may be reversed. The hope of immortality, therefore, is useful to give a loftier view of human nature, but not materially to alter its professions.

Whether the change of sentiment thus described be or be not a subject for congratulation is a wide question: but it suggests the criterion which should decide whether we have or have not a right to the ancient title. There are, in fact, two courses which may be taken by those who believe in the continued vitality of Christian ideas. They may retain or reject what may be briefly called the ascetic element of the creed; all the beliefs, that is, which gather round the doctrine that man's duty here is not to make the best of this world, but to prepare himself for another. The ultramontane party boldly adhere to the first plan of action,[15] and assert, as Dr. Manning has lately done,[16] that their doctrines are not incompatible with progress. And of course it is undeniable that Romanism, like most other known forms of belief, denounces drunkenness, cruelty, and stealing, and is, so far, favourable to the honesty, sobriety, and other virtues which are essential conditions of progress. But the true difficulty of reconciling themselves to what is meant (so far as anything definite is meant) by progress remains in full force. There is, of course, the intellectual difficulty—the utter impossibility of reconciling science and history as taught by the impartial inquirers, with the science and history as countenanced at Rome. But from that root spring difficulties of still wider and deeper character. First is the difficulty of giving real vitality to a faith which cramps and ultimately destroys all genuine love of speculative truth. The mob care little, it may be, for difficulties which affect Strauss or Mr. Darwin; their brains are too torpid to be directly sensitive to the disturbances in a region of the atmosphere inaccessible to them. And yet when the brain is paralysed, even the organs which enjoy a mere vegetative existence gradually feel the change. Practically, what is proposed is a compromise degrading and ultimately corrupting. The cultivated classes are invited to acquiesce in a creed which they do not believe, or, in plainer language, to sanction systematic lying on consideration that the priests will keep the dangerous classes quiet. The dangerous classes are to give up their objectionable schemes and to receive in exchange a good comfortable religious narcotic. Playing with the old-fashioned ecclesiastical toys, they are to forget their dreams of turning the world upside down. Undoubtedly there are many easy-going people who would be only too glad to accept that compromise for the sake of peace—that is to say, of their own comfort. Unluckily, there are difficulties in the way. In the first place, systematic lying does not answer in the long run; and in the next place, the compromise turns out to be a delusion, for the strongest party is not to be so easily hoodwinked. If the revolutionary party would accept priestly guidance, it would only be on condition that the priests would guide them in the direction they desire. That the priest may become a demagogue, he must appeal to the passions upon which the demagogue works; and the only question would be which party to the alliance would be making tools of the other. If the priests were the dupes, our last case would be worse than the first, and we should be soon protesting against the most degrading tyranny which ever yet entered the world; but in the other, the highest success must be won at a price fatal not only to democracy, but to progress in any intelligible sense. Imagine, in fact, a state of things in which the religion of all cultivated men is an organized hypocrisy, and in which the religion of the lower means that they are drilled to obey a priestly order; that humility is to be preached instead of independence, that poverty is to be consecrated instead of extirpated, and every spark of intellectual activity carefully troddon out for fear of an explosion. Practically that means that the population is to be emasculated in order that it may be kept quiet; and that society is to consist of a superstructure of effeminate rich men with a foundation of contented and superstitious paupers. Certainly some virtues might flourish under such a state of things. Sobriety, honesty, and chastity might abound, as they abound in some priest-ridden countries; but directly they bore their natural fruit, and gave rise to truthfulness, independence, and the masculine virtues, fresh opiates must be applied to lull the masses once more into indifference. That such a consummation should be contemplated by cowards who have been frightened out of their belief in mankind, or in a divine superintendence of the world by the apparition of the red spectre, is intelligible though it is melancholy; but it cannot be tolerated by any one who has some remaining faith in the old precept of telling truth and shaming the devil. Like Goldsmith, indeed, many people want to be well out of the reach of his claws before trying the experiment.[17] They would rather soothe him by a little judicious equivocation, than fight him face to face.

Meanwhile, however, such a scheme, though tacitly assumed, is not often openly propounded. We generally propose, then, to adopt the alternative, and to preach Christianity in such a way as not to run counter to the best aspirations of mankind. The question remains

whether it is possible to do so and to have a fair claim to the old title:
that is, to ask whether the doctrines preached by many admirable men
are really Christian doctrines reconciled to reason, or rationalism
thinly veiled under Christian phraseology, and the answer must
depend upon our view of more difficult but closely connected problems. Does that theory of the universe which all our preachers accept
in words, really supply a basis for the virtues which are most needed
at the present day? Is the course which they advise us to adopt that
which would be naturally suggested by the position in which they say
that we are placed? They admit that the prospect of gaining heaven and
avoiding hell is not to be urged as a motive for weaning us from
interest in this world, but only as a motive for encouraging us to make
a nobler use of it. The removal of a belief in a future world would not
be to take the sun from the skies, though it will dim his light. Is it possible still to retain more than a verbal belief in doctrines which have
been so far emptied of their old meaning, and to convert what was
once a disturbing force into a force identical in its direction with those
of earthly origin, though more elevating in its character? Or, again, is
there any meaning in holding to a supernatural origin of our religion,
whilst you admit that it is identical in kind, though differing in degree,
from all the other religions which have moved the world? Is it possible
to retain any sense of the special divinity of our creed whilst recognising the divine element, more shrouded and disturbed, in all others?
Upon our answers to these and similar questions must depend our
opinion as to whether we now are or are likely to remain Christians in
any intelligible sense of the word. If our answers be in the affirmative,
the new stream may run in the old channels; but it must be admitted
that its quality will be materially changed.

NOTES

1. [David Friedrich Strauss (1808–1874), German theologian whose
Leben Jesu (1835; The Life of Christ) denied the historical foundations of the

supernatural elements in the Gospels. Stephen refers specifically to *Der alte und der neue Glaube* (1872; translated as *The Old Faith and the New*).]

2. [William Ewart Gladstone, *Address Delivered at the Distribution of Prizes in the Liverpool College, Dec. 21, 1872* (1873).]

3. [The First Council of Nicaea, held in 325 CE, resolved numerous theological controversies of the time, including the rejection of Arianism, and established many of the central doctrines of the Christian Church.]

4. [Alfred, Lord Tennyson, "The Two Voices" (1842), ll. 86–87 ("crystal silence" for "sunrise" in Tennyson).]

5. [Charles Bradlaugh (1833–1891), British freethinker and politician. In 1880 he was elected to Parliament, but he was prevented from holding his seat until 1886 because he refused to take the oath of office on a Bible.]

6. [The Athanasian Creed, once attributed to St. Athanasius (296?–373), Bishop of Alexandria, is a widely used profession of faith in Western Christianity, especially in the Lutheran and Anglican churches. It expounds the doctrines of the Trinity and the Incarnation and asserts that belief in the creed is necessary to salvation.]

7. [The Thirty-nine Articles is a set of doctrinal formulae accepted by the Anglican Church in 1563 as a means of distinguishing itself from other churches.]

8. [Positivism is a school of philosophy associated with the French thinker Auguste Comte (1798–1857). It asserts that human thought has evolved successively from the theological to the metaphysical to the scientific.]

9. [The South Kensington Museum was established in London in 1852 as the Museum of Manufacturers at Marlborough. It was moved to South Kensington in 1857 and renamed the Victoria and Albert Museum in 1899. Strawberry Hill is an eccentric neo-Gothic structure built by British author and dilettante Horace Walpole (1717–1797) in Twickenham, beginning in 1750. It anticipated the Gothic revival of the nineteenth century.]

10. [Charles Haddon Spurgeon (1834–1892), British Baptist preacher and author who became a celebrity for his sermons in the 1850s and at the Metropolitan Tavern (1861f.). He became a leader of the British Evangelical movement, but he cared little for doctrine or dogma.]

11. ["If in this life only we have hope in Christ, we are of all men most miserable." 1 Cor. 15:19.]

12. [Shakespeare, *Measure for Measure* 3.1.129–32.]

13. [La Grand Chartreuse is the mother house of the Carthusian monks,

situated in a group of mountains 4,300 feet above sea level in a valley of the Alps near Grenoble, France. The Carthusians are extreme ascetics.]

14. [Alexis de Tocqueville (1805–1859), French political scientist and author of *De la démocratie en Amérique* (1835–40; translated as *Democracy in America*).]

15. [Ultramontism refers to a tendency in the Roman Catholic Church to centralize all authority and influence in the pope and the Papal Curia. It achieved its greatest triumph in 1870, when the First Vatican Council declared the pope infallible.]

16. [Henry Edward Manning (1808–1892), British theologian who converted to Roman Catholicism and became a cardinal. He was a major supporter of the doctrine of papal infallibility at the First Vatican Council, expressing his views in the volume *Petri Privilegium* (1871). He later wrote the treatise *The Vatican Decrees and Their Bearing on Civil Allegiance* (1875).]

17. [The reference is to a discussion between British writers Oliver Goldsmith and Samuel Johnson, recorded in James Boswell's *Life of Johnson* (1791), under the date April 15, 1773: "GOLDSMITH: For my part, I'd tell truth, and shame the devil. JOHNSON: Yes, Sir; but the devil will be angry, I wish to shame the devil as much as you do, but I should choose to be out of the reach of his claws. GOLDSMITH: His claws can do you no harm, when you have the shield of truth."]

18

THE TWILIGHT OF CHRISTIANITY

Harry Elmer Barnes

[Harry Elmer Barnes (1889–1968), American historian and sociologist, graduated from Syracuse University and later obtained a PhD from Columbia; he
taught successively at Clark University, the New
School for Social Research, Smith College, and
Amherst College. A prolific author and journalist,
Barnes wrote more than thirty books and hundreds of
essays and reviews. In *The Genesis of the World War*
(1926), Barnes blamed that conflict more on the Allies
than on Germany. An advocate of the "New History,"
which stressed the social and economic underpinnings
of historical events, Barnes wrote such works as *The
New History and the Social Sciences* (1925) and *The
History of Western Civilization* (1935). In the 1930s he
wrote a widely syndicated column called "The Liberal
Viewpoint," but when World War II broke out, he
attempted to exculpate Hitler from blame for starting
the conflict. In the following chapter, titled "Religion

Harry Elmer Barnes, *The Twilight of Christianity* (New York: Vanguard Press, 1929), pp. 426–46.

in a Secular Age," Barnes writes that religion must change in several fundamental particulars in order to be viable in the modern age: it must give up adherence to outmoded dogmas, it must accept the latest findings of science, and it must lend its weight to moral and social advancement.]

Today a great Spirit is passing over the earth which says, "I take my stand upon the present and mean to dominate it; and if I destroy the past, it is for the sake of the future."

(Elwood Worcester)[1]

I. THE CASE FOR RELIGION IN THE MODERN WORLD

Many scientists would hold that in the future there will be no need for religion and that science will be able to supply all the insight and controls essential to human well-being. This may well be true, but the writer is inclined to concede that a secularized social religion like Unitarian Humanism or advanced Christian Socialism may be of great value in the future in organizing group sentiment in support of decent and just causes. It is probable that man's emotions, as well as his intellect, must be exploited in the service of social control, and religion is better adapted to performing this function than science. The main thing to emphasize is that the new secular religion will not of itself attempt to supply the information and guidance essential to the most perfect realization of human happiness, but will derive this knowledge from the best science and aesthetics of the age. In inculcating the desirable attitude toward alcohol, for example, the new religion would consult Raymond Pearl, Starling and other scientific students of the effect of alcohol on man.[2] In dealing with sex it would

follow Forel, Havelock Ellis, Freud and Robinson.[3] Books like
Parshley's *Science and Good Behavior* and Edman's *The World, the
Arts and the Artist*,[4] would be regarded as at least harbingers of the
Old and New Testaments of the new religion. Durant Drake would be
accorded more respect than St. Augustine.[5] We would rid ourselves of
the perennial emphasis of the religionist on the antithesis between
intelligence and character.

Inasmuch as there is little or nothing in common between the old
supernaturalism and the new secular religion, it has been proposed that
we drop the term "religion" as applied to the latter and denominate it
social ethics, humanitarianism or something of the sort—Comte called
it "Positivism." There is much to be said for such a suggestion, but to
retain the term religion may have certain pragmatic value in for-
warding the transition from the old to the new régime.

No sensible person would contend that natural and social science,
coöperating with a secular religion, will be able to end all human ills
and terminate all human unhappiness. There is much unhappiness
inherent in the very nature of man and his social relations. Yet, we can
at least say that in the new secular régime we shall cease to suffer from
fear of imaginary dangers and evils. We shall no longer be incapable
of making the best possible use of all available secular agencies in rid-
ding ourselves of actual menaces to health and happiness. The sources
of misery and suffering which remain will ultimately be only those of
the insoluble or ineradicable type.

II. WHAT RELIGION MUST ABANDON
TO COMMAND RESPECT AND
CONFIDENCE TODAY

If we cannot be too dogmatic or confident in regard to what forms religion may take in the future, we can at least be fairly positive about
those things which any successful and reasonable religion in the future
must abandon in order to command the respect and enlist the interests

of those who actually live, intellectually speaking, in the twentieth century. If Modernism is to save religion, it must surrender such of its present tenets as do not square with those scientific discoveries and scholarly researches which are not open to challenge.[6] If it compromises and wavers, it is bound to lose its most intelligent and indispensable supporters; for those who might constitute the core of its forces will be driven out of the churches to seek intellectual freedom and consistency elsewhere. It profits Modernism nothing to abandon one sinking craft to take refuge on another that is just as certainly foundering. Religion must abandon its hopeless effort to adapt ancient categories and concepts to new knowledge of entirely different nature and connotation. Rather, it must base its reconstruction upon the facts of the cosmos, of the world, and of man as we now know them, and then determine what valid religious concepts and practices can be worked out in harmony with the new knowledge and perspective. Never has there been a more pertinent example of the futility of attempting to force new wine into old bottles than we find in conservative Modernistic apologetic.

In the course of this book we have indicated the nature and extent of the untenable beliefs and attitudes supported by the Fundamentalists and the Devout Modernists. Therefore, it will not be necessary to repeat and reiterate at length on this subject. We may content ourselves with a bare enumeration of those older dogmas and interests which must most certainly be surrendered before we can begin any intelligent consideration of the possibility of formulating a religion which will be compatible with modern knowledge and truly serviceable to contemporary society. These intellectual and cultural anachronisms, which have played a basic part in the older religion and religious philosophies but must now be abandoned, may be summarized as: (1) insistence upon dogmatic certainty of the existence of God; (2) any primary interest in the question of God; (3) the doctrine of the divinity, infallibility or unique religious significance of Jesus; (4) absorption with considerations of the Infinite and The Absolute; (5) support of transcendental and idealistic philosophy, which attempts to establish truths and values independent of time and space, as well as of human factors and situations; (6) all assumptions of a supernatural world, alien to man's natural conditions and inscrutable by the methods of science and secular knowledge; (7) the personality obsession, particularly as relates to the effort to personify the cosmos and God, though we may concede the supreme importance of a secular consideration of the human personality and its development; and, finally, (8) the outstanding theological fossils, such as the conceptions of the soul, immortality, sin, the spirit world, prayer, and the sense of sanctity and the sacred.

Some of these suggestions as to what must be surrendered in the light of modern knowledge raise issues of sufficient importance to justify brief discussion. A basic question arises as to whether a belief in God is actually necessary to man or a vital religion. The belief in God has been regarded as indispensable in the past: (1) because God was believed to be essential to protect us from supernatural powers and dangers; (2) because His Grace alone was able to save us from Hell; and (3) because of the sense of dependence upon the Heavenly Father. None of these three reasons will appear to the scientist to be longer valid. Even the continued belief in God as the basis of security and protection has been shown by the psychologists to be the result of our unfortunate projection of parental imagery and symbolism into our interpretation of the cosmos. More and more, people are being able to go along quite securely and serenely without any sense of divine support.

People who feel dependent upon God do so because they have been taught to seek security in His protection. It is, to use Watson's terminology, not an inherent necessity but rather a "conditioned response."[7] There is little or no doubt that man can successfully deal with the impending necessity of facing experience and reality without any conviction that he possesses a cosmic guide or companion. The more rapidly he effects this emancipation the more immediately and more certainly will he be able to cope with his mundane problems in a sane, direct and rational fashion.

The chief objection to any vivid interest in or thoroughgoing acceptance of the conception of God is to be found in its contribution to intellectual confusion in dealing with fundamental religious and moral issues. In other words, whereas Descartes assumed that we could not produce any clear and logical thinking without the initial premise of the existence of God, we have now come to see that we can actually have no real intellectual lucidity and logical consistency in treating basic questions of morals and religion as long as we insist upon retaining any vivid interest in the God concept. The intellectual confusion produced by the theistic attitude arises primarily out of the introduction of an absolutely indeterminate element in dealing with the question of the good life. For example, some of the Reconcilers, among them Professor Mather,[8] hold that the chief aim of religion is to promote interest in and loyalty to the cause of the good life. But they go on to specify that the good life which they envisage is not the best possible life from the standpoint of man's interests and activities here on earth, but that life which is "most pleasing to the Administrator of the Cosmos."

Once any such contention as this is admitted we face absolute chaos and confusion in working out practical suggestions as to the nature and achievement of the good life. As long as we view the question from the standpoint of the nature of man and his social needs, we can approach the problem of the best life for man with some degree of precision and logic. We know a great deal about human nature and social institutions at the present time, and we are well on our way towards discovering much more in this field than we know at the present time. In other words, we are making rapid progress towards real ability to work out a valid and consistent philosophy of human life in strictly secular terms. Once we bring into the picture, however, the notion of attempting to please the Administrator of the Cosmos, we are thrown into interminable chaos, and the whole search for the good life is confused if not, indeed, paralyzed. No person can say with assurance that there is any Administrator of the Cosmos, and even if we are willing to concede that there is such a Being or force, there is no method whereby we can ascertain His identity or wishes. Therefore, to set up any such goal as winning the approval of the Administrator of the Cosmos is to destroy at once any prospect of working out a rational and satisfactory conception of life. Still further, if one is interested in pleasing the Administrator of the Cosmos, it would seem logical to hold that we are most likely to do so if we attempt to secure the most perfect realization and expression of our inherent capacities. Those who believe in an Administrator of the Cosmos must admit, if they are consistent, that the traits of man are those with which God has endowed him. Therefore, the surest way of pleasing the Administrator of the Cosmos would seem to lie in the best possible use of the equipment which He has conferred upon mankind. Indeed, it would appear that there is no other possible manner whereby one might hope to win the approval of the cosmic God if there be one.

Especially vicious and deplorable, in the light of modern psychology, is the tendency of most Modernists to retain the conception of God as the "Father" of man and the human race and to envisage him in terms of parental symbolism and imagery. Children have trouble enough in adjusting themselves to the situation of earthly parenthood. To encumber them with still greater burdens in the shape of the even more ominous and difficult symbolism of celestial parenthood is poor pedagogy and psychology and has wrecked many a personality. Further, it tends to keep one's reactions in the field of religion on an essentially infantile level. If our stereotypes, imagery and symbolism are infantile, our thinking in such fields must likewise remain fundamentally childlike. Again, this type of symbolization of God creates unusual difficulties and psychic lesions when the disillusionment comes, as it is likely to in the case of every educated person today. When the untenable dogmas and infantilisms of orthodoxy are undermined in school or college or by reading, the person who has been accustomed to react to God and religion in terms of the parental symbolism suffers keenly from a psychic malady akin to homesickness. The psychological distress involved in the reconstruction of religious beliefs is greatly and quite unnecessarily increased thereby. In this connection it is interesting to remember that ninety-eight per cent of both the ministers and the theological students investigated by Dr.

Betts felt that God could best be envisaged in terms of a sublimated earthly parent and could be quite literally regarded as a "Father."[9]

In the *Forum* for August, 1929, Max Eastman brings forward against the belief in God what may be called the argument of psychic or amatory economy. He says:

> I would define religion as a belief that there is Something in the objective world, aside from other people, to which you can direct your emotions of love and adoration, and that you will be helped by loving this Something. If this definition is acceptable, I am prepared to defend the proposition that religion is a hindrance to progress. The idea that we are all children of God and that we must love God with all our strength uses up just that much love which we might turn to the loving of our neighbor.[10]

If the loss of a belief in a dogmatic certainty of the nature and existence of God is no great menace, what about the possible danger of the uprooting of supernatural religion? History shows that the great objection in every age to the progress of enlightenment has been the gloomy prediction that social chaos would ensue. At the end of the sixteenth century one of the most learned of Frenchmen, John Bodin, felt that society would collapse if we surrendered the belief in witchcraft.[11] Yet witches have passed and humanity goes on unshaken from the loss. Controls based on scientific knowledge and conviction are being created to supplant those grounded on fear of the unknown. We no longer need a papal encyclical to induce an individual to avoid contagious diseases and poisonous herbs. There is no reason to believe that social control based upon scientific knowledge cannot be made to pervade every aspect of human behavior. A secular religion may well reinforce guidance of this sort. Indeed, the real danger is that the new secular guidance will not be supplied rapidly enough to supplant the fading supernaturalism. The latter is passing for reasons quite apart from the sporadic attacks of courageous individual scientists; chiefly, the incidence of contemporary secular and mechanical civilization. We must either prepare for an age guided by science and aesthetics or be willing to contemplate an era without any positive guidance and social control, which would be chaos indeed.

Man can only survive on condition that he is able to extend the range of science throughout every department of knowledge and make science pervade every level of society. How far a new type of religion can aid in this process time alone will tell. Meanwhile every sane scientist will welcome the collaboration of every religious expert of enlightened outlook and humanitarian sentiments. The desirable goal of both has been well expressed by Max Otto:[12]

> Accept the stern condition of being physically alone in all the reach of space and time, that we may then, with new zest, enter the warm valley of earthly existence—warm with human impulse, aspiration and affection, warm with the inconquerable thing called life; turn from the recognition of our cosmic isolation to a new sense of human togetherness, and so discover in a growing human solidarity, in a progressively ennobled humanity, in an increasing joy in living, the goal we have all along blindly sought, and build on earth the fair city we have looked for in a compensatory world beyond.

Our repudiation of supernaturalism must include not merely the crass supernaturalism of men like Mr. Bryan, John Roach Straton and Cardinal Hayes but equally so the sophisticated and rationalized supernaturalism of the Devout Modernists.[13] What we mean is well enough indicated in the article by Professor Henry N. Wieman on "Is Sin Out of Date?", in the *Christian Century* for March 14, 1929. Here Professor Wieman says that: "Morality is the living of life in such a way as to adjust human interests to one another. Religion is the living of life in such a way as not only to adjust human interests to one another, but also to adjust human interests to the requirements of that cosmic process, or extra-human factor, upon which we are dependent." As far as the writer can see, nothing whatever is gained by giving up the Fundamentalist aspiration to do something immediately pleasing to Yahweh and substituting this Modernist aspiration to serve the extra-human factor in the cosmos. This extra-human cosmic factor of Professor Wieman is just as indeterminate and just as confusing as the Fundamentalist God or Professor Mather's Administrator of the Cosmos. Man cannot work intelligently or constructively with materials the nature and manifestations of which he does not know. Man must confine himself absolutely and resolutely to considerations arising out of his own nature and the adjustment of that nature to the physical environment and the social surroundings. We need not deny that there are extra-human elements existing in the cosmos, but we can only make intelligent and constructive use of those factors and influences which are evident in the nature of man, the processes of life, and the observed facts relative to the physical universe. It is difficult for the writer to be very favorably impressed by the contention of Professor Wieman that when he is talking about the "extra-human factor" in the universe he is not thinking at all of the supernatural. In the end, it comes down to the same thing as the cosmic God or the Administrator of the Cosmos. Even if Professor Wieman does not regard this concept as supernatural, it has the same vicious effect in diverting the attention of man from secular and human affairs.

The only extra-human factors which can be envisaged with any intelligence or precision are, of course, the physical environment and the plant and animal kingdoms. If we were to seek guidance in adjusting ourselves to the extra-human factors we should turn, then, not to the theologians but to the anthropogeographers, the botanists and the zoölogists. If we were to take Professor Wieman literally at his word we would not have recourse to a Kant, Schliermarcher, Harnack, Brown or Wieman but to a Ritter,[14] Ratzel, Vidal de la Blache, Lucian Febvre, Ellsworth Huntington, J. Russell Smith, Patrick Geddes, De Vries, W. M. Wheeler, T. H. Morgan, H. M. Parshley, J. A. Thomson and the like.[15] In actual practice today, with man's triumph over the other members of the animal kingdom, the only extra-human factor of any significance is the geographical setting of a culture.

We shall not make much progress by abandoning dogmatic theism and supernaturalism unless we likewise relinquish loyalty to their bastard child, the transcendental and idealistic philosophy which has come down to us in ever more elaborate form from the time of Socrates. Just as long as we admit the validity of entities and categories in human life which are held to have existed anterior to man and to operate entirely independently of time, space, the nature of man and the character of human institutions, we are bound to remain on the threshold of theism and supernaturalism. If one allows a Modernist to toy with transcendentalism and absolutes, he may be assured that it will not be long until he has made a God for himself.

III. THE NEW PERSPECTIVE AND RELIGIOUS READJUSTMENT

It follows as a matter of course that such epoch-making changes as we have described above with relation to the status of orthodox religion and Devout Modernism in the light of modern science and critical thought, make necessary a searching re-examination of the place and function of religion in modern society. In the first place, the new view of matters makes it very evident that the clergyman can no longer pretend to be a competent expert in the way of discovering the nature, will and operations of the new cosmic God. If undertaken and solved at all, this is a problem for the coöperative endeavors of the natural scientist and the cosmic philosopher of the Dewey tradition.[16] The theologian at best can only be a competent second- or third-hand interpreter of the facts and implications gathered about the cosmos and its laws by specialists in science and philosophy. In the old days, when it was thought that God might be reached and understood through prayer, sacrifice or revelation, the clergyman or theologian was indeed "the man of God" who could make clear the will of the Deity to believers. But now, when God must be sought, if at all, in terms of the findings of the test-tube, the compound microscope, the interferometer, the radium tube and Einstein's equations, the conventional clergyman is rather hopelessly out of place in the premises. Therefore, it is apparent that the intelligent and educated theologians must surrender their age-long pretension to special, if not unique, competence in clearing up the problem of the nature of God and His laws. They can at best be little more than ringside spectators of the observatory and the laboratory, doing their best in the way of an amateurish appreciation of what is going on therein.

We may concede the contention of Dr. Dieffenbach that theology is a very important phase of religion but we can scarcely admit that there longer remains any function for the independent theologian.[17] The presentation of "orderly and systematic ideas about religion" must now be looked upon as the province of the social scientist and social philosopher. We should, of course, grant Dr. Dieffenbach the right to continue his useful work in the new religious era. We would merely insist on his adopting the correct professional label.

Next to the revelation of the nature of God and his ways, the most time-honored function of the so-called "man of God" has been to unravel God's will with respect to human conduct and to inculcate the absolute and inflexible principles which should guide personal morality, in order that the soul of the individual might be assured of an ultimate refuge in the New Jerusalem. This was a perfectly rational and logical function for religion when it was commonly assumed to be axiomatic: (1) that the purpose of moral conduct was to insure the salvation of the soul, and (2) that the supreme and complete guide to moral living was to be discovered in Holy Scriptures. Neither of these postulates can be sustained today. There seems to be no ground whatever for the orthodox views of a bodily or spiritual immortality and the imminence of a literal heaven and hell. Hence, the basic objective of right living can no longer be regarded as the insurance of spiritual salvation. On the contrary, the fundamental purpose of the good life is to secure the maximum amount of happiness for the greatest possible number here upon this earth. Therefore, it is readily apparent that accurate guidance to the good life can not be sought in ancient Scriptures or provided by specialists in Holy Writ. The moral code of the future must be supplied by the specialists in mundane happiness, namely: biologists, physiologists, psychiatrists, educators, social scientists and students and practitioners of aesthetics.

Some who frankly admit the incompetence of the clergyman and the theologian in the way of providing original and conclusive guidance to moral conduct contend, nevertheless, that religion can exercise a very valuable service in interpreting and popularizing the findings of the specialists in human happiness. This may be true, to a certain extent, but many qualifications would have to be noted. Many phases of guidance to complete human happiness would necessarily be a highly technical and individual matter, to be handled by medical and other experts in relation to individual cases and problems, and would scarcely be adapted to comprehensive general interpretation or exhortation.

A much better case can be made for the service which may be rendered by religion in inculcating an interest in and respect for such broad and scarcely debatable moral conceptions as justice, honesty, pacifism, coöperation, kindliness, beauty, etc. Professor Kirsopp Lake has well stated the case for the desirability of having religion relinquish interest in sumptuary moral control and assume responsibility for the advancement of more profound and general moral principles:[18]

One man may find much comfort in tobacco, while another may injure himself by smoking: one may err by playing too much, and another by never playing at all. I doubt whether the men of tomorrow will try to interfere with each other on these points, knowing that the thing which matters is ability to do good work, and that one man can do his best work in one way, another otherwise. Many of the things Puritans condemn are strictly indifferent. The religion of tomorrow will recognize this, it will give good advice to individuals, but not lay down general rules for universal observance.

On the other hand, it may have a sterner standard in business, industry and finance. It may insist more loudly that honesty applies to the spirit of business, not merely to its letter. It may even demand that men must be as trustworthy in advertisements, business announcements and journalistic reporting as they are in private affairs. For these are the questions of morals which are the issues of life and death for the future. They are not covered by the teaching of Jesus or of historic Christianity, for neither ever discussed problems which did not exist in their time. Some of the principles which have been laid down by them will play a part in the solution of these problems but probably others will also be needed, certainly the actual solutions will contain new elements, and the religion of tomorrow will have to look for them.

One can scarcely quarrel with Professor Lake on theoretical and logical grounds, but there is an important practical consideration, namely, that the modern social and economic order is based to no inconsiderable degree upon intrigues, shrewd business enterprise, relentless competition, unreasoning patriotism and class selfishness. It can scarcely be expected that the custodians of the modern order, who provide the chief pecuniary support for our religious institutions and organizations, will contribute with enthusiasm to a movement designed to cut at the root of many of the principles and practices which they hold most sacred and indispensable. Before religion could achieve much in this field it would be necessary to organize and carry on a very definite program of education in the principles of social ethics broadly conceived. Thus far, however, few clergymen so orientated and motivated have been able to maintain their position long enough to make much headway in this educating process. As far as the writer is aware, there has been no marked or organized effort to draft the services of Sherwood Eddy, Norman Thomas, Kirby Page, Bouck White, Jerome Davis, Ralph Harlow, Harry Ward, David D. Vaughan and others of their kind and induct them into the pastorates of great metropolitan churches.[19]

The supervision of religion over recreation, which has in the past been exercised chiefly in making arbitrary decisions as to what are immoral and what are moral forms of recreation and in closely scrutinizing and controlling the activities of individuals in these fields, must now be sharply challenged. The orthodox religious criteria as to moral and immoral forms of recreation were not based upon physiological, psychological or social grounds, but upon theological considerations which have little or no validity in the light of modern knowledge. Religion, having no competence in the matter of determining the nature of moral and immoral conduct in the light of modern secularism, obviously can not apply its decisions in this field to the realm of recreation. Recreation, like morality, with which it has been so closely associated in the past, is a field for the secular expert and must be handed over to biologists, medical experts, psychologists, social scientists and aesthetes. Religion at most could scarcely go further than to proclaim the general desirability of healthy and adequate exercise and the exhibition of a proper spirit of good sportsmanship.

Another function of religion in the past which has received much support relates to its aesthetic services. It is held that the ritual, pageantry and liturgy of the church provide a relatively economical and highly valuable aesthetic service to humanity. This is, of course, an argument which can be far better justified from the Catholic standpoint than from the Protestant, as the Protestant churches have given up most of the splendor of the Catholic service. This argument boils down to the allegation that the church is in a position to "put on a better show" for the populace and at a lower cost than any other comparable secular organization. While there is much to be said in support of this view in regard to the services of the church in earlier periods, it would seem that this function may be, and indeed is, now achieved more adequately and cheaply by various secular enterprises, such as the grand opera, the theater, the movies and various types of public pageantry. Further, many contend that the attitude of fear, awe and solemnity generated by religious ritual and pageantry produces a fundamentally unhealthy state of mind which, to a large degree, offsets the aesthetic service contributed thereby.

We have already referred in several connections to the poetic interpretation of religion set forth by Mr. John Cowper Powys.[20] He believes that the function of religion is to provide the sceptic with a method of poetic contemplation of the great illusions of humanity during the life history of the race. This certainly constitutes a noble and dignified statement of the case for religion, and there are doubtless many who find that religion, thus conceived, gives life a deeper and richer content. Yet one can scarcely imagine that this view of religion will be able to give satisfaction to any large number of individuals. Not one person in a thousand who approaches religion from a sentimental point of view can attain Mr. Powys' scepticism, and it is equally true that few who are as sceptical as Mr. Powys are capable of a sentimental attitude toward religion. Further, if one believes that religion should be the dynamic basis of effective social reform, it is obvious that Mr. Powys' negativistic conception of religion is completely unadapted to fulfilling this function.

Therefore, it would seem definitely established that the conventional functions of traditional religion have well-nigh completely evaporated in the light of contemporary knowledge and intellectual attitudes. It must be conceded that the theologian is not longer needed to chart out and control the supernatural world and supernatural powers, inasmuch as the existence of such entities can scarcely be established. It is equally apparent that the theologian can not by himself locate, describe or interpret the new cosmic God believed by some to be implied in the discoveries of modern science. Neither can the theologian supply detailed moral guidance in the way of indicating how man must live in order to achieve the maximum degree of happiness here on earth. Nor can the church support its ancient pretensions to guiding and controlling recreation or in supplying popular pageantry. This raises the important question as to what religion can legitimately engage upon in harmony with the tenets of an open-minded and contemporaneous secular attitude.

It would seem that the most reasonable field for the functioning of religion in contemporary society is in the way of providing for the mass organization of the group sentiment of mankind in support of the larger principles of kindliness, sympathy, right, justice, honesty, decency and beauty. Just what constitute the essentials of right and justice and the like would have to be determined by the appropriate scientific and aesthetic experts, but these experts have little potency or opportunity in the way of arousing ardent popular support for their findings. Religion has thus far been the most powerful agency in stirring and directing the collective will of mankind. Therefore, we may probably contend with safety that the function of a liberalized religion, divested of its archaic supernaturalism, would be to serve as the public propaganda adjunct of social science and aesthetics. The social sciences and aesthetics would supply specific guidance as to what ought to be done, while religion would produce the motive power essential to the translation of abstract theory into practical action. There would, however, be ever present the problem of restraining this educational propaganda and keeping it in thorough conformity with the recommendations of science and art. The function of religion, then, would be to organize the mass mind and group activities in such a fashion as to benefit secular society and not to please God, at least not God as he has been understood and expounded in the orthodox religions of the past.

It would appear to the writer that the problem is not so much one of the nobility or the validity of this function of religion or one of its value to society, but rather the question of whether or not religion can successfully carry out such a type of social service. The issue is primarily one of whether an organization, hitherto almost exclusively devoted to the understanding, control and exploitation of the supernatural world, can be completely transformed into an institution designed for the purpose of increasing the secular happiness of mankind here on earth. Such a transformation would imply a complete revolution in the premises and activities of religion, and we have little or no evidence from the past to give us any definite assurance that so profound a transition is practicable or attainable. The issue is fundamentally whether organized religion can be held together and can operate without a sense of mystery and a fear of the unknown. The thrill from the mysterious has been the core of all past religion, and we have nothing to give any final assurance that religion can persist without this dominating element of mystery and fear. Certain writers contend that there will always remain a certain fringe of mystery, particularly in the way of unsolved problems, as well as the general mystery inherent in the riddle of the universe. Yet, as Professor Shotwell has well indicated in his *Religious Revolution of Today*,[21] the mysteries of modern science are quite different in their premises, manifestations and psychic effects from the conventional religious mystery based upon an emotional reaction to a hypothetical supernatural world. The reaction to the mysteries of science does not promote that group-forming tendency which Ward, Hankins, Durkheim and others have shown to be so characteristic an effect and accompaniment of supernatural religion.[22] Abstruse scientific perplexities and the riddle of the universe may promote advanced forms of cerebral effort but they are not likely to evoke a sentimental thrill or to generate a crusading passion in human assemblages.

Indeed, some leading social scientists contend that the divergence between the old supernaturalism and the new secular program is so great that no real common ground can be found. Hence, they argue that we should not contaminate and confuse the new secular type of ethical enterprise by denominating it religion. This is certainly a consideration which is entitled to receive serious thought. The chief defense which can be made of the retention of the term religion, as applied to the new secular conception of a dynamic urge to social betterment, is that it will soften the shock of the transition if we are able to preserve the older terminology with new implications and outlook. Whether or not this is an adequate justification for the retention of the term religion to cover a conception quite different from its past connotation, the writer will not assume to say. Another argument for preserving the religious terminology is that we should thereby be able to make use of existing ecclesiastical organization and equipment. The problem which arises here is as to whether existing religious institutions are not so inseparably attached to outworn conceptions and practices as to make them more of a liability than an asset to religious reconstruction. Certainly, there has been much confusion engendered in the minds of those who have surrendered traditional notions of religion and yet are unwilling to admit that religion must become nothing more or less than the inspirational basis of social ethics. Such writers have tended to flounder hopelessly in search of that hypothetical but non-existent area, intermediate between adjustment to the supernatural world and the betterment of human society. Such confusion has particularly been the bane of the more radical wing of the Devout Modernists.

There are many who believe that religion of whatever variety is bound to pass away and that its place will be taken by various secular cults organized about some particular social reform program; in short, that religion will be supplanted by devotion to the ideals of Capitalism, Rotary, Kiwanis, Service, Socialism, Anarchism and the like. Certainly, there is much to be said for this point of view. These secular programs have the power to enlist that group-forming tendency and to invoke those group loyalties which Hankins, Ward and others look upon as the essential core of religion. Further, many of the Russians seem to have found as much satisfaction in devotion to the Bolshevist principles as they formerly did in subservience to the dogmas of the Greek Catholic Church. We can only say in this regard that time alone will tell whether the socio-economic dogmas and cults will usurp the position formerly occupied by religion. It is too early to speak with any assurance on this point.

NOTES

1. [Elwood Worcester (1862–1940), American theologian and rector of Emmanuel Church, Boston (1904–29).]

2. [Raymond Pearl (1879–1940), American biologist who studied the effects of food and alcohol upon birth and death rates. Ernest Henry Starling (1866–1927), British physiologist who studied the secretion of lymph and other bodily fluids.]

3. [August-Henri Forel (1848–1931), Swiss neuroanatomist and crusader against syphilis. Havelock Ellis (1859–1939), British physician and author of the landmark treatise *Studies in the Psychology of Sex* (1897–1928). William J. Robinson (1867–1936), American editor of the *American Journal of Sexology and Psychoanalysis* and author of numerous treatises on sex.]

4. [H. M. Parshley, *Science and Good Behavior* (1928); Irwin Edman (1896–1954), *The World, the Arts and the Artist* (1928).]

5. [Durant Drake (1878–1933), American professor and author of books on philosophy, religion, conduct, and other subjects.]

6. [For Modernism, see n. 17 to Westermarck's "Christianity and Morals."]

7. [The reference is to John B. Watson (1878–1958), American psychologist and founder of behaviorism.]

8. [Kirtley F. Mather (1888–1978), American professor of geology at Harvard (1927–54) and author of *The Impact of Science upon Religion* (1925) and *Science in Search of God* (1928).]

9. [See George Herbert Betts, *The Belief of 700 Ministers* (1929). Betts (1868–1934) was an American professor of education who wrote frequently on religious subjects.]

10. [Max Eastman, "Does the Modern World Need Religion? A Socratic Dialogue," *Forum* 82, no. 2 (August 1929): 72–76 (quotation from p. 72). Eastman (1883–1969) was an American political and social radical who edited the *Masses* (1912–17), the *Liberator* (1918f.), and other leftist journals.]

11. [Jean Bodin (1530–1596), French political philosopher whose *Six Livres de la République* (1576; translated as *The Six Bookes of a Commonweale*, 1606) argued for the divine right of kings and the literal enforcement of the Ten Commandments.]

12. Otto, *Things and Ideals*, p. 290.

13. [William Jennings Bryan (1860–1925), American political and religious figure who spearheaded the prosecution's case in the Scopes evolution trial in 1925. John Roach Straton (1875–1929), Southern Baptist preacher and opponent of Modernism, the Social Gospel, and other liberal movements. Patrick Joseph Hayes (1867–1938), American theologian and archbishop of New York (1919–38). Although theologically conservative, he quietly supported the social policies of Franklin D. Roosevelt during the Depression.]

14. [Friedrich Schleiermacher (1768–1834), German philosopher and disciple of Kant. For Adolf Harnack, see n. 11 to Westermarck's "Christianity and Morals." Thomas Brown (1778–1820) was a British philosopher who discussed the philosophy of mind.]

15. [Barnes refers to a succession of leading scientists in the fields of biology, zoology, and anthropology.]

16. [John Dewey (1859–1952), American philosopher, propounded a philosophy of naturalistic empiricism in such works as *Experience and Nature* (1925).]

17. [Albert Charles Dieffenbach (1876–1963), American theologian and author of *Religious Liberty: The Great American Illusion* (1927).]

18. Lake, *The Religion of Yesterday and Tomorrow*, p. 173. [Kirsopp Lake (1872–1946), British biblical scholar who taught at Leiden and at Har-

vard. *The Religion of Yesterday and Tomorrow* (1925) discusses theological controversies in prior ages and in the modern world.]

19. [Sherwood Eddy (1871–1963), national secretary of the YMCA. Norman Thomas (1884–1968), socialist candidate for president (1928–48). Kirby Page (1890–1957), author and social evangelist. Bouck White (1874–?), radical pastor of the Church of the Social Revolution in New York City. Jerome Davis (1891–1979), professor of practical philanthropy at Yale Divinity School (1924–37). Ralph Volney Harlow (1884–1956), professor of history at Yale and Syracuse. Harry Frederick Ward (1873–1966), pastor and social worker. David Davies Vaughan (1876–?), Methodist minister and professor of social ethics at Boston University (1919–43).]

20. [John Cowper Powys (1872–1963), Welsh novelist. See his treatise, *The Religion of a Sceptic* (1925).]

21. [James Thomson Shotwell, *The Religious Revolution of To-day* (1913), which put forth the view that modern religion has freed itself from superstition. Shotwell (1874–1965) was a professor of history at Columbia University (1900–42).]

22. [For Ward, see n. 19 above. Frank Hamilton Hankins, American sociologist and author of *An Introduction to the Study of Society* (1928). Emile Durkheim (1858–1917), French social scientist and author of *Les Formes élémentaires de la vie religieuse* (1915; translated as *The Elementary Forms of Religious Life*).]

19

GOD IN THE MODERN WORLD

Walter Lippmann

[Walter Lippmann (1889–1974), American journalist and essayist, was born into a Jewish family but rejected his religion at an early age. He studied at Harvard with William James and George Santayana, leaving in 1910 to become a reporter for the *Boston Common*, a socialist newspaper. He soon became an assistant to Lincoln Steffens and wrote his first book, *A Preface to Politics* (1913); in his next work, *Drift and Mastery* (1914), he renounced socialism in favor of a planned society run by a public-minded elite. He urged the United States to enter World War I and helped draw up what became Woodrow Wilson's Fourteen Points for postwar reconstruction. In later political books, such as *Public Opinion* (1922) and *The Phantom Public* (1925), Lippmann questioned the general public's ability to resist political propaganda and prejudice, leading to a questioning of the very principle of democracy. In 1922 he joined the *New York World*, setting the

Walter Lippmann, *A Preface to Morals* (New York: Macmillan, 1929), pp. 21–36.

tone for its liberal editorial page. His *A Preface to Morals* (1929) attempts to find a meaning in life for those who have lost their faith in a benevolent god. When the *World* folded in 1931, he joined the more conservative *New York Herald-Tribune*, becoming the leading political commentator of his day. His later books, such as *The Method of Freedom* (1934) and *The Good Society* (1937), steer a middle ground between liberalism and conservatism. He strongly urged the United States to battle Hitler in World War II, but opposed the American doctrine of "containment" toward the Soviet Union. His last major work was *Essays in Public Philosophy* (1955). Lippmann received the Presidential Medal of Freedom in 1964 and became a celebrity as a television commentator. He was notorious for speaking out against the Vietnam War, becoming a leader of the antiwar movement in the later 1960s. In the following chapter titled "God in the Modern World," Lippmann contends that the god envisioned by modern philosophers such as Alfred North Whitehead are so nebulous and abstract that they cannot command the devotion of the average person.]

1. IMAGO DEI

By the dissolution of their ancestral ways men have been deprived of their sense of certainty as to why they were born, why they must work, whom they must love, what they must honor, where they may turn in sorrow and defeat. They have left to them the ancient codes and the modern criticism of these codes, guesses, intuitions, inconclusive experiments, possibilities, probabilities, hypotheses. Below the level of reason, they may have unconscious prejudice, they may speak with a loud cocksureness, they may act with fanaticism. But there is gone that ineffable certainty which once made God and His Plan seem as real as the lamppost.

I do not mean that modern men have ceased to believe in God. I do mean that they no longer believe in him simply and literally. I mean that they have defined and refined their ideas of him until they can no longer honestly say that he exists, as they would say that their neighbor exists. Search the writings of liberal churchmen, and when you come to the crucial passages which are intended to express their belief in God, you will find, I think, that at just this point their uncertainty is most evident.

The Reverend Harry Emerson Fosdick has written an essay, called "How Shall We Think of God?",[1] which illustrates the difficulty. He begins by saying that "believing in God without considering how one shall picture him is deplorably unsatisfactory." Yet the old ways of picturing him are no longer credible. We cannot think of him as seated upon a throne, while around him are angels playing on harps and singing hymns. "God as a king on high—our fathers, living under monarchy, rejoiced in that image and found it meaningful. His throne, his crown, his scepter, his seraphic retinue, his laws, rewards, and punishments—how dominant that picture was and how persistent is the continuance of it in our hymns and prayers! It was always partly poetry, but it had a prose background: there really had been at first a celestial land above the clouds where God reigned and where his throne was in the heavens."

Having said that this picture is antiquated, Dr. Fosdick goes on to state that "the religious man must have imaginations of God, if God is to be real to him." He must "picture his dealing with the Divine in terms of personal relationship." But how? "The place where man vitally finds God . . . is within his own experience of goodness, truth, and beauty, and the truest images of God are therefore to be found in man's spiritual life." I should be the last to deny that a man may, if he chooses, think of God as the source of all that seems to him worthy in human experience. But certainly this is not the God of the ancient faith. This is not God the Father, the Lawgiver, the Judge. This is a highly sophisticated idea of God, employed by a modern man who would like to say, but cannot say with certainty, that there exists a personal God to whom men must accommodate themselves.

2. AN INDEFINITE GOD

It may be that clear and unambiguous statements are not now possible in our intellectual climate. But at least we should not forget that the religions which have dominated human history have been founded on what the faithful felt were undeniable facts. These facts were mysterious only in the sense that they were uncommon, like an eclipse of the sun, but not in the sense that they were beyond human experience. No doubt there are passages in the Scriptures written by highly cultivated men in which the Divine nature is called mysterious and unknowable. But these passages are not the rock upon which the popular churches are founded. No one, I think, has truly observed the religious life of simple people without understanding how plain, how literal, how natural they take their supernatural personages to be.

The popular gods are not indefinite and unknowable. They have a definite history and their favorite haunts, and they have often been seen. They walk on earth, they might appear to anyone, they are angered, they are pleased, they weep and they rejoice, they eat and they may fall in love. The modern man uses the word 'supernatural' to describe something that seems to him not quite so credible as the things he calls natural. This is not the supernaturalism of the devout. They do not distinguish two planes of reality and two orders of certainty. For them Jesus Christ was born of a Virgin and was raised from the dead as literally as Napoleon was Emperor of the French and returned from Elba.

This is the kind of certainty one no longer finds in the utterances of modern men. I might cite, for example, a typically modern assertion about the existence of God, made by Mr. W. C. Brownell,[2] a critic who could not be reproached with insensitiveness to the value of traditional beliefs. He wrote that "the influence of the Holy Spirit, exquisitely called the Comforter, is a matter of actual experience, is solid a reality as that of electro-magnetism." I do not suppose that Mr. Brownell meant to admit the least possible doubt. But he was a modern man, and surreptitiously doubt invaded his certainty. For electro-magnetism is not an absolutely solid reality to a layman's mind. It has a questionable reality. I suspect that is why Mr. Brownell chose this metaphor; it would have seemed a little too blunt to his modern intelligence to say that his faith was founded not on electro-magnetism, but as men once believed, on a rock.

The attempts to reconstruct religious creeds are beset by the modern man's inability to convince himself that the constitution of the universe includes facts which in our skeptical jargon we call supernatural. Yet as William James once said, "religion, in her fullest exercise of function, is not a mere illumination of facts already elsewhere given, not a mere passion, like love, which views things in a rosier light. . . . It is something more, namely, a postulator of new *facts* as well." James himself was strongly disposed toward what he so candidly described as "overbeliefs"; he had sympathy with the beliefs of others which was as large and charitable as any man's can be. There was no trace of the intellectual snob in William James; he was in the other camp from those thin argumentative rationalists who find so much satisfaction in disproving what other men hold sacred. James loved cranks and naifs and sought them out for the wisdom they might have. But withal he was a modern man who lived toward the climax of the revolutionary period. He had the Will to Believe, he argued eloquently for the Right to Believe. But he did not wholly believe. The utmost that he could honestly believe was something which he confessed would "appear a sorry underbelief" to some of his readers. "Who knows," he said, "whether the faithfulness of individuals here below to their own poor overbeliefs may not actually help God in turn to be more effectively faithful to his own greater tasks?" Who knows? And on that question mark he paused and could say no more.

3. GOD IN MORE SENSES THAN ONE

But even if there was some uncertainty as to the existence of the God whom William James described, he was at least the kind of God with whom human beings could commune. If they could jump the initial doubt they found themselves in an exciting world where they might live for a God who, like themselves, had work to do. James wrote the passage I have quoted in 1902. A quarter of a century later Alfred North Whitehead came to Harvard to deliver the Lowell Lectures. He undertook to define God for modern men.[3]

Mr. Whitehead, like William James, is a compassionate man and on the side of the angels. But his is a wholly modernized mind in full command of all the conceptual instruments of scientific logic. By contrast with the austerity of Mr. Whitehead's thinking, James, with his chivalrous offer of fealty to God, seems like one of the last of the great romantics. There is a God in Mr. Whitehead's philosophy, and a very necessary God at that. Unhappily, I am not enough of a logician to say that I am quite sure I understand what it means to say that "God is not concrete, but He is the ground for concrete actuality." There have been moments when I imagined I had caught the meaning of this, but there have been more moments when I knew that I had not. I have never doubted, however, that the concept had meaning, and that I missed it because it was too deep for me. Why then, it may be asked, do I presume to discuss it? My answer is that a conception of God, which is incomprehensible to all who are not highly trained logicians, is a possible God for logicians alone. It is not presumptuous to say of Mr. Whitehead's God what he himself says of Aristotle's God: that it does "not lead him very far toward the production of a God available for religious purposes."

For while this God may satisfy a metaphysical need in the thinker, he does not satisfy the passions of the believer. This God does not govern the world like a king nor watch over his children like a father. He offers them no purposes to which they can consecrate themselves; he exhibits no image of holiness they can imitate. He does not chastise them in sin nor console them in sorrow. He is a principle with which to explain the facts, if you can understand the explanation. He is not himself a personality who deals with the facts. For the purposes of religion he is no God at all; his universe remains stonily unaware of man. Nothing has happened by accepting Mr. Whitehead's definition which changes the inexorable character of that destiny which Bertrand Russell depicted when he wrote that

> we see, surrounding the narrow raft illumined by the flickering light of human comradeship, the dark ocean on whose rolling waves we toss for a brief hour; from the great night without, a chill blast breaks in upon our refuge; all the loneliness of humanity amid hostile forces is concentrated upon the individual soul, which must struggle alone, with what of courage it can command, against the whole weight of a universe that cares nothing for its hopes and fears.[4]

It is a nice question whether the use of God's name is not misleading when it is applied by modernists to ideas so remote from the God men have worshiped. Plainly the modernist churchman does not believe in the God of Genesis who walked in the garden in the cool of the evening and called to Adam and his wife who had hidden themselves behind a tree; nor in the God of Exodus who appeared to Moses and Aaron and seventy of the Elders of Israel, standing with his feet upon a paved walk as if it were a sapphire stone; nor even in the God of the fifty-third chapter of Isaiah who in his compassion for the sheep who have gone astray, having turned everyone to his own way, laid on the Man of Sorrows the iniquity of us all.

This, as Kirsopp Lake says,[5] is the God of most, if not all, the writings in the Bible. Yet "however much our inherited sentiments may shrink from the admission, the scientists are to-day almost unanimous in saying that the universe as they see it contains no evidence of the existence of any anthropomorphic God whatever. The experimentalist (*i.e.*, modernist) wholly agrees that this is so. Nevertheless he refuses as a rule, and I think rightly—to abandon the use of the word 'God.'" In justification of this refusal to abandon the word 'God,' although he has abandoned the accepted meaning of the word, Dr. Lake appeals to a tradition which reaches back at least to Origen who, as a Christian neo-platonist, used the word 'God' to mean, not the King and Father of creation, but the sum of all ideal values. It was this redefinition of the word 'God,' he says, which "made Christianity possible for the educated man of the third century." It is this same redefinition which still makes Christianity possible for educated churchmen like Dr. Lake and Dean Inge.

Dr. Lake admits that although this attractive bypath of tradition "is intellectually adorned by many princes of thought and lords of language" it is "ecclesiastically not free from reproach." He avows another reason for his use of the word 'God' which, if not more compelling, is certainly more worldly. "Atheist" has meant since Roman times an enemy of society; it gives a wholly false impression of the real state of mind of those who adhere to the platonic tradition. They have been wholly without the defiance which "atheism" connotes; on the contrary they have been a few individuals in each age who lived peaceably within the shelter of the church, worshiping a somewhat different God inwardly and in their own way, and often helping to refresh the more mundane spirit of the popular church. The term "agnostic" is almost as unavailable. It was invented to describe a tolerant unbelief in the anthropomorphic God. In popular usage it has come to mean about the same thing as atheist, for the instinct of the common man is sound in these matters. He feels that those who claim to be open-minded about God have for all practical purposes ceased to believe in him. The agnostic's reply that he would gladly believe if the evidence would confirm it, does not alter the fact that he does not now believe. And so Dr. Lake concludes that the modernist must use the word 'God' in his own sense, "endeavoring partly to preserve Origen's meaning of the word, and partly shrinking from any other policy as open to misconstruction."

I confess that the notion of adopting a policy about God somehow shocks me as intruding a rather worldly consideration which would seem to be wholly out of place. But this feeling is, I am sure, an injustice to Dr. Lake who is plainly and certainly not a worldling. He is moved, no doubt, by the conviction that in letting 'God' mean one thing to the mass of the devout and another to the educated minority, the loss of intellectual precision is more than compensated by the preservation of a community of feeling. This is not mere expediency. It may be the part of wisdom, which is profounder than mere reasoning, to wish that intellectual distinctions shall not divide men too sharply.

But if it is wisdom, it is an aristocratic wisdom. And in Dean Inge's writings this is frankly avowed.[6] "The strength of Christianity," he says, "is in transforming the lives of individuals—of a small minority, certainly, as Christ clearly predicted, but a large number in the aggregate. To rescue a little flock, here and there, from materialism, selfishness, and hatred, is the task of the Church of Christ in all ages alike, and there is no likelihood that it will ever be otherwise."

But in other ages, one thing was otherwise. And in this one thing lies the radical peculiarity of the modern difficulty. In other ages there was no acknowledged distinction between the ultimate beliefs of the educated and the uneducated. There were differences in learning, in religious genius, in the closeness of a chosen few to God and his angels. Inwardly there were even radical differences of meaning. But critical analysis had not made them overt and evident, and the common assumption was that there was one God for all, for the peasant who saw him dimly and could approach him only through his patron saint, and for the holy man who had seen God and talked with him face to face. It has remained for churchmen of our era to distinguish two or more different Gods, and openly to say that they are different. This may be a triumph of candor and of intelligence. But this very consciousness of what they are doing, these very honest admissions that the God of Dean Inge, for example, is only in name the God of millions of other protestants—that is an admission, when they understand it, which makes faith difficult for modern men.

4. THE PROTEST OF THE FUNDAMENTALISTS

Fundamentalism is a protest against all these definitions and attenuations which the modern man finds it necessary to make. It is avowedly a reaction within the Protestant communions against what the President of the World's Christian Fundamentalist Association rather accurately described as "that weasel method of sucking the meaning out of words, and then presenting the empty shells in an attempt to palm them off as giving the Christian faith a new and another interpretation." In actual practice this movement has become entangled with all sorts of bizarre and barbarous agitations, with the Ku Klux Klan, with fanatical prohibition, with the "anti-evolution laws," and with much persecution and intolerance. This in itself is significant. For it shows that the central truth, which the fundamentalists have grasped, no longer appeals to the best brains and the good sense of a modern community, and that the movement is recruited largely from the isolated, the inexperienced, and the uneducated.

Into the politics of the heated controversy between modernists and fundamentalists I do not propose here to enter. That it is not merely a dispute in the realm of the spirit is made evident by the President of the Fundamentalist Association when he avers that "nothing" holds modernists and fundamentalists together except "the billions of dollars invested. Nine out of ten of these dollars, if not ninety-nine out of every hundred of them, spent to construct the great denominational universities, colleges, schools of second grade, theological seminaries, great denominational mission stations, the multiplied hospitals that bear denominational names, the immense publication societies and the expensive societies were given by fundamentalists and filched by modernists. It took hundreds of years to collect this money and construct these institutions. It has taken only a quarter of a century for the liberal bandits to capture them. . . ."

Not all the fundamentalist argument, however, is pitched at this level. There is also a reasoned case against the modernists. Fortunately this case has been stated in a little book called *Christianity and Liberalism* by a man who is both a scholar and a gentleman. The author is Professor J. Gresham Machen of the Princeton Theological Seminary.[7] It is an admirable book. For its acumen, for its saliency, and for its wit this cool and stringent defense of orthodox Protestantism is, I think, the best popular argument produced by either side in the current controversy. We shall do well to listen to Dr. Machen.

Modernism, he says, "is altogether in the imperative mood," while the traditional religion "begins with a triumphant indicative." I do not see how one can deny the force of this generalization. "From the beginning Christianity was certainly a way of life. *But how was the life to be produced?* Not by appealing to the human will, but by telling a story; not by exhortation, but by the narration of an event." Dr. Machen insists, rightly I think, that the historic influence of Christianity on the mass of men has depended upon their belief that an historic drama was enacted in Palestine nineteen hundred years ago during the reign of the Emperor Tiberius. The veracity of that story was fundamental to the Christian Church. For while all the ideal values may remain if you impugn the historic record set forth in the Gospels, these ideal values are not certified to the common man as inherent in the very nature of things. Once they are deprived of their root in historic fact, their poetry, their symbolism, their ethical significance depend for their sanction upon the temperament and experience of the individual believer. There is gone that deep, compulsive, organic faith in an external fact which is the essence of religion for all but that very small minority who can live within themselves in mystical communion or by the power of their understanding. For the great mass of men, if the history of religions is to be trusted, religious experience depends upon a complete belief in the concrete existence, one might almost say the materialization, of their God. The fundamentalist goes to the very heart of the matter, therefore, when he insists that you have destroyed the popular foundations of religion if you make your gospel a symbolic record of experience, and reject it as an actual record of events.

The liberals have yet to answer Dr. Machen when he says that "the Christian movement at its inception was not just a way of life in the modern sense, but a way of life founded upon a message. It was based, not upon mere feeling, not upon a mere program of work, but on an account of facts." It was based on the story of the birth, the life, the ministry, the death, and the resurrection of Jesus Christ. That story set forth the facts which certify the Christian experience. Modernism, which in varying degree casts doubt upon the truth of that story, may therefore be defined as an attempt to preserve selected parts of the experience after the facts which inspired it have been rejected. The orthodox believer may be mistaken as to the facts in which he believes. But he is not mistaken in thinking that you cannot, for the mass of men, have a faith of which the only foundation is their need and desire to believe. The historic churches, without any important exceptions, I think, have founded faith on clear statements about matters of fact, historic events, or physical manifestations. They have never been content with a symbolism which the believer knew was merely symbolic. Only the sophisticated in their private meditations and in esoteric writing have found satisfaction in symbolism as such.

Complete as was Dr. Machen's victory over the Protestant liberals, he did not long remain in possession of the field. There is a deeper fundamentalism than his, and it is based on a longer continuous experience. This is the teaching of the Roman Catholic Church. From a priest of that church, Father Riggs, has come the most searching criticism of Dr. Machen's case. Writing in the *Commonweal* Father Riggs points out that "the fundamentalists are well-nigh powerless. They are estopped, so to speak, from stemming the ravaging waters of agnosticism because they cannot, while remaining loyal to the (Protestant) reformers . . . set limits to destructive criticism of the Bible without making an un-Protestant appeal to tradition."[8] Father Riggs, in other words, is asking the Protestant fundamentalists, like Dr. Machen, how they can be certain that they know these facts upon which they assert that the Christian religion is founded.

They must reply that they know them from reading the Bible. The reply is, however, unsatisfying. For obviously there are many ways of reading the Bible, and therefore the Protestant who demands the right of private judgment can never know with absolute certainty that his reading is the correct one. His position in a skeptical age is, therefore, as Father Riggs points out, a weak one, because a private judgment is, after all, only a private judgment. The history of Protestantism shows that the exercise of private judgment as to the meaning of Scripture leads not to universal and undeniable dogma, but to schism within schism and heresy within heresy. From the point of view, then, of the oldest fundamentalism of the western world the error of the modernists is that they deny the facts on which religious faith reposes; the error of the orthodox Protestants is that although they affirm the facts, they reject all authority which can verify them; the virtue of the Catholic system is that along with a dogmatic affirmation of the central facts, it provides a living authority in the Church which can ascertain and demonstrate and verify these facts.

5. IN MAN'S IMAGE

The long record of clerical opposition to certain kinds of scientific inquiry has a touch of dignity when it is realized that at the core of that opposition there is a very profound understanding of the religious needs of ordinary men. For once you weaken the belief that the central facts taught by the churches are facts in the most literal and absolute sense, the disintegration of the popular religion begins. We may confidently declare that Mr. Santayana is speaking not as a student of human nature, but as a cultivated unbeliever, when he writes that "the idea that religion contains a literal, not a symbolic, representation of truth and life is simply an impossible idea." The idea is impossible, no doubt, for the children of the great emancipation. But because it is impossible, religion itself, in the traditional popular meaning of the term, has become impossible for them.

If it is true that man creates God in his own image, it is no less true that for religious devotion he must remain unconscious of that fact. Once he knows that he has created the image of God, the reality of it vanishes like last night's dream. It may be that to anyone who is impregnated with the modern spirit it is almost self-evident that the truths of religion are truths of human experience. But this knowledge does not tolerate an abiding and absorbing faith. For when the truths of religion have lost their connection with a superhuman order, the cord of their life is cut. What remains is a somewhat archaic, a somewhat questionable, although a very touching, quaint medley of poetry, rhetoric, fable, exhortation, and insight into human travail. When Mr. Santayana says that "matters of religion should never be matters of controversy" because "we never argue with a lover about his taste, nor condemn him, if we are just, for knowing so human a passion," he expresses an ultimate unbelief.

For what would be the plight of a lover, if we told him that his passion was charming?—though, of course, there might be no such lady as the one he loved.

NOTES

1. [Harry Emerson Fosdick (1878–1969), American theologian who was ordained as a Baptist minister but tended toward theological liberalism. "How Shall We Think of God?" appeared in his book, *Adventurous Religion and Other Essays* (1926).]

2. [W. C. Brownell (1851–1928), American literary and cultural critic.]

3. [Alfred North Whitehead (1861–1947), British mathematician and philosopher who cowrote *Principia Mathematica* (1910–13) with Bertrand Russell. Whitehead's Lowell Lectures of 1926 were published as *Religion in the Making* (1926).]

4. [For Russell, see p. 79. The quotation is from "A Free Man's Worship" (1903).]

5. [For Lake, see n. 18 to Barnes's "The Twilight of Christianity."]

6. [For Inge, see n. 18 to Westermarck's "Christianity and Morals."]

7. [J. Gresham Machen (1881–1937), Presbyterian minister who taught at Princeton Theological Seminary (1906–37) and attacked theological liberalism in *Christianity and Liberalism* (1923) and other works.]

8. [T. Lawrason Riggs, "Fundamentalism and the Faith," *Commonweal* 2, no. 15 (19 August 1925): 344–46 (quotation from p. 346).]

Part VI.

THE AGNOSTIC
WAY OF LIFE

20

SECULARISM

The True Philosophy of Life

G. W. Foote

[George William Foote (1850–1915), British journalist
and secularist, was raised as an Anglican but joined the
Unitarians when he was fifteen. He soon became
involved in radical freethought, founding the Young
Men's Secular Association in London in 1869 and
contributing to Charles Bradlaugh's *National
Reformer.* He later broke with Bradlaugh; started his
own paper, the *Secularist*; and, with George J.
Holyoake and Charles Watts, formed the British Secular Union. In 1881 he began the weekly paper the
Freethinker, attacking Christianity in both articles and
cartoons. In 1883 he was sentenced to a year in prison
for blasphemy, but the sentence was later overturned.
Foote reconciled with Bradlaugh, taking over from
him as president of the National Secular Society in
1890. His voluminous writing largely took the form of
articles and polemics in the numerous magazines he
edited; some of his articles were collected as *Flowers*

G. W. Foote, *Secularism the True Philosophy of Life* (London: Freethought, 1879), pp. 7–22.

of Freethought (1893–94). In the following extract, Foote argues that secularism advocates a moral and social philosophy superior to that of any religion, by focusing on vital issues relating to human life as it is actually lived.]

W ere I obliged to give an approximate definition of Secularism in one sentence I should say that it is naturalism in morals as distinguished from supernaturalism; meaning by this that the criterion of morality is derivable from reason and experience, and that its ground and guarantee exist in human nature independently of any theological belief. Mr. G. J. Holyoake,[1] whose name is inseparably associated with Secularism, and who has done so much to illustrate and enforce it, says: "Secularism relates to the present existence of man and to actions the issues of which can be tested by the experience of this life." And again: "Secularism means the moral duty of man deduced from considerations which pertain to this life alone. Secularism purposes to regulate human affairs by considerations purely human." The second of these quotations is clearly more comprehensive than the first, and is certainly a better expression of the view entertained by the vast majority of Secularists. It dismisses theology from all control over the practical affairs of this life, and banishes it to the region of speculation. The commonest intelligence may see that this doctrine, however innocent it looks on paper, is in essence and practice revolutionary. It makes clean sweep of all that theologians regard as most significant and precious. Dr. Newman, in his "Grammar of Assent,"[2] writes: "By Religion I mean the knowledge of God, of his will, and of our duties towards Him"; and he adds that the channels which Nature furnishes for our acquiring this knowledge "teach us the Being and Attributes of God, our responsibility to Him, our dependence on Him, our prospect of reward or punishment, to be somehow brought about, according as we obey or disobey Him." A better definition of what is generally deemed Religion could not be found, and such religion as this Secularism will have no concern with. From their point of view orthodox teachers are justified in calling it irreligious; but Secularists themselves, agreeing with Carlyle that whoever believes in the infinite nature of Duty has a religion, repudiate the epithet *irreligious* just as they repudiate the epithet *infidel*, for the popular connotation of both includes something utterly inapplicable to Secularism as understood by those who profess it. Properly speaking, then, Secularism is not irreligious, but untheological; yet, as it entirely excludes from the sphere of human duty what most people regard as religion, it must explain and justify itself.

Secularism rejects theology as a guide and authority in the affairs of this life because its pretensions are not warranted by its evidence. Natural Theology, to use a common but half-paradoxical phrase, never has been nor can be aught but a body of speculation, admirable enough in its way perhaps, but quite irreducible to the level of experience. Indeed, one's strongest impression in reading treatises on that branch of metaphysics is that they are not so much proofs as excuses of faith, and would never have been written if the ideas sought to be verified had not already been enounced in Revelation. As for Revealed Religion, it is based upon miracles, and these to the scientific mind are altogether inadmissible, being trebly discredited. In the first place, they are at variance with the general fact of order in nature, the largest vessel or conception into which all our experiences flow; adverse to that law of Universal Causation which underlies all scientific theories and guides all scientific research. Next, the natural history of miracles shows us how they arise, and makes us view them as phenomena of superstition, manifesting a certain coherence and order because the human imagination which gave birth to them is subject to laws however baffling and subtle. All miracles had their origin from one and the same natural source. The belief in their occurrence invariably characterises certain stages of mental development, and gradually fades away as these are left farther and farther behind. They are not *historical* but *psychological* phenomena, not *actual* but merely *mental*, not *proofs* but *results* of faith. The miracles of Christianity are no exception to this rule; they stand in the same category as all others. As Mr. Arnold aptly observes: "The time has come when the minds of men no longer put as a matter of course the Bible miracles in a class by themselves. Now, from the moment this time commences, from the moment that the comparative history of all miracles is a conception entertained, and a study admitted, the conclusion is certain, the reign of the Bible miracles is doomed."[3] Lastly, miracles are discredited for the reason insisted on by Mr. Greg[4]—namely, that if we admit them, they prove nothing but the fact of their occurrence. If God is our author, he has endowed us with reason, and to the bar of that reason the utterances of the most astounding miracle-workers must ultimately come; if condemned there, the miracles will afford them no aid; if approved there, the miracles will be to them useless. Miracles, then, are fatally discredited in every way. Yet upon them all Revelations are founded, and even Christianity, as Dr. Newman urged against the orators of the Tamworth Reading-Room, "is a history supernatural, and almost scenic." Thus if Natural Theology is merely speculative and irreducible to the level of experience, Revealed Religion, though more substantial, is erected upon a basis which modern science and criticism have hopelessly undermined. The practical relation of Secularism to Theology will be dealt with later on; its intellectual relationship is all we are concerned with at present.

Now if we relinquish belief in miracles we cannot retain belief in Special Providence and the Efficacy of Prayer, for these are simply aspects of the miraculous. Good-natured Adolf Naumann, the young German artist in "Middlemarch," was not inaccurate though facetious in assuring Will Ladislaw that through him, as through a particular hook or claw, the universe was straining towards a certain picture yet to be painted;[5] for every present phenomenon, whether trivial or important, occurs here and now, rather than elsewhere and at some other time, by virtue of the whole universal past. All the forces of nature have conspired to place where it is the smallest grain of sand on the sea-shore, just as much as their interplay has strewn the aether-floated constellations of illimitable space. The slightest interference with natural sequence implies a disruption of the whole economy of things. Who suspends one law of nature suspends them all. The pious supplicator for just a little rain in time of drought really asks for a world-wide revolution in meteorology. And the dullest intellects, even of the clerical order, are beginning to see this. As a consequence prayers for rain in fine weather, or for fine weather in time of rain, have fallen almost entirely into disuse; and the most orthodox can now enjoy that joke about the clerk who asked his rector what was the good of praying for rain with the wind in that quarter. Nay more, so far has belief in the efficacy of prayer died out, that misguided simpletons who persist in conforming to apostolic injunction and practice, and in taking certain very explicit passages in the Gospels to mean what the words express, are regarded as Peculiar People, in the fullest sense of the term; and if through their primitive pathology children should die under their hands, they run a serious risk of imprisonment for manslaughter, notwithstanding that the book which has misled them is declared to be God's word by the law of the land. Occasionally, indeed, old habits assert themselves, and the nation suffers a recrudescence of superstition. When the life of the Prince of Wales was threatened by a malignant fever, prayers for his recovery were publicly offered up, and the wildest religious excitement mingled with the most loyal anxiety. But the newspapers were largely responsible for this; they fanned the excitement daily until many people grew almost as feverish as the Prince himself, and "irreligious" persons who preserved their sanity intact smiled when they read in the most unblushingly mendacious of those papers exclamations of piety and saintly allusions to the great national wave of prayer surging against the Throne of Grace. The Prince's life was spared, thanks to a good constitution and the highest medical skill, and a national thanksgiving was offered up in St. Paul's.[6] Yet the doctors were not forgotten; the chief of them was made a knight, and the nation demanded a rectification of the drainage in the Prince's palace, probably thinking that although prayer had been found efficacious there might be danger in tempting Providence a second time. Soon after that interesting event Mr. Spurgeon preached a sermon wherein he modestly observed that philosophers were noisy enough in peaceful times,[7] but shrank into their holes like mice when imminent calamity threatened the nation; which may be true without derogation to the philosophers, who, like wise men, do not bawl against popular madness, but reserve their admonitions until the heated multitude is calm and repentant. Professor Tyndall has invited the religious world to test the alleged efficacy of prayer by a practical experiment, such as allotting a ward in some hospital to be specially prayed for, and inquiring whether more cures are recorded in it than elsewhere.[8] But this invitation has not been and never will be accepted. Superstitions always dislike contact with science and fact; they prefer to float about in the vague of sentiment, where pursuit is hopeless and no obstacles impede. If there is any efficacy in prayer, how can we account for the disastrous and repeated failure of righteous causes and the triumph of bad? The voice of human supplication has ascended heavenwards in all ages from all parts of the earth, but when has a hand been extended from behind the veil? The thoughtful poor have besought appeasement of their terrible hunger for some nobler life than is possible while poverty deadens every fine impulse and frustrates every unselfish thought, but whenever did prayer bring them aid? The miserable have cried for comfort, sufferers for some mitigation of their pain, captives for deliverance, the oppressed for freedom, and those who have fought the great fight of good against ill for some ray of hope to lighten despair; but what answer has been vouchsafed?

What hope, what light
Falls from the farthest starriest way
On you that pray?

*   *   *   *

Can ye beat off one wave with prayer,
Can ye move mountains? bid the flower
Take flight and turn to a bird in the air?
Can ye hold fast for shine or shower
One wingless hour?[9]

The dying words of Mr. Tennyson's Arthur—"More things are wrought by prayer than this world dreams of"[10]—are a weak solace to those who recognise its futility, and find life too stern for optimistic dreams. Salvation, in this life at least, cometh not by prayer, but by valiant effort under the guidance of wisdom and the inspiration of love. Knowledge alone is power. Ignorant of Nature's laws, we are broken to pieces and ground to dust; knowing them, we win an empire of enduring civilisation within her borders. Recognising the universal reign of law and the vanity of supplicating its subversal, and finding no special clause in the statutes of the universe for man's behoof, Secularism dismisses as merely superstitious the idea of an arbitrary special providence, and affirms Science to be the only available Providence of Man.

Thus theological conceptions obtruded upon the sphere of secular interests are one by one expelled. We now come to the last, and, as the majority of people think, the most serious and important—namely, the doctrine of a Future Life and of Future Reward and Punishment. Mr Gladstone says that, putting this world and the next into two scales of value, the Secularist finds that the one weighs much, the other either nothing, or nothing that can be appreciated. This is very near the truth. Secularism, as such, neither affirms nor denies a future life; it simply professes no *knowledge* of such a state, no information respecting it which might serve as a guide in the affairs of this life. The first question to be asked concerning the alleged life beyond the grave is, Do we know aught about it? If there were indisputably a future life in store for us all, and that life immortal, and if we could obtain precise information of its actualities and requirements, then indeed the transcendence of eternal over temporal interests would impel us to live here with a view to the great Hereafter. But *have* we any knowledge of this future life? Mere conjectures will not suffice; they may be true, but more probably false, and we cannot sacrifice the certain to the uncertain, or forego the smallest present happiness for the sake of some imagined future compensation. Have we any *knowledge* of a life beyond the grave? The Secularist answers decisively No.

Whatever the progress of science or philosophy may hereafter reveal, at present we know nothing of personal immortality. The mystery of Death, if such there be, is yet unveiled, and inviolate still are the secrets of the grave. Science knows nothing of another life than this. When we are dead she sees but decomposing matter, and while we live she regards us but as the highest order of animal life, differentiated from other orders by clearly defined characteristics, but separated from them by no infinite impassable chasm. Neither can Philosophy enlighten us. She reveals to us the laws of what we call mind, but cannot acquaint us with any second entity called soul. Even if we accept Schopenhauer's theory of will, and regard man as a conscious manifestation of the one supreme force, we are no nearer to personal immortality; for, if our soul emerged at birth from the unconscious infinite, it will probably immerge therein at death, just as a wave rises and flashes foam-crested in the sun, and plunges back into the ocean for ever. Indeed, the doctrine of man's natural immortality is so incapable of proof that many eminent Christians even are abandoning it in favour of the doctrine that everlasting life is a gift specially conferred by God upon the faithful elect. Their appeal is to Revelation, by which they mean the New Testament, all other Scriptures being to them gross impositions. But can Revelation satisfy the critical modern spirit? When we interrogate her, discord deafens its. Every religion—nay, every sect of every religion—draws from Revelation its own peculiar answer, and accepts it as infallibly true, although widely at variance with others derived from the same source. These answers cannot all be true, and their very discord discredits each. The voice of God should give forth no such uncertain tidings. If He had indeed spoken, the universe would surely be convinced, and the same conviction fill every breast. Even, however, if Revelation proclaimed but one message concerning the future, and that message were similarly interpreted by all religions, we could not admit it as quite trustworthy, although we might regard it as a vague foreshadowing of the truth. For Revelation, unless every genius be considered an instrument through which eternal music is conveyed, mast ultimately rely on miracles, and these the modern spirit has decisively rejected. Thus, then, it appears that neither Science, Philosophy, nor Revelation affords us any knowledge of a future life. Yet, in order to guide our present life with a view to the future, such knowledge is indispensable. In the absence of it we must live in the light of the present, basing our conduct on Secular reason, and working for Secular ends. How far this is compatible with elevated morality and noble idealism, we shall presently inquire and decide. Intellectually, Secularism is at one with the most advanced thought of our age, and no immutable dogmas preclude it from accepting and incorporating any new truth. Science being the only providence it recognises, it is ever desirous to see and to welcome fresh developments thereof, assured that new knowledge must harmonise with the old, and deepen and broaden the civilisation of our race.

In morals Secularism is utilitarian. In this world only two ethical methods are possible. Either we must take some supposed revelation of God's will as the measure of our duties, or we must determine our actions with a view to the general good. The former course may be very pious, but is assuredly unphilosophical. As Feuerbach insists, to derive morality from God "is nothing more than to withdraw it from the test of reason, to institute it as indubitable, unassailable, sacred, without rendering an account *why*."[11] Stout old Chapman's protest against confounding the inherent nature of good is also memorable:

> Should heaven turn hell
> For deeds well done, I would do ever well.[12]

Secularism adopts the latter course. Were it necessary, a defence of utilitarian morality against theological abuse might here be made; but an ethical system which can boast so many noble and illustrious adherents may well be excused from vindicating its right to recognition and respect. Nevertheless, it may be observed that, however fervid are theoretical objections to utilitarianism, its criterion of morality is the only one admitted in practice. Our jurisprudence is not required to justify itself before any theological bar, nor to show its conformity with the maxims uttered by Jesus and his disciples; and he would be thought a strange legislator who should insist on testing the value of a Parliamentary Bill by appealing to the New Testament. Secularism holds that whatever actions conduce to the general good are right, and that whatever have an opposite tendency are wrong. Manifold objections are urged against this simple rule on the ground of its impracticability; but as all of them apply with equal force to every conceivable rule, they may be peremptorily dismissed. The imperfections of human nature must affect the practicability of any moral law, however conceived or expressed. Christians who wrote before Secularism had to be combated never thought of maintaining that reason and experience are inefficient guides, although they did sometimes impugn the efficacy of natural motives to good. So thoughtful and cautious a preacher as Barrow, whom Mr. Arnold accounts the best moral divine of our English Church, plainly says that "wisdom is, in effect, the genuine parent of all moral and political virtue, justice, and honesty."[13] But some theologically-minded persons, whose appearance betrays no remarkable signs of asceticism, wax eloquent in reprobation of happiness as a sanction of morality at all. Duty, say they, is what all should strive after. Good; but the Secularist conceives it *his* duty to promote the general welfare. Happiness is not a degrading thing, but a source of elevation. We have all enjoyed that wonderful catechism of Pig-Philosophy in "Latter-Day Pamphlets."[14] What a scathing satire on the wretched Jesuitism abounding within and without the Churches, and bearing such malign and malodorous fruit! But it is not the necessary antithesis to the Religion of Sorrow. It is the mongrel makeshift of those "whose gospel is their maw," whose swinish egotism makes them contemplate Nature as a universal Swine's-Trough, with plenty of pig's wash for those who can thrust their fellows aside and get their paw in it. The Religion of Gladness is a different thing from this. Let us hear its great prophet Spinoza, one of the purest and noblest of modern minds: "Joy is the passage from a less to a greater perfection; sorrow is the passage from a greater to a less perfection."[15] No; suffering only tries, it does not nourish us; it proves our capacity, but does not produce it. What, after all, is happiness? It consists in the fullest healthy exercise of all our faculties, and is as various as they. Far from ignoble, it implies the highest normal development of our nature, the dream of Utopists from Plato downwards. And therefore, in affirming happiness to be the great purpose of social life, Secularism makes its moral law coincident with the law of man's progress towards attainable perfection.

Motives to righteousness Secularism finds in human nature. Since the evolution of morality has been traced by scientific thinkers the idea of our moral sense having had a supernatural origin has vanished into the limbo of superstitions. Our social sympathies are a natural growth and may be indefinitely developed in the future by the same means which have developed them in the past. Morality and theology are essentially distinct. The ground and guarantee of morality are independent of any theological belief. When we are in earnest about the right we need no incitement from above. Morality has its natural ground in experience and reason, in the common nature and common wants of mankind. Wherever sentient beings live together in a social state, simple or complex, laws of morality must arise, for they are simply the permanent conditions of social health; and even if men entertained no belief in any supernatural power, they would still recognise and submit to the laws upon which societary welfare depends. "Even," says Dr. Martineau,[16] "though we came out of nothing, and returned to nothing, we should be subject to the claim of righteousness so long as we are what we are: morals have their own base, and are second to nothing." Emerson, a religious transcendentalist, also admits that "Truth, frankness, courage, love, humility, and all the virtues, range themselves on the side of prudence, or the art of securing a present well-being."[17] The love professed by piety to God is the same feeling, though differently directed, which prompts the commonest generosities and succours of daily life. All moral appeals must ultimately be made to our human sympathies. Theological appeals are essentially not moral but immoral. The hope of heaven and the fear of hell are motives purely personal and selfish. Their tendency is rather to make men worse than better. They may secure a grudging compliance with prescribed rules, but they must depress character instead of elevating it. They tend to concentrate a man's whole attention on himself, and thus to develop and intensify his selfish propensities. No man, as Dr. Martineau many years ago observed, can faithfully follow his highest moral conceptions who is continually casting side-glances at the prospects of his own soul. Secularism appeals to no lust after posthumous rewards or dread of posthumous terrors, but to that fraternal feeling which is the vital essence of all true religion and has prompted heroic self-sacrifice in all ages and climes. It removes moral causation from the next world to this. It teaches that the harvest of our sowing will be reaped here, and to the last grain eaten, by ourselves or others. Every act of our lives affects the whole subsequent history of our race. Our mental and moral like our bodily lungs have their appropriate atmospheres, of which every thought, word and act becomes a constituent atom. Incessantly around us goes on the conflict of good and evil, which a word, a gesture, a look of ours changes. And we cannot tell how great may be the influence of the least of these, for in nature all things hang together, and the greatest effects may flow from causes seemingly slight and inconsiderable. When we thoroughly lay this to heart, and reflect that no contrition or remorse can undo the past or efface the slightest record from the everlasting Book of Fate, we shall be more strongly restrained from evil and impelled to good than we could be by supernatural promises or threats. The promises may be mistrusted, the threats nullified by a late repentance; but the natural issues of conduct are inevitable and must be faced. Whatever the future may hold in store, Secularism bids us be true to ourselves and our opportunities now. It does not undertake to determine the vexed question of God's existence, which it leaves each to decide for himself according to what light he has; nor does it dogmatically deny the possibility of a future life. But it insists on utilising to the highest the possibilities that lie before us, and realising as far as may be by practical agencies that Earthly Paradise which would now be less remote if one tithe of the time, the energy, the ability, the enthusiasm and the wealth devoted to making men fit candidates for another life had been devoted to making them fit citizens of this. If there be a future life this must be the best preparation for it; and if not, the consciousness of humane work achieved and duty done, will tint with rainbow and orient colours the mists of death more surely than expected glories from the vague and mystic land of dreams.

There are those who cannot believe in any effective morality, much less any devotion to disinterested aims, without the positive certainty of immortal life. Under a pretence of piety they cloak the most grovelling estimate of human nature, which, with all its faults, is infinitely better than their conception of it. Even their love and reverence of God would seem foolishness unless they were assured of living for ever. Withdraw posthumous hopes and fears, say they, and "let us eat and drink for to-morrow we die" [1 Cor. 15:32] would be the sanest philosophy. In his grave way Spinoza satirizes this "vulgar opinion" which enjoins a regulation of life according to passions by those who have "persuaded themselves that the souls perish with the bodies, and that there is not a second life for *the miserable who have borne the crushing weight of piety"*; "a conduct," he adds, "as absurd, in my opinion, as that of a man who should fill his body with poisons and deadly food, for the fine reason that he had no hope to enjoy wholesome for all eternity, or who, seeing that the soul is not, eternal or immortal, should renounce his reason, and wish to become insane; things so preposterous that they are scarcely worth mention."[18]

Others again, deny that a philosophy which ignores the Infinite can have any grand ideal capable of lifting us above the petty tumults and sordid passions of life, and worthy to be called religious. But surely the idea of service to the great Humanity, whose past and future are to us practically infinite, is a religious conception vast enough for our finite minds. The essence of all true religion, says Carlyle, is "reverence for human worth." But reverence is not all, love and service are also elements. The instincts of Love, Reverence, and Service may be fully exercised and satisfied by devotion to a purely human ideal, without resort to unverifiable dogmas and inscrutable mysteries; and

Secularism, which bids us think and act so that the great Human Family may profit by our lives, which enjoins us to labour for human progress and elevation here on earth, where effort may be effective and sacrifices must be real, is more profoundly religious than any supernatural creed and holds the promise of a wider and loftier beneficence.

NOTES

1. [George Jacob Holyoake (1817–1906), British freethinker and a leading secularist of the period. See his *Origin and Nature of Secularism* (1896).]

2. [John Henry Newman, *A Grammar of Assent* (1870).]

3. [For Matthew Arnold, see n. 16 to Fawcett's "Agnosticism."]

4. [William Rathbone Greg (1809–1881), British industrialist and author of *The Creed of Christendom* (1851) and other skeptical works.]

5. [In George Eliot's novel *Middlemarch* (1871–72), Adolf Naumann is a friend of the religious skeptic Will Ladislaw. Eliot herself was a skeptic and a freethinker; see the essay "Evangelical Teaching" (1855), reprinted in *Atheism: A Reader*, ed. S. T. Joshi (Amherst, NY: Prometheus Books, 2000), pp. 147–70.]

6. [The reference is to the future King Edward VII (1841–1910), who as the Prince of Wales fell ill of typhoid fever in 1871 and came close to dying but recovered in early 1872. Prime Minister William Ewart Gladstone arranged a thanksgiving service at St. Paul's Cathedral on February 27, 1872.]

7. [For Spurgeon, see n. 10 to Stephen's "Are We Christians?"]

8. [John Tyndall (1820–1893), renowned British physicist and a leading exponent of scientific naturalism. He debated the efficacy of prayer at meetings of the Metaphysical Society in 1872.]

9. A. C. Swinburne, *Félise*. [Algernon Charles Swinburne, "Félise" (1866), ll. 214–15, 266–70.]

10. [Alfred, Lord Tennyson, *Idylls of the King* (1862–73), "The Passing of Arthur," ll. 415–16.]

11. [Ludwig Feuerbach (1804–1872), German philosopher. Foote quotes from *Das Wesen des Christentums* (1841; translated by George Eliot

as *The Essence of Christianity*), which interpreted Christianity as a subjective myth.]

12. [George Chapman (1559?–1634), British poet. The quotation is from *The Tears of Peace* (1609), ll. 61–62.]

13. Sermon on "The Pleasantness of Religion." [Isaac Barrow (1630–1677), Anglican divine and mathematician, and a well-known preacher of his day. Foote quotes from the sermon "The Pleasantness of Religion."]

14. [Thomas Carlyle (1795–1881), *Latter-Day Pamphlets* (1850), in one section of which ("Jesuitism") the notion of Pig-Philosophy—the universe as seen from the perspective of swine—is put forth as a satire on the limited vision of the Jesuits.]

15. [Benedict Spinoza, *Ethics* (1677), Part III, Proposition XI.]

16. *Nineteenth Century,* April, 1877. [James Martineau, "A Modern 'Symposium': The Influence upon Morality of a Decline in Religious Belief," *Nineteenth Century* 1 (April 1877): 341–45.]

17. Essay on *Prudence.* [Ralph Waldo Emerson, "Prudence," in *Essays: First Series* (1841).]

18. [Spinoza, *Ethics*, Part V, Proposition XLI.]

21

ON HAPPINESS

H. L. Mencken

[Henry Louis Mencken (1880–1956), American journalist and essayist, gained a foothold in journalism as
a teenager and continued in the profession for the next
fifty years. A longtime columnist for the *Baltimore
Evening Sun*, Mencken also edited the *Smart Set*
(1914–23) and founded and edited the *American Mercury* (1924–33), making it one of the leading magazines of political and social commentary of its time.
His incisive essays and reviews—some collected in the
six-volume series *Prejudices* (1919–27)—made him
the most influential American critic of the 1920s. Early
in his career, Mencken wrote a pioneering study, *The
Philosophy of Friedrich Nietzsche* (1908), and later
translated Nietzsche's *The Antichrist* (1920). His longtime hostility to organized religion was most exhaus-
tively expressed in *Treatise on the Gods* (1930). His
coverage of the Scopes "monkey trial" in 1924 gained
him both celebrity and notoriety for the pungency with

From the *Baltimore Evening Sun* (May 9, 1927): 17.

which he lampooned fundamentalist religion. For an extensive sampling of his writings on religion, see *H. L. Mencken on Religion* (Prometheus Books, 2002). In the following essay, Mencken addresses the issue of whether a person can be happy without a belief in God.]

I.

The following letter, apparently quite genuine, comes to me from a young man who says that he was born a Jew, and into an orthodox family:

> I am 25 years old. Not an old man, as old men are considered; not a wise man, as wisdom is counted. But life has changed for me. I am almost an atheist. Almost, because I cannot discard the fear of the Unknown that was drilled into my young heart. I still faintly fear that Something. Yet I cannot believe the Bible; I cannot accept it as God-given. My simple reason tells me that death is the end of all; that the force that propels life is Nature, a Nature that does not perform miracles. And with this new idea has come misery, unhappiness, the desire to forsake this life. Does enlightenment mean misery? Does non-belief mean unhappiness?

Why this young man sends his problem to me instead of to a clergyman I don't know, save that he recognizes my colossal theological gift. My advice to him does not differ appreciably from that he would receive from a regular practitioner of the ghostly art. (When I say a regular practitioner, of course, I mean a true believer, not one of the shameless frauds who try to conceal their agnosticism by calling themselves Modernists.) I advise him to give his new skepticism six months trial. If, at the end of that time, he finds that its effects upon him are still indistinguishable from those of a bad case of cholera morbus, I advise him to go the nearest orthodox rabbi, tell his troubles, pay his fine (if fines are levied in such cases), and reconcile himself to the faith of his fathers.

Why not, indeed? What ails him is simply pride, which Holy Church long ago put among the seven deadly sins. Unfitted by training, and perhaps also by nature, for a life of doubt, and seduced into it at twenty-five by the rhetoric of men of a quite different kidney, he now finds himself ashamed to admit that he longs to go back whence he came. But why should he be ashamed? Some men are born religious as others are born with long legs or outstanding ears. If that is the bent of their nature, they should follow it. More, I believe that they are inevitably bound to do so. The moment they step outside the borders of faith they are unhappy. And if they try desperately and against their inner inclination to remain there, their unhappiness becomes unendurable. The colleges of the land turn out thousands of such sad cases every year. A few of the victims hang themselves. But the vast majority, at thirty, are again comfortably within the fold, as they were in early youth, and as their fathers were before them.

II.

Now and then, desiring to be unpleasant to persons who dislike me, I propose that a vast campaign of so-called education be launched in the late Confederate States, to acquaint the youth of the region with the elements of the physical sciences, and so rescue them from the naïve and negroid theology of their elders. But that proposal is never taken seriously by anyone who actually knows me, for every such person knows that I never do anything to execute it. More, they know that I'd protest if it were executed by others.

Why, indeed, should it be executed? Why should I (or anyone else) get into a sweat about what is believed by the boys and girls of Georgia, or Mississippi, or Tennessee? Above all, why should anyone want to change what they believe into something else? Is their religion idiotic? Then their science would also be idiotic. If they are actually mainly numskulls, as appears to be probable, then there is no known way to cure their numskullery. Every attempt to do so, by the devices of the logician, can have only the result of making them unhappy. And why make them unhappy?

I am, indeed, against all proselyters, whether they be on my side or on some other side. What moves nine-tenths of them, I believe, is simply the certainty of the result that I have just mentioned. Their lofty pretensions are all tosh. The thing they yearn for is the satisfaction of making some one unhappy: that yearning is almost as universal, among them, as thirst is in dry Congressmen. Sometimes they deceive themselves, but probably not often. The wowser is a wowser the whole world over, no matter what banner he flies.[1] What he craves above all is resistance. He wants to break it down, to force his ideas upon his victims, to watch them writhe and suffer. If the Chinese asked for missionaries, it would be hard to find recruits for the dreadful trade. But the Chinese resist them and are made unhappy by them, and so every Y. M. C. A. tank in the land is gorged with candidates.

III.

In this department, by God's grace, my own conscience is perfectly clear—perhaps my own plausible boast at a moral agent. I have never consciously tried to convert anyone to anything. Like any other man bawling from a public stump I have occasionally made a convert; in fact, in seasons when my embouchure has been good I have made a great many. But not deliberately, not with any satisfaction. Next to a missionary, a convert is the most abhorrent shape I can imagine. I dislike persons who change their basic ideas, and I dislike them when they change them for good reasons quite as much as when they change them for bad ones. A convert to a good idea is simply a man who confesses that he was formerly an ass—and is probably one still. When such a man favors me with a certificate that my eloquence has shaken him I feel about him precisely as I'd feel if he told me that he had started (or stopped) beating his wife on my recommendation.

No; it is not pleasant to come into contact with such flabby souls, so lacking in character and self-respect. Their existence embitters the life of every man who deals in ideas. The hard-boiled fellows are far more agreeable, no matter what their concrete notions. Some of those who appear to depart the farthest from the elements of sense are the most charming, for example, certain varieties of pastors. I have known many such pastors, and esteemed not a few of them. But only, I should add, the relatively unsuccessful, who seldom if ever achieved the public nuisance known as saving a soul. They believed their depressing rubbish firmly, but they did not press it upon either their inferiors or their superiors. They were not wowsers.

Unluckily, there are very few such pastors in the average Christian community, especially in the United States. The great majority, forgetting their office of conducting worship, devote themselves mainly to harassing persons who do not care to join them. This harassing is bad enough when it fails of its purpose; when it succeeds its consequence is simply an increase in the sum of human degradation, publicly displayed. It is well known that natural believers are always suspicious of converts. No wonder. For precisely the same reason sober automobilists are suspicious of drunken drivers, and Prohibition agents of Prohibitionists.

IV.

My correspondent raises a question that cannot be answered here at any length: it would take five or six columns. It has to do with the emotional effects of skepticism. Is the skeptic ever happy, in the sense that a man who believes that God is watching over him is happy? Privately, I often doubt it. Here the pious seem to have a certain bulge on the doubters. Immersed in their faith, they enjoy a quiet contentment that is certainly never apparent in a man of restless, inquisitive, questioning mind. The happiest people in the world, accepting this definition of happiness, are probably Christian Scientists—that is, until they come down with appendicitis or gallstones.

But there is a kind of satisfaction that is quite as attractive, to certain rugged types of men, as this somewhat cow-like form of contentment. It is related to the latter just as the satisfaction of a soldier on active duty is related to the satisfaction of a man securely at home. The man at home is quite safe, and the soldier runs a considerable risk of being killed or wounded. But who will argue that the man at home, on the whole, is happier than the soldier—that is, assuming that the soldier is a volunteer? The one is tightly comfortable, and hence happy. But the other, though in grave peril, is happy too—and I am inclined to think that his happiness is often of a palpably superior variety.

So with the skeptic. His doubts, if they are real, undoubtedly tend to make him uneasy, and hence unhappy, for they play upon themselves quite as much as upon the certainties of the other fellow. What comforts him, in the long run, I suppose, is his pride in his capacity to face them. He is not wobbled and alarmed, like my correspondent; he gets a positive thrill out of being uneasy, as the soldier gets a thrill out of being in danger. Is this thrill equal, as a maker of anything rationally describable as happiness, to the comfort and security of the man of faith? Ask me an easier question! Is a blonde lovelier than a brunette? Is *Dunkles* better than *Helles*?[2] Is Los Angeles the worst town in America, or only next to the worst? The skeptic, asked the original question, will say yes; the believer will say no. There you have it.

NOTES

1. ["Wowser" is an Australian slang term of which Mencken was very fond. He quotes a definition of it by one John Norton: "a fellow who is too niggardly of joy to allow the other fellow any time to do anything but pray." Mencken, *The American Language*, 4th ed. (New York: Alfred A. Knopf, 1936), p. 265n.]

2. ["Dark" beer and "light" beer.]

22

THE ETHICS OF HUMANISM

Corliss Lamont

[Corliss Lamont (1902–1995), American philosopher and educator, received a BA from Harvard in 1924 and a PhD from Columbia in 1932. He taught philosophy at Columbia (1928–32), the New School for Social Research (1940–42), and again at Columbia (1947–59). He was a longtime director of the American Civil Liberties Union (1932–54). The son of the well-known banker Thomas William Lamont, the partner of J. P. Morgan, Lamont rejected his upper-class upbringing and devoted himself to humanism and socialism. He visited the Soviet Union in the early 1930s and wrote the travel diary *Russia Day by Day* (1933), becoming active in promoting reconciliation between the United States and the Soviet Union. He ran for office on the American Labor Party ticket in 1952 and on the Independent Socialist Party ticket in 1958. Lamont was cited for contempt of Congress in 1953 by Joseph McCarthy, but the case was later dismissed in federal

Corliss Lamont, *The Philosophy of Humanism* (1949; 4th ed. New York: Philosophical Library, 1957), pp. 189–95, 200–207.

court. Lamont was a prolific author, writing such works as *The Illusion of Immortality* (1935), *You Might Like Socialism* (1939), and many other volumes. His collected essays appeared as *Voice in the Wilderness* (1974) and his memoirs as *Yes to Life* (1981). He received the Gandhi Peace Award in 1981. In the following extract from a chapter titled "The Ethics of Humanism," Lamont explains the difference between the Humanist and the religious way of life, especially in regard to sexual morality and altruism.]

In the Humanist ethics the chief end of thought and action is to further this-earthly human interests on behalf of the greater happiness and glory of man. The watchword of Humanism is service to humanity in this existence as contrasted with the salvation of the individual soul in a future existence and the glorification of a supernatural Supreme Being. Humanism urges men to accept freely and joyously the great gift of life and to realize that life in its own right and for its own sake can be as beautiful and splendid as any dream of immortality.

The philosophy of Humanism constitutes a profound and passionate affirmation of the joys and beauties, the braveries and idealisms of existence upon this earth. It heartily welcomes all life-enhancing and healthy pleasures, from the vigorous enjoyments of youth to the contemplative delights of mellowed age, from the simple gratifications of food and drink, sunshine and sports, to the more complex appreciation of art and literature, friendship and social communion. Humanism believes in the beauty of love and the love of beauty. It exults in the pure magnificence of external Nature. All the many-sided possibilities for good in human living the Humanist would weave into a sustained pattern of happiness under the guidance of reason.

In this Humanist affirmation of life the monistic psychology again plays a most significant role. For this view means that in whatever he does man is a living unity of body and personality, an interfunctioning oneness of mental, emotional and physical qualities. Humanism adheres to the highest ethical ideals and fosters the so-called goods of the spirit, such as those of culture and art and responsible citizenship. At the same time it insists that all ideals and values are grounded in this world of human experience and natural forms. As Santayana puts it in summing up his conception of human nature, "everything ideal has a natural basis and everything natural an ideal development."

Much of the emphasis in supernaturalist ethics has been negative, calling on men continually to deny many of their most wholesome impulses in order to keep their souls pure and undefiled for that life after death which is so very much more important than life before death. In this ethics the prospect of supernatural rewards and punishments in the future overshadows present conduct; the values decreed by supernatural authority override those of the natural and temporal order in which man actually lives.

By contrast, the emphasis of Humanist and naturalistic ethics is *positive*.[1] It is an ethics in which conscience does not merely play the role of a vetoing censor, but is creative in the sense of bringing to the fore new and higher values. This system of morality recommends the greater and more frequent enjoyment of earthly goods on the part of all men everywhere; it repudiates ascetic other-worldliness in favor of buoyant this-worldliness; it is against all defeatist systems which either postpone happiness to an after-existence or recommend acquiescence to social injustice in this existence.

An excellent example of the typical religious defeatism that Humanism decries is the following consolation offered by Pope Pius XI in his encyclical of 1932, at the height of the Great Depression: "Let the poor and all those who at this time are facing the hard trial of want of work and scarcity of food, let them in a like spirit of penance suffer with greater resignation the privations imposed upon them by these hard times and the state of society, which Divine Providence in an ever-loving but inscrutable plan has assigned them. Let them accept with a humble and trustful heart from the hand of God the effects of poverty, rendered harder by the distress in which mankind now is struggling. . . . Let them take comfort in the certainty that their sacrifices and troubles borne in a Christian spirit will concur efficaciously to hasten the hour of mercy and peace."

Humanism sweeps aside the confusing and corrupting Dualism of the past in which "the natural life of man with its desires and pleasures became something to be shunned as evil and degraded, something to be forsaken for higher things. Man's true nature was of a different quality, his destiny lay in another realm. . . . It is this Dualism running through all of man's actions that has left its impress on the commonly accepted moral codes of the West to this day, and seems even yet to make impossible that whole-hearted and simple enjoyment of the goods of a natural existence that men now envy in the Greeks of old. It is not that men have ever refrained from action or from these pleasures, but that they have never been able to rid themselves of the notion that there is something essentially wrong about them." (Professor Randall.)[2]

The Humanist ethics is opposed to the puritanical prejudice against pleasure and desire that marks the Western tradition of morality. Men and women have profound wants and needs of an emotional and physical character, the fulfilment of which is an essential ingredient in the good life. Contempt for or suppression of normal desires results in their working themselves out in surreptitious, coarse or abnormal ways. While it is true that uncontrolled human desires are the prime cause of evil in the world, it is equally true that human desires directed by reason toward socially useful goals are a prime foundation of the good. They provide the drive and energy that eventuate in individual and group achievement contributing to the good society.

The reasonable self-restraint that Humanism favors has little in common with the constant sense of guilt encouraged by the traditional Christian ethics. A central proposition in that ethics is the original sin and inherent wickedness of man; and one of its special stresses is that the sex impulse in human beings is essentially base and bad, Adam's original sin being transmitted from generation to generation through the act of procreation. Thus the Christian Church, in order to establish the complete purity of Jesus, felt obliged to assume that he was born of a virgin in violation of ordinary biological laws. Due in large part to the influence of Christianity, immorality in the minds of most people in the West became synonymous with improper sex conduct.

Humanist ethics of course recognizes the necessity of high standards in relations between the sexes, but it does not regard sex emotions in themselves as in any sense evil. It insists that from a moral viewpoint the sex life of an individual is no more important than his political or economic life. In fact, Humanism asserts that perhaps the most pressing ethical need of our time is the establishment of higher standards of action in the fields of politics and economics. A man can be an exemplary husband and father and at the same time be dishonest in business affairs or engage in political graft. Past over-emphasis on the sex aspect of morals has led to a neglect of its other aspects and a narrowing of its range.

The realm of ethics is pre-eminently social in scope and application; within its sphere lies all human conduct in which socially significant alternatives are possible. Many small everyday acts have no ethical significance, though any type of action may under certain circumstances carry such significance. In origin and development ethics is likewise social, the term itself coming from the Greek word *ethos*, meaning custom or usages. Ethical values and standards evolve in the interaction between individual and individual, between the individual and the group, and between group and group. The sympathetic impulses in human nature, such as the parental, the sexual and the gregarious, become socially transformed and broadened in human association.

The advantages of mutual cooperation, support and protection lead to the social functioning and utilization of basic instincts such as those of self-preservation and reproduction. Conscience in human beings, the sense of right and wrong and the insistent call of one's better, more idealistic, more social-minded self, is a social product. Feelings of right and wrong that at first have their locus within the family gradually develop into a pattern for the tribe or city, then spread to the much larger unit of the nation, and finally from the nation to mankind as a whole. Humanism sees no need for resorting to supernatural explanations or sanctions at any point in the ethical process. A supernatural First Cause or Sustaining Principle is no more necessary in the sphere of ethics than in that of physics or metaphysics.

In making ethical decisions the Humanist relies, as in any endeavor to solve a problem correctly, upon the use of reason approaching as closely as possible to the method of science, instead of upon religious revelation or any sort of authority or intuition. Since moral judgments, like judgments of aesthetic quality, are a species of value-judgments, it is most difficult to obtain general intellectual agreement as to what is right and what is wrong. Nonetheless, the Humanist contends that a true science of ethics is possible and will yet be established.

For Humanism no human acts are good or bad in or of themselves. Whether an act is good or bad is to be judged by its *consequences* for the individual and society. Knowledge of the good, then, must be worked out, like knowledge of anything else, through the examination and evaluation of the concrete consequences of an idea or hypothesis. Humanist ethics draws its guiding principles *from* human experience and tests them *in* human experience. Since, as I pointed out in the last chapter, knowledge of anything is in the first instance never immediate, there can be no immediate knowledge of the right. However, once we have established or accepted a regulative principle of morality, we are able to use it immediately thereafter.

In Humanism's stress upon the need and value of intelligence in the ethical enterprise, its approach differs once again from that of the traditional Christian ethics. Though Humanism naturally incorporates certain of the generous social ideals voiced by Jesus, it finds little in the New Testament that can be considered as an appeal to reason. The appeal of Jesus was primarily designed to bring about a change in the heart of man; and this transformation was to be wrought by individuals receiving insight and inspiration from a personal God. Deeply imbedded in the Christian tradition was an antagonism toward the intellect, expressed originally in the myth that God punished Adam for disobeying the divine prohibition against eating the fruit of the tree of knowledge. And supernatural religions in general have been very distrustful of human reliance on reason. The ethical tradition in which the human mind, unprompted by any supernatural agency, was regarded as able to attain moral truth came down from ancient Greek philosophy, notably that of Aristotle, and from modern thinkers like Spinoza.

The Humanist submits every ethical precept of the past to the searching analysis of reason, operating in the light of present circumstances. For the Humanist well realizes that all ethical laws and systems are relative to the particular historical period and to the particular culture of which they are a part. What was good for the Old Testament Hebrews some 4,000 years ago or for the Greeks in 400 B.C. or for Europeans only 100 years ago is not necessarily good for Americans living in the second half of the twentieth century. Furthermore, in the world today there are a considerable number of different nations and peoples, some of them in quite dissimilar stages of historical development. Ethical standards generally accepted in the United States today may be in their formative phases in less developed countries or consciously frowned upon among peoples with a different socio-economic system. These remarks do not mean, of course, that moral standards are merely subjective or that we cannot learn a great deal from the ethical systems of the past.

Clearly, however, ethical rules of conduct become out-of-date as conditions change and time marches on. In general the advance of science and invention has affected ethical philosophy to an immense degree. Modern medicine, for instance, has demonstrated that many undesirable human traits which used to be ascribed to original sin or bad character are actually attributable to glandular insufficiencies or deep-seated emotional frustrations. The discovery and dissemination of scientific birth control techniques are naturally of vital significance in the sphere of sex behavior. The growth of mechanized, urban civilization in recent centuries has both altered long-established ethical standards based on a primitive agricultural civilization and given rise to innumerable new ethical problems. A twentieth-century invention like the automobile demands a new and special code of ethics for the millions of drivers; reckless driving that threatens life and limb has become one of the major immoralities. This is a field in which the law rightly steps in to regularize and enforce proper standards of safety.

The multiplication of fresh ethical problems of a complex character in our present-day society shows the need not only for the moral flexibility that Humanism advocates, but also for the use of intelligence in determining what action or actions are right and good in each case. The function of basic moral principles, expressing the funded wisdom of human experience, is not to provide absolute rules of conduct that will automatically tell men just what to do under all circumstances. Their function "is to supply standpoints and methods which will enable the individual to make for himself an analysis of the elements of good and evil in the particular situation in which he finds himself." That analysis should always take into consideration the surrounding circumstances, the total context of a specific situation.

Humanism teaches the formation of sound moral habits as well as of guiding moral principles, but believes that neither habits nor principles should grow too set or rigid. The highest ethical duty is often to discard the outmoded ethics of the past; it is a truism to say that the merely good is the enemy of the better. The Humanist refuses to accept any Ten Commandments or other ethical precepts as immutable and universal laws never to be challenged or questioned. He bows down to no alleged supreme moral authority either past or present. [. . .]

The attribution of low motives to people whose ideas or conduct you do not like is a favorite pastime throughout the world. It should be obvious, however, that it is rather difficult to gauge with accuracy the complex subjective states that lead a man to this or that action or opinion. Humanists, therefore, are chary of passing sweeping moral judgments on other people. Even the wisest of men hardly possesses the knowledge and impartiality to render a Last Judgment on himself or anyone else. Nevertheless, increasingly during these trying times men adopt the attitude that those differing with them on some current issue are absolute scoundrels and utterly damned. Yet needless to state, it is possible for reasonable and morally worthy persons sincerely to disagree on the great controversies of the day. The human mind being a somewhat imperfect instrument, even outright inconsistency is seldom a sure sign of hypocrisy. Intellectual intolerance and moral arrogance on the part of those who may themselves ultimately be proved mistaken are at the opposite pole from the true spirit of philosophy.

The whole question of motivation is fundamental to the Humanist philosophy for another reason. One of the great aims of Humanism is the transformation and socialization of human motives. This is a sector where human nature can be drastically reconditioned and reshaped. What the scientific study of human motives shows is that human nature is neither essentially bad nor essentially good, neither essentially selfish nor essentially unselfish, neither essentially warlike nor essentially pacific. There is neither original sin nor original virtue. But human nature is essentially flexible and educable. And the moulding or re-moulding of human motives is something that takes place not only in childhood and youth, but also throughout adult life and under the impact of fundamental economic institutions and cultural media that weightily influence mind and character. The social development and conditioning of human beings, their training, direct and indirect, by means of all sorts of educational techniques, can be so extensive that the hoary half-truth, "You can't change human nature," becomes quite irrelevant.

Humanism believes that in ethical training, while sufficient attention must naturally be given to the process of self-cultivation, equal emphasis should be laid on the individual's relation to society, his unending debt to the collective culture of mankind and his corresponding obligation to serve the common good. Humanism holds that even highly developed intelligent self-interest, such as Plato discusses in his *Dialogues*, is not sufficient as an ultimate ethical sanction. For intelligence operating on behalf of an evil will is precisely the definition of Satan. A first-rate mind always acting at the behest of self-interest does not necessarily result in a person's furthering the welfare of the community. There may and do occur situations that ethically demand the very last measure of personal sacrifice and in which, therefore, no form of mere individual self-interest will be adequate. Neither the capable mind nor the good will acting alone and in isolation can be depended upon for genuine ethical achievement; both functioning together make the ideal partnership from the Humanist standpoint.

The theory that everyone invariably acts from self-interest, direct or indirect, is psychologically unsound. The simple fallacy behind that theory consists, as Dewey states, "in transforming the (truistic) fact of acting *as* a self into the fiction of always acting *for* self." Now obviously a man does act frequently on behalf of himself alone; but also he can and does act on behalf of other people and large social objectives. He may well obtain personal satisfaction in so doing, but the gaining of that satisfaction may be a by-product and is not necessarily his original and primary goal.

There are many situations demanding courage or heroism in which a man has time to think through the main implications and consequences before taking action. If the final decision involves his risking or even giving up his life in a good cause, you may say that he is pursuing his self-interest because he is a believer in supernatural religion and expects to receive his reward in heaven. Traditional Christianity has indeed preached and encouraged a self-interest ethics in this sense of building up credits for an after-existence. But suppose the individual has no faith in immortality and yet follows a course that he knows is quite certain to end his earthly career. How can we possibly reduce to self-interest his decision to surrender what he considers his one and only life?

Throughout history and especially during modern times, there have been millions of men and women with some sort of Humanist philosophy who have consciously given up their lives for a social ideal. Of course they have wanted to devote themselves to that ideal and have been willing to make the supreme sacrifice for it. Yet because an individual desires to do a thing does not prove at all that he desires to do it from mere self-interest. In the case of dying for a cause, such as the welfare of his country or of humanity, he may truly desire the good of country or mankind above everything else, even above his own self-preservation. Or in the narrower setting of close personal relationships a man may care for his wife, his child or his friend literally more than he cares for himself.

Intense interest in other people or in society as a whole is, to be sure, an interest manifested by a self, but that does not make it synonymous with self-interest. To call genuine self-sacrifice or patriotism or public service forms of self-interest is to stretch the connotation of *self-interest* to cover its opposite, so that it loses its distinctive meaning. And there can be no doubt that much of the age-long controversy on this subject of self-interest has been due to verbal confusion and to the illegitimate practice of the self-interest school in trying to get rid of altruism by defining it out of existence.

The self-interest theory has been closely tied up in the history of thought with the ethical view that pleasure is and should be the goal of human endeavor. This pleasure ethics is founded on a false analysis of human nature. For psychology demonstrates that we do not in the first instance desire an object because it gives us pleasure, but that it gives us pleasure because we desire it. We enjoy a tender, well-cooked steak because we desire it in terms of bodily need and hunger; if we are already satiated with food, we have no appetite for a steak. It is really objects that we immediately desire, the accompanying pleasure being a welcome by-product and a sign that the object is one that we fundamentally want, something that is basically congenial to our nature. Feelings of pleasure cannot be automatically produced, since they are inseparably bound up with our experiencing of objects that are agreeable to us and that we positively desire only under certain conditions. This is a decisive reason why the direct and self-conscious pursuit of pleasure is not likely to succeed and to bring lasting satisfaction. Herein lies what has long been known as the Hedonistic Paradox.

Applying this analysis to the larger problem of ethical reflection and decision in regard to the general good, we see that an individual certainly possesses the psychological power of setting up social aims as among his primary objects of desire; the pleasure or happiness that may result from his furthering those aims is then secondary and derivative. Thus Humanism affirms the psychological possibility and the ethical desirability of intelligent altruism. There is nothing more shallow than those sophisticates who insist on reducing all human conduct to personal self-interest and who persist in saying that egoism is more "natural" than altruism.[3] Neither egoism nor altruism is an original characteristic of human nature; both, however, are potential dispositions of the personality. Thinkers who claim that complete selfishness is an inborn quality of human beings are taking over and expressing in different language one of the great errors of Christian ethics, namely that man is inherently sinful and depraved.

The more extreme forms of self-interest are, in truth, equivalent to ordinary selfishness, in which there is a deficiency of consideration for others and in which an individual fulfils his needs and desires to the detriment of someone else. Obviously self-regard in the sense of keeping healthy, acquiring an education, earning a living and finding a congenial life partner of the opposite sex is something to be encouraged. Self-cultivation in general and during youth in particular is by no means opposed to the social good; indeed, it helps to build a personality which can render greater service to society. Similarly a sense of personal pride in fine workmanship redounds to the advantage of the community. It is not Humanism's intent that an individual should belittle the value of his own self in affirming that of other selves.

The significant point ethically speaking is not the truism that it is always some self that has interests; it is the *kind* of interests that any self has. The self or personality is not a fixed, simple and ready-made entity standing behind a man's activities and directing them; that idea is a holdover from the supernatural doctrine of a divinely created soul—complete in all essentials—entering the body from on high. The human personality is a fluid, developing, growing complex of habits, impulses and ideas that is never finished and is always in the making *through* its activities and interests.

The unity of the self is not something one starts with, but something one may achieve, and even then only in a relative sense. Of course the self can change for the worse as well as for the better. In any case the range and quality of an individual's interests come to define in large measure the nature of his self. A man *is* what he does and likes to do. The Humanist concept of a growing, expanding personality, which comes to include social aims and ideals as an integral part of the self, cancels out the false antithesis of the individual *versus* society.

The concept of an always selfish self is a cultural product and today goes hand in hand with a social system that sets up economic self-interest in the form of money-making and profit-making as the primary motive capable of stimulating men to productive effort. In philosophy the self-interest theory of ethics received its most precise and mature formulation in the writings of the nineteenth-century Utilitarians, Jeremy Bentham and John Stuart Mill. In this regard their work, though quite humanistic in its total effect, was the philosophic counterpart of the profit-motive theory of Adam Smith and other exponents of laissez-faire economics.

In America's present capitalist society, with its constant emphasis on the profit motive and competitive individualism, there is a tendency to look upon those who support a broader and more scientific view of human motivation as intellectual crack-pots; and to consider those who try to practice altruism as impossibly naive or afflicted with a martyr complex. Amateur psychoanalysts and half-baked Freudians are fond of explaining away manifestations of social idealism in terms of some obscure neurosis. They assume that normal people function on the basis of self-interest and that therefore militant social idealism must be due to peculiar quirks in the human personality. Yet it is obviously fantastic to maintain that a deep desire for social justice, any more than a passion for truth, necessarily springs from some sort of personal neurosis or maladjustment.

Despite its criticism of the self-interest morality, the ethics of Humanism is cognizant of how deeply rooted in our economic and cultural situation are both the theory and practice of crude self-interest. Humanism is realistic in that it fully recognizes to what an extent men are bent in a wrong direction by propaganda and cultural conditioning which appeal to, reinforce and spur on the selfish and violent impulses. Humanism is further realistic in understanding that in the last analysis "the refutation of egoism consists in the eradication of egoism, that is, changing the actual feelings, desires and attitudes of those who are egoists." (Professor Edel.)[4] This clearly cannot be done simply by trying to preach, talk and argue men out of habits and actions that run counter to the social good.

Hence Humanism considers it most essential to carry through a systematic and skilful program of training the motives and the emotions so that the social and sympathetic tendencies of human beings will be encouraged rather than the more egoistic ones. Without exception the great thinkers on the subject of morality have agreed that a cardinal aim of ethical education is to develop men and women who find pleasure and happiness in doing right, and pain and unhappiness in doing wrong. Social conditioning, working upon plastic human nature with all the new techniques of twentieth-century teaching, communication and advertising, can accomplish wonders either for good or for bad.

The role of reason in this situation is not to act as a force contrary to the emotions and to assume the impossible task of driving them out or suppressing them; that would be partly to adopt the ethics of the old supernaturalism. The function of individual and community intelligence is to guide and redirect emotional life; to replace anti-social passions, motives, ambitions and habits by those that are geared to the common good. Even those deep-seated tendencies of hate and aggression that psychoanalysts say practically all human beings harbor within can be harnessed to a constructive purpose and directed against such evils as poverty, disease, tyranny and war.

Emotion and reason are not, as popularly believed, opposed to each other; they are complementary and inseparable attributes of human beings. Some degree of intellection is associated with every identifiable human emotion, for any definite emotion has a consciously distinguishable object. Fear of being blown to bits by an atomic bomb is not the same as the fear of getting a ticket for illegal parking. The difference in the quality and strength of these two fears depends upon the cognitive recognition and estimate of what is being feared. In general, the greater the measure of sound reasoning associated with the individual's emotions, the greater is the chance of his attaining the good life.

A widespread misconception is that powerful emotions are to be deplored. Professor V. J. McGill points out: "It is hard to find a psychological text which does not warn against *intense emotion* in general, as if it were deleterious to feel too strongly about anything. The public takes the same view, disparaging strong emotions, yet esteeming love and certain other passions beyond anything in the world. It seems pretty clear, however, that whether a strong emotion is desirable or deleterious depends on its cognitive object, the attitude toward it, the rationale of the situation. It is perhaps sufficient to note that mother-love, love between the sexes, the passionate quest of the scientist or humanitarian, are praised only when they are intense." (*Emotions and Reason.*)[5]

Returning once more to the role of the intellect, I wish to point out that in Humanism's general scheme of education nothing is more important from an ethical viewpoint than teaching boys and girls, men and women, how to reason correctly and to use their minds in dealing with the myriad problems of life. Such teaching must be aware that reason is "not a ready-made antecedent which can be invoked at will and set into movement. . . . It is the attainment of a working harmony among diverse desires . . . a laborious achievement of habit needing to be continually worked over." The irrational impulses of human beings have played an enormous role in bringing recurrent disasters upon mankind and remain a sinister danger in contemporary affairs. For the Humanist, stupidity is just as great a sin as selfishness; and "the moral obligation to be intelligent" ranks always among the highest of duties.

NOTES

1. Whereas, eight of the Old Testament's Ten Commandments, for instance, are phrased in negative terms.

2. [John Herman Randall Jr. (1899–1980), American philosopher and

historian who taught at Columbia University (1921–67). Lamont quotes from *Religion in the Modern World* (1929), cowritten with his father, John Herman Randall (1871–1946).

3. This is a good example of "the reductive fallacy," in which philosophers or others over-simplify by illegitimately classifying certain multiple phenomena under one category.

4. [Probably a quotation from Abraham Edel (1908–?), author of numerous books on social and ethical philosophy.]

5. [V. J. McGill, *Emotions and Reason* (1954).]

FURTHER READING

Bithell, Richard. *The Creed of a Modern Agnostic.* London: George Routledge & Sons, 1883.

Bruce, Steve. *God Is Dead: Secularization in the West.* Oxford: Blackwell, 2002.

Christianity and Agnosticism: A Controversy. New York: D. Appleton, 1889.

Cohen, Chapman. *A Grammar of Freethought.* London: Pioneer Press, 1921.

Darrow, Clarence, and Wallace Rice, ed. *Infidels and Heretics: An Agnostic's Anthology.* Boston: Stratford, 1929.

Flint, Robert. *Agnosticism.* New York: Charles Scribner's Sons, 1903.

Haldeman-Julius, E. *The Militant Agnostic.* Amherst, NY: Prometheus Books, 1995.

Harris, Sam. *The End of Faith: Religion, Terror, and the Future of Reason.* New York: W. W. Norton, 2004.

Kadison, Alexander. *Through Agnostic Spectacles.* New York: Truth Seeker, 1919.

Kennedy, Ludovic. *All in the Mind: A Farewell to God.* London: Hodder & Stoughton, 1999.

Kenny, Anthony. *What I Believe.* New York: Continuum, 2006.

Kurtz, Paul. *In Defense of Secular Humanism.* Buffalo, NY: Prometheus Books, 1983.

Leon, Philip. *Beyond Belief and Unbelief: Creative Nihilism.* London: Victor Gollancz, 1965.

Lightman, Bernard. *The Origins of Agnosticism: Victorian Unbelief and the Limits of Knowledge.* Baltimore: Johns Hopkins University Press, 1987.

Longman, Heber A. *The Religion of a Naturalist.* London: Watts, 1914.

Merrill, William Pearson. *Faith and Sight: Essays on the Relation of Agnosticism to Theology.* New York: Charles Scribner's Sons, 1900.

Oppy, Graham Robert. *Ontological Arguments and Belief in God.* Cambridge: Cambridge University Press, 1995.

Ray, Matthew Alun. *Subjectivity and Irreligion: Atheism and Agnosticism in Kant, Schopenhauer and Nietzsche.* Aldershot, UK: Ashgate, 2003.

Rinaldo, Peter M. *Atheists, Agnostics, and Deists in America: A Brief History.* Briarcliff Manor, NY: DorPete Press, 2000.

Russell, Bertrand. *Why I Am Not a Christian and Other Essays on Religion and Related Subjects.* Edited by Paul Edwards. New York: Simon & Schuster, 1957.

Schurman, Jacob Gould. *Agnosticism and Religion.* New York: Charles Scribner's Sons, 1896.

Spalding, J. L. *Religion, Agnosticism and Education.* Chicago: A. C. McClurg, 1902.

Stephen, Leslie. *An Agnostic's Apology and Other Essays.* London: Smith, Elder, 1893.

Vahanian, Gabriel. *The Death of God: The Culture of Our Post-Christian Era.* New York: George Braziller, 1961.

Ward, James. *Naturalism and Agnosticism.* London: A. & C. Black, 1899.